10/15

Books by Jack Olsen

"SON": A PSYCHOPATH AND HIS VICTIMS   (*1983*)

HAVE YOU SEEN MY SON?   (*1982*)

MISSING PERSONS   (*1981*)

NIGHT WATCH   (*1979*)

THE SECRET OF FIRE FIVE   (*1977*)

MASSY'S GAME   (*1976*)

ALPHABET JACKSON   (*1974*)

THE MAN WITH THE CANDY   (*1974*)

THE GIRLS IN THE OFFICE   (*1971*)

SLAUGHTER THE ANIMALS, POISON THE EARTH   (*1971*)

THE BRIDGE AT CHAPPAQUIDDICK   (*1970*)

NIGHT OF THE GRIZZLIES   (*1969*)

SILENCE ON MONTE SOLE   (*1968*)

"SON"

"SON"

A Psychopath and His Victims

JACK OLSEN

New York   1984   ATHENEUM

Picture consultant: Chris Anderson

Excerpts from *Psychopaths* by Alan Harrington, Copyright © 1972 by Alan Harrington, reprinted by permission of International Creative Management, Inc. Excerpts from *The Mask of Sanity* by Hervey Cleckley, Copyright © 1982 by The Mosby Medical Library, reprinted by permission of C.V. Mosby Company, 11830 Westline Industrial Drive, St. Louis, Mo. 63146

Library of Congress Cataloging in Publication Data

Olsen, Jack.
   "Son": a psychopath and his victims.

    1. Coe, Fred. 2. Rapists—Washington (State) —
Spokane—Biography. 3. Coe, Ruth. 4. Mothers and
sons. 5. Psychology, Pathological. 6. Revenge.
I. Title.
HV6565.W2047 1983   364.1'532'0922 [B]   83-45082
ISBN 0-689-11408-7

Copyright © 1983 by Jack Olsen
All rights reserved
Published simultaneously in Canada by McClelland and Stewart Ltd.
Composition by Westchester Book Composition, Inc., Yorktown Heights, New York
Manufactured by Fairfield Graphics, Fairfield, Pennsylvania
Design of illustrations by Mary Ahern
Illustrations printed by Philips Offset, Mamaroneck, New York
Designed by Harry Ford
First Printing October 1983
Second Printing November 1983
Third Printing December 1983
Fourth Printing January 1984
Fifth Printing February 1984

For Scott Meredith

There walk among us men and women who are in but not of our world....Often the sign by which they betray themselves is crime, crime of an explosive, impulsive, reckless type.

ROBERT LINDNER, M.D.

Psychopathic personality: a disorder of behavior toward other individuals or toward society in which reality is usually clearly perceived except for an individual's social and moral obligations and which often seeks immediate personal gratification in criminal acts, drug addiction, or sexual perversion.

WEBSTER'S SEVENTH NEW COLLEGIATE DICTIONARY.

Hiya kid. Tis I, your great buddy. It looks like we made it and I know I've got quite a ways to go. I hope you didn't have such a hard time as I will encounter. Good luck Bill.

FRED COE, 1965 HIGH-SCHOOL YEARBOOK.

ILLUSTRATIONS

"SON"

Prologue: The Lilac City

Spokane seems to be a place that doesn't evoke strong passions in people....I personally have never had any feeling whatsoever for Spokane—good or bad—I've merely sought to sell the area.... I spent 40–60 hours a week for four years selling Spokane as "a recreational wonderland"..."Gateway to the lush Intermountain Northwest lake country!" I puffed it as a pristine region featuring "relatively inexpensive real estate...little smog, traffic or crime...a great place to raise a family!"—Fred Coe, Jan. 15, 1982

Most Americans lump Northwest cities together—Seattle, Spokane, Portland, Tacoma. Rainy towns, gray and damp, dreary. But Spokane isn't dreary, at least climatically. It draws only a few more drops of rain than Los Angeles and less than half as much as Seattle or New York. The sun beats so hard on the landlocked "Lilac City" that some of its railroad signal lights are solar-powered.

Dry Spokane is as far from soggy Seattle as Richmond is from New York, and just as different. Perched at the eastern edge of Washington State, twenty minutes from Idaho by freeway, the self-described "Hub of the Inland Empire" is a good-hearted marketplace and railhead, a welcoming kind of place where cabdrivers get out and open your door and wish you luck, and home-town boosterism has been raised to an art.

Spokane is blue-collar and first-name country (Reagan country too, though many of its 177,000 citizens consider the president too liberal). It lies in a natural amphitheater surrounded by hilly wheatlands, mined-out coal and silver digs, salty draws and moonscape badlands sprinkled with dust from Mt. St. Helen's. Deep woods are nearby; cougars infiltrate the city limits and eagles occasionally soar high above the downtown buildings. Marmots preen on a rock above Spokane Falls and whistle at the clients of a downtown bar.

The town is not without a share of industrial ugliness, blackened remnants of a railhead past. But most of the recycled Spokane is verdant, flower-scented, deserving of the municipal awards heaped on it since the successful world's fair of 1974.

Americans who have forgotten the forties and fifties would find it hard to envisage the place and its spirit. An out-of-towner wrote to one of the local newspapers:

> I would like to thank the Spokane bus driver who turned in the package I left on the bus the other day, and also to say that I've noticed how courteous all of the drivers are. They have been most helpful during my stay in Spokane. It's good to know that there are still thoughtful and kind people.

Thoughtful and kind people are the norm in Spokane. The locals take pride in helping and sharing; the driver with a flat tire isn't alone for long. Circumstance and geography have combined to preserve bygone folkways. Women are called "girls" until their breasts begin to droop, and then they become "ladies." Ozzie and Harriet, Beaver Cleaver, the Brady Bunch stroll these unmean streets. The town is the perfect size: big enough to offer cosmopolitan amenities, small enough to sustain neighborliness and pride. Streets are wide, traffic jams unknown. Pedestrians wave their thanks when cars stop at crosswalks; the citizens exude a blend of ingenuousness and bonhomie, subspecies of naïveté perhaps, but nonetheless refreshing. Attempts at smart-ass humor are wasted:

> Cashier at fast-food restaurant: "Thank you! Would you like to play our word game?" Visitor: "I'm not very athletic." Cashier: "Oh, you don't have to be athletic!"

For hard-working Spokanites, time permits few abstruse discussions over Brie and Sauterne. Wives clean house and then hop buses for jobs downtown; weary husbands drive home from Kaiser Aluminum or the Burlington Northern yards or the hundreds of small businesses along the river and up the hillsides. Life is lived close to the bone, and comfortable tribal rites are preserved. On weekend nights post-adolescent Spokanites "cruise the gut," driving gleaming pickup trucks and big old Detroit cars along Riverside Avenue honking at young women—a fossil scene from *American Graffiti*. For most of these teenage boys, the ultimate in delinquency is to de-pants a fraternity brother or paint out the "G" at the Black Angus restaurant. More mature citizens unwind by jogging or skiing or drinking beer, and a few seniors entertain themselves by dropping into Big Brothers Bingo on N. Monroe, where regular games pay a hundred dollars and you can win a thousand if you bingo on your first/last ball number.

In some ways time seems to have congealed in Spokane and created habitat groups suitable for study by physical anthropologists. At the Sunday brunch in the baroque lobby of the Davenport Hotel, women of a certain age appear fresh from church in stiletto heels, upswept spectacles with rhinestone insets, bouffant hair-dos and wigs with curls reaching skyward in towers and cones. Among the men, the odd crewcut is seen along with the layered look and the slicked-back pompadour. Wheatmen just in from the Palouse wear satin shirts and lariat ties, and millionaire businessmen heft their tired feet on the potted plants to reveal new $500 cowboy boots with embroidered swirls and curlicues.

The theme-restaurant fad has barely arrived, and it is still possible to dine out without an asparagus fern in your ear. Restaurant food is basic and cheap;

signs advertise "Beef Strog, Veal Parm" and "Fill Your Belly at Paul's Deli."
Waitresses chirp the obligatory "There ya go" when serving each course, refill
your coffee cup every few minutes, and pronounce words like "Chablis" and
"vichyssoise" as spelled, even when they know better. The locals are fond of
well-worn expressions like "It's three o'clock straight up," and "It's Tuesday
all day," and when you thank them, they smile and say, "You bet," or "You
betcha," and mean it. There are a few unfriendly loudmouths and boors, but
they know their place.

Very little of national interest happened in the smoky old railhead town in the
five decades after Harry Lillis "Bing" Crosby departed in the 1920s. The relaxed
Crosby style was pure Spokane, and locals remember him fondly. There is a
Crosby museum and a statue of the singer on the campus of his alma mater,
Gonzaga University. The bronze pipe in the statue's mouth presents a challenge to a few freshmen who, according to the school president, "haven't quite
caught the spirit of Gonzaga yet." Pilfered pipes cost the school $100 apiece
and in recent years have been removed each night by campus guards and
replaced when the sun comes up, like the flag.

The popular TV sitcom *Taxi* made a rare national mention of the old
hometown in an exchange between cabbie Jim Ignatowski, a burnt-out ex-
hippie, and a female visitor to the New York City taxi garage. Ignatowski asks,
"Are you new in town?"

"Yes."

"Where do you come from?"

The woman answers, "Spokane."

"Spokane!"

"Have you been there?"

"No. *Wait!* What am I saying? I *come* from Spokane—eh, I think. Say,
that's a nice dress. Where did you get it?"

"In Spokane." He studies her figure closely. "Wow! Long time since I saw
a dress from Spokane."

The late *Spokane* magazine deplored the dialogue. "Boise is funny," the
magazine editorialized. "Tacoma is funny. Walla Walla is good for a laugh any
day of the year. Spokane, however, is not even vaguely amusing."

No reasonable observer would argue. Spokane, pleasant and livable, is an
introspective white Anglo-Saxon Christian community that takes itself and its
piety seriously. A typical sign stretches across a front porch: "God Bless America Peace on Earth," and a billboard says simply, "Acts 1:8." Winos sun themselves outside the Union Gospel Mission under a scrawled sign: "Christ Our
Creed, Love Our Law." St. John's Cathedral, an architectural masterpiece that
looks transplanted from the Loire Valley, looms over the city like a watchful
Episcopalian father.

Less than two percent of the local population is black, and there hasn't
been an influx of ethnics since the Chinese railroad laborers came (and went)
before 1900. There used to be two synagogues in town, but Interstate 90 wiped
one out and there were too few Jews to bother rebuilding. A goodly number
of Scandinavians were assimilated long ago, but one seldom hears an Eastern
European name or an Italian or Greek or Oriental name or picks up the sound
of an accent. There are no foreign-language radio stations or ethnic neigh-

borhoods. Imported films close on Saturday night; Clint Eastwood and Burt Reynolds are the big draws but Disney tops them both. Porno houses do a moderate business, and cinema lovers slip into them sideways.

The city's moral tone is set by an old-money conservative establishment backed by banking, mining, logging and farming interests and personified by the brothers Bill and Jim Cowles, multimillionaire publishers, philanthropists and property owners. Both under fifty, they are teetotaling Republican Presbyterian Yalies who have been known to return bottles of Christmas cheer. Their grandfather arrived from Chicago in 1880 when "Spokan Falls" was a sawmill next to an Indian camp.

Spokane is one of the largest U.S. metropolitan areas in which a single family owns the only morning and evening newspapers as well as radio and TV stations. For almost a century the Cowles family used its wealth and power to impress an old-fashioned sense of morality on the city. For years the papers refused to run divorces. "The family's always been in love with the past," says a local businessman. "Their attitude was—we don't have crime in Spokane; we don't have vice and God help us we don't have scandal. Nobody here but us Christians."

The sexual revolution stalled at the city gates. In the 1940s city policemen rooted out an enclave of gays, and the scandal reached such proportions that the newspapers were obliged to take notice. More than one Spokanite phoned the library to ask the meaning of "homosexual." The townspeople were appalled; a furniture dealer was disgraced and a doctor killed himself. The feeling was that he had done the only decent thing.

Almost four decades later, the ancient shoeshiner in the Davenport Hotel acknowledged the changing times by laying out copies of *Penthouse* and *Hustler*, but he carefully played a religious radio station as though to cleanse the air. City fathers continued to pass rigorous anti-obscenity laws (and state courts continued to strike them down). At election time, authorities made traditional raids on massage parlors and other dens of lukewarm debauchery—while the Cowles press clucked its applause. But vicious sex crimes like rape were uniformly downplayed. Newsprint was better used to characterize "the All-American City" as an ideal setting for business.

Spokane seemed to thrive on such pride and insularity. If observers hinted that looking inward and backward was a risky municipal habit, boosters drowned them out, insisting that the old home town was a safe and pure place in an unsafe, impure world. The image held up till Fred and Ruth Coe came along.

1978-79

AUTHOR'S NOTE

Certain persons depicted in this book have requested that their names be concealed, some through fear of retaliation and some through embarrassment at having been the victims of sex crimes and other indignities. Fictitious names will be set in italic type (e.g., *Lois Higgins*) the first time each appears.

1

To use the very colorful prison language—I assure you that "taking pussy" is not my game. I have never had to do so. And I would not do so. I adore <u>women</u>—have no animosity whatsoever toward them— have no weird hang-ups about my mother—am totally normal sexually.—Fred Coe, April 5, 1982

Lois Higgins pushed aside her coffee cup and stomped out of the restaurant. The silly argument had lasted long enough—now she had to get off by herself for a while. She didn't want to sit one more second with her husband or his biker friends. All they ever did was argue.

Lois hadn't yet turned twenty, but she'd been through abortion and divorce and poverty and enough family turmoil to fuel one of her favorite soap operas for months. The last thing she needed on this April night in 1978 was more hassles. Three weeks earlier she'd attempted suicide, and her head still wasn't right. She was eating one meal a day, sometimes none. At five feet five inches she weighed eighty-six pounds.

She hurried through the Burlington Northern underpass, putting space between herself and Vip's restaurant. When she reached the far end, she realized that Al wasn't coming after her. A freight train approached, its generators throbbing. She watched the oscillating yellow headlight paint the backsides of buildings as the train clattered overhead. Like every other Spokanite, she was accustomed to the great dark shapes that reminded the old railhead town of its origins.

The frame house that Lois and Al and the baby shared with a friend was three miles north of the river, but the prospect of the long uphill walk didn't bother her. Growing up in the apple orchards of Washington—"always poor, beans most of the time, meat twice a week if we were lucky"—she thought nothing of walking five or ten miles. Doctors had convinced her that walking was her safest exercise. She had a history of pleurisy, pneumonia and asthma, and vivid memories of being rushed to hospitals.

She hurried past the brightly lighted Opera House and came to Riverfront Park, a grassy improvement that only a few years earlier had been a sooty tangle of tracks and trestles and sheds, inhabited largely by rats. She decided to take a shortcut across the lawns originally planted for Expo 74. Al could go to hell. If he came after her he'd never find her here. The open roof of the International Pavilion curved over her head in graceful arcs and planes. She flopped on a bench to think.

They had met in this park during the fair. Al was a muscular Vietnam vet with surprising reserves of compassion and emotion. How excited he'd been when she turned up pregnant! "Now stay in the house, and no lifting!" he'd warned her. "Goddamn, I'm gonna have a son! Me—a daddy!" He made plans to return to school.

Two months into the pregnancy, Lois slid on a patch of ice and fell hard on her spine. Al blamed her for the loss of "my son." When she became pregnant again, he demanded that she have an abortion, but she refused. He stopped speaking to her. "He's all tore up," she told friends in her little-girl voice with a slight lisp. "His attitude is—go away, you lost my son, this one won't live either."

But Becky, five pounds thirteen ounces at birth, had lived—a lovely healthy child. Al hardly acknowledged her. He had taken up a new hobby: chasing teenage girls on his motorcycle. Lois went into a post-partum depression—"the mother blues," she called it.

Sitting on the park bench a year later, she still felt betrayed, lost. A light blinked off in one of the glassy new buildings downtown, reminding her that Wednesday was almost over. No one was in sight as she stepped onto the bridge. The Spokane River burbled beneath her; spring runoff filled the gorge from bank to bank. Every day lately, townspeople had been crowding the Monroe Street bridge to watch the brownish-green water shoot Spokane Falls with a roar that drowned speech and sent cloudlets of spray to catch the sun in miniature rainbows—a spectacular sound-and-light show in the heart of town. Once Lois had appreciated the lavish wild beauty, but now she was beset by her troubles. She began the long uphill trudge past drab, uninspiring storefronts. She hardly noticed the first pedestrian to pass her since Vip's. This was her own neighborhood in safe old Spokane. Besides, men didn't bother women who barely cast a shadow.

She remembered the terrible Saturday night three weeks ago. After dinner, Al had headed for the door. "Can't you stay home with me and Becky?" Lois had begged. "You promised, Al! You said you'd stay with us tonight."

"Well, if I promised."

He sat silently all evening, his nose in a book. Around midnight, Lois went to bed. A few minutes later, she heard him leave on his bike. At dawn he came home and rushed her to the hospital, where doctors pumped out the overdose of Percodan and penicillin—all she'd been able to find in the medicine cabinet. Ever since, she'd been going to a mental health clinic. Al and the doctors had warned her that she would lose Becky if she didn't get straight.

Walking up the long hill, she tried to figure out why he had lost interest in their marriage. She wondered: Am I so damned ugly? She was thin, but she still had a good figure, set off by the tiniest of waists—sixteen inches the last time she'd measured. Luminous auburn hair trailed to her slender thighs; her face was narrow, almost pinched, but enhanced by smooth pale skin, full lips, and liquid brown eyes. For tonight's rare date, she had worn her best outfit: new blue jeans, a brown and white blouse, a navy-blue denim jacket, and a soft new pair of brown snowboots, a surprise gift from her sister. Before Al had started sniping at her in Vip's, he'd told her that she looked nice, rare praise from him.

A car slowed, then sped off. Guess I don't look like a pickup, she told herself. The clock at Hazen & Jaeger's Funeral Home said 11:43. She'd covered twenty blocks in a half hour.

Was Al looking for her? More likely he was cruising the young stuff on Riverside Avenue. Once she'd been young stuff herself, but now she was a sickly nineteen-year-old who'd mismanaged the birth of her husband's son. She thought, Thank you, God, for my sweet baby girl! In a few days Becky would have her first birthday party. Al had promised to attend.

As she passed the Savage House Pizza Parlor, she thought about removing her jacket. A motorcycle swerved onto Northwest Boulevard, and she looked without turning her head. It wasn't Al. She wondered why he hadn't come after her. How many men would let their wives walk out of a restaurant late at night and not give a damn where they went? She wished she could stop thinking about him.

She turned west on Indiana Avenue, bordered in maples and sycamores and lined with small homes built flat to the ground. The sweet scent of lilacs filled the air. In a pocket of darkness midway between streetlights, a man appeared like a jack-in-the-box from behind a white parked car. He looked a little like her mother's next-door neighbor. Before she could figure out why he was blocking her path, he grabbed her by her arms below the shoulders.

She saw that he had long blondish hair, sideburns and a mustache: a collegiate type. He was neatly dressed in a blue-jean outfit—pants and heavy jacket—and he was broad-shouldered and much taller than her own five-five. She looked into his colorless eyes and thought, My God, I'm gonna be raped.

She screamed.

He pressed his hand over her face and muffled the sound. "If you don't scream I'll take it away," he promised. She nodded agreement in pained little jerks.

His hand slid away and she yelled, "Oh, God, he's gonna rape me! Please! Oh—"

He rammed his left hand halfway down her throat. As she fought for breath, his face brushed hers and she noticed a smell of bath soap and peppermint. She fought for air and wondered crazily why a rapist would take pains not to offend.

"If you don't scream," he said, "I won't hurt you." She tried to say "Okay" but only succeeded in grunting. He shoved her toward a grassy plot between two dark houses.

A car passed. He held her tightly as the light slid over his face. She got a better view of a square chin and cold eyes of blue or green. They didn't blink, and they seemed full of hatred. She wondered why. She'd never seen him before. Why would he hate her so? When another car approached he shoved her toward the back of the narrow yard. She fell in the damp grass. He rammed his hand back into her mouth and straightened her up with his other arm. She realized that he was strong and decided not to struggle.

He maneuvered her toward a patch of black. She fell again. He dragged her six or eight feet across the wet grass and lifted her to her feet. She saw small flower beds on both sides and a fresh-painted wooden fence. He took his hand from her mouth as though he knew that she wouldn't scream again. He reached under her blouse, shoved her white cotton bra up around her neck and kneaded her breasts.

After a few minutes he said, "Now I'm gonna clean you out." He slid to his knees, ripped open the zipper on her jeans, and wrenched them to her ankles. He pulled down her red underpants and removed her tampon. Still kneeling, he reached up and jammed his left hand back into her mouth, clawed at her breasts with his free hand and stuck his tongue in her vagina.

She stood immobile, talking silently to him: *Don't do this crazy thing to me. This is my body, not yours. You don't have the right! Stop! You don't have the right!* She succeeded in feeling nothing physical, nothing more painful than a hand jammed into her mouth. She willed herself not to move, not to pull away. Let him do—whatever he wanted.

Then she realized that he'd stopped. She felt herself being pulled down. Good, she thought, now he'll take his hand out of my mouth. But he rammed it deeper, till she felt his nails scratch her throat. This is not happening, she told herself. *What a crazy thing to do!* This is a dream. I am...somewhere else. Oh, God, let me breathe!

He was trying to kill her. She jerked her head away and rolled on her stomach. He climbed on top as another car passed; she raised an arm, knowing it was futile. He said, "Come on, come on," as he straddled her. She saw that he had lowered his pants and was yanking at his penis. "Come—*on!*" he repeated.

After a few minutes he turned her over and entered her from the front. "Like it?" he asked. She wished she could humor him, but she was still gagged. She started to scream and his hand seemed to expand in her throat. "Don't try that again," he ordered, raising his fist. He began a steady patter of questions: "Do you like this? Do you like to fuck? Are you married? Do you have children? Do you live around here? *Do you like this?*" She wondered why it was important to him that she like it. Then she thought, Am I going to walk away from this? Will I see Becky again? God, please, make him leave....

He lifted himself from her body and began rubbing his penis rhythmically against the jeans around her ankles. He groaned a few times and quivered. She opened her eyes and saw tulips in a neat bed a few inches away. How odd, she thought, my favorite flowers. At the corner of the house she could make out the outline of a lilac bush ten or twelve feet tall. The scent made her think about coffins.

He was rearranging his clothes. "Don't tell the police or anybody else," he said. "I'll come back and kill you. Do you understand?"

"I understand," she said, trying to sound meek. He stepped over her body and disappeared toward Monroe. She wondered, Is it safe to get up now? Is it safe for me to get help? She remembered what her grandmother had told her years ago: If you're ever in trouble, run to the nearest house. A tiny thing like you—people will help you.

She hobbled to the white frame house next door at 1219 Indiana and banged loudly. No one answered. She realized that she was half naked. She pulled up her underpants and jeans, buckled her belt, pulled down her shirt. Her bra was around her neck; she didn't bother to refasten it. She lifted her long hair off her face and noticed that it was gritty. Her chest felt hollow and her skin cold. She hurried to the house on the other side of the yard, a bungalow with imitation brick facing, and again got no response.

She stepped back on the sidewalk and looked both ways. It occurred to her that the man might be watching from the shadows. She began to run, a crazy-legged sprint on the lumpy sidewalk.

She spotted a light on a wooden house in robin's egg blue, and pounded on the door with both hands. It opened an inch. She asked, "Can I use your telephone?" Her voice was a croak; she could feel blood dribbling down her throat.

A woman's voice said, "No."

"My God, I've just been raped; I've gotta use the telephone." As she said the words it dawned on her for the first time: I've been raped! *Raped!* She tried not to faint.

Inside, the woman pointed to the phone. Lois dialed "0" and blurted into the mouthpiece, "Give me the police! I was just raped!" It was a long time before the operator acknowledged her request. By the time the next voice came on the line, she was no longer sure where she was. She remembered that there was an Albertson's supermarket a block or two west on Indiana; she asked if someone could meet her there.

The woman's son drove her to the store in his pickup, and Lois clutched the first policeman she saw as though he were a lifeguard. He pulled away and she grabbed at his arms. She felt that if someone didn't comfort her she would scream and never stop. "Please," she said. "Hold me. *Hold me!* I've just been raped."

The officers guided her into the rear of the blue and white patrol car and shut her inside. The sound of the slamming door made her feel ashamed. She asked to be driven home—maybe Al would be there, maybe Al would hold her. She was covered with dirt and grass stains when she stumbled into the house. "My God," Al said. "What happened?"

One of the policemen said, "She's been raped."

Al grabbed her by the upper arms, exactly as the rapist had.

She yelled *"Don't!"* and collapsed. When she came to, the policemen drove her back to Indiana Avenue, where she stumbled through the geography of the rape while they took notes. They found out why no one had answered her knocks; both adjoining houses were vacant. The officers played their long black flashlights over the swatch of lawn and looked for evidence.

At Deaconess Hospital, one of three big hospitals lined up on the hill south of the Spokane River, everyone was pleasant and professional. A nurse asked her to undress, and when Lois said she never wanted to touch her clothes again—they were beyond laundering—the nurse undressed her like a child. Her body was caked with dirt; the nurse cleaned her up. Technicians made their swabs and smears. There was seminal fluid in her vagina and on the right leg of her blue jeans, but the first microscopic inspections showed no sperm cells. One of the doctors theorized that the rapist had been able to perform only the preliminaries of the sex act, short of full ejaculation. She listened but heard only dimly. All she knew was that she felt like a blob of filth.

* * *

She stayed in her bathtub till nearly 3 a.m., the hot water turning her skin pink. Al came in, but she asked him to leave—she needed to think. When she finally climbed into bed she had Becky with her. Al signaled his intentions by stroking her nipples with his fingertips. She thought, My God, not tonight! "Al, please," she whispered.

When he tried again in a few minutes she jerked away. "Don't—lay a hand—on me," she said slowly. "Just leave me—*alone*. Let me just lay here!"

At 5:30 the alarm went off. She hadn't slept. "Go to work," she whispered. "Go! We'll be okay."

He left at 6 a.m., just as her mother was arriving to help out. A few hours later there was a loud rap on the front door. "Don't answer!" she whispered. She grabbed a kitchen knife, peeked outside and saw no one. "Who is it?" she called through the door.

A muffled voice came back. The rapist! Well, he wouldn't lay a hand on Becky. *Not one hand!* "If you don't show yourself," she yelled, "I'm gonna take this knife to you!"

A man's face appeared at the window. He was holding a badge. She opened the door a crack and he said, "Police officer." She took a good look; he was too old to be the rapist. Still trembling, she let him in. He led her to the sofa and lifted the knife from her hand.

2

Yes, F H "Kevin" Coe is a rara avis. Objectivist, libertarian, radical capitalist, political polemicist, positive growth activist, marketing and communications specialist — witty, eloquent, an egoist, a supreme materialist! A lover of clothes, cars, luxury, women, art, sports, good health ... LIFE! Yet epistemologically metaphysical — a nature and animal lover! A paradoxical paradigm of all humankind ... striving for excellence! — Fred Coe, April 5, 1982

That summer of 1978 Jeni Coe began to entertain the slightest hope that things might work out. She'd been with her ex-husband off and on for six years, and she'd learned that life with Frederick Harlan Coe could be a bumpy ride, even now that they seemed headed for reconciliation. He'd helped her find an apartment but continued living with his parents a block away on Spokane's lovely South Hill. He made conjugal visits — sometimes sneaking over for the night — but after nearly a year of this unusual arrangement he still hadn't told his mother and father what he was doing.

That's so typical of him, Jeni thought. He loves to be devious, to go from A to B by way of X and Y. But, good Lord — hiding a woman from his parents at the age of thirty-one? *His own ex-wife?*

She was pretty sure she knew what was frightening him. Mamie Ruth Enfield Coe tyrannized her son Fred and her husband Gordon, managing editor of the Spokane *Chronicle*, and she'd tried her damnedest to tyrannize Jeni. In her former role of mother-in-law, Mrs. Coe had traveled back and forth to Las Vegas and Los Angeles, endlessly meddling in their marriage. On a drive across the Nevada desert the short-fused woman had reached across the front seat and raked Jeni's cheek with her fingernails. The scar was permanent; she had to use cover-up when she did her face. The only apology had come from Fred: "Mother Bear forgot to take her thyroid pills."

Mother and son had always been close. He lovingly called her "Barefax" or "Mother Bear" and she called him "Freddiecoe," "Coco," "Rickie," and "Son." She had some kind of whammy on him; there was no doubt about that. They were twenty-six years apart — Ruth was fifty-eight now, although she still dressed like a young woman — but the two of them acted more like boyfriend and girlfriend, even to the point of spats and reconciliations. Jeni wished the woman would just butt out.

She'd never understood the relationship between Ruth and Gordon Coe, either. Fred's gray-haired father, a retired Reserve Army colonel, had been on the *Chronicle* for something like forty years and married to Ruth for over thirty. He was quiet and hardworking, a typical Spokanite. Ruth hectored and badgered the poor man, wasted his money, called him a bore and a stick in the mud and punished him with frequent threats of divorce. Sometimes she left his bed and board for months. Jeni wondered why he bothered to hang on.

Whatever the parental problems, Fred and Jeni were still in love—at least she was, and Fred certainly acted like it, bringing her flowers and gifts and pleading for another chance. Their sex life was good—he'd always insisted she was the best partner he'd ever had—and they both seemed ready to settle down, with Jeni working as a bookkeeper and Fred raising money for a disco. But what were the chances of a reconciliation if the mother-in-law kept interfering? Nil, Jeni told herself.

She wished she knew what had gone wrong between her and Ruth Coe. She had theories. She knew that Ruth considered her too old for her godlike son. But were six and a half years an unbridgeable gulf? Or maybe it was because she'd been married before—but so had Ruth. Jenifer knew for a fact that Ruth described her as "white trash." It was one of the woman's pet expressions, culled from *Gone With the Wind*, her favorite source of wisdom.

Jenny Linnea Coe, renamed "Jenifer" and "Jeni" by her ex-husband Fred, was the devoted mother of fine twin sons from an earlier marriage and she definitely did *not* consider herself "white trash." The hip-shooting mother-in-law had always been quick to pass judgment. She liked to misquote Bible verses, mostly about hellfire and the wrath of God, but Jenifer wished she would re-read Matthew on judging.

Sometimes she wondered if Ruth Coe knew what was going on behind her back. Not only were Jeni and Fred meeting nightly, but he'd begun transferring his belongings from his parents' condominium to her place. The latest item was his electric typewriter. In a few nights he intended to move in permanently.

Jenifer still wasn't completely relaxed about the idea. But he'd promised that it would be different this time. His novels would be successful, his disco would go big, and he would put his money to work in real estate and build a fortune. She knew better than to buy his forecasts outright. He had always lived in the future, but the present never seemed to work out. She thought of all the lost nights sitting in Vegas discotheques like Dirty Sally's and the Troubador watching him charm a bunch of silly women tittering around his disc-jockey console. She remembered the time he told her out of the blue that he was going to make a fortune as a gigolo, catering to both sexes. She remembered the mornings he hadn't come home, the lies she'd caught him in, his eccentricities, his peculiar ideas about dress and life. He was always changing his look, tinting his hair, getting it permed. Sometimes he shaved his head and wore wigs. The Coes were obsessed with their looks; Fred and his sister Kathleen had each undergone cosmetic surgery. Jeni couldn't imagine why they'd bothered. With or without improvements, the whole family looked like movie stars.

Most of all Jeni remembered how Fred could rationalize his most outrageous actions and almost make her agree with him. Out of work in Santa Monica, they'd gone a month without paying for a single restaurant meal— he taught her to slip outside and start the car during dessert so he could make a fast getaway. He explained that a person without money has an ethical right to steal. She couldn't imagine how she'd allowed herself to become involved in such scams. But he was convincing, and he used big words.

Now that they were back in conservative Spokane, she could see why she'd needed to drink. But alcohol had made her hostile, and she'd been off the stuff for almost a year now. She wondered if she really wanted to go back to a life where booze was almost a necessity. There were alternatives: other cities, other jobs, other men. *Plenty* of other men. At thirty-seven, she was a slender woman of five-nine with a straight profile and prominent cheekbones set in an oval face. Her large blue eyes were widely spaced. Her hair, once dyed black in a misguided attempt to make it resemble Ruth Coe's, was now back to its natural light auburn. She spoke in a husky voice and carried herself with a model's grace. She hadn't lacked for male attention since her days as student body leader, star golfer and National Honor Society member in high school.

Sometimes she wondered if there would be enough money to support the planned reconciliation; Fred hadn't drawn a salary in a couple of years. She had a steady income from her job at the rest home, but he lived by parasitizing his father's modest salary as an editor. It was unnerving that the man she loved had never succeeded in the business world. He'd been a theater usher and DJ and radio announcer; those were his total credits at age thirty-one. And yet he acted as though he were one of the outstanding young businessmen of his era. "I'm a media man," she'd often heard him boast. He sometimes referred to himself as "a former radio news editor," but she was under the impression that his radio news experience consisted of reading wire-service roundups between selections by Chubby Checker and the Who.

He also claimed that he was an author, but the books he'd churned out in his spare time—hunching over the typewriter for hours without a break— had never come close to acceptance by a publisher. His novels, *Snowy* and *Shirley* and *Outrage*, his satirical magnum opus, *Sex in the White House*— all had been failures. After *Sex* had been turned down thirty or forty times, he'd published the book in paperback with a loan from his loyal father. Then no major distributor would handle it.

Jeni knew Fred to be a funny man, especially in his scathing send-ups, but she hadn't found a humorous line in the work. She figured she wasn't sophisticated enough to appreciate word play like "cuntree" and "Amareeka" and "unWashedington" and tableaux like "President Richyard Obb Noxious" masturbating in "the Ovary Office." Whole passages seemed sophomoric:

> Only those of the highest caste were allowed to reside at the Pearly-gate. There were no Jewz permitted...and no Catlicks, no Proud-estunts, no blacks, reds, yellows or ethnics—only Episscopaleyuns,

atheists and there were two Hindus (Brahmans, Oxford-edu-
cated...don't you know!).

Thousands of copies of the paperback were mildewing in storage, and he still
insisted he would turn them into cash. Jeni thought, He's a permanent resident
of outer space, living on dreams. But that was Fred, and if you took him, you
took his eccentricities, his enthusiasms, his wild ideas. Recently he'd gone on
a diet involving strict avoidance of food additives and dangerous "poisons" such
as the ones in tapwater. He provided various explanations for the regimen:
that it helped relieve his allergies, that it would raise the low sperm count that
had prevented him and Jeni from having children, and that it mellowed his
"broadcast voice."

Jeni couldn't understand the constant concern about his voice. He spoke
with a studied coolness reminiscent of his idol Hugh Hefner, but there was
nothing noteworthy about his style or his delivery. He could lower his voice
to sound like Santa Claus and he could "punch it up" like Ted Baxter, the
fatuous newscaster on the old *Mary Tyler Moore Show*, but these were mim-
icries. He'd been fired from his radio DJ job at KENO in Las Vegas after one
of the bosses had re-auditioned him on a bad day. And now he was stuffing
himself with sardines and baked potatoes and Perrier water to protect his
precious voice. To Jeni it seemed like the act of a duffer wasting time buffing
his woods.

But there was so much she didn't understand about the man she loved.
She'd always tended to be self-critical; maybe their troubles had been as much
her fault as his and the two of them were natural partners after all: Coco and
Jeni, Son and Sweet Bird, Rick and Pooky. Then there was Ruth, old Barefax;
sooner or later she would cut herself in on the deal. Good God, Jenifer thought,
we're a cast of thousands! How will it ever work out?

3

Two months after she'd been raped alongside a tulip bed, Lois Higgins still hadn't resumed menstruating. At first she thought she might be pregnant, a possibility that frightened her almost as much as the rape. She made an appointment with a doctor to see about aborting the madman's child.

Every night before she fell asleep she felt his hands gripping her breasts, his arm lifting her from the grass, his fingers sliding down her throat. She saw his large face and his square chin and his angry eyes, smelled his soap and his peppermint breath. She would fall asleep after an hour or two and dream about rape. At first her dreams were reconstructions of the event, as though her mind were trying to come to grips with what had happened. Then she began a series of dreams in which she would repulse the rapist. She blew his head off with a pistol; she pounded him with hammers; she severed his penis and dropped it into the rapids below the Monroe Street bridge and yelled, "Go get it!" Then she flung him over the rail.

She apologized over and over to her husband, admitted that it was her own fault for stomping out of the restaurant and putting herself at the mercy of the first maniac who came along the street. Al told her that she wasn't to blame, but he was strangely unresponsive when she tried to discuss the details. "I guess he doesn't understand," she told her mother. "His attitude is—I don't want to hear it, I don't want to discuss it. But talking about it is what I need!"

She drew closer to Becky—too close, she realized later, for the infant's welfare. Al would come home and find her sobbing in a corner with the year-old child in her arms. "She's my only salvation," Lois explained. "She's sweet and innocent and—I can trust her." He would shake his head and turn away.

He seemed to want sex more than ever. She wondered what had made her so desirable. Surely not the rape? The prospect of making love to any man, even her husband, made her want to throw up. When Al increased the pressure after a few weeks, she was afraid he would leave her for one of his teenyboppers, and she took her fears to a therapist. "He can't understand the rape," Lois explained. "He can't understand why I don't want him near me for a while, why I hurt inside, why I'm so bitter."

They discussed her past. She admitted that she'd always been apprehensive about sex. In her short lifetime she'd endured abortion, abuse, several attempts at force. "This rape is the end of the line," she told the counselor. "My sex life is over."

But the therapy worked. Two months after the rape she said to herself, Hey, neat, I think I can actually *stand* it. She sent some signals, crawled into bed and took off her nightgown. Al turned in surprise and said, "Are you . . . ready?"

"Yes," she said. He aroused her with his hands, then slid on top. It felt good. Then she looked into his eyes and saw the rapist. She threw him off and bolted from the bedroom. When he followed she picked up Becky and held the child like a cross between them. Finally he dressed and went out.

That was where matters stood. A standoff. Al was getting his sex elsewhere and she was sure she was pregnant with the rapist's child. A day before her appointment to discuss an abortion, her period began. Thank God, she thought. Now I won't have to have that madman's baby. Or anybody else's.

4

Jenifer's and my relationship was one of, uh, I'd say at least on my part it was almost entirely one of more of a brother and sister type thing....—Fred Coe, Dec. 27, 1981

[The psychopath] cannot achieve true and abiding loyalty to any principle or person.—Hervey Cleckley, M.D., *The Mask of Sanity*

One warm June evening Jenifer Coe opened the door of her small apartment to admit her ex-husband Fred. From this night on they would be together— no more sneaking back and forth from his parents' condo and pretending that he wasn't seeing her.

Lying on their air mattress later, he warned her that his mother might be angry when she found that the carefully arranged lump in his bed was not her beloved "Son." Jeni didn't have to be told about her former mother-in-law's temper. She only hoped that the woman would learn to live with the fact that her thirty-one-year-old son had cut the cord at last.

But had he? As she listened to him go on and on about his mother and how much he hated to "break her heart like this," she wondered if he would ever be free. The maternal attachment went too deep—and it went both ways. She remembered a scene four or five years back when they'd been vacationing at his parents' old house on the South Hill. One night Ruth announced that she was going to trim his shoulder-length hair. She approached with the scissors and Fred wrested them away.

The enraged woman stuffed a couple of traveling bags and her yearling Samoyed in her new Chrysler Imperial and announced that she wouldn't spend another night under the same roof with such a disobedient son. She slept at a motel sixty miles away, losing the frisky pup in the process, and then drove on to Nevada. A few days later she returned home by air, leaving the Chrysler behind. At the time, Jeni had wondered about the woman's mental state. In the ensuing years nothing had changed her opinion that Ruth Coe was mentally ill and her relationship with Fred was essentially sick.

What would the woman do in the morning when she found that "Son" was gone? Lying on the mattress, Jeni could see nothing but trouble ahead.

She listened as Fred told how frightened he'd been sneaking away. He said that he hated to hurt his parents, that he owed them a lot—including several substantial loans—but he'd risked it for love of his "Sweet Bird."

Jenifer had heard similar endearments for six years. She consoled him by saying that Ruth would soon adjust. "What else can she do?" She wished she was as sure as she sounded.

The next day Fred called his mother and confessed. Ruth cursed him out and demanded to know where he and Jeni were living. When he refused to give her the address, she told him he could consider himself disowned. His lower lip quivered as he recounted the conversation.

Ruth Coe soon learned that Jeni was working at St. Joseph's Care Center, a nursing home. Jeni began receiving disturbing phone calls, often when one of the nuns was at her elbow. Ruth would say, "Why don't you get out of Son's life?" Sometimes she would attack Jeni for leaving Fred in the first place and then having the nerve to return to Spokane to bother him again.

Jenifer made it plain that she resented the intrusions, and the calls turned anonymous and silent. She would hear breathing, but no one would be on the line. She was sure it was Ruth—checking on her or Fred. Several times Jeni whispered, "Ruth, please! *This is an office!*" For weeks the calls continued.

5

A mobile-home salesman named D. Jay Williams glanced at the clock and grabbed the ringing phone. Who could be calling at 1:30 in the morning?

"Ja-ay?" He recognized the tortured vowel: two clear musical notes on an instrument called the larynx.

"Yes, Mrs. Coe."

"Ja-ay, I'm *very* upset with you. Do you want to know why? *You* let that horrible woman back into Fred's life!"

"*I* let her—?"

"*You* helped him bring her back to Spokane and *you* helped them get together. *You* were the go-between, Jay." All musicality fled the voice, and it took on the quality of a shriek. "*Don't lie about it!*"

The trouble was, she was mostly right. Active churchman Jay Williams was Fred Coe's closest friend—they'd met in grammar school and sworn eternal loyalty. They'd played together, worked together, fought together, drunk beer together and dallied with women together, although those days were now so distant that Williams could hardly imagine himself as a participant. Despite various separations their mutual slogans remained in full force: "*semper fideles*" and "*esprit de corps*," which Coe insisted meant boosting each other in every way and at every opportunity.

"Ja-ay?"

"Yes, Mrs. Coe?"

"Suppose you just explain yourself." Her voice took on an imperious quality. "You *can't*, can you? I rather thought not."

Williams couldn't think. Fred must have told his mother everything. He wondered why. Finally he said, "Talk to Fred about it, will you, Mrs. Coe? He asked me to do what I did."

This wasn't the first call from Ruth Coe, although it was the first after midnight and the first since Fred had moved back in with Jenifer. Williams wished he'd never become involved. He was no Jeni Coe fan—he wasn't happy with the way she alternated between gushing over Fred and raving about other men from her past. He also felt uneasy about the vague charges she made against Fred from time to time and a certain lack of coherence in her personality. He didn't need to be reminded of Coe's peccadilloes—he'd been involved in too many of them himself.

A former Golden Gloves titlist and Vietnam Marine, Williams had become a devout Seventh Day Adventist, an elder of his church in the Spokane Valley. He wasn't righteous or pushy about his religion, but his faith was total. To Williams there was a difference between Christians and true Christians. And true Christians understood and forgave. He thought of II Corinthians: "To whom ye forgive any thing, I forgive also."

Besides, Christian or not, he admired his old friend Coe, found him brilliant, witty, imaginative, alive with exciting ideas, an unsung genius who had insisted all through the years of their friendship that someday he would be one of the richest men in the world. Williams still saw no reason to doubt him, despite a slow start. His friendship with the atheistic Coe was a cornerstone of his life. You didn't dump a friend like that just because he was a little eccentric. To Jay Williams, loyalty to friends came second only to loyalty to God. Sometimes his wife warned him that Coe took advantage of these twin beliefs; Jay always answered that she didn't understand.

That was why he'd agreed to help Fred and Jeni arrange their meetings and relayed messages back and forth. It hadn't been easy, with Fred living at his parents' condo and Ruth ready to disavow her only son if he so much as glanced at Jenifer again. But Williams had accepted the assignment in the sacred name of friendship.

A few days after the late-night call from Ruth Coe, he got another call at his office. This time Mrs. Coe sounded like her old friendly self. "Jason, I'm looking for Fred," she purred. "I've misplaced his address."

She's trying to trick me, Williams realized. The last thing Fred and Jeni want right now is a visit from her, and she knows it. They even hide their car. "I'm sorry, Mrs. Coe," he said. "I can't help you."

The calls continued for days. Ruth Coe knew how tight the two friends were, and she knew that Williams wouldn't lie. She tried to pry the address out of him and flatter it out of him and when nothing else worked she tried to threaten it out of him. In desperation he went to Fred. "Listen, I'm not gonna lie to your mother. So from now on don't tell me anything more than necessary about you and Jeni, okay? I don't want to know where you're living; I don't want to know anything more than the minimum."

Fred had always scoffed at Jay's dedication to truth—words were tools, he'd patiently explained to his churchly friend, and if lies achieved a beneficial purpose, they were not only acceptable but moral. Coe called this approach "situational ethics," and said it was derived in part from the Russian-emigré author Ayn Rand.

Now Fred promised to keep him as much in the dark as possible—at least till Ruth Coe quieted. Everything would be on a need-to-know basis for a while. Jay hoped it wouldn't be long.

6

Jeni could tell that Fred was still worried sick about his mother's angry reaction. He would make long detours to keep from going near his parents' condominium, and he spoke often of moving to another part of town—one block wasn't much of a buffer zone. But it cost money to move and they were broke except for Jeni's modest salary. All they could do was wait. Ruth was famous for her mood changes—"a fast recycler," as her husband Gordon liked to describe her.

Fred usually parked his '77 Cutlass a few blocks away so that his mother wouldn't spot it. But one evening a few weeks after he'd moved back in with Jeni, he parked in the lot behind the apartment building. During the night the car was vandalized—windows broken, lights knocked out, silver-gray finish dented and scratched, upholstery ripped. The insurance company paid $1500 for repairs.

Two weeks later, the Cutlass was damaged again. This time Coe's yellow vanity plate "DISCO" drew particular attention. The insurance investigator said some of the damage looked as if it might have been inflicted by a woman's stiletto heel. Fred cautioned Jeni to be silent and told the agent he couldn't imagine who would do such a thing. The insurance company paid again.

Later Jeni asked, "What's your mother trying to prove?"

"Gordo told me she's back with her shrink," Fred explained. "He said she, uh, flipped out."

"Your father said that?" The words didn't sound like Gordon Coe. "What made her flip out?"

Fred didn't answer. He frequently ignored difficult questions. Jeni knew it was a waste of time to probe.

The newly reunited couple moved several miles away to a small apartment a few blocks from the Lincoln Heights shopping center, still on the South Hill but three miles removed from Ruth and her spike heels. She might find them there—a favorite gift shop was in the vicinity—but it wouldn't be as easy this time.

* * *

Jay Williams was troubled when Fred told him about the war against the Cutlass. He had known the family since 1953 and always found Fred's mother a likable mix of Auntie Mame and Zelda Fitzgerald. He'd heard her criticized as overdressed and overstated with her pedigreed collies straining at the leash and her furs and diamonds and grape-sized pearls, but he didn't regard flamboyance as a sin. She'd always been kind and loyal to Fred's friends, sometimes overly so.

But trashing a car! The mobile home salesman couldn't comprehend such hateful behavior.

He thought about Jeni and Fred. As charitable as he wanted to be toward them, they didn't seem any more natural together than when they'd first married six years ago. Jeni still gazed into Fred's eyes and called him "Coco," and Fred still picked out her wardrobe and kept after her to change her style. Once when he'd revamped her to his own specifications, he'd paraded her around the Williamses' living room like a show dog. "Jenifer, turn around! Show Sue and Jay how much weight you've lost. Jenifer, show them how that jacket reverses for evening wear."

Jeni had made the graceful moves she'd learned as a store model at The Crescent, and Jay had felt obliged to comment, "Yeah, Jeni, you really look good."

"Do you like her hair?"

"Yeah, Fred. Looks great that way."

Sue Williams, herself a chic and attractive woman, couldn't abide the home fashion shows. She would find an excuse to disappear till the Coes had left. She told Jay that she wasn't the least surprised by what had happened to the Cutlass. She reminded Jay that they'd watched Jeni and Ruth together in the short period when mother-in-law and daughter-in-law had been friendly. "Both of them overdo everything—remember that, Jay? If they like you, they're all over you. If they hate you, they're ready to punch you out. Remember that night they were trying to outcompliment each other? Anybody could tell they hated each other."

Jay said, "But why would Ruth wreck his car?"

"It was the jilted sweetheart routine, Jay. Do you realize how Ruth acted? Like the other woman!"

He said he would have to think about that.

7

For a time I had an agent in Chicago who was convinced I was the next Hemingway—-the next Shakespeare—-the next——the next— —I cannot tell you!!!! But then.... right at the apex of my ca- reer.... this Jew fukker died!! Dirty little cocksuckin yid, heb, kike, M-F!!!!—Fred Coe, Jan. 30, 1973

Jenifer Coe busied herself around the apartment as she tried to imagine where her missing husband could be. It was 10 o'clock; he'd promised to be home by 7 to take her to dinner.

She couldn't believe how quickly things had soured. She'd been back with Fred for four months and his behavior was driving her to distraction. He'd replaced the battered Cutlass with a new air-conditioned Pontiac a half mile long. "What are *we* doing with a car like this?" she'd asked. "We can't even pay the rent." His plans for bringing disco to Spokane were as nebulous as ever. His latest novel had been turned down again. How could they afford another car-lease payment?

He kept telling her to relax. "I'll always take care of you, Pooky," he insisted. "You don't have a thing to worry about." She must have heard that a thousand times. He claimed that his business dealings required a classier image, and what was classier than a new Grand Prix? She couldn't imagine what "business dealings" he was talking about. His potential disco backers and associates stopped returning his calls. Some were probably put off by his manner. He always referred to himself as Mr. Coe. "Uh, yes indeed, this is Mr. Coe speaking. To whom am I speaking, please?" He didn't seem to un- derstand the easy familiarity of American businessmen—the joshing and ban- ter that masked the intensity underneath. Once she'd heard him giving brisk instructions to a literary agent. "With Jews," he'd explained to her, "you've got to be aggressive." She felt three inches tall as she listened to him on the phone. "Hello, Lindeman? F. H. Cohen here. Have you read my manuscript yet? No? *Well, read it!*" The agent rejected the script and Cohen reverted to Coe.

Fred's old friend Jay Williams claimed to have a theory that explained everything. He joked that Fred was a space invader trying to imitate earthlings. There were times when Jeni could swear he was right. That damned Grand

Prix, she said to herself as she waited in their new apartment. Every time you drive it around the block it's another gallon of gas. He was out in the car now—God only knew where. He'd probably never intended to take her to dinner. What would he use for money? His father's credit card, she supposed. That was his usual method of payment. Ruth still wasn't speaking.

Jeni wondered how much longer they were going to have to sneak around Spokane worrying that Fred's mother was going to catch up and—what next? Fire-bomb their apartment? She shook her head angrily. How frustrating that a mother-in-law could create so many problems, even *in absentia*.

She looked at her watch. Fred was over three hours late. She phoned a place he'd said he might visit. A male voice told her that no one named Coe had been there, and was she sure she had the right number?

Oh, God, she thought, it's a repeat of Vegas. Was everything going to unravel again? Her self-esteem was gone; she didn't even have her own style anymore. He kept trying to remake her in another image. A few years back he'd bought her an Afro wig, and she'd worn it till her sister Sonia, a former fashion coordinator, told her, "Jeni, you look *awful!*" Then he'd decided she should be a blonde, so she lightened her hair, and a few weeks later he'd suggested that dark brown would be nice.

Why wasn't he satisifed with her natural look? Or his own, for that matter? He still changed his hairstyle frequently. Sometimes he shaved and showered twice a day; sometimes he didn't bother for three or four days. His old wispy DJ moustache and sideburns came and went. There were times when he looked gaunt, times when he looked bloated. When he wasn't fasting or subsisting on steak and corn and Perrier water, he was gorging on junk food. He called this aspect of his new diet "flooding" and had an explanation—something about testing his body, finding its limits—but Jeni knew there wasn't a diet on earth that called for alternate starving and stuffing. Maybe he'd misread the instructions; she'd known him to do that before. Of course he had an explanation for every damn fool thing he did. If he fell off the top of St. John's Cathedral, he'd be explaining before he hit the ground that it was a planned trip.

Now where was he? It was 10:30. She felt anxious. This wasn't the first time since their reconciliation that he'd been hours late. They'd argued about it. Wouldn't his mother be pleased! Jeni wandered to the living room and picked up a sheet of his newest business stationery: "SPOKANE METRO GROWTH. Activists for a Bigger and Better Spokane." Lately he'd been using the letterhead to write unsolicited municipal advice, mostly to the *Spokesman-Review*'s letters column. He signed the letters "X. Drew Butler," a pseudonym inspired by happy hooker Xaviera Hollander and Rhett Butler of *Gone With the Wind*. To the businesslike Jeni the project was a poor substitute for a job.

He'd also made a decision to go into real estate, and he'd been spending hours in men's shops buying a working wardrobe—four suits, twenty-five shirts, three sweaters, four pairs of shoes and a dozen silk ties. He couldn't work a day as a realtor till the collection was assembled. "Fred," she'd pleaded, "just go to work. Sell a house. *Then* buy your clothes."

It was like talking to a store dummy. He'd always been a perfectionistic dreamer. Jeni knew that the plans he drew up in his head were more real to him than the messy world outside, and in his head now he was seeing himself whirring around town in his new silver-gray Grand Prix—the best-dressed realtor in Spokane. People would come to him for the sheer pleasure of being around someone so fashionable.

He'd explained it all to her, but unfortunately—as he'd also explained— she didn't understand the subtleties. He'd learned all about business psychology from Robert J. Ringer's *Winning Through Intimidation*, Michael Korda's *Power: How to Get It, How to Use It*, and similar books. Jeni wondered when he'd done his reading. As far as she could tell, he never finished a book. He drew his knowledge from magazine articles and newspaper items, from flyleaves and blurbs.

She thought she knew who was behind his latest ideas about fashion. Jay Williams was the Johnny Carson type, a short lean man who could look stylish in a sack. Up to now, Fred had been wearing his old Las Vegas wardrobe— designer jeans, nylon shirts, gaudy shoes, no ties—but Jay had shown him John J. Molloy's book *Dress for Success*, and now all he could think about were three-piece suits and custom-made silk shirts without pockets. The new wardrobe would cost over two thousand dollars, and he was buying it with a supply of bank cards made out to "Fred H. Coe," "F. Harlan Coe," "Harlan Coe" and other combinations. When he overdrew a card, he would apply for another, using a different name. Even with a bad rating, credit wasn't hard to get if your father was managing editor of the *Chronicle* and your references were straight-arrow businessmen like D. Jay Williams.

But what would happen when the bills came in?

She thought, What a mess! What chaos! The utter irresponsibility of it all! She wished she had a drink.

8

I resent being described as "conservative."...Spokane may be "conservative-looking," as you assert. I most definitely am NOT! I dress in expensive, high-style clothing...and being a gregarious type I think I'd far closer fit the adjective "flamboyant."—Fred Coe, Jan. 15, 1982

The friendly folks at the James S. Black real estate agency could hardly believe their luck when a young man stepped from the pages of *Gentleman's Quarterly* and into their lives in October, 1978. The real estate market was still strong in Spokane, and no one in the busy office, least of all the females, resented the competition from Frederick Harlan Coe. "My God, he's the best-dressed young man I will *ever* see!" a middle-aged staff member told a friend. "And he takes such good care of himself. I'm so envious of his hair—he must have it cut and blown. That costs a mint!" She sighed and said, "How I wish I had the time."

Another employee asked him how old he was, a subject of interest around the busy office. He looked to be in his early twenties, but there was something about his eyes that suggested he might be older. The realtor was puzzled by his reaction to her question. "He acted like it was a deep dark secret," she said later. "I only know one other person who's that secretive about age, and she's eighty-seven!"

After a few weeks the manager, a bearded dynamo named Jim Cory, took notice that Coe's real estate career seemed to be getting off to a slow crawl, but that wasn't unexpected. Rookie realtors were supposed to be like freshman legislators and new cars—quiet and untroublesome during the break-in period. Coe seemed to know what was expected of him. And of course he was only a part-time employee; he was still doggedly working on a disco deal with the Sheraton. He'd been up front about it in the interview, admitted that the project might take six or eight more months to settle one way or the other. Jim Cory had admired Coe's honesty. There'd never been much doubt about the hiring. James S. Black himself, owner of the firm, had announced that his friend Gordon Coe's son was coming over and if he looked any good to give him a shot. The young man had introduced himself to Black by writing a long letter in which he praised the company as "the best in town."

As the work weeks went by, Coe seemed to be spending most of his time staring into space, except when he was off on his disco venture. One day he struck up a conversation with Mary Jo Macy, a veteran realtor. "I'm gonna be the greatest listing salesperson in Spokane," he said after a few preliminaries about the attractive outfit she was wearing. "Just watch me. I mean—*the greatest.*"

Mrs. Macy, a jovial woman with a laugh that rattled windowpanes, started to suggest that he stop talking and start selling, but she refrained. No sense in dampening those high spirits. A short while later the new employee strolled over to her desk in his jaunty walk, flashed a white-toothed smile and said, "Are you busy?"

"No," she lied.

He asked a complex question about closing real estate deals—the sort of inside detail that couldn't be learned in short training courses like the one he'd taken. She tried her best to answer, but after a few minutes she began to feel that he wasn't listening. In the middle of a sentence he said, "Thank you," and walked away.

She leaned back and tried to remember something from six or eight years back: a luncheon, or was it a charity thing? She had gone to a house on the South Hill and met an attractive woman with black-on-black hair and lavender fingernails. A young man had stared sullenly from a living room chair. He had long hair, sloping eyes and an outfit straight from Hollywood: silk shirt open to the navel, tight-fitting pants and fruit-boots in purple or plum, she forgot which. She remembered thinking at the time, Why doesn't that kid get up and say how do you do? He looked like a drug-taker or boozer, and she hoped her own kids never gave that kind of impression to anybody.

Now she remembered that the woman's name had been Coe and the son must have been Fred. Why hadn't she realized it before? But he looked so different now. And acted so friendly and pleasant and outgoing—until these last few minutes.

Mrs. Macy had done charity work in psychiatric wards. As she sat musing at her desk the word "schizoid" leaped to mind. But that was a huge jump to a drear conclusion, and she knew she wasn't qualified to make it. Still, she wondered if she had seen the real Fred Coe, or if a real one existed at all.

9

The psychopath never adjudicates the situation with reference to the future. He just plunges ahead....They will also be more bored than the average person. They have to constantly escalate in order to get a kick out of life. And at times they escalate to the point of being arrested.
—Thomas P. Detre, M.D., Yale University professor of psychiatry

They seem to live only for the moment.—Karl Menninger, M.D.

Late on the night of November 26, 1978, six weeks after Fred Coe had embarked on his real estate career and seven months after the Lois Higgins rape, a young woman was walking along a street near police headquarters. Chilled air swirled up from the Spokane River a few blocks to the south, and as she kicked her way through fallen leaves a man approached. She wasn't concerned. West Broadway was a busy street. He was tall, on the slender side, and wore a dark leather jacket and white pants. When he came even he grabbed her by the breasts.

She jerked away and cried, "I'm gonna call the police!" A car approached and the man ran. Witnesses saw him jump into a silver-gray Pontiac Grand Prix. They followed him to the Savage House Pizza Parlor, a few blocks from the scene of the Higgins rape, and called the police. By the time officers arrived the young man was gone. But witnesses had made a note of his license plate, "DISCO," and a rough description: six-three, 185, with medium-length curly hair.

The case was assigned to a veteran homicide detective. After handling nearly a hundred murders in his long career, Bill Beeman wasn't overjoyed about catching a misdemeanor, but it was easier to handle the petty case than beef about it. All he had to do was run the tag through the State Department of Licensing and arrest the owner for "indecent liberties."

The Grand Prix turned out to be leased to a "Fred Coe" of Box 421, Airway Heights, Wash. Beeman checked out the box when the post-office substation opened the next day. It was registered to an organization called "Spokane Metro Growth."

He dug into police files and found an old listing for "Frederick Harlan

Coe, 1015 W. 29th, D.O.B. 2-2-47." The address was near the top of the South Hill, a good neighborhood. The date of birth meant the subject was now thirty-one. The witnesses had guessed he was younger, and the nature of the offense suggested a wild teenager, perhaps one with an inability to hold his liquor.

There were four entries on the file card. The first said, "Mentioned in Prop. Damage—Swimming Pool Rpt. 8-21-63." Coe would have been sixteen then. A chippy case, Beeman realized: greasy kid stuff. He hadn't even been charged.

The next notation read, "Mentioned, Carnal Knowledge 6-7-65." Coe would have been eighteen by then, probably in his senior year of high school. Under those conditions "carnal knowledge" could mean a lot of things, none of them of deep criminal significance. Again no charge had been filed.

The third entry was more serious: "Poss. Assault 5-1-66." No formal charges were listed. The fourth and final citation was for "Indecent Liberties and 1st Degree Burglary 5-28-71." This time a charge had been brought—and dropped.

In a separate folder Beeman found a 1977 Disorderly Person report. An airline stewardess had sworn that Fred Coe, then thirty years of age, had peeped over the toilet wall in the women's room of Vip's Restaurant on Third Ave. and told her, "You sure have a nice cunt." No disposition was shown, which probably meant that the case had been dropped like the others.

Before the detective could look further, he caught a hot felony. When he returned to the indecent liberties case, he could locate neither suspect nor victim. A fresh murder pinned him down for another week. He wanted to check with the prosecutor's office to see why none of the earlier charges against Coe had stuck, but he couldn't find time. With no prior convictions, the worst possible sentence would be a wrist slap.

When still more felony cases fell into his in-box, Beeman marked the Coe case "inactive" and filed it. Maybe someday. . . .

The Spokane police department had numbered 250 officers, give or take a handful, for as long as anyone could remember. Per capita, the city had half as many policemen as the national average. In days gone by the short staff had been more than sufficient to keep the peace, but in recent years the detectives and uniformed personnel had become sorely overburdened. "The business people who run things, they like to pretend we don't need more cops because there's no real crime here," a retired detective explained. "That makes it easier to bring in new industry and keep up our image as the market town of the Inland Empire, all that bullshit."

The SPD was so chronically shorthanded that traffic enforcement barely existed. Minor automobile accidents were ignored; red-faced drivers stood in the streets and argued while policemen cruised past and waved. An unending topic of conversation on call-in radio shows was the lateness of police response, or the failure to respond at all. Canny Spokanites dialed the fire department when they needed help fast.

A detective supervisor observed later, "What the hell was Beeman supposed to do with that chippy indecent liberties case? We're so overloaded we're *always* inactivating. Inactivating is our way of life. And not just misdemeanors."

Fred Coe was free to go on his way.

10

GINI PERHAM—A nice, very sensitive, unstable woman. Bright and artistic. I had profound interest in her as a human being... but little or no interest in her romantically.—Fred Coe, March 29, 1982

The newcomer made only the faintest impression on Gini Perham when he entered the laundromat. She was too busy making change and operating the dry-cleaning machines and seeing that no one nudged ahead in the line. The Manito Highlander on Spokane's South Hill had seldom been so crowded. It was late December and the citizens of the South Hill were sprucing up their wardrobes for the holidays.

After a while the newcomer sidled over to the cash register and asked, "What do you think of this weather?"

Gini hadn't thought much about it. Spokane was suffering through one of its weird foggy spells, which alternated with biting cold to form the city's typical winter weather. She looked up at a nice-looking young man with a trace of a smirk on his face. "I like it," she said perversely.

"I don't," he said. "I'm from Las Vegas. Well, L.A., really. You know—sunshine and palm trees?"

She knew. As the daughter of the retired deputy commander of Spokane's Fairchild Air Force Base, Virginia Kay Perham was well traveled. And of all the places she had seen, she would take Spokane at its worst to the rest of the world at its best. The Perhams were an old Spokane family. There was a Perham Hall at nearby Washington State University; one ancestor had been a Standard Oil executive in Spokane and another the first Methodist minister in the Northwest.

At twenty-six Gini considered herself lucky to be back in her home town. She had more friends than anybody she knew. When she'd graduated from high school in 1970, a student newspaper had described her as "one of the most wonderful people around, a beautiful person, you can't find anyone who knows her that doesn't love her." She'd been an Army medic in Texas and a short-term Jesus freak. She'd helped harvest soft summer wheat in northwest Washington and waited on tables in Spain. Wherever she went she played tennis and rode horseback and dated men who were more serious about her than she was about them. By preference she always returned to Spokane. Her two brothers lived here and so did her divorced parents. Her mother had been institutionalized three times for depressions and hallucinations, and Gini helped take care of her in between studying art, writing and philosophy at a nearby junior college and working nights at the laundromat.

None of which was any of this young man's business. But here among the swishings of the yellow-gold Maytag machines and the sanitary smell of Tide and bleach and cleaning fluid, he seemed inspired to talk. He told her his name was "Coco" and didn't bother to ask hers. She took a better look and realized he hadn't lied when he'd said he was from out of town. He had light-brown hair almost to his shoulders and a velour shirt that opened at the collar, showing a few tendrils of hair. His fingers and hands looked small for his size, and when he spoke he waved them about strangely, the gestures not always fitting the words. He griped again about the local weather. "If you like L.A. so much," she asked, "what are you doing here?"

She hadn't intended the question rudely, and she was surprised when he stared back at her without answer. She tried to read his eyes to see if he was annoyed, but they were a kind of slate color that didn't reflect mood or light. She was reminded of four-year-olds who ignored questions they didn't feel like answering.

He switched to the subject of Spokane women and said they were prudish, backward, hard to date. Back home in L.A. and Vegas, he said, women were relaxed about dating and sex. He acted frustrated about being stuck in such a dump. She was too busy to listen. A few minutes later she overheard him talking to someone else waiting in line. He was saying that the women in Spokane were sticks and the local weather was lousy.

The Spokane-hater returned in a few months. His light-brown hair had been chopped short. He had a basket of women's and men's laundry neatly folded and stacked. There were so many towels that she wondered if he might be the coach of a children's team. "Remember me?" he asked.

"Uh, yes," she said.

"I'm Kevin," he said, offering a formal handshake.

Kevin? Hadn't he called himself something else the last time? Yes— "Coco." She'd known some people in the Jesus movement like that—"Pete" one week, "Forbearance" the next. After a while, he told her his name was Coe.

"Coco Coe?" Gini asked. He replied that his name was Kevin Coe and Coco was an old nickname.

In this conversation he didn't seem as negative and she wasn't as busy, and things went more smoothly. He told her that he'd been born in Las Vegas and had gone to school there. He told her about his days as a radio disc jockey under the name "Mark Mitchell." She thought, what a lot of names you have.

He walked to one of the Maytags and she noticed a cockiness in his stride, a saunter that didn't come off as natural. When he returned to the counter she noticed that his right eyebrow arched higher than the left and there was a small scar just to the right of one eye. "My wife's," he said, holding up a pair of nylons. He explained that he was living with his ex-wife and hinted that there was trouble between them. Ho-hum, Gini thought. Another misunderstood husband.

She'd heard just about all possible lines from married and single both. She was in the bloom of life, with dark auburn hair piled high on her head and eyes that were gray-green in winter and a vivid emerald when the outdoor foliage appeared (her mother called them "summer green eyes"). She had a light-olive complexion and a femininely sturdy figure built up by thousands of hours on tennis courts and horses. In Spain she'd been mistaken for Ava Gardner. There'd been only two lovers in her life but dozens of boyfriends. Once she'd wanted to be a cowgirl, later a doctor or nurse, and now she was thinking about marriage and motherhood. Which left out the unhappily married young man with the slightly sloping eyes and the neat stack of dirty clothes and the line of chatter.

She had no objection to listening. In his new mellow mood he was rattling on about his wife, a seeming preoccupation with him—how she was really a very lovely woman, but she, uh, she had an alcohol problem. Himself, he didn't drink—he thought too much of his body to abuse it. As he spoke he lifted some nylon dainties and fluffed them for the washer. Gini tried not to laugh—the poor thing seemed so henpecked. She could tell from the way he talked that his wife was dominant. Well, let him blow off steam. It wouldn't be noticed in the laundromat.

"Kevin" began appearing twice a week, each time striking up a conversation. She'd always been a good listener, and she had to admit she was beginning to enjoy him—he was soft-spoken and bright, never again as overbearing as on his first visit. Occasionally he used unusually long or esoteric words. She felt that he was trying to impress rather than communicate and took it as a compliment. One day he showed up with a growth of beard and disheveled hair. He was wearing a gray jogging suit, a change from his usual T-shirts or velour top. He apologized and told her it was important that she see him someday "in my usual clothes—three-piece suits and nice-looking shirts and shoes."

She wondered why it was important. A few days later she heard that he'd come in all dressed up and was sorry she was off.

Through the spring of 1979, he kept revealing more about himself. He brought in a paperback by "Superfry" called *Sex in the White House* and told her that he'd had a hand in the writing. She saw that the work was full of toilet humor and sexual perversion but decided not to judge him. Her eyes fell on the epigraph:

Blind Man Went Down to the Sea to See
What He Could See...But on the Beach
He Stepped on a Beer Can and Cut His Toe!

She guessed this was what the experts called wry humor. She glanced across the page and saw that the copyright was held by "F. H. Coe." She asked who that was.

He hesitated. "Well, F. H. is the guy I wrote it with, and Coe is me." It seemed an odd way to copyright a book, but she didn't press for details.

After a month or two Gini got the impression that things were looking up in the real estate business and wondered if she shouldn't think about plunging in herself. Kevin had begun arriving at the laundromat in three-piece suits cut in the European style; he looked like a male model in *Paris Match* or *Vogue*. He seemed unusually pleased when she complimented him.

"You have a great deal of taste, Gini," he told her. "Not everybody in Spokane appreciates flair."

He talked about how hard he'd been working and showed her a typed daily schedule: He'd broken his day into fifteen-minute segments, starting at 5:30 a.m. with a segment of exercise, followed by a segment in the shower and two segments for breakfast. After working till 5, he would come home for fifteen minutes of exercise preceding a thirty-minute dinner and an evening of work. He went to bed at 10 sharp. Gini wondered why he had to take such pains. Was his life so out of control? Around the laundromat he seemed in control of everything he did, down to the least arch of his eyebrow.

He spoke often about his relationship with his ex-wife Jenifer. He said the marriage had begun to disintegrate in Las Vegas after fights over the groupies who'd flocked around him when he was a disco DJ. Once she'd come at him with a knife. They'd moved to Santa Monica to try to save the marriage, but by that time Jeni was drinking heavily and seeing other men and it seemed best for him to get a divorce. But after he'd moved back to Spokane he'd heard that the poor woman was "an alcoholic basket case rattling around Southern California," and out of pity and compassion he'd arranged to bring her back to her home town of Spokane with the help of his best friend Jay Williams.

Gini listened attentively as he told how pleased his mother had been when he'd divorced Jeni and how annoyed she'd been when they'd re-established the relationship. His dear mother had only recently started talking to him after a long hiatus. He didn't love Jeni, he said, but felt responsible for her. She was an alcoholic and probably shouldn't have become involved with him in the first place. "No woman should."

"Why not?" Gini asked, mildly intrigued.

"Well, it's my life style, and just the type of person I am." She wondered what that meant. He'd begun to seem likable—a little henpecked and troubled but undeniably an interesting man. When he seemed depressed about his bills she offered to lend him money, and a few days later he asked for three hundred dollars. It was a larger amount than she'd had in mind, but she knew he was good for it.

Soon after accepting the money, he announced that he wouldn't be in as often. He was plunging full-time into real estate and his wife would be doing the family laundry. When he left she felt unaccountably depressed. She suspected that her feelings had passed beyond friendship.

11

Jenifer Coe flopped in the easy chair and stared across the room at her husband. He hadn't sold a square inch of real estate after months of racketing around town in his silver-gray Pontiac Grand Prix, and now he wanted to lease a new Oldsmobile. "What's wrong with the Grand Prix?" she asked.

"Nothing, Trinket," he said, pacing the floor excitedly. "I'll use the new car and you can drive the Grand Prix."

"We'll have two cars?"

"We *need* two cars! I'm gonna be the biggest listing salesperson in Spokane! Listen, I've got plans, ideas...."

His voice droned in the background as she contemplated their financial situation. She'd had to quit her job at St. Joseph's Care Center because bankcard collectors had begun harassing her at work and Ruth Coe's frequent calls disturbed the nuns. Jeni still hadn't found another job and they were months behind on their bills. "No more riding dirty old buses, Pooky!" Fred was saying. He described the car he had picked out: "A brand new Toronado, pure white, with air conditioning—"

"What's the lease fee?"

"—a tape deck, air conditioning, speakers all around, red leather seats, opera lights, power windows—"

"What's the monthly payment?"

"Oh, I don't know. Two-eighty, three hundred."

"Fred, we're broke!"

"It's a question of perspective," he said, and began a long explanation. She stopped listening when she heard the word "epistemological," one of his favorites. She wasn't sure what it meant and doubted if he knew himself. She let him ramble on till his pep talk was finished. There was no point in arguing; he was going to do what he'd decided anyway, and then bully her into agreement with his "superior" intellect.

Soon she heard the tapping of his typewriter. The sound stopped momentarily while he cursed himself loudly for making a mistake and rolled in a new sheet of paper. After a while he showed her his latest effort. It was a letter on Spokane Metro Growth stationery from "X. Drew Butler," advising the mayor of Airway Heights to prepare for major expansion over the next decade. She wanted to ask what that had to do with making a living, but she held back.

As spring gave way to the hot dry days of a typical Spokane summer, Jeni began feeling more and more mopey and unreal. Once when they'd lived in Las Vegas she'd gone to the Nevada Mental Health Clinic for depression, and a psychiatrist had told her, "Get interested in something." She hadn't then and she didn't now. Dealing with Fred Coe was a full-time job. It took all her energy just to try to understand him, and she wasn't any closer now than she'd been before their divorce in 1976.

She went out looking for jobs in her personal Grand Prix, but it was heavy on gas and their credit card had been voided. She killed time by hitting a bucket of golf balls and found that the click was gone. She dropped into a bingo parlor and didn't even buy a card. She spent hours at the bedside of her sister Sonia, a wonderfully patient woman racked with rheumatoid arthritis, and more hours visiting her mother—a living saint, the emotional support of her family. Jeni loved and trusted the two of them more than anyone on earth, but she couldn't bear to admit that her marriage was in trouble again.

Sometimes she walked the three-mile round trip to her parents' house just for something to do. One day she turned in at a bar.

12

Lois Higgins spent the first anniversary of her rape wondering how to kill herself. She still had Becky—sweet Becky, almost two now, a loving, lovely child—but otherwise life was meaningless. By force of will she had brought herself to the point of allowing her husband an evening of sex once a month or so. If he touched her on the upper arms—the sensitized area that the rapist had grabbed—she would begin a choking anxiety attack that sometimes passed into asthma and made her wonder if she would ever draw another breath.

Al's eyes resembled the rapist's; that was the problem. She wondered what made God play a dirty trick like that. Would it have been any big deal to give the rapist brown eyes, or wide-open evenly leveled eyes? Did they have to be exactly the same gray-blue color and slightly slanted shape as Al's? Yes, they did. God's idea of a joke.

She'd read about the psychological problems of Vietnam veterans, and she was sure she was experiencing delayed stress syndrome. Al would glance at her shoulders and she would grab Becky and hold tight. Nothing else could allay her fears. The sex act was joyless. She could have read a book and eaten an apple. She told herself that no one with a shred of self-respect would go on living like this. She reviewed her first suicide attempt: a handful of Percodans and penicillin tablets. They'd probably canceled each other out. This time it would be different. She would take Becky to her mother's, kiss both of them good-bye, and then go back home to—what? A slug from Al's .38? Gas? She would make sure there was no one around to save her.

13

I adore women...and they adore me. I am lucky—females have just always been superattracted to me! It is kind of a joke in the family!— Fred Coe, April 5, 1982

Gini Perham looked up from the laundromat counter and saw a familiar face. Only two or three days had passed since Kevin Coe had announced that his ex-wife would be doing the laundry from now on, and here he was with a basketful, the dirty clothes meticulously stacked as usual. She said, "I thought you told me—"

"I lost the argument," he said, grinning sheepishly and showing his even white teeth.

Gini was glad. He sat down and resumed where he'd left off: talking about Jenifer, how he was trying to help her and of course there was nothing physical between them and never would be. Sad to say, the poor woman was drinking heavily. As he was leaving, Gini touched his arm. He seemed so hassled.

She found herself thinking about him often; she saw a fundamental decency in the man, for all his idiosyncrasies like folding his dirty laundry and changing his look from time to time. When he didn't show up for a few days she missed him. Then one balmy April evening his car arrived at the laundromat and somehow she knew he had come to ask her out. The idea was exciting.

He waited till she was finished with a customer, then shyly asked her to dinner. She remembered that she was meeting a girlfriend. "I can't," she said. "I'm—sorry. I'd love to."

He patted his chest and said, "You're gonna break my heart. I've wanted to do this for a long time."

"Well, look," she said, hating herself for being too available, "maybe I can change things."

He picked her up when the laundromat closed at 10 p.m. On the way down the South Hill he drove so fast that she held on to the door handle. "Please," she said after a while, "couldn't you just slow down a little?" She didn't want to sound fearful—she drove fast herself, like most Spokanites— but this was positively dangerous.

"Oh, sure!" he said. A few minutes later they were speeding again.

They ate at the St. Regis Café, a warm little place with good food and cozy atmosphere. She didn't want to drive him deeper in debt, so she ordered an omelet. He surprised her by eating a large meal including dessert. His choices seemed heavy for someone who claimed to be on such a radical diet. He talked about himself in a disarmingly honest way while she doodled expertly on the butcher-paper tablecloth. He admitted that he'd been attracted to her for a long time. Some day, he promised, he would take her to a Las Vegas show, drive her through the streets of Beverly Hills at night, run with her on the sands of Santa Monica at sunset. "You're trying to impress me, aren't you?" she said, interrupting her doodling.

"Well, uh—yeah." She liked the way he admitted it.

"Don't bother. You've already impressed me. I mean you yourself, not what you can offer me. I've been to enough places already."

Over coffee he slid his hand on hers. It felt good—a proper gesture. Earlier she'd worried about being a homewrecker, but she felt no guilt. His marriage was dead; he'd made that plain. She'd doubted him at first, but the story made sense. In an age when so many men walked out on their troubles, he faced up to his. You had to admire his decency. After coffee he told her that he had to take her straight home—he didn't want to aggravate Jenifer by coming in too late. Maybe someday things would be different.

He dropped Gini off at her sick mother's house, where she planned to spend the night. She felt lightheaded as she walked across the lawn. After a long succession of grabbers and clutchers she'd finally met a gentleman. It almost seemed superfluous that he was handsome, tall, athletic and—no, he wasn't light on his feet, sort of klutzy really, but the slight ungainliness in his rolling walk only made him more attractive. For the first time in years she felt stimulated by a man.

Her mother was asleep when she went inside. Thank God, Gini thought, that's exactly what she needs. Lately the schizophrenia seemed worse than ever—for no reason at all she would order Gini from the house and then call her back, all apologies. She seemed to be losing track of her own thoughts. She would hug Gini and cry and then Gini would cry until the next aggressive period began.

To make matters worse, forty-seven-year-old Shirley Perham had gone deaf. Her once-lovely face was puffed out from medication, her tongue a lump. Sleep, mother, Gini said to herself. Dream about the old days. Her mother had never been happier than when she was helping others, and now this most loving woman in the world could barely help herself. Gini didn't consider her mother a burden—just a good friend in trouble. Her closest friend ever. She kissed her cheek and went home to her own apartment with Kevin on her mind.

Within a week they went out again. It was a repeat of their first date—an interesting conversation and a quick drive home. He told her it might be a while before he could see her; he was working on some big real estate deals and his wife was giving him constant trouble. Gini said she could wait.

Two days later she'd just checked in at the laundromat when one of her mother's neighbors phoned. There was trouble; could she come to her mother's house right away?

When she arrived she saw a squad car with flashing lights parked in front. "What happened?" she asked a uniformed policeman.

"Lady inside shot herself in the chest."

She tried to go in but the cop turned her back. "I'm her daughter," she insisted.

"It's sealed till the coroner leaves," he said politely. A neighbor held her tight. Out of the corner of her eye she saw a stretcher being wheeled through the front door.

A policeman showed her the suicide note: "I believe in reincarnation. I'm deaf, I don't want to be elderly with all these problems including mental illness. I'm leaving. Please—I'm sorry—forgive me." There was a scribbled sentence for her own mother, Gini's grandmother: "You know about the arrangements." Those were the last words from Gini's best friend on earth.

After the burial, she returned to her mother's house on the South Hill and lay on the bed where her mother had died. The old house was empty, and at first she was afraid. After a few minutes she began screaming, then talking out loud: "I'm mad, Mother. *I'm damned good and mad at you.* Why'd you do a thing like that? I'd have helped you! I'd have stayed with you, Mother! *Who cared if you were deaf? I was your ears! I was glad to do—anything you wanted.*"

She went from talking to sobbing. A peace came over her, and when she left the house she felt that she'd begun to come to grips with her mother's suicide. "It wasn't a tragedy," she told a friend later. "Mother sincerely wanted to go. It was like buying a ticket and leaving on a train. She didn't want to be here and she took off. I respected her wishes." She would always miss Shirley Perham, but it wouldn't be a permanent pain, just a bittersweet longing from time to time.

Kevin called and offered to help in any way. When he saw her he said he was disturbed that she hadn't chosen him to lean against. He told her he was impressed by her strength, her character, and admitted a deep admiration for independent women who breezed through crises. She began to suspect that he wanted someone like that for his own.

At 10:15 p.m. on the last day of that April, 1979, a young woman jogged along the tree-shaded streets of the South Hill. As she passed a quiet intersection a man tried to drag her down. She broke loose, and later described her assailant as a white male, twenty-five, six-two, 180, medium-length brown hair either blow-dried or permed, wearing a khaki GI jacket, a light shirt and jeans. She said he tried to ram his hand and fingers down her throat.

14

A Jewish businessman from Las Vegas was interested in investing in the massage market. I studied the massage parlor market thoroughly. They figured I was some horny guy and didn't know I had a business interest.—Fred Coe, May 26, 1982

The Tiger's Den personnel never stopped kidding the "parlor girl" Misty about the way she'd broken into the business. Now that she'd been working for six months, she could even see the humor herself. They must have thought she just fell off the turnip truck. How naïve can you get?

She'd come from a lower-class Spokane family where love was apportioned a teaspoon at a time and her truck-driver father and barfly mother both sought it elsewhere. By mutual consent Misty had left home at fifteen. Since then she'd knocked around at minimum-wage jobs: waitressing, housecleaning, laboring. She wasn't strong; at five-six, she'd never weighed over a hundred pounds. But she had a slender figure and a pretty face with small, delicate features, penciled eyebrows and brownish-red hair.

One day she spotted a want ad for a "bathhouse attendant" in the *Spokesman-Review*. She figured the job had something to do with saunas or whirlpools and she would be bringing towels and doing laundry. The owner told her in an interview that nineteen was a little young, but his partner okayed a trial. "So I went to work," she explained later, "and I was, uh...initiated. It was shocking." She slapped the first man and threatened to call the police on her second. Then the other girls clued her in.

If a clergyman or one of the straitlaced Cowles brothers had stepped into a Spokane massage parlor, he would have been informed that a sauna or whirlpool massage cost $25 per half hour and $40 per hour. But for most customers there was another set of figures: "straight lay" $60; "half and half" $80, and "hand finish" $40. Each "girl" was on her own after she took the customer to the massage room, but there was a tacit agreement that the job entailed more than just rubbing backs. It was also understood that a girl didn't have to do any customer she didn't want to. As the owners kept pointing out, this wasn't slavery, and there were plenty of applicants. They arrived by the busload from the dying old mining towns and sheep spreads of nearby Idaho and Montana.

Misty went for the money. She and her boyfriend, a high-school dropout named *Pete Johnson*, were buying a small home in the Spokane Valley, and this new job would help. Their long-range hope was to own a business someday, maybe a gas station with a couple of racks. Shy, quiet Pete was a genius with cars and engines.

Misty especially liked the colleague she was working with this muggy Sunday afternoon of June 17, 1979. She went by "Louise," and she was the baby of the Tiger's Den, the smallest of the girls who rotated among the four massage parlors under the same ownership. "She's a little old blond-headed gal," Misty had told Pete. "Maybe four foot ten, ninety pounds drenched. Funner than hell. A really neat lady."

Louise usually overdid her makeup on purpose. When she fixed up her eyes and put on her extra-long lashes and smudged her cheeks with rouge, she looked like a doll in a puppet show. She was barely nineteen, but she'd been working the parlors for two years. There'd been several busts while she was on the payroll, but luckily she'd been off or there would have been trouble about her age.

Neither Misty nor Louise liked the looks of a man who showed up around noon. He had the general appearance of a late teen, but his gray-blue eyes looked ten years older. His hands were dirty and he needed a shave, but there was a rich-kid look about him. He seemed nervous and anxious. Two months earlier one of the parlor girls, pregnant at the time, had been assaulted by a man who waited around till she was closing and tied her up. Since then, the Tiger's Den had been getting up to seventy-five obscene calls a day. Misty and Louise had answered more than their share, and they eyed the newcomer warily. A frizz of light hair curled from under his dark-blue stocking cap, as though he might be growing out a permanent. He wore loafers, jeans, a flannel shirt and a down vest. The girls wondered, Why such hot clothes in the summertime? Louise acted on instinct. "We're booked up," she told him.

The man returned five or six times and finally stood in the alleyway staring at the door. After their last customer left, Misty said, "He'll come in now. He knows we're alone. You book him in, Louise. I just can't."

The little cowbell tinkled. "I'd, uh, rather not," Louise said.

Misty stretched out on the sofa in the small entrance room and grabbed a magazine. "It's your up," she said firmly.

The man entered and stood at the counter. Louise reluctantly asked his name. He muttered something and gave a downtown address. She jotted down his approximate height, weight, color of eyes and hair, just in case. She told him, "I'll book you in for a whirlpool. I don't do massages."

He murmured, "Anything." Louise's eyes caught Misty's. Men didn't come to the Tiger's Den for "anything." Without being asked, he counted $25 from his wallet.

Louise led him to a massage room and told him to undress for the required shower. The usual mood music wasn't playing. She leaned down to plug in the radio and felt a pair of arms grab her from behind. "As long as you do what I want," the man said, "I won't hurt you."

He turned her around. A black pocket knife with open blade glittered in his hand. "Why me?" she asked in her small voice. "*Why?* I just got out of the hospital. I had a fallopial tube taken out."

In a strangely deep voice he ordered her to put her arms behind her back. He turned her around and tied her hands with soft, rubbery tape, mumbling, "I'm sorry, I'm sorry." He pulled her terrycloth top off and shoved her to the floor. She tried not to scream.

He yanked down her shorts. "I'm sorry," he repeated. She told herself, *He can end your life right now, Louise. Right now*! She trembled and felt cold. She was afraid she was going to lose control of her bladder.

He tied a towel over her mouth. "I'm sorry," he said again. She closed her eyes and waited for the knife. Minutes passed. A scream reverberated from the front hallway. God, she thought, I wonder what he's doing to Misty?

Misty had just told herself that Louise had been in the back room for quite a while when the guy with the old eyes appeared in the hallway. "Something happened to your girlfriend," he said.

Her first thought was that Louise had started bleeding from her recent female trouble. She headed for the back and the man grabbed her as she tried to pass. He put his hand across her mouth and knocked her cigarette to the floor. "Don't scream and I won't hurt you," he said. "All I want to do is rob you."

She ordered herself not to resist. He was a half foot taller and twice her bulk. He tied her hands behind her with insulating tape. "I'm not gonna hurt you," he said in a low voice. "I just need money."

She said she would show him where there was lots of money, up front near the windows. She had a vague idea that someone might see them and call the cops. Then he admitted, "Money's not what I want."

"Whatever," she said, trying to keep her voice level.

He pulled down her top and jerked her by her hair. She fell to her knees. She didn't know a single massage parlor girl who hadn't been manhandled by some freak; now it was her turn. Would he hurt her? God, don't let him! Then she thought, What did he do to Louise? She went limp as he dragged her toward Room C, hurting her thin wrists. She called out, "Louise!"

There was no answer from the back. Not a peep. Poor Louise—she must be dead. The dinger sounded on the door to the alleyway. A customer. She yelled till her throat hurt. The outer door clicked shut and the place was quiet again.

The man threw her across the massage table and tried to straddle her, but she twisted away. "Louise!" she cried. "*Louise!* Help me!"

"Bitch!" he said. He yanked her around by the hair and slapped her hard several times. "You're gonna pay for this!"

He hauled her to her feet. "I'll kill you!" he said. She saw a knife.

He grabbed her hair and twisted her back down to her knees. "If you don't want that," he said, "then you're gonna give me some head." His half-erect penis nudged her mouth.

She jerked away. He slammed her to the floor. She tried to yell and he said, "Shut up!" When he covered her mouth with his hand, she knew she was going to be murdered. It had happened before in the parlors. Louise was dead in the other room. Now it was her "up." She tucked her chin down so he couldn't cut her neck. Her wrists hurt behind her back. Oh, God, she thought, why did we let him in?

He was talking again. "You dirty bitch. You—whore! Dirty bitch! *Whore!*" She raised her eyes to see what he was doing. He was playing with himself but he wasn't stiff. "You deserve this," he said hoarsely. He was staring at the wall. "You'll pay for this!" He sounded as though he were talking to someone else.

She started to cry. He said, "If you won't shut up, I'll shut you up!" He tied a towel tightly across her mouth and flopped on her scrawny body. Once again he tried unsuccessfully to enter her, this time from the front. He gave up and began jerking at himself, keeping up a stream of talk: "You cunt! You *whore!* I'm gonna fuck your cunt. Just wait, bitch! You're gonna get it."

She sobbed against the towel in her mouth. His words grew louder and faster, and a warm spurt of fluid dribbled down her bare thigh. He pushed himself to his knees and said weakly, "I—I'm sorry." The pitch of his voice had risen; he sounded on the verge of tears. "I'm sorry," he went on, getting to his feet. "I'm terribly sorry. I'm *really* sorry."

He took the towel from her mouth and wiped the semen from her leg and himself. He pulled a Kleenex from the box on the shelf and patted her tears. His face was directly over hers and she got a good look. He looked like a rich punk, a sicko. Talked like it, too, now that his macho act was over. "I'm real sorry," he whined. He sounded like a sick child.

He pulled her to her feet and started dressing her clumsily. She couldn't stop crying. He put her dress on inside out; she reversed it as he mumbled apologies. He lifted her to a sitting position on the massage table and began tidying up, talking as he worked. "I didn't mean to hurt you," he said as he put the baby oil back on the shelf and lined up the bottles. "I didn't mean to scare you."

He wiped everything: doorknobs, counter, the floor where he'd raped her, the massage table. Then he left the room. "If you come out before five minutes are up," he said over his shoulder, "I'm gonna kill you." His voice had turned mean and deep again. "I'll cut you good," he said.

For ten minutes she heard him in the reception area. Then the little bell tinkled and the outer door shut. She yelled, "Louise?" There was no reply.

She stood up, hands still taped behind her back, and walked from room to room. All five doors were closed. She called again, and again there was no answer. As she was trying to decide what to do, the phone rang. She hurried out front and shoved it off the hook with her nose. The handset fell to the floor and she leaned over and said, "We're in trouble. Help us. We're in trouble!" A masculine laugh pealed from the earpiece.

She walked down the hall and began opening the doors one by one. Louise sat naked in the middle of Room D. A towel had been stuffed into her mouth, her ankles crossed and bound and her hands taped behind her back. The two women helped each other get free, and Louise said, "Oh, Misty, I heard you screaming. I thought you were dead."

They hugged, and Misty said, "I thought you were, too."

Out in the entrance hall they discovered that the rapist had stolen back his $25 fee, plus about $65 and a driver's license from Louise's purse and

$100 from Misty's. He had left the reception area spotless. Misty looked for the cigarette that had fallen from her mouth when he jumped her. It was in a basket, snuffed out.

The dinger sounded. "It's him!" the two women yelped. The door opened and they both screamed. The bookkeeper walked in. She took one look and dialed the police.

Two days later the girls of the Tiger's Den, Valley Viking, Den of Foxes and The Bath were called to a meeting by the owners.

Misty and Louise, still tearful, told the twenty women what had happened and described the rapist. The owners advised the girls not to panic if he returned but to stall him and call the police. Then the floor was thrown open for ideas on who he might be.

Everyone had a candidate. A girl from The Bath said a man of the rapist's description had been a steady customer until a few months back when he left angrily after the bank turned down the telephone check on his father's credit card. He was a rich-looking dude, took great care of himself, used creams and lotions and sometimes makeup, looked a lot younger than his age. His name was Fred Coe.

"Oh, *him*!" said a masseuse named Bobbi. "He's my customer now. Likes me to dress up like a little girl and talk babytalk. Hey, get off his case! He's a good tipper."

"Any chance he could be the rapist?" someone inquired.

"He's never rough with me," Bobbi said. The group passed on to more likely candidates.

At 10:15 on the night of July 30, 1979, five weeks after the massage parlor rape, a woman was attacked at the corner of Seventh and Oak in the steepest part of the South Hill. She broke loose when her attacker tried to grab her by the throat.

Police put out a description: "W/M, 17-22 yrs., 5'10", med. build, shoulder length brown hair, unknown color vest, unknown color shirt, blue jeans." Once again, it wasn't much to go on.

15

Sooner or later when the classic psychopath comes on stage, things will go wrong....Patterns of temporary success or at least stability are followed by strangely brutal and irresponsible behavior, stupid and unnecessary falls from grace for which there can be no rational explanation....The hurt and astonished mate, friend, or business associate who has suffered at the hands of the psychopath may well be persuaded that he or she, not the other, has been temporarily out of his mind.—Alan Harrington, *Psychopaths*

Fred and Jenifer Coe moved again, to a small mustard-colored ranch house at the corner of Twenty-ninth and Rebecca. The South Hill's fanciest homes were clumped along its far-western edges, the quality deteriorating as one traveled east, and the Coes' new address was almost as far to the unstylish east as one could go before a series of low hills and gullies marked the dropoff to the Spokane Valley. But Fred seemed glad to be living on busy Twenty-ninth, the playstreet of his childhood, though three miles and a far cry from the old family residence by Comstock Park.

The local homes ranged from bedraggled fixer-uppers with tarpaper walls to fifty-thousand dollar post-war houses like the one they were renting at $325 a month. The house had a sunny kitchen with sliding glass doors leading to a deck, beige carpeting, a full basement and a two-car garage. Jeni's bedridden sister Sonia had told her, "You have everything now, Jeni. I'll bet you're really happy."

But of course she wasn't. She had Fred to contend with, and he hadn't changed. By midsummer their life was one long spat, mostly about his absences and her drinking. They were poorer than ever, expecting any day to have the phone cut off. He'd finally managed to sell a house—a cross-deal on another realtor's listing—but the split commission had barely paid off the debt he'd run up in the office for fees and expenses.

Unperturbed, he was still bringing home steaks, Portuguese sardines, Perrier water and other gourmet items, and Jeni figured he must be using his parents' credit cards or borrowing again from his father. The managing editor's patience seemed unlimited. He'd advanced Fred a bundle to publish the unsuccessful *Sex in the White House*, and since then there'd been thousands of dollars in Christmas handouts and pocket loans and little taps in the office.

Fred spent hours devising bail-out schemes, and they were all about as successful as the ad he'd once placed in the *National Enquirer*: "How to Succeed at Anything! How to be a Success Beyond Your Wildest Dreams! How to Make a Fortune!" If the ad generated enough interest, he'd explained, he would produce a quickie book. Five orders had come in.

A dead-solid zero—that's how Jeni rated his schemes in her bookkeeper's mind. He was busier than ever with Spokane Metro Growth, but no one had seen a penny from all those pseudonymous letters minding other people's business. She looked back at his dreams and schemes and saw the same collision approaching that had flattened her in Las Vegas three years before. And she was making the same mistake—first a few nips, then one or two glasses of wine during the daytime, and finally full-flight escape to alcohol. She knew there must be a better way to handle her problems, but she hadn't been able to find it.

The blow-up might have come sooner except for Sonia McNeill. Jeni's sister lay almost immobile in a nursing home at the base of the South Hill. Powerful medications for rheumatoid arthritis had darkened her lovely blond hair and the disease had canted her fingers at odd angles. She'd fought pain smilingly for twenty years, clinging to hope and living by the Bible that was always at hand. She routinely won blue ribbons in open needlework competitions. She was scratching out a long manuscript with imported inch-thick pens that she gripped with her twisted fingers. Her nails were long and neatly done; she kept a makeup table alongside her bed with perfumes and colognes aligned in perfect precision as though she were ready for an evening on the town. Once she had been fashion coordinator of The Crescent, Spokane's toniest department store, and Jeni had worked for her as a model. Now, in adversity, the two of them were closer than ever.

Sometimes Fred tagged along on Jeni's visits to the nursing home, and sometimes he dropped in alone with chocolate candy or flowers or perfume, a rare bright spot in Sonia's existence. She had a shelf of Ayn Rand books he'd given her; he always called himself an Ayn Rand objectivist. She told Jeni, "You know, with all that flattery and attention, he makes me feel like a woman, and it's very seldom I feel like a woman anymore." Dressed in his vested suits and silk ties and expensive shoes, he would talk about the fortune he and Jeni would make and how they would buy a van with a hydraulic lift for Sonia's heavy wheelchair and go cruising down to the Palouse wheat country or over to Montana, an hour's drive, or out to one of the eighty or ninety lakes that ringed Spokane. He told gaudy and bawdy tales about the thousand-dollar-a-night whores who'd thrown themselves at his feet when he'd been a DJ in Las Vegas, told her how one of the most stunning courtesans on earth used to smother his face with her snowy breasts when she bent to kiss him at the console.

Sonia pretended to believe every word, even egged him on. She complimented him on his attire and his ever-changing appearance; she boosted his ego and dignified his pipe dreams. In private she told her sister, "I love to watch him, don't you? He can't stand being an average Joe. He has his own rules of conduct. He's above it all." Yes, Jeni said patiently, she knew.

One August day Sonia's mother brought Sonia's eleven-year-old son to the nursing home to visit, and while they were enjoying one another's company Fred and Jeni dropped in. It was so hot that Sonia's bedsheets crackled as though freshly ironed. A pitcher of ice lay on a table in the middle of the three-bed ward, and Fred and the boy began flipping little shards over Sonia and onto the beds of two women in their nineties.

Sonia asked, "What on earth are you *doing*?"

The pranksters giggled and Fred said to the child, "Come on, let's get some more ice at the machine."

One nurse was on duty on the floor. She saw the two of them walking along the hall. A few seconds later she heard an elderly patient cry out, "I am *hot!*" Then she heard a scream.

She rushed into the room and found ice sprinkled on the helpless woman. Coe was walking away with a glass in his hand. The angry nurse ordered him and his giggling nephew to wait. The child said later that Fred had promised to pay him off in candy bars if he would take the blame. So he confessed.

The nurse told him, "Look, you've still got your glass of ice in your hand. Fred told you to lie for him, didn't he?" She ordered Coe to leave for good.

The incident added to Jeni's feeling that catastrophe was imminent. She began patronizing downtown bars that catered to drifters. Fred would come home and find her wobbly; sometimes he would track her from bar to bar. Sometimes she admitted that maybe she was an alcoholic looking for an excuse, but then how explain the year that she'd lived by herself without taking a drop? And the absolute certainty that she could kick booze tomorrow if only she were alone? She'd once read that marriage was like two cats tied together by the tails and thrown over a clothesline. That was bad enough, but what if one cat was crazy? What would that do to the other cat?

On a breezy summer night Fred came home from the office in his three-piece suit and asked if she had any money for groceries. She showed him her empty purse. He headed for the garage and their two big cars. A half hour later he returned with a thick tenderloin steak—more than the two of them could eat. "Where'd you get that?" she asked.

"Lifted it," he answered.

"Oh, Fred." She couldn't eat. She'd never been able to get over the shame of the hit-and-run dinners they'd stolen in Southern California and the poor waitresses who'd had to make good on their unpaid bills. Now this! She was disgusted with him but far more disgusted with herself. She knew that no matter what they did, this would be their all-time low together, lower even than the night in Vegas when he'd announced he was becoming a bisexual gigolo.

After a while he put on his gray sweatsuit and left for his regular evening jog, and she drove her silver Grand Prix to a bar. When she came home late that night he wasn't home. No surprise. His absences had become longer and more frequent. Morning and night, even at midday when he was supposed to be out selling real estate, no one could locate him. The office was always wondering where he was.

Something was going to happen. Something bad. It was like living under a giant meat ax. She began to plan her escape.

16

The accountants at James S. Black & Co. reckoned that it cost the company four hundred and eighty-five dollars a month to maintain each desk, and the investment in Fred "Kevin" Coe wasn't paying off. By the middle of 1979 he was lagging far behind his colleagues. One told another, "Kevin's a complete blank on things that he should have picked up by now. I have to show him how to do the paperwork step by step, and he needs constant reassurance about petty details."

Coe's boss, Jim Cory, confided to a friend, "His problem is he tells the buyer what he wants to hear and the seller what *he* wants to hear. That's no way to sell anything."

Cory had demanded little from the rookie for the first six months of his employment, but at least he'd been expected to pay his out-of-pocket expenses. On the first of the month the accounting department billed each agent for his share of the various office expenses. Each month the accountants would complain that Coe hadn't paid, and the same conversation would ensue, with minor variations:

Cory: I heard from the accountants again.

Coe: You mean you didn't get my check?

Cory: Kevin, listen, this isn't fair to anybody. I have to ask you every time.

Coe: But I sent you a check!

Cory: Why didn't you just pay in the office?

Coe: It seemed simpler to mail.

Cory: Well, I never got the letter.

Coe: I must've made a mistake on the address.

After several more complaints, a back-dated check would arrive. Sometimes it would bounce. Cory didn't understand. Coe came from a good family, drove an expensive car, dressed like a store manikin, but now everything seemed to be deteriorating. He'd show up for floor time unshaven and sweaty, wearing open shirts and sweatsuits. When he was asked to explain, he said, "It doesn't matter. Nobody ever comes in off the street anyway."

"Well, what if somebody does?" Cory asked.

"I'll handle 'em, don't worry."

"Kevin, I don't want to see you in this office in your sweats, okay?"

"Okay, *okay!*"

Cory wished he'd given up on the young man months ago, back when Coe had been out of the office more than he'd been in, ostensibly putting together a big disco deal. But it wasn't easy to fire the son of a powerful newsman. One day Cory asked how the disco deal was going, and Coe, uncharacteristically glum, said, "It's dead."

"Okay," Cory said, slapping him on the shoulder. "Then we'd better start thinking about real estate."

A few days after that conversation Cory received a lengthy letter from Coe, declaring, "I am working on a timetable that will soon make me the top salesman in the South Side office, in the James S. Black organization, in the city of Spokane and in the state of Washington."

Cory awaited developments. Then he noticed that Coe wasn't showing up for floor time and had become unreachable at home. Phone calls would go unanswered or someone would pick up the phone after five or six rings and disconnect. "Something wrong with your phone, Kevin?" Cory asked.

"It must be my wife. She's on the phone all the time."

"What happens if we need you on a weekend?"

"I'm always there."

"But we've tried."

"I must've been out for a few minutes."

The connection remained poor. Potential customers would complain that they couldn't reach Coe. One of the realtors speculated that the problem was related to Kevin's mother. She would park in front of the real estate office in a yellow Cadillac and wait for him, and off they would go for the afternoon or the day. Now and then, both mother and father would arrive, and the father would hang back while Mrs. Coe did the talking. When Kevin held an open house, his mother showed up in furs and jewels and pirouetted about the room making everyone aware that she was the mother of the listing realtor and the wife of a big editor on the *Chronicle*. At a weekend real estate convention Kevin made a grand entrance with his mother, both of them dressed as though they had just left the Sunday brunch at the Davenport. The other realtors noticed how out of place she looked, draped in furs in a roomful of real estate salesmen seated on folding chairs. "She must be lonely," said one of them, "if she has to rely on her son for her social life." Kevin catered to her, treated her like visiting royalty while ignoring the business at hand.

An office mate got up the courage to ask, "Don't you feel kind of funny with your mother always hanging around?"

"What an odd question," Coe replied. "Of course not."

On the last day of the convention Mrs. Coe made a beeline to the podium and offered to drive the keynote speaker to the airport. Fred and another realtor went along and Ruth monopolized the conversation.

Even outside his mother's presence Kevin seemed odd to the other salespeople. He spoke constantly about nutrition and diet, but every few weeks he would start eating chocolate and potato chips and candy bars, sometimes breaking out in pimples like a teenager. Then he would fast till he looked ill.

Once in a while he would be seen jogging at a pace just above a walk.

Several times he came into the office scratched and injured. Once he said a German shepherd had attacked him in a park. When he showed up with a black eye, Jim Cory quipped, "What happened, Kevin? Did you run into a door?"

"No," Coe said. "A St. Bernard attacked me while I was running." Another time he explained that his "unstable" wife had scratched him with her nails.

When the company assembled its one hundred and twenty employees for an advertising picture in front of an old clock tower, Kevin refused to be photographed. "My Las Vegas contracts won't permit it," he explained, turning away from the cameraman.

Jim Cory thought the reaction peculiar, and one realtor whispered, "How feminine!" But after each such incident, along would come another letter promising that "next week" or "next month" Coe would initiate a selling program that would make him the top realtor in Spokane and the West, and the easygoing Cory would shake his head and give him one more chance.

Mary Jo Macy, one of the veterans of the staff, had never stopped looking askance at the new employee. She had a friend who'd lived near the Coes when Kevin was a small boy on Twenty-ninth Avenue. "He was like a robot," the friend told her. "He never varied from one day to the next—always polite, always clean, never particularly happy or unhappy. Just... the same. His mother trained him that way. Once when he was in his teens Ruth told me that he'd been a perfectionist even as a little kid, in his clothes, his eating habits. She was very proud of that."

On a sunny afternoon in August, Jim Cory's secretary, Cheryl Ferguson, strolled up to Hamblen Park, high on the South Hill. The city recreation department was sponsoring a dance program for children, and radio station KJRB had promised to send one of its star disc jockeys, a woman who called herself Sunshine Shelly.

As Cheryl approached the park her eye caught a well-dressed man watching from a fringe of trees. He seemed to be trying to conceal himself behind the trunks, slipping from tree to tree to keep abreast of the dancing children and the energetic DJ. Since two of the Ferguson children were among the dancers, Cheryl sidled up for a closer look. The man was wearing dark glasses and eating from a box. "Oh, hi, Kevin," she said, relieved. Coe had been working at James S. Black & Co. for ten months now and she'd found him pleasant enough.

He jumped. "Oh," he said, "I, uh—I'm not eating these. I'm just carrying them around." He swallowed hard and shoved the chocolates into a pocket.

She wondered why he found it necessary to lie; she wasn't his mother. "What's up?" she asked with a smile.

"I'm just watching," he said, looking away.

She made another attempt to be friendly. "Cute, aren't they? Say, where's your car?" There was a long row of empty parking spaces on the street.

Sunshine Shelly had moved from one side of the dance group to the other, and his eyes seemed to follow. "My car?" he said. "I parked it down the street." She caught the coolness in his voice and wandered over near the dancers. She'd never known him to be rude, but everyone had off days. Once in a while she glanced toward the edge of the park. He was still moving from tree to tree, keeping the dancers in sight forty or fifty feet away. After a half hour he walked toward the church parking lot across the street. She wondered why he'd parked his car where it couldn't be seen. He drove away fast.

17

A few nights later, on August 15, a young married woman was walking on the South Hill when she noticed a man on the other side of the street walking in the same direction. Patricia O'Malley had blue eyes, freckles, a button nose and two physical characteristics in common with the rape victims Lois Higgins and Misty—she was short and had auburn hair, almost a dark red.

Warming down after a jog, she slowed her stride till a half block had opened up between her and the stranger. The man crossed to her side of the street; she noticed but wasn't disturbed in this populous neighborhood, where the biggest problems for joggers were dogs and a few potholes. She lost him in the twilight. When she came to a small U-shaped driveway, he stepped from behind a hedge.

He didn't seem threatening; he looked like "the kid next door," as she said later. He wore a jacket and jeans and was hatless. His hair was a dusty blondish brown, parted on one side, and he had a square chin and even features. As she tried to pass he smiled and grabbed her breast.

She shoved him away with both hands and kicked at his knee. He gave way and she ran. When she came in sight of her house she looked back. He hadn't followed. Safe inside, she became almost hysterical, finally calmed enough to dial the police. "Were you hurt?" the man on duty wanted to know.

"No."

"That's good. We've been getting a few rapes up around your way."

"Rapes?" She froze at the word.

"Yeah. But—you're okay?"

"O—kay?"

"You don't need assistance or anything, right? I mean, he just reached out and touched you?"

"Uh, right," she said.

"Well, we're swamped tonight, ma'am. I'll file this as an indecent liberties case. Let us know if you see the guy again." She heard nothing further.

The next night at 9:30 a woman was raped on the street at Twenty-ninth and Southeast Blvd., a mile east of the spot where Pat O'Malley had been grabbed by the breast. No one made a connection.

18

My relationship with my mother is perfectly normal. We get along great. There most certainly is nothing sexual in our relationship.— Fred Coe, Mar. 11, 1982

On the way to her first encounter with Gordon and Ruth Coe, Gini Perham couldn't imagine what to expect. Kevin had often spoken proudly about his mother, but there were contraindications too.

"Won't your parents think it's nervy bringing a woman over there?" she'd asked. "With you still living with your wife?"

He'd said, "They'll love you, Baby Bunny." It was his latest name for her. She noticed that he renamed a lot of people: Jay Williams was "Jayhammad" after Muhammad Ali; his old high-school friend John Nyberg was "Humpy," "Humpturd" or "Humptoid"; Gordon Coe was "Gordo" and Ruth "Barefax" or "Mother Bear." Gini wondered why he objected to calling people by their real names, or at least by their usual nicknames. She put it down to an excess of imagination, part of his charm.

At his suggestion they were taking Katy, the late Shirley Perham's collie, as a peace offering to Ruth. Fred had argued that such a big animal would suffer in Gini's small apartment. She asked him why his mother required a peace offering. "Oh, she thinks I'm a failure," he said as he drove at his usual high speed toward his parents'. "I've been back here three years now and she thinks I haven't accomplished anything. And she's never forgiven me for marrying Jenifer. She didn't speak to me for months after we got back together."

Gini had to laugh. "Who could possibly think of you as a failure?" All she'd seen in these first few months of dating was a well-turned-out young realtor who seemed to have time on his hands, so much time, in fact, that she'd decided to go into real estate herself and enjoy the same easy living.

"My mother thinks I'm a flop," he said in a low voice. "And my father probably does, too."

She remembered one acrimonious conversation between Ruth Coe and her son. Kevin had spent thirty minutes yelling into the telephone—a complete change from the mild-mannered young man she'd been dating. He cursed his mother and called her "cheap" and "miserly." After he slammed down the phone he looked at Gini as though surprised she was there. "I'm sorry," he said. "It's just—she aggravates me. My sister gets everything. Can you believe it? My mother sold her own diamonds to get her into college! Kathy *always* got more than I did." Gini thought it was strange talk for a full-grown adult, but she withheld judgment.

The condominium was impressive. It was in a fir-landscaped three-story building on the corner of Seventh and Monroe, one of the oldest residential sections of the South Hill. Spokane's logging and mining barons had built their first mansions in this neighborhood: boxy frame lumps with Georgian fronts and Doric columns and balconies, cameo-cut stained-glass windows that reflected and refracted bright colors in the afternoon sun. Some of the old homes had servants' quarters in the rear, plantation style. At ten, little Gini Perham had begged her father to drive her on these roller-coaster streets.

"That's their unit," Kevin said proudly, indicating a top-floor apartment in the rear. "At night they can look down and see the whole town—the newspaper building and everything." He opened the door with his own key. They led the dog into a small living room and Gini blinked. Blue was dominant, starting with royal blue wall-to-wall carpeting. There was a rock fireplace in one corner, a large crystal chandelier and crystal pendants hanging from five or six lamps, and so much French provincial-style furniture that one piece abutted another. The walls were hung with prints, each surrounded by a gilt frame with scrolls and curlicues. "This is nothing," Kevin said. "You should have seen our old house up on Twenty-ninth. Mom made it into a palace." Gini could imagine.

A woman appeared and filled the room with her presence. Gini thought, My God, what a sight! She wore a royal-blue suit, spike heels, ropes of jumbo pearls and a diamond clip. Her hair was a spiral nebula of raven-black curls. Kevin had said his mother was fifty-nine and a certain softness confirmed the age, but underneath a chalky patina of geisha makeup she had perfect features, full lips and dark eyes of the deepest blue, slightly slanted like Kevin's. And as if God hadn't awarded her more than her share of endowments, he'd also given her a figure by Rubens. Gini was impressed.

"Ah'm Ruth Coe," the woman said, extending a handful of rings above burgundy nails. "*So* nice to meet you. Fred's told me *so* much about you." Momentarily Gini wondered who Fred was, but she shook hands and nodded.

"Do sit down," the hostess said, and began chattering to Kevin about personal business. At first Gini couldn't place her accent, but then it came back to her. It was pure Alabama, where Gini's father had been stationed at Maxwell Air Force Base. Why hadn't Kevin told her his mom was from the South?

Mrs. Coe was effusively friendly. "And here's Katy!" she said, kneeling down to pat the collie. She peered at the animal like a judge at a dog show. "Ah dearly love that coloring," she said, stepping back and tilting Katy's head. According to Kevin, the family had owned pedigreed collies since his earliest childhood, and his mother was an expert on the breed.

The faint sound of radio or TV emanated from another room. Soon it stopped and a man entered wearing a small compressed smile. He was a solidly built six-footer, about as tall as Kevin and six or seven inches taller than Mrs.

Coe. He had wavy gray hair and a sharply chiseled profile, but Gini was surprised to see deep sad eyes and the furrowed face of a man with problems. She told herself that running a newspaper must be grueling.

Mrs. Coe barely stopped talking and flitting about the room long enough for Kevin to make the introductions. She was describing with great intensity the recent euthanasia of a beloved Samoyed: "just like losing a child of mah own!" She paused as she told how the dog had been put to sleep in her arms. "Ah was *never* so upset," she said, sounding as though she were going to burst into tears. "Only thing that *saved* me was mah precious daughter. The great children? She flew *all* the way from Seattle to be at mah side. Remember, Pottilee?"

Gordon Coe nodded.

Gini's face must have revealed her confusion, because Kevin quickly said, "'The great children'—that's what Mother calls my sister Kathy." Gini had never heard individuals described in the plural, but she didn't inquire—it wouldn't have been easy to get a word in anyway. Mrs. Coe insisted that they tour the condo and she apologized as they walked from room to room. "It's nothing like mah old house on Twenty-ninth. Such a *luuuv*ly place. Ah had a yard *full* of lilacs. Ah brought 'em up from the South." Gini wondered why anyone would bring lilacs to the Lilac City.

Mrs. Coe led the way into the kitchen with a little sideways dance step on tiptoe. Gini had seen Kevin make similar moves, though with less grace. Whirling about, the woman spoke of the magnolia-scented plantation of her childhood, the great oak-lined halls of the main house, the faithful black retainers with their trays of juleps and lemonade. Gini wondered why Kevin had never mentioned the place. She got the impression the family had owned a big property in Georgia; Mrs. Coe had mentioned that her kinsmen were close friends of the "Co'Cola folks" in Atlanta. "Thank the deah Lord we recovered from what the North did to us," the woman said. "They just *ravaged* us, those awful Yankees." The woman's full lips widened and her bright white teeth showed; it seemed to Gini that she was suppressing a great rage. Gini started to make a comment—she had strong feelings of her own about the Civil War—but a dark glance from Kevin silenced her. Mrs. Coe had turned to racial problems. "We just showed 'em their place and made sure they stayed in it. Not like these northern Nigras."

Gordon Coe said, "Ruth, come on now."

She returned to the subject of Kevin's childhood home high on Spokane's South Hill. "You wouldn't have be*lieved* how Ah transformed that place. Ah replaced the front door with French doors. Double doors with brass knobs in the middle? Ah had blue velvet tacked on panels hanging in the entrance-way"—she clapped her hands like a child—"and a velvet rope for a banister. And the cutest water fountain in the corner, and bright silver stars set into the ceiling, and glitter on the basement ceiling. Ah surely do miss that old house!"

Gini wondered why the woman sounded so much like a caricature of a Southerner, and why father and son seemed so edgy about the performance. Ruth Coe was one of those intense people who draw the energy out of everyone around them. Gini tried to imagine a give-and-take discussion with her. What a challenge!

In the end, it was the woman's way with Katy that made the most lasting impression; she treated the dog with babytalk and hugs and nose rubs and patience. You could tell a lot from the way a person treated dogs. Before the short visit was over, Mrs. Coe proved to be outgoing and courteous, interested in Gini and warmly loving to her son, despite their long estrangement. Gini left the apartment slightly overwhelmed. No one could say Kevin's mother was dull. On the way home she asked, "Do you have an older brother named Fred?"

Kevin started and stopped his explanation several times and finally admitted that he was F. H. "Fred" Coe.

"Where'd 'Kevin' come from?"

"I always liked male names that started with K. One night Jeni and I were making up names and I hit on Kevin. It had a nice sound to it, so I decided to keep it."

He admitted that he was the F. H. Coe who had written *Sex in the White House.* He said another reason for changing his name was to confuse his creditors in Las Vegas. "I didn't mean to lie to you about my name, Gini," he said. He told her that his money problems stemmed from trying to start a disco business in Spokane and working only part-time as a realtor. He said his father had pushed him into real estate. He said he felt sorry for his mother and the boring life that Gordo had forced her to live. He said he wished he could arrange a Las Vegas life-style for her. "She'd fit right in," he explained. Gini agreed.

She asked about the southern accent. He said that his mother had been born and brought up in Spokane. "She likes to pretend, that's all. She enjoys making up stories."

"A few times she sounded like a Shakespearean actress," Gini observed. "Eyether for either, tomawto for tomato—"

"She calls that the King's English. I guess she picked it up in school."

"School?"

"She got bored and went to charm school. She really didn't have much to learn. She's been modeling since she was twelve. She teaches charm and modeling, you know."

Gini couldn't imagine Mrs. Coe in the role. "Where?" she asked.

"Oh, women's clubs. Charity affairs. She's lectured at the YWCA. She teaches underprivileged girls how to sit, stand, walk, things like that. She's done a lot of fashion coordinating for the stores." He paused. "Hey, what'd you think of Gordo?"

"Very distinguished," she said. "He *looks* like a managing editor. In a lot of ways he reminds me of you. Did anyone ever tell you that?"

"You're not very observant," Kevin said coldly. "I look like my mother. Everybody says so."

Everybody except me, Gini thought. Where did he think he got his face? The line of his chin was exactly like his father's. So was the way one eyebrow arched when he talked, and the way he gritted his teeth and stretched his lips between phrases. But if it was important to him to think that his good looks were maternal in origin—well, fine. She liked him too much to argue. She'd come to enjoy their long talks; he was the most stimulating man she'd known. Often he seemed overconcerned with money and possessions—the string of Caddies he would own, the mansion on the South Hill and the co-op apartment in New York and the Learjet for commuting back and forth—but Spokane was a mercantile city and he couldn't be blamed for taking on the hometown attitudes. How many times must he have heard his father speak of the wealthy Cowles brothers and his mother's tales about the family's lost fortune? Kevin had never denied that he was a materialist, "a radical capitalist" as he put it. He liked green ink because it was the color of money, and he kept a plastic dollar sign—symbol of his guru, Ayn Rand—on the dashboard of his car. Gini had known plenty of local men who were obsessed with money; it was part of being from Spokane. At least Kevin admitted it.

As their friendship grew he began showing her letters that he wrote to the *Spokesman-Review* with suggestions for municipal improvement and growth. He displayed his work proudly, and she noticed that his messages were always perfectly typed, grammatical, and phrased with professional skill. One morning she picked up the paper and read a letter about the city's need to attract new industry. She recognized the name "X. Drew Butler, Spokane Metro Growth," and typed up a joking letter of her own, concluding with "Who is this crazy X. Drew Butler with his crazy ideas?" She signed the letter "P. P. Piles." Kevin commented bitterly when it ran in the paper; for a long time she couldn't bear to tell him that she was the author. Spokane Metro Growth and X. Drew Butler were no joking matter to him.

She realized that whatever direction he chose, he had enough raw material for a lifetime—daring, imaginative concepts, ideas of breadth and substance. All that was lacking, as he'd explained many times, was financial backing—and perhaps a little "focus," one of his favorite words. Time and hard work would pay off big for him; she was as certain of that as he was.

She was thankful that his political views turned out to be close to her own. He referred to himself as an ethical objectivist. She considered herself a moderate conservative: She had read the objectivist philosophy of Ayn Rand years before—agreed with it for the most part—and had campaigned for Gerald Ford. Coe seemed surprised and pleased at the news.

Occasionally she wondered how it happened that such a paragon had come into her life. He seemed to charm everyone with his boyishness and shyness and sense of humor. He was skilled with his "radio voice" and could deepen it for comic turns with waiters and ushers and gas-station attendants who seemed to find him as entertaining as she did. He knew everything about radio, especially DJ shows, and made her laugh with his critiques of the locals. He expressed admiration for KJRB's Sunshine Shelly, a bubbly young woman with a machine-gun delivery and a highly personal style: "This is Sunshine in the nighttime and I'm spinning this record for *you!*" He admitted that he was fascinated by her voice, but *all* women fascinated him—he admitted that, too. And Gini, he said again and again, fascinated him the most.

She liked his laid-back style, so different from other Spokane men she'd known. He would take her arm or lightly drape his arm across her shoulder as they walked. He brought her a gold-leaf cat and a porcelain cat to add to the three live cats she already owned, and dozens of knickknacks and re-membrances. Now and then she would arrive at the laundromat and find that he had delivered a single yellow rose.

She admired his personal habits. He smelled pleasantly of his favorite soap: Redken's Men's Bar, a pH-balanced product that he bought at beauty salons. He washed his hair and skin with Redken's every day, sometimes two or three times. She thought it was a lovely habit and he was a lovely man.

So she was surprised when, after four or five dates, sex proved to be something of a letdown. He couldn't get hard and slid down her body to perform orally. The act was new and strange to her, but it had the effect of stiffening his penis. He entered her from the front, straightening his arms to push away from her upper body. He seemed annoyed that he couldn't climax. The love-making was over in minutes, from his first touch to his leaping from bed as though an alarm had gone off. She was left with the feeling that somehow he'd found the whole thing abhorrent. She decided she'd expected too much. They would work it out together.

One night as they were driving along he told her that he loved her. She didn't trust her own excited reaction, so she didn't react at all. It was August, and in a few days she would be taking her vacation time from the laundromat to go away and harvest wheat at $50 a day—an annual tradition that she couldn't afford to abandon. She was at her best in the vast openness, with the August sun beating down on her. By the time she returned to Spokane she would have a better reading on whether she had found the perfect man.

A few nights before she was to leave, the new lovers bumped into one of Gini's friends, a woman she hadn't seen in months. Coe acted truculent, almost hostile. Gini couldn't understand. Sue Barbee was a brilliant woman; she and Kevin should have hit it off from the beginning.

The next morning Gini phoned her old friend. "Oh, Gini," Sue said, "I wanted to talk to you but I didn't want you to think I was—you know—pushy. Gini, honey, listen to me! I saw something in that man. And he saw that I saw it too. Did you notice the way he reacted? Don't ask me to explain. It's beyond explaining. Listen to me, Gini. There's nothing there!"

"Nothing...there?" she repeated in amazement.

"He's a shell."

Gini was baffled and hurt. She'd never known Sue to be so wrong.

19

Tom Dolan, a powerfully built young welder with a full beard and the hawklike visage of an ancient Celtic warrior, was hoisting a few at the end of a hot August day and telling a friend about the wild thing that happened to him earlier. "I was clearing some brush at my new house and this Grand Prix pulls up in the driveway across Rebecca and a woman gets out and goes inside. A few minutes later she runs across the street screaming—a good-looking lady, dark hair, big blue eyes, looks like she coulda been a movie star. She come right at me and says, 'Hey, help me! My husband's crazy!'

"I'm going, 'Wow!' To myself, ya know? She smelled like she'd been drinking. I'm standing there with a pitchfork in my hands and she says, 'I need some help. Do you have a phone in your house?'

"I says, 'No. What's the matter?'

"She says, 'This guy. He's crazy, he's crazy!'

"Then who comes walking out of the house but a guy I seen there before—a very freaky dude. One day he'd be all greasy and grungy, and the next day he'd be washed up with his hair blowed. In and out all hours of the night. A guy down the street had the house figured for a dope station, said he looked inside once and there was nothing but a phone. And cars coming and going all the time: a Toronado, a big yellow Cadillac. Somebody else said he heard voices in there one night like, 'Don't touch me! Stop! Don't do that!' Crazy stuff!

"Anyway, he comes walking out his back door in a three-piece suit. He's got a pink shirt, pink-tinted shades, a pink tie, and there's not a hair out of place. Picture perfect! He walks up to me, we're all standing at the edge of my lot, and he says, 'Don't worry about her. She's putting on a good show, but she just escaped from a mental hospital.' He sounded like he was trying to sell me something. *Smooooth.*

"The lady starts to say something and he turns and yells at her, and then he puts his arm around me like we're buddies, and he says, 'Don't worry about it, they're coming to pick her up.' Then he turns and yells at her again. I mean, his voice would just click from one style to another, back and forth.

"I ducked out from under his arm and I says, 'Wow, man, get *away* from me! What're you *doing*?' I mean, this guy's acting like we been friends for years!

"Then he grabs her and says, 'Come on, Jenifer, we're going inside.' She hung back, like she didn't want to go, and they got into a scuffle on the way across the street.

"She says, 'Gimme my car keys, you bastard!' I kind of hung around on my side of the street. I had a weird feeling, ya know? Like—what's gonna happen now? She's asking for the keys again, and he tells her to shut up. She calls out, 'Would you come over here and keep this guy away from me? *Come on!*'

"He drags her into their driveway and she says, 'You're crazy! You're the devil!' She grabs his pink shirt and pops a button. He freaked! He grabbed her by the hair and threw her in the beauty bark next to the fence. *Hard!* He's stronger than he looks.

"I got kind of pissed. I thought, You're strange, buddy, picking on women. I called out, 'Boy, you do that again I'm gonna throw you right through that fence!'

"He puts on that calm voice again, like he's got a special voice for talking to people like me, and he says, 'Well, look what she did to my shirt.'

"'That's no reason to be throwing a lady around. You look like you got more sense'n that.'

"She picks up a piece of hose and starts whaling on him, and I ran across the street and jumped in between 'em. I says to her, 'Hey, if you want to go inside and call the police, go ahead. You live here too.'

"She says, 'Yes, I do, goddamn it,' and she starts inside. He was on her like a cat, grabbed her and twisted her down. He says, 'You touch that phone and I'll—'

"I says, 'Wait a minute!' I says, 'Hey, I don't want to get into this marriage hassle, but don't be grabbing her and throwing her around like that!'

"He turns to me real calm again and he says, 'I told you not to worry about her. She just escaped from a hospital.'

"I said, 'I don't wanna hear about it. Let her call the police if she wants to. You don't got nothing to hide?'

"She was almost in the house and *bam!* he jumped in and grabbed the phone. He bared his teeth like an animal, just spread his lips and showed his fangs! He says, 'We don't need cops to help us with this little problem.'

"I says, 'Let her call anybody she wants.' I took a look around. That house, it was clean! I mean, everything waxed and polished. All his suits on a rack, like a clothing store. There was a broom in the kitchen and a coffeemaker, not another thing. I could see into the living room and it was empty.

"They're still hassling over the phone and then he reaches out and hands her the keys to her car. He says, 'Get outa my house and don't ever come back!'

"She says, 'Don't worry.' I walked back across the street and she comes over and thanks me. She says, 'I already left him. I just came back today for some of my clothes.' She says, 'If you know what's good for you, you'll stay away from this guy. He—is—*strange!*'

"I says to myself, Thanks for the tip, lady. She drove away in the Grand Prix and he comes flying out of the garage in his Toronado. The last I seen he was following right behind."

20

On September 7, a pleasant windless night in Spokane, an eighteen-year-old girl was attacked in the 1200 block of South Monroe. A detective's follow-up report said:

> The complainant stated that she left her parents' home somewhere around 11:15 p.m. and that it takes her about 10 to 12 minutes to get to her apartment. She stated that she was wearing her jogging shorts and states that she does walk a lot and jogs a lot and when she got around 13th and Lincoln, she observed a suspect walking towards her and it seemed to her that he had just entered Monroe Street, coming from either Cliff or 12th Avenue, which join together at Monroe.
>
> As he walked towards her, she looked at him twice and she had a strange feeling about him and, as he was about to pass her and about mid-block between 13th & Cliff, he grabbed at her legs and knocked her down off to the side of the sidewalk, which is quite rocky, and there are shrubs there.
>
> He had her on the ground on her back and was pulling at her shorts, trying to pull them down and she was screaming and he kept hitting her and kept telling her to open her mouth and she stated he was holding his hand in such a way as if he had a pill or something small in his hand, to put in her mouth. She stated she would not open her mouth and, when she did, she would keep her teeth together....
>
> She described the suspect as being W/M, early 20s, more like 6' tall, square, blocky build, not heavy set, and his hair appeared to be dark at night and as there was not too much light there, she stated his hair could have been sandy colored, although it was not blond. She stated that the hair was short and straight and somewhat shaggy.
>
> During the assault, a lady called out, "Are you all right out there?" and she thought this voice came from across the street; however, she does not know for sure and she thought a porch light went on across

the street; however, she did not see anybody. After she continued to yell, the suspect then took off running and ran north on Monroe and then west on 12th. . . . She said that she sustained a cut lip, abrasions on her left forehead, as well as left shoulder and back.

As in most nighttime street crimes there were varying descriptions of the assailant. The victim herself had first said he was six three. Three male witnesses who spotted him fleeing said he was shorter and had blond collar-length hair and a blue down vest. The woman who yelled out the window said she'd glimpsed the man as he fled and he was a stocky brown-haired six-footer wearing jeans and a blue jacket.

Days after the incident the same victim called the police emergency number and reported that she had spotted her assailant near the scene of the crime. This time he was wearing gray sweats and a dark blue down vest and tennis shoes. She said he'd walked up from behind and said, "Whoa, baby!" Squad cars searched the area but couldn't find the man.

An experienced policewoman, Detective Joan Schmick, made a vigorous and lengthy investigation of the attack—even developing a strong suspect who turned out to have an unassailable alibi. Eventually the case was marked "No Leads" and inactivated.

21

Gini Perham couldn't remember a better harvest. The farmer had planted a double crop, 1900 acres, and a threat of thunderstorm had lent excitement. They brought in mountains of soft white wheat without losing a bushel, and she headed back to Spokane and the Manito Highlander laundromat and her new relationship with the wondrous Kevin. She wondered when she would fit everything in. Her real estate test was scheduled for September 15, and she'd barely started to study. That wouldn't leave much time for a social life.

The day after she got home, she phoned Kevin at the James S. Black office and left a message. She'd missed him and wanted to see him. But he didn't return the call. A few evenings later he arrived in his white Toronado. As near as she could recall later, it was sometime in the first two weeks of September.

They took a short walk in the darkness. He seemed preoccupied. He told her that Jenifer had left and he was getting drunken calls every night from Las Vegas and L.A. He seemed alternately enraged and hurt by his ex-wife's departure.

"Who'll take care of her now?" he asked, sounding bereft. "She depended on me." Gini wondered if he'd told the truth about the relationship. If he didn't really love Jeni, what was the big deal?

He complained that the real estate business was bad and he wasn't earning any money. She said that she intended to go ahead with her test anyway; nothing could be less lucrative than working in a laundromat. She told him she intended to pass the test on her first attempt and that she wouldn't have much free time till then. He said that was okay with him and asked if he could drop over later that night. She said of course he could. They hadn't seen each other in weeks.

When he showed up she met him at her front door. "Where's your car?" she asked.

"I parked around the block."

Inside she saw that he was scratched and bruised on his hands and face. Several of his fingernails were discolored, and one was badly torn. There were scrapes along the top of his hands. "My God," she said, "were you in a fight?"

A familiar half smile rippled across his face, and he didn't answer. She repeated the question.

He dropped into a chair. It took her five or ten minutes to get him to tell her what had happened. A dog had jumped him in Manito Park. After his peculiar reluctance to talk, he went into lavish detail about the struggle and how he'd finally repulsed the animal.

She didn't believe him for a second. She'd seen him with dogs—he got down on his hands and knees and talked to them in their own language, whimpering like a reincarnated Airedale. No, he'd had a fistfight and didn't want to say so. It was just like him—he was so concerned with his image. She said, "Kevin, no dog would mark you up like that. Those are slits, not punctures or tears or rips. They look like fingernail scratches."

The smirk returned to his face. For the sake of his pride she dropped the subject. He tuned her radio to KJRB, but Sunshine Shelly wasn't working. After a while he went home.

The next few days she put the incident out of her mind and studied hard. She told herself that when he called she would explain that she couldn't see him for a while—this test was just too important to her future.

22

Rape is always a symptom of some psychological dysfunction, either temporary and transient or chronic and repetitive. It is usually a desperate act which results from an emotionally weak and insecure individual's inability to handle the stresses and demands of his life....It is not sexual arousal but the arousal of anger or fear that leads to rape.—A. Nicholas Groth with H. Jean Birnbaum, *Men Who Rape*

After the station break Shelly Monahan thrust her pretty face into the mike and tried to show an exuberance she didn't feel. "It's ten o'clock," she said cheerily, "and time for—sunshine in the nighttime!"

Seventy-two hours had passed since the abortive attack at Twelfth and Monroe, but Sunshine Shelly was unaware of that incident. She was feeling low for another reason: That afternoon her parakeet Sunshine had died. She remembered him now as a puff of pure yellow.

On that Sunday night, September 9, 1979, Shelly Monahan was twenty-one years old and a veteran broadcaster. Every weekday she drove the station's VW Rabbit seeking cars with yellow KJRB decals in their windows. She would pick up her mobile phone and say in her thousand-word-a-minute delivery, "This is Sunshine Shelly and I'm following license number U-G-F 0-3-5. If they'll just pull over I've got a hundred dollars cash for them! *They're pulling over!* We've got another winner on the SUNSHINE AND WINNING STATION!"

Each Saturday and Sunday night she became "Sunshine Shelly," female DJ. In a competition "rock-off" with other disc jockeys she'd drawn two hundred calls in ten minutes. When she was stricken with pneumonia and did her broadcasts from a hospital bed, the whole city listened and people donned Sunshine Shelly T-shirts. More Spokanites knew her name than the mayor's. Around the clock the station blared promos: "This is seven ninety KJRB—and don't forget to be looking for SUNSHINE SHELLY! She'll be out and about looking to make YOU a winner if you have a yellow sunshine sticker in YOUR window, and DON'T FORGET—this Saturday SUNSHINE SHELLY will be doing a remote at King Norman's Kingdom of Toys...."

Competitors couldn't maintain her pace. Her routine workweek was six-

and-a-half days; once she went seven straight weeks without a day off. She'd been doing the sticker-promotion job for nearly five years, right out of high school, and she still got more excited about finding a winner than most of the winners themselves. On weekdays she would work all day in the Rabbit, rush home for a meal and a nap, then return to the station from eight to ten p.m. to tape commercials. In her spare time she gave talks as the station's "public service director" and made appearances for charity. Her base pay was eleven hundred dollars a month, adequate by Spokane standards, slave wages for most U.S. broadcasters, but she would have worked for nothing.

Her DJ style was naturally bubbly, rapid-fire, upbeat—she made no attempt to exploit her femininity with a bedroom voice. It was enough to be herself. She never had to strain for sincerity or high spirits like so many other DJs. At five-four and barely a hundred pounds, she usually described herself as "no boobs and short legs—I'm going to go through puberty any day now." Once she'd wanted to be a dancer—"a short dancer but a dancer"—and she still tried to spend an hour at the barre every day. Her well-defined Irish-Cherokee face was highlighted by large blue-gray eyes, and her hair was a profusion of light-brown ringlets and curls with touches of auburn and red. In any company she attracted stares, "no boobs and short legs" notwithstanding.

On this unseasonably cold night in September she had shared some egg rolls with her father in between spinning records. She was the oldest of seven children, brought up on the unfashionable north side of Spokane, and she was still close to her parents. A few minutes after her father left, the all-night DJ came in, and for once she was happy to be getting off. It had been a grueling week, marred by the death of her bird. She had plain run out of energy, and her next shift would begin in the morning at 10.

At 11 p.m. she turned the control panel over to her successor and grabbed her coat. Her husband would be home in an hour from his job, and she had laundry to do before he came in. She stepped around loose bricks and tools and broken-down walls; KJRB was being remodeled. A few weeks earlier she had looked up and seen a stranger standing outside the glass staring at her; headphones had kept her from hearing him enter. She was used to handling obscene callers, but this time she'd been alone in the studio. The man watched her for a while and then disappeared. When the same thing happened a few nights later, she told the station manager, "I don't mean to be a baby, but weird men have been showing up at all hours. Could you maybe put a latch on the control room door so I can lock myself in?" She also asked for a floodlight on the field that served as a parking area. The station was on a windswept moor beyond the residential section of the South Hill, just outside the city limits. Neither request was granted.

She shivered as she stepped into the darkness. The calendar said it was late summer, but a cold wind whined through the area with the deep *mmmmmmm* usually heard only in forests—a typical South Hill sound. There was no light. She tightened her coat about her as she walked toward her VW Beetle. She'd told her listeners a few minutes earlier, "It's a chilly night in Spokane—thirty-four and falling. Dress warm in the morning!" The radiance of summer had come to an end. She glanced upward at a sprinkling of stars.

Something moved in the parking lot. "Hon?" she called out. "Is that you?" Sometimes her husband came to meet her.

She thought she saw a silhouette. She took another step and a hand clutched her neck. A male voice said, "Don't make a sound or I'll kill you."

She kicked and squirmed as the man tightened his grip on her throat and began dragging her into the field. The thong snapped on her sandal and it dropped off. The only person who could help her was seated inside with headphones clamped across his ears. She screamed and her assailant tried to ram his hand into her mouth. She bit hard and he punched her in the face. A tooth pierced her lower lip from the force of a blow.

She kicked and tried to scream, and he said, "Shut up!" Halfway across the field, about forty yards from the lightly traveled Fifty-seventh Avenue, she managed to get his hand out of her mouth and yelled again. When he hit her in the nose, she felt it crunch.

She tried to get a look at him but there wasn't even a glimmer of light. She was battling an invisible force, a presence. She thought of the Nanette Martin case in her childhood; parts of the missing schoolgirl's body had been found in plastic bags all over Spokane. Dear God, she prayed to herself, don't let me be another Nanette Martin. If you save me, Lord, I'll make you *so* proud of me. . . .

In the middle of the field the man threw her on the ground and jumped on top. She was choking on blood. "Wait!" she gasped. "What's going on? Hold on, please! *Please, wait, stop!*"

He hit her on the left side of the face. She kept turning on her stomach to let the blood run out of her nose and mouth so she wouldn't gag, and he kept yanking her on her back and slugging her again. Pink bubbles popped from her mouth. She was covered with dirt and weeds. It felt as though the whole left side of her face had been smashed in.

She tried to concentrate on a star. She began to tremble from the cold. The man fumbled with her clothes, but she could hardly feel his fingers on her skin. She stared at the star and prayed, Please, God, let me make it out of this alive. He pulled off her jeans, popping the button. He ripped off her shirt and her underpants and yanked her bra up around her neck. Then he tried to spread her legs. She kept squeezing them together, and each time she resisted he reached back and hit her hard—on the face, the side, the arms, on her shoulders, her thighs, her back, an unceasing rain of blows.

He spoke in a soft voice. "Your breasts are small but they're nice. What do you wear to bed at night?"

She mumbled, "Footie pajamas."

"Do you have a boyfriend?"

The thought of her husband made her moan, and the man said, "Shut up! I'll kill you if you don't shut up!" She thought, My God, dead? I'll be dead. I'll let him do anything he wants. *I DON'T WANT TO BE DEAD. . . .*

He tried to enter her and failed. As he leaned over her body she saw that his hair extended over his ears in a shag haircut. His skin had the smell of a rinse or after-shave. He tried to enter her rectally but couldn't. He said, "Then you're gonna give me a blow job." He held his penis to her lips, but she was shaking so hard she couldn't open her mouth. He rubbed it against her body, and she tried to ignore him by concentrating on her husband. Oh, my God, she said to herself, he'll be upset if I don't get the clothes folded. Then she thought, Oh, man, I've got to get those commercials done. . . .

The madman was going from one end of her body to the other, rubbing himself against her, fingering her, licking and nibbling her nipples and her genitals, rising to his knees to play with himself and then dropping back on her small body trying to force his way inside. She tried to be back with the nuns in grammar school; they were making her balance an eraser on her hand as she practiced handwriting.

Loud instructions returned her to the weeds and the field. "Pee on me! Yes you can! *Pee on me!*" She was beyond shame—her whole body throbbed with pain, and she felt as good as dead. As though to reassure her he said, "It's a little kinky, isn't it? Makes you feel dirty." Then he told her to masturbate. She went through the motions while he raised up on his knees and yanked at himself. He complimented her on "a nice ass, nice tits." When he slid his tongue into her mouth, she tried not to feel the slimy thing. He raised back up again, yanked at himself and flopped on her with all fours. She felt a spurt of liquid, more outside than inside her, and then he was still.

After a while, he turned her on her stomach so she still couldn't see his face, then patted her on the backside and stroked her thigh. "I didn't mean to hurt you," he said. He confessed that he sometimes masturbated to her DJ show. He told her how much he admired her broadcasting ability. "I'd hate for this to happen to you again," he said sympathetically. He spoke in the calm tones of a lover enjoying the afterglow, of someone who had her best interests at heart.

She twisted her head to see his face, but all she could discern in the deep darkness was the outline of his eyes. They seemed slightly slanted, but she couldn't be sure. All she could tell was that he was bigger than she, perhaps in his early twenties, with longer-than-average dark brown hair and smaller-than-average hands and fingers. He was wearing a plaid shirt, a dark-colored down vest and light-colored pants. The smell about him wasn't Brut or Aqua Velva or any of the popular after-shaves or colognes, but it was on that order. She knew that when every other memory faded she would remember that smell.

"I know where you live, you know," he was saying. It sounded as though he were adjusting his clothes as he spoke. "If you tell anybody, I know where to get ahold of you. I'll come back and kill you."

"I won't," she said, her voice quaking. "Honest to God, I swear I won't tell a soul."

He patted her again. "I'm gonna leave pretty soon," he said. "What're you gonna do?"

She tried to think of a pleasing answer. "I'll, uh—I'll just get in my car and go home."

"Okay. Listen, I didn't mean to hurt you. But you shouldn't have fought me. I had to hit you." She lay on her stomach, her face pressed into the weeds. She heard his voice again. "One more question. How do you plan to further your radio career?" He spoke in the superior voice of an executive.

She couldn't answer. She tried, but her mouth was choked with blood and dirt and the words wouldn't come. She waited a few minutes till she could no longer hear his pantlegs brushing the dried weeds and then sat up. When she saw that he was gone her fear turned to rage. She wished she had a gun. She'd hated guns from childhood, but she knew that she'd have shot him square in the back and then stood over him and killed him again—a hundred times over. A *thousand*.

His smell hung in her nostrils. She picked up her clothes, pulled herself to her feet and staggered toward the studio door. She had taken a few steps inside the building when she realized she was naked. She put her pants and shirt on and told the overnight DJ she'd been raped. Then she crawled to a corner and drew herself into a ball.

State police and sheriff's deputies arrived in a few minutes. Her teeth were chattering. "Please," she asked, "wrap me in blankets." She looked at the big studio clock. It was a few minutes after midnight. She'd been outside in thirty-four-degree weather for over an hour, naked.

She was rushed to Deaconess Hospital. Her wedding band and engagement ring were stuck together with blood. A nurse cleaned the blood off her face and tried to clear her nose. Her left eye was swelling shut. Her husband arrived ready to do battle. He squeezed her hand hard and asked, "What'd he look like?"

"I don't know," she murmured. "Maybe five nine, five ten. Stocky, dark hair, kind of slanty eyes."

"I'm gonna kill him," he said. "Where is he? *I'm gonna kill him!*"

She was in X-ray for a long time and when she came out her father and mother were waiting. It was the first time she'd seen her father cry. He said, "If only I'd stayed, baby. If only I'd stayed...."

Her parish priest arrived, then the program director and the station manager. The program director held her and kissed her and looked on the verge of tears. Everyone stared at her battered body. Technicians put her under black light and scraped semen off her legs and clothes, then took cultures of her bloody mouth and throat and other body cavities. She couldn't stop throwing up. Doctors tried to give her pills, one to keep her from getting pregnant and another to ward off VD, but she vomited them one by one.

At police headquarters she was asked to disrobe for photographs. An older man with a camera patted the back of her shaky hand and said, "Don't worry, I usually take pictures of dead bodies, so anything you have to show me I've already seen." In his own clumsy way he made her feel a little better.

On the way home in a sheriff's car she had the dry heaves. They kept up every ten minutes for five or six hours and turned her into a dishrag. She couldn't control her body. She was afraid she would never be able to function again. The rapist had said he would come back and kill her. In a way he already had.

23

A few James S. Black staffers were waiting for the others to assemble for a Tuesday morning meeting in September when the man they knew as Kevin Coe appeared at the door in his gray sweatsuit. Jim won't like this, Cheryl Ferguson said to herself as Coe entered in his customary jaunty stride. Cory had warned him about appearing in the office in sweats.

Then she took another look. There were scratch marks on his neck and along his heavy jawline. One hand appeared to be cut. As several women gathered around him he raised his pantleg to show more scratches on his calf.

"A dog," he said. "A big German shepherd in Manito Park."

The injuries didn't look like dog bites to Cheryl or several other women in the office. Dogs didn't usually make deep scratch marks under the eye, like the one on Coe's face. One realtor said, "Kevin, you better get to a doctor."

"It's okay," he said. "I've been bitten before." Everyone remembered his singular bad luck on the jogging trails.

"I'll bet that hurts," one of the women said, examining his gashed hand.

"No problem," Coe said. He seemed to appreciate the sympathy.

24

The nature of my lifestyle included a high degree of mystery.
—Fred Coe, April 15, 1982

Dining alone in her apartment, Gini Perham couldn't imagine what had gone wrong with her big romance. Kevin hadn't phoned for almost a week and hadn't returned her calls—very rare for him in their six or seven months of dating. He usually called a few times a day just to talk.

She wondered if it had anything to do with that scary scene at his house a week or so ago. All evening long he'd lamented Jenifer's departure, her drinking and carousing. When Gini told him he was overreacting he raised a fist. She backed off in surprise and he fled to the bathroom. She heard the click of the door lock and an anguished cry: "*You don't know what the situation is!*" For the first time in their relationship she felt like the other woman. She tiptoed to the door and drove home.

But tonight she missed him terribly. Everybody was entitled to an off moment, and she'd already forgiven him his outburst. After all, Jeni was a problem of long standing.

She washed and dried the dishes and tuned to KJRB. One of the disc jockeys was talking to Sunshine Shelly on a remote from her home. Shelly was loquacious and cheerful as always, explaining that her "flu" was almost cured and she'd be back soon with more "Sunshine in the nighttime." Kevin was right: She was a pro. Gini listened for a while and wondered if he was listening too, wherever he was.

After a while she hit on another explanation for his failure to call. Several months back he'd borrowed $300 from her. She hadn't mentioned the loan, but it was past due. The silly twit, she said to herself. He doesn't have the money and he's ashamed to face me. And he still feels dumb about that scene at his house. Well, somebody has to give a little. I'll drive up there and tell him what I think of his stupid pride.

It was late in the evening when she knocked on the front door of the little yellow house at Twenty-ninth and Rebecca. She was glad that Jenifer was gone; there was no chance of a confrontation. Of course Kevin had always insisted that there was nothing physical between them, but who knew how she would react to a visit from another woman? From everything Kevin had said, Jenifer Coe wasn't the most peaceable woman in the world.

No one answered her knock. Where *was* he? As she drove west on busy Twenty-ninth Avenue, she wondered if he'd left town or been hit by a truck or something. She was thinking of checking with the Coes when her headlights picked up a large white car approaching at high speed. As it passed, she caught a glimpse of a vanity license plate. Kevin's plate "DISCO" was still on the Grand Prix, but she knew that he'd covered the plates of his Toronado with a film of yellow plastic to make them look personalized.

Gini spun the wheel of her little yellow Datsun and made a U-turn, but she lost the speeding Toronado in a dip in the road. Approaching a busy intersection, she saw the big white car tucked in a driveway next to a small building. What was the man *doing*? A bus went by and he stared at it.

She felt smarmy. Maybe he'd seen her, maybe not, but it was obvious that his plans for the evening didn't include her. She decided to go home. Then she saw the Toronado pull out and head east on Twenty-ninth.

Her tires squealed as she turned sharp at the next corner. She was going to drive so fast she would beat him to his place. Then she'd find out what the hell was going on.

He arrived first. She might have known. No one drove the streets of Spokane like Kevin Coe. He had himself confused with the Snevas, the city's auto-racing family. She parked and knocked on the door of the lighted house. When he didn't answer she looked around. His Toronado was in the garage. Jeni had taken the Grand Prix when she left. So he *had* to be home.

She knocked again. Footsteps clomped up from the basement. Kevin opened the door and peered through the crack. "Some other time, okay?" he said in a high-pitched voice. "I'll see you later. I'll, uh, I'll call you!"

Why was he acting so squirrelly? "I've been trying to get in touch with you," she said.

"Not now. Now now!" He sounded almost hysterical. "*I don't want you to come in!*" The door closed in her face.

She drove home. She started to call him and thought better. He didn't deserve a call. What he deserved was retribution for being such a horse's ass. What about the hearts and flowers, the little kindnesses, the candelit dinners? *Jerk!* Shutting the door in her face! Maybe he was still upset about Jeni. But why take it out on somebody else?

When several days passed without word, she drove to the elder Coes' condo on the South Hill and asked Mrs. Coe if Kevin had a bank account. Ruth wanted to know why, and Gini spilled out the story. As she spoke she grew angrier. She saw herself as a patsy for the fancy-dressed realtor with his luxury car. She wondered how many other female marks he had on his list.

"Can you believe this, Mrs. Coe?" she said out of spite. "He's got a new car!" She knew Kevin had been keeping the news from his parents, lest they demand repayment of the thousands of dollars he owed them. "It's an Olds Toronado. With red leather seats and air conditioning and a sun roof. He's—"

Ruth Coe said, "He—*what*?"

"He's got a new car. He's had it for five or six months."

The woman let out a shriek and began stomping around the apartment. "He's a louse!" she yelled. She picked up a pillow and threw it down. "He's a coward!" She shook her fists. "Jenifer ruined him!" She turned and said, "Gini? I want my dog back!"

"*Your* dog?"

"Yes! My collie. Katy!"

Gini decided not to debate the question of ownership. Katy had belonged to Gini's mother. After the suicide Kevin had suggested that they give her to Mrs. Coe as a "peace offering," but after a few months the woman had passed her back to Kevin—the condo had proved too small for a mature collie. Since then Kevin and Jenifer had been raising Katy in his house. Somehow in that progression of events Katy had become Ruth's.

"You, uh—you want her back?" Gini asked.

"I don't want *him* to have her. He doesn't deserve a nice dog like that."

"But wasn't she too big for your condo?"

"Look, Gini, let's get her out of his house. Then we can decide what to do with her."

They drove to Kevin's rented house in the yellow Cadillac. The door was locked and the two-car garage was empty. Ruth led Gini to the owner's mother's house next door. When the woman answered, Mrs. Coe introduced herself as "Fred's mom" and said, "We just want to go inside and pick up a package he left for us."

The woman gave them a key. They grabbed Katy and took her to Gini's brother's house, and Mrs. Coe seemed pleased with the arrangement. "As long as Son doesn't have her," she said. She smiled sweetly and added, "Thank you, Gini. We've done something good today." As they headed toward the condo, Gini wasn't so sure.

Back home, Ruth announced that she was going to keep dialing her son till he answered. She jabbed at the phone with long plum-colored fingernails. Gini tried to cool her down. She had expected a measure of annoyance, but not this dognapping frenzy. "Mrs. Coe, please—don't make Kevin mad. All I want is the money he owes me. If you could just—"

The woman muttered, "The Coe men are no good." She dialed another number and told whoever answered that she wanted to speak to Gordon Coe *this instant*. She briefed the managing editor at the top of her lungs and this time she didn't call him Pottilee. "Come on!" she said to Gini. The two women made a quick downhill drive to the *Chronicle* office. Mr. Coe was waiting outside and climbed into the car.

Ruth did the talking on the return trip to the condo. To Gini's surprise she blamed her husband—quiet, passive Gordon, who hardly ever spoke, and certainly not at the moment. "It's your fault, giving him money!" she yelled. "That's what you've been doing, haven't you? How many times have I told you not to? How many times have you promised me? *How many times?*"

Back inside, the woman seemed to lose all control. Gini was frightened; it was like being in the same room with a wild animal. *Damn, hell, son of a bitch*—she was using words Gini hadn't heard her use before. "You've been supporting the bastard again, haven't you?" Mrs. Coe screamed at her husband. "*Haven't you? HAVEN'T YOU?*"

Mr. Coe admitted that he had.

"Oh, God," she said, clutching her head with both hands. "The Coe men! What a group! What unreliable—"

"Now, Ruth," he said, looking embarrassed.

"Don't 'Now Ruth' me! The Coe men are no damned good!" She shook her finger at him. "The Coe men don't provide!"

He stood with his hands in his pockets. When his wife stepped into the other room he pulled out his wallet and offered Gini five twenty-dollar bills. "No, Mr. Coe," Gini said.

"Take this for now," he begged her.

She backed away. Angry yells came from the other room.

"Gini, I insist," he said. He looked ashamed and guilty. She got the impression he was accustomed to scenes like this, that he had often helped his son and been berated for it.

"I can't take your money," she said. "I want Kevin to pay me back."

The managing editor pressed the bills into her hand and closed her fingers over them. Both of them heard Mrs. Coe dialing in the other room, then her voice saying sweetly, "Fred?" She spoke softly for several minutes. "All right, Son," she said. "We'll be there in a few minutes." Thank God, Gini said to herself. She's calmed. Or—she's setting him up.

Mrs. Coe came back into the room and began muttering something. "What?" Gordon asked.

"I said we saw Son's new car, Gordon. You and I. We saw that Toronado! Don't you remember? The night he was here and we went for a walk and it was parked outside? And he said it wasn't his? He lied to us, Gordon. *He's a no-good goddamn liar!*"

She grabbed the phone and began dialing again. "You rotten thing!" she babbled into the mouthpiece. "You lied to us about that car. You've always been a liar! And you borrowed money from Gini! How dare you borrow from a woman? You call yourself a man? Hah! You bought that car and never told— *What*? Leased? Well, it's the same thing! You wimp, you owe us and you owe Gini!" She slammed the phone on the cradle and said, "Let's go!"

When they pulled up, Gini noticed that the Toronado was out of sight. Kevin must have parked it around the block. But he was there to answer the door. He smiled at his parents and said warmly, "Hey, come on in!" Then he spotted Gini hanging back. "I'm not speaking to you," he said loudly. She wondered what her offense was. Lending him money? Telling the truth?

"Get out of the way!" Mrs. Coe yelled. Kevin stepped aside and all three entered. In the small living room Mrs. Coe began kicking at everything in sight with her gold lamé high heels. She kicked pillows, chairs, doorjambs and walls while excoriating her son. Once in a while Gordon Coe would say, "Now, Ruth," and she would turn on him and continue her tirade. Watching the three of them, Gini could imagine Kevin's childhood: his mother as judge, jury and executioner, Gordon as futile peacemaker, and a child called Son in the middle. Pathetic. She almost felt sorry for him. No wonder he acted weird once in a while.

Mrs. Coe asked about the new white Toronado and he insisted that he didn't know what she was talking about. But a few minutes later he let slip that he had leased a new car.

"Ah-*hah!*" Mrs. Coe yelped. "See? You're a chronic liar!" The woman's arms flailed as she stalked toward the door. "As soon as we get home I'm calling your office!" she shrieked. She lurched across the lawn in her backless heels. "It's time they found out how rotten you are. You're no good! A louse! Disgusting! You make me—*sick!*"

Gini was glad to get inside the shelter of the car. She took one last look and saw Kevin standing at the front door as they pulled away. He looked far calmer than she expected.

25

On the road Jenifer Coe moved steadily southward. Cold sober in Spokane, with Fred heavy in her gravitational field, she'd had only two close friends: her mother and her sister Sonia. But now she could walk into a bar, order a drink and float away on a sea of camaraderie. And not just with men—women liked her, too. Still a year under forty, she retained her slender figure and the facial planes of a professional model. Often as not she would finish the evening surrounded by admirers and wind up going to someone's house to party till dawn. She'd never had so many friends.

The night she'd left Spokane for Las Vegas she'd aimed the silver-gray Grand Prix straight for the Cascade Mountains two hundred miles west. Something had told her that she wouldn't be safe from Fred till she put a wall of solid rock between them. She drove on Interstate 90 through fields of standing wheat and down into the valley of the Columbia, then climbed to Snoqualmie Pass and began the long descent toward Puget Sound and the Pacific. In Seattle she turned south toward the part of the world she had enjoyed so much a few years before. She relaxed a little; she was getting away from Fred and his crazy ways.

But still she phoned him collect every day, like a servile employee. He would say passionately, "Pooky, come home. Come back! Things'll work out. I'll take care of you, Sweet Bird!"

"Yes," she would say. "Yes! I'm coming home." And then she would get in the car and continue south. One night in Las Vegas she looked up to see a man in white standing over her. All she could remember was that she'd been drinking and an angry woman had tried to poison her. Something like that. She was told she was in a detoxification tank. She said she had to get to a phone to call her husband, and when they wouldn't open the door she put up a fight.

Summoned by doctors, Coe arrived in the white Toronado and signed her out. Before they could tandem back to Spokane in the two cars, he told her they had to raise travel money. "Go out and beg," Fred instructed her. "It's easy for a woman. Just smile and say, 'Could you help me out?'"

She detested the idea but he insisted. With her last few dollars she went into a bar to stoke up her confidence, then hit the streets. As she accepted coins and smiles mixed with leers and a few propositions, she realized that every time she thought she had reached the lowest point in her life, a lower low came along. And Fred was always the instigator, teaching her to lie, to steal, now to beg. It was a wonder he'd never asked her to whore. This was the man who'd promised on the phone that she would always be safe with him.

As she brooded about the situation on the drive back to Spokane, the old resentments and fears returned. She was beginning to see her ex-husband as a hustler laying his jive on everyone on earth including his family. She felt like an escapee being returned to a mental hospital to which she'd been committed unjustly. She decided to shake him off and leave again. But no matter how hard she flogged the Grand Prix, Fred's Toronado stuck to her tail. At Ritzville, sixty miles west of Spokane on the Interstate, she hit the off ramp at a hundred miles an hour and broke away. Then she drove into Spokane on back roads.

He found her later and returned her to their little yellow house. He didn't reproach her or bawl her out. That wasn't his way. She realized later that it was easier for him to keep up his con.

It might have worked if it hadn't been for the stolen collie. They'd had the beautiful Katy for only a few months, but Jenifer had come to love her. And so had her twin sons, living now with their father and going to high school in the Spokane Valley.

"Where's Katy?" she asked as she entered the house.

"My mother took her," Fred explained.

"Your mother? Why?" Fred didn't answer.

"I know why," Jeni said, fighting tears. "Because she's God Almighty, that's why!"

She cried herself to sleep. In the morning she realized that the house held nothing for her—not even her dog. No husband lived here; she'd never had a husband, only an image. Underneath the three-piece suits there was a wailing infant frightened of his mommy. The realization struck deeper that afternoon when they drove downtown to buy her some jeans. They'd gone a few blocks when he said, "Duck. Quick! *Duck!*"

"What—?"

"Mother and Gordo. They're right behind us."

She slumped in her red leather seat, angry with herself for complying. Would she have to spend her whole life hiding from Ruth Coe? "The Caddie's still behind us," Fred said after a few minutes. "They must've been watching the house." Six or eight high-speed turns later, she felt the Toronado slow down. "Close call," he said, as though he'd just outrun a death squad.

When Jeni had been back in Spokane a few days, all the old arguments resumed. Sometimes the words turned to blows, and often as not she was the one who started it. She'd become sensitized to his unreason, his unpredictability. His slightest word ticked her off; she had nightly dreams about punching him out and tried to live the dream when she awoke.

It hadn't taken him long to return to his old ways: disappearing without explanation, lying, not working, running up bills. Several times he came home with expensive food that she knew he couldn't afford. Probably shoplifting again. Any day she expected to pick up the phone and find that he'd been arrested.

She began spending more of her time at favorite haunts like the Fresh Air Tavern and the Woodshed. It was Las Vegas and Santa Monica all over again. What she couldn't get from Coe she got from others: attention, consideration, respect. Now and then she met a desirable man, and now and then she stayed out all night. Let Fred find out how it felt. He had wrecked her life, twisted her mind the way arthritis had twisted her sister's fingers, and she no longer gave a damn.

26

"I guarantee that even in this town here I can produce a half-dozen psychopaths, men and women, who if the average Yale professor was left alone with them, you know, head to head, for any length of time, they would destroy him. I don't just mean beat him up either. Mentally too! They would know how to confuse and frighten him until he'd break down."—A police detective, quoted by Alan Harrington in *Psychopaths*

For a week or so after the angry confrontation over the borrowed $300, Kevin had called Gini Perham almost daily to complain and dig at her. "Gini," he would say, "you have set me back im*mea*surably! Don't you realize Gordon was my steady source of money? Now he's cut me off! On account of you! What a stupid thing, going to my mother like that. Where were your brains, Gini? Do you have any? What a *stu*pid bitch you are!"

Usually he would reduce her to tears. There wasn't the least softening from one call to the next, or the least sign that he'd once said he loved her. He called to hurt, and succeeded.

At last Gini told him to stop pestering her. He yelled over the phone that she had brought it on herself, that this was the end. When he called an hour later, she hung up.

She heard from her unlikely ally, Ruth Coe. "Don't let Son upset you," Ruth advised, slipping in and out of her southern drawl. "He's not worth worrying about, honey. Gordon and I learned that *age*s ago." She called her son a liar and a bum and told how he'd demanded a handout at Christmastime the year before. When she'd turned him down, he'd lost his temper and shoved her so hard she'd almost fallen. "Don't get me wrong, Gini," Ruth went on. "Gordon and I know we're not perfect. We've made mistakes with him. We *are* trying—we do want to understand the boy. But he makes it so *hard!*" She thanked Gini for dating him. "You were *such* a good influence, dear."

Gini was surprised when money orders began arriving in Spokane Metro Growth envelopes. She was sure he was repaying the debt only to get back in his mother's good graces, showing her the receipt stubs. The poor man seemed to live and die for her approval. The final installment of the pay-off arrived with a two-page letter. It began with a declaration that she'd been unfair and unjust from the beginning and that every action he'd taken had been correct and businesslike. A few phrases would stick in her mind forever: "You are uncontrollable, emotionally unstable. . . . You're a barracuda, Gini. . . . *Your action proves you're as crazy as your mother was.*"

Something about his tone convinced her that she was in danger. She still had deep feelings about him, but Prince Charming had turned unstable. She borrowed a hunting rifle and kept it by her bed for moral support. It wasn't loaded.

27

...The offender typically reports being in an upset and distressed frame of mind at the time of the offense. His predominant mood state appears to be a combination of anger, distress, frustration, and depression, and the offense itself is typically preceded by some upsetting event, often, but not invariably, involving some significant woman in the assailant's life.—A. Nicholas Groth with H. Jean Birnbaum, *Men Who Rape*

Jeni Coe drove toward Spokane's Joe Albi Stadium to watch one of her sons play in a high-school football game. She had been drinking, but she didn't feel drunk. On a straight stretch of road she blacked out and woke up slumped over the steering wheel. She saw that she was in a yard. The police told her that the Grand Prix had knocked over a fire hydrant, rolled across a lawn between a tree and house, caromed off a porch and scattered a stack of logs. They ticketed her for negligent driving and informed Frederick Harlan Coe, the lessee of record, that his badly damaged car needed a tow. He was understandably upset.

At 1:15 a.m. that night another woman was raped on the streets of the South Hill.

28

A few weeks later, *Millie Lukens* laid her suitcase in the trunk of her old brown Cadillac and tried to close the lid without making a sound. It was 6 a.m. on a chilly Saturday and she was acutely aware that she was alone and defenseless in the big empty parking lot outside her apartment building on the South Hill. She told herself to be calm. She was on her way to spend a weekend with her ex-husband in San Francisco, and there was a chance they might reconcile. She should be happy and excited, and she *would* be—as soon as she drove away.

At forty-seven Millie Lukens was still regarded by her many friends as youthful. She was five-six, slight and small-boned, with auburn-highlighted brown hair and a becoming nip of gray in the front. She turned the key and the engine caught. She opened the glove compartment for a pack of cigarettes and noticed a flicker of motion to her left. A man stood so close that his body almost brushed the car.

She slapped at the switch that locked the doors. Thank God, she thought, they clicked. She pressed on the horn but it didn't work. Then she screamed.

Alongside her window, the man had begun to masturbate. She pounded again on the horn. It still didn't work. The man's face pressed against her window. Any second now he would break down the door and rape her. And no one would ever know. She raced the engine to attract attention. His face filled the glass. He looked to be in his twenties, with a square chin and straggly blondish hair. She yelled, "Help! Help! *Somebody help me!*" She started to back out, to try to pin him against another car. In her state of mind it was kill or be killed.

The face faded like a film dissolve. She looked through the rear window. He was walking away, doing a clumsy little kootchie as he pulled up his pants. His bare buttocks were white blobs in her back-up lights. She tried to make a run at him, but he had reached a fringe of trees. She drove into the street. Two blocks away she heard a wailing sound. It was her own voice.

The first policeman she saw was a guard at the airport. He promised to make a report. She spent a ruined weekend in San Francisco. All she could think of was the face at the window. Her ex-husband was understanding.

When she returned Sunday night she told an airport guard that she was afraid to walk to her car. She called the Spokane Police while he searched the Cadillac. Two uniformed officers were waiting at her parking lot when she drove up. They checked her apartment and took a report. Fifteen minutes after she went to bed she heard scratching noises at her window. She called the police again and they searched outside with flashlights. The underbrush had been trampled.

A few nights later the prowling incident was repeated, and then again. Technicians dusted her window ledges for fingerprints, and a detective told her, "Millie, it looks like you got a sex nut *and* a burglar."

She gasped, "Oh, dear. Can't you do something?"

"We're trying." The detective told her that her reaction to the parking-lot masturbator had been exactly what the man wanted. "You should have laughed at him. Now he'll keep coming back."

She sat up all night. In the morning she called her boss and said she would have to work different hours for a while: arriving after sunup and leaving before sundown. She flatly refused to go out at night. She parked her car on the street, afraid to use her own parking space. The sleepless nights stretched into weeks. When she was almost ill with fatigue, her father drove over from Idaho. She slept around the clock while he sat up in her living room—and heard nothing. After he'd gone back to Idaho someone started throwing pebbles at her windows at 4 in the morning.

Not long afterward she reconciled with her ex-husband and moved to California. She would have left one way or the other. She reported her new address to the Spokane P.D. and said she would be willing to testify if they caught the man. But she heard nothing further.

29

The psychopath doesn't suffer so much as he makes others suffer. Since he is freed of inhibitions, his impulses are said immediately to spill over into action. He takes what he wants when he wants it. . . . He may lie glibly and show little if any embarrassment when caught out. The classic psychopath leaves a trail of misery, fighting, fraud, running up debts; he may abandon his wife and children, perhaps returning now and then if he feels like it, or leave a job without notice, or suddenly, for no reason, begin to perform so poorly or dishonestly that the company fires him.—Alan Harrington, *Psychopaths*

By the end of October Jim Cory decided he had gone as far as he could with the editor's son. Kevin Coe had been with James S. Black & Co. for a year and accomplished next to nothing. He wasn't showing up for floor time, he wasn't answering his home phone, and he wasn't paying his office expenses. The last straw was Jenifer Coe. She was making a thorough pest of herself. She would call Kevin and he would yes her to death, then hang up the phone and throw a fit. Sometimes he would leave the office and not show up for two or three days. And while he was unreachable, Jeni would call and demand in a slurry voice that they produce him immediately—or else.

Soon the lady began appearing in person. Sometimes she looked well groomed and attractive; sometimes she looked as though she'd slept on a bench. One morning she walked in and said, "Tell that no-good bastard I'm gonna send my twins after him. They're over six feet now. Tell him if he doesn't get me some money my boys'll take care of him."

To Jim Cory the situation seemed irretrievable. The real estate market was depressed enough without family problems spilling into the office. "Kevin," he said, feeling uncomfortable, "I'm sorry to have to tell you this, but—you've got to go."

Coe's brow furrowed. "Why?" he asked.

"You're not gonna make it in this business, Kevin. Your mind just isn't on it. Besides that, we can't afford you."

"Jim, listen. I can do it!"

Cory thought of the upbeat letters and notes Coe had sent him. "Kevin," he said, "you've been saying that all along. But nothing's changed."

"I can do it, Jim!" Coe pleaded.

"Maybe you can. But not with James S. Black."

A few days later Cory heard from the general sales manager, who had received a lengthy letter from Coe. "In about ten thousand words he says you're a jerk, Jim," Cory's boss said over the phone. "Says you never gave him a chance. Let me quote: 'I have the undisputed potential to be the greatest salesman at James S. Black and anyplace else. I could be top listing salesman at any agency in the world!' Hey, you really shook the poor guy up!"

"Well, I—"

"Don't bother to explain," the man interrupted. "I'd've fired him six months ago."

Coe came back to clean out his desk. Cory asked him, "Are you gonna take your lockbox key over to Multiple Listing or would you like me to?"

"I don't trust you to do it," Coe said.

"Okay, but take it over soon, will you?" There was a thousand-dollar fine for loss of a lockbox key. With one of the keys a realtor could enter any vacant home in Spokane. There'd been a series of empty-house burglaries, and the police suspected that entry had been made with a lockbox key.

A week after the conversation Multiple Listing called to locate Coe's key. "He said he'd bring it over," Cory explained.

"Well, he hasn't, Jim, and you're responsible."

Cory called Coe's telephone number. As usual there was no answer. He and his secretary, Cheryl Ferguson, kept after the number. Sometimes the phone was picked up and disconnected. Once a voice said, "Metro!" and fell silent. Often breathing could be heard. But no Kevin. Cory dialed Coe's parents.

"Hel-*lo*-oo!" a voice sang.

"Mrs. Coe?"

"*Yeh*-es?"

"This is Jim Cory at James S. Black."

"How *dare* you call me?"

Cory wondered what had been said. "Mrs. Coe, I can't find Kevin and I'm concerned about the key he was supposed to return. I just wondered if you could have him call me."

"Why should I have him call *you*?"

The woman sounded furious; Cory couldn't imagine why. Did she really think he'd been unfair to her son? "Well," he said, still keeping his voice down, "if he doesn't want to call me, have him turn that key in, would you?"

"Why?"

"Because it's worth a thousand dollars, Mrs. Coe. Either he's gonna have to pay it or I am."

"That key's *no* concern of yours," the icy voice responded. "Son is com-*plete*ly trustworthy. One—hundred—per*cent*! He's making arrangements to go with Main Realtors."

"That's fine, Mrs. Coe, but the key is in our name."

There was a pause, and then, "Why do you insist on picking on Son?"

"Picking on him?" he said. "I don't pick on him."

"I rather think you do."

Cory couldn't believe his ears. Did a one-year tryout constitute "picking on" her son? "Who's picking on him?" he asked, raising his voice a little. "He told me he was gonna take that key to Multiple Listing and he didn't do it. If he'd done what he promised, we wouldn't be having this conversation. Now if you'll just—"

Mrs. Coe broke in with a denunciation of Cory, of James S. Black, of anyone who would doubt the integrity and ability of Son. As Cory tried to figure out a graceful way to break off, it occurred to him that the woman didn't sound quite right. Did she drink? He didn't think so. But she was saying things that didn't correspond with reality. Kevin had the same problem.

At the end she agreed that she would try to influence her son to return the key and pay the $251 in office expenses he still owed. He never did either.

30

Sometimes Jeni Coe slept at her parents' home on the South Hill, sometimes elsewhere. She no longer visited Kevin's house alone. She would enlist the services of a beefy barmate and brief him on the situation: "I've got to pick up some stuff, but my ex-husband's there and he always beats me up."

Coe complained to friends that he would answer his door and be confronted by Jeni and her musclemen. Sometimes he would let them in and sometimes he would take the male aside and explain that she was insane. If he wasn't home she would call all over town looking for him.

Jay Williams took a call from Ruth Coe at his office. She said in her singsong voice, "Jay-ay, we're both Christians, aren't we?" Williams conceded the point. "Well, Jay-ay," the woman went on, "Christians stick together. If that horrible Jeni *ever* calls you looking for Fred, don't help her!" Jay said he would do his best.

One night Jeni drank a few glasses of Riesling and went straight to the Coes' condo looking for her ex-husband. "I know he's here," she told Gordon Coe at the door.

Ruth Coe elbowed Gordon aside and said, "Son doesn't want to see you. Get away from that door or I'll call the police!"

Jenifer strolled outside to the parking lot. She found a brick and went to work on the fender and headlights of the Coes' Cadillac. She heard later that the damage was $860. It seemed only fair.

31

"Now you or I looking at a woman as a sexual objective won't im-
mediately, with no preliminaries, expect to take her—because she's a
cultural subject as well. But the sociopath is either untrained in social
values or they mean nothing to him, so why pause? He'll not hesitate
to go after her and immediately try to seduce her. That, of course, in
some cases will mean rape."—Dan Sakall, probation officer, Tucson,
Arizona, quoted by Alan Harrington in *Psychopaths*

The last months of 1979 were traumatic for certain women on Spokane's South
Hill, home of half the city's inhabitants. The idle visitor wouldn't have spotted
anything unusual as he picked his way along wet, icy streets or strolled picture-
book parks strewn with pine cones and maple leaves. The two Cowles newspapers and the Spokane Police Department gave no sign that anything unusual
was happening. Only the victims knew, each in her own shame and solitude.

In the early-evening darkness of Monday, November 19, a woman was
dragged into the brush by a jogger who grabbed her as she climbed from her
car. The rapist was described in police reports as "W/M, 22-24 yrs., 6', 180
lbs., brown hair, blue-gray jogging jacket, gray jogging pants w/pockets, tennis
shoes, neat, clean." The terse report described what had happened: "Exposed
himself, cunnilingus, intercourse anal & frontal, fondle breasts, masturbate,
unable to climax...asked 'What think of it?' (Mast.); used word 'cunt,' asked
about her getting off on oral sex; if she mast...." Just before running off, the
rapist patted his victim's bare buttocks and said, "Be more careful the next
time. I've been watching you."

At 5:45 a.m. on the last day of November a woman walked out of her
South Hill home toward her car. On the sidewalk she was grabbed by a man
she described as a white male, five-ten, 170 pounds, wearing a dark shirt,
gray sweatpants, and a stocking cap over his face. She fought him off and
locked herself in her car. The man masturbated in front of her and fled.

Just after nightfall six days later, a rapist bulldogged a jogger in the
southeastern part of the Hill, hit her several times in the face and dragged
her into a yard. A police report noted, "Unzip coat, pull up shirt and bra, he
pulled down her pants...asked about sexual experiences, told her to say 'fuck

my cunt,' used word his 'juice' and asked if husband had big penis, asked her to urinate/would turn him on, ask if made her feel degraded... put finger in anus, rub on chest, made vict. touch; asked vict. to move bowels... cunnilingus, feces on chest, att. rectal and vaginal intercourse unsuccessful; mast. and ejaculated on buttocks." The assailant was described as "W/M, 25-30 yrs., 5'8-10", 170-190 lbs, fine features, square chin, no facial hair; quilted lt. tan jacket, sweat pants, jogging shoes." No weapon had been seen or mentioned.

Twenty-four hours later a woman was raped two miles away by a young jogger who rammed his thumb down her throat and said he had a knife. "Don't scream," he whispered as he dragged her between two houses. He asked questions like "Do you masturbate? Do you enjoy sex? How old are you?"

He entered her from the front, then pulled out and rolled her on her stomach. She felt him jerking at himself and his semen oozing onto her bare backside. "You're a nice little lady," he said. He pushed her face to one side, patted her bottom and ran off. The woman told police he had light brown hair to his collar, a squarish face and unusually small hands for a man of his height.

On December 11, along hospital row at the base of the South Hill, a woman walking to work was attacked by a young man with "dishwater blond hair" and a black stocking cap. He shoved his fingers down her throat and warned that he had a knife. When she told him she was menstruating he fingered her vagina and ejaculated on her breasts.

Two days before the end of the year the young daughter of a prominent Spokanite stepped from a South Hill bus on a foggy Saturday afternoon. After she had walked several blocks a jogger wearing leather gloves with raised welts hit her so hard that she thought her jaw was broken. He demanded her age and if she "ever fucked before." When she screamed he warned that he had a knife. Keeping his face lowered so she couldn't get a good look, he tried to harden his penis by hand, but two attempts at penetration failed and he spurted on her genitals. Before he ran away he told her that he would get her if she called the police.

It was the sixty-ninth rape of the year. For a city the size of Spokane, the number was not unusually large.

32

Shelly Monahan was happy to see 1979 end. She thought of it as "the year of the bummer," the supreme test of her natural joyfulness and high spirits. She passed—but barely.

A few weeks after her rape in September a man had called KJRB when she was on the air and told her, "I'll bet you thought I forgot about you, didn't you, Sunshine?" He started laughing, and she recognized the resonant tones of the rapist. He went on, "Hey, I read in the paper that a South Side female disc jockey was raped. You told me you wouldn't call anybody. I'm coming back for you when you least expect me. It may be a week, it may be a year, it may take ten years. This time you're not gonna make it out alive." She ran from the control room, then returned to finish her show.

After the rape her happy life had turned around. Her husband took the attack personally, his anguish slowly devolving into something different, something so complex that he didn't understand it himself. As he said later, "The night of the rape was the maddest I've ever been in my life. I felt like it violated our personal life and our marriage and everything that our life was about. It was traumatic for both of us. We'd had a good marriage, and after that we just started to go apart."

Shelly kept insisting that he listen to her story of the rape. Lying in bed at night, she said, "I've got to tell you about this from front to back. Every gory detail, every dirty word. That's the only way I can start to get over it. Listen to me, babe, *please!*"

He tried but couldn't. The subject was too painful. In her anguish Shelly accused him of regarding her as soiled property, and he tried to explain that those weren't his feelings at all. She insisted that he at least study the sheriff's report, so he would know what she'd been through. He made the attempt but couldn't finish. At night he had to rouse her from dreams of rape, and once she attacked him with fists and feet, thinking he was the man with the clean smell.

The first time she'd seen her husband undressed after the rape she'd been shocked. She said to herself, He's a man just like that other man! It was so confusing. They made love about a week after the rape, and it felt fine. But... first she'd had to think about it.

The marriage bent and cracked. Early in December he told her he didn't love her anymore. No, he didn't know why. They'd dated since she was a sixteen-year-old Catholic virgin and married when she was nineteen. She'd never loved another. She begged and pleaded and cried, but he was adamant.

They had to decide who would stay in their large apartment and who would go. She couldn't afford the rent and took a small place of her own. She phoned him every day and spent a night with him in an attempt at reconciliation, but it didn't take.

The investigation of the rape dragged on. Sheriff's deputies developed a suspect and searched his room. They found two notebooks full of neatly printed quotes from her broadcasts, word for word—*"This is 790 KJRB Sunshine in the Nighttime. Spokane area weather coming right up."* The man admitted masturbating while listening, but he turned out to be a pathetic soul with an airtight alibi.

Living alone now, Shelly couldn't stop thinking about the rapist's threat. She dreamed the worst. Two or three times a night she was raped and murdered—waking up in a sweat with the bedding twisted. Then she passed into a series of dreams in which the rapist chased her through corridors of locked doors. He would start to jam his thumb down her throat and she would wake up screaming.

When she arrived home late each night, she slid a butcher knife from her purse and checked out every inch of the apartment. Then she crawled into a closet and covered herself with loose clothes. She slept that way for weeks, and then one night she stopped, because she knew that no matter what she did, the man would find her and kill her anyway.

Christmas came and went. She didn't buy a tree.

33

Misty told a friend about life after rape. "For three or four days afterward I wouldn't go back to the Tiger's Den. But I had to make some money. Pete and I were paying on our house in the Spokane Valley and we had big bills. I figured if I'd been raped in a grocery parking lot I wouldn't quit my job, so I went back to work. I wouldn't book anybody I didn't know or hadn't seen before—unless they were too old to rape. But I still had a mind problem with the job. I wasn't gonna get hurt. I left the door open a little bit when I took somebody into a room. And I made the other girls swear to me on God's honor that if any of their customers tried anything weird they'd scream so I could run away. It annoyed a couple of the girls for a while, but then I, uh—I got back to normal."

Not quite. After the rape Misty made a slow transformation from drug dabbler to junkie, taking her faithful Pete with her. He lost his job as a mechanic and they had to sell their house. Another masseuse accused her of stealing from a purse and beat her so badly she had to go to the hospital. When she was released Misty asked the girls if they knew anyone who was holding Dilaudid or heroin, morphine—*anything*. Just before the end of 1979 she was fired.

Misty's co-worker Louise stayed scared for a long time after being trussed up and gagged and left in a back room to listen to the screams. "I'd just turned twenty, and I couldn't stop having dreams about this guy coming in and tying me up and saying he's sorry while he kills me. A couple of times I actually felt the sensation of the knife going in my back. That's what the rapist was, you know—a backstabber and a chicken. It's pretty cowardly to attack a girl of four-ten from behind."

By the end of the year she was back in her home town, eighty miles from the Tiger's Den. She swore she would never return.

34

...The astonishing power that nearly all psychopaths and part-psychopaths have to bind forever the devotion of women.—Hervey Cleckley, M.D., *The Mask of Sanity*

The year ended happily for the newest female member of the James S. Black staff. Gini Perham was sales-pitching a house over her apartment telephone when there was a knock on her door. She excused herself and called out, "Who is it?"

"Coco." At the familiar name she began to tremble. She didn't know whether to let him in or climb out a window. Her protective rifle had long since been returned.

She opened the door a crack. Kevin stood there in a brown leather coat, flared jeans and a sweet smile. She steered him to the sofa and resumed her phone conversation, saying one dumb thing after another. She wondered, What does he want?

After the breakup in September she'd become so involved in her new career that she didn't want to see Kevin or anyone else. She discovered quickly that there was a living to be made in real estate, contrary to Coe's experience, but only by working hard. She lost herself in the job. After a while thoughts of Kevin had returned. Without him she felt incomplete. Hour after hour she'd mulled over the unhappy ending and decided that the fight over borrowed money had been a smokescreen. Kevin had *wanted* to dump her. Despite his disclaimers he was still in love with Jenifer. She thought how awful it must be to love someone who drinks and runs around. She felt a maternal pity for the poor man. No wonder he'd acted so strangely. She was sure he wouldn't be back, but she couldn't stop reliving the exciting nights when he'd mesmerized her with his charm and his goals and his big ideas.

And now he was sitting on her sofa while she tried to get off the phone. When she hung up she discovered she was shaking. She managed to say, "What are *you* doing here?"

He told her she'd spoiled his entrance. "I was going to sweep you into my arms and kiss you, but that telephone call wrecked my plan."

She said she was surprised to see him after what had happened in September. "Oh, that," he said, dismissing with a flip of his hand the fight and his enraged calls and his hurtful letter. "That was nothing." He hugged her lightly, then stepped back and touched his chest. "Look!" he said. "My heart's pounding."

She admitted she was glad to see him; she'd never been good at the little lies of courtship. But when he told her after a while that they ought to get back together, she cut him off. "You love Jenifer, Kevin. I realize that now."

"Love...*Jeni?*" He grinned. "Well, of course! I see her as a sister. Always will."

"Kevin, it's more than sisterly."

"That's not true."

He reasoned and insisted. He clutched her hand and told her how much he'd missed her. She remembered how she'd loved the touch of him, the way he draped his arm over her shoulder as they walked. "Look, Gin," he said, sliding so close on the sofa that their legs touched, "I'm not like other men. Once I'm committed to a woman, I *stay* committed. It's a sacred obligation. I feel it toward Jeni. But with you, it's...deeper."

It took him two hours to convince her. Before he left he suggested that they think about marriage. They made arrangements to date again, starting with the James S. Black year-end party in a few days. They kissed goodnight. She lay in bed for a long time, exhausted but wide awake. She decided that true love must consist of constant, persistent, consecutive tests. It was like being initiated into a sorority. She sat up in bed and smiled.

That's what made it so sweet.

The party was a joy, although Kevin didn't seem to think so.

He wandered around keeping out of the way of his nemesis Jim Cory. Now and then Gini would look up and see her lover standing by himself, smiling wanly. He had fasted for nearly a week, and the skin was drawn over his cheekbones and square chin. She heard one of the female realtors tell him, "God, Kevin, you look sick!" After a while Gini dragged him onto the dance floor, but it was like dancing with a cod.

She joined a professional entertainer in boisterous songs and skits. As she took her bows she scanned the room for Kevin; he stood in the shadows in the back, touching his palms in listless applause.

Jim Cory had noticed Coe and Gini Perham entering the party room at the Spokane Club. He wasn't displeased to see Gini—he'd heard the new employee was doing well—but that other SOB wasn't welcome. My God, Cory muttered to himself, we're paying for his food and entertainment and he owes us two hundred and fifty-one bucks and a lockbox key that's worth a thousand!

As he watched Coe standing around looking ill at ease, it occurred to Cory that the young man had never seemed to understand the consequences of his acts. His arrival with Gini wasn't so much an act of contempt as an act of ignorance, of bald indifference. Coe had always lived in dream space all his own, as everyone in the office could attest. Cory thought, I wonder if the guy has a learning disorder.

1980

35

Was there really a clear-cut commonality to all 43 rapes? From what I read in the reports—and granted, I'm not a criminal or a criminalist—one has to stretch pretty far to see the common strands.—
Fred Coe, Jan. 15, 1982

January 1980 opened to jungle drums on Spokane's South Hill as nervous residents exchanged information and gossip about the wave of rapes. Descriptions of the rapist and his MO passed quickly from the modest houses down near the freeway to the half-million-dollar homes perched above Hangman Creek. He was said to be neat and clean, although sometimes he looked as though he hadn't shaved in days, perhaps in an effort to throw police off. He was variously estimated at five-eight to six-three but most often as around six feet, and his build was described a few times as muscular and stocky but usually as slender, almost gaunt. He often wore a gray sweatsuit, a down vest and a stocking cap. His hair was sometimes slightly disheveled, sometimes neatly layered, and was usually described as brown or dark blond.

Although no two rapes were identical, they were all outdoors and almost all in the hours of darkness. The attacker often shoved his hand down his victim's throat and punched her if she resisted. He usually asked a string of questions about her sex life and showed a fascination with oral sex and toilet functions. He frequently commented on his victim's figure and seemed obsessed by the word "cunt." He tried to penetrate front and back, then masturbated. If he failed to reach a climax, another woman would be attacked within a few days. Sometimes he turned his victim over and patted her thighs or her bottom, and he often warned that he would return with his knife if she made a report.

None of the gossipers had the slightest idea how many victims the rapist had claimed. For weeks the city's newspapers and broadcasting stations had ignored tips about the rapes. A jogging enthusiast called the *Spokesman-Review* to say that the wife of a Spokane policeman had alerted him to a series of South Hill rapes involving runners, and an unsigned letter complained about the lack of publicity on "at least five attempted rapes within a two-mile radius in southwest Spokane." Unreported victims were showing up at the Rape Crisis Clinic for therapy.

Most residents felt like Kathy Berry, a checker at a supermarket, who told a neighbor that she feared for the safety of her teenage daughters. The Berry house was on a dark block of Twenty-fourth Street, a thickly landscaped neighborhood where sycamores touched overhead and nearly every house had a big pine or spruce or arborvitae in the front yard. "This is such an easy neighborhood to hide in," Mrs. Berry said. "It's a wonder he's missed us. It's one man, or two or three; I don't know—but there's *somebody* out there."

Amid the mounting anxiety, the afternoon *Chronicle* emulated its managing editor, Gordon Coe, who suffered from a mysterious tendency to fall asleep at his desk. The other Cowles paper took notice of the rape situation in an article published on Sunday, January 6. Under the headline "*Sex Assaults Alert Police*," the *Spokesman-Review* noted, "A rapist who masquerades as a jogger may be responsible for a number of attacks on women in Southwest Spokane." The article included a series of statements by Det. Capt. Richard A. Olberding. As though acutely aware of the city's commercial need to be viewed as a safe place for shoppers and visitors, he insisted that there was no trend toward rape in any part of the Lilac City. "What we do not want to do is alarm the residents," he said. "We don't want everyone talking about a South Side Rapist." He advised women to walk in pairs and jog in daylight but noted that there would be times when this would be impractical. He said, "There are going to be women who find themselves out alone, either getting off a bus or for some other reason, and I don't want to alarm them by guessing at a trend now."

The detective captain had an explanation for why citizens of the South Hill seemed to know more about the rape wave than the police. At a recent meeting, he said, a detective had noted similarities between rapes on the South Hill and others in the city. "What apparently was happening was that each of the reports was being sent to a different area or to different officers, because of the various crimes involved, and because of the ages of the victims. Assaults involving minors were sent to Young People's Bureau, the rapes were assigned to one detective, the assaults to another, attempted rapes to another. Because of the number of investigators involved, no trend was clearly evident."

Other police departments avoided such oversights by assigning intelligence units to sift daily reports and make connections. But the Spokane PD, long underbudgeted by city fathers, couldn't afford to pay policemen to sit around and cogitate. Olberding promised that his men would catch up.

He didn't mention that police already had a hot suspect. Months earlier John Blake Mounsey, twenty-three-year-old member of a prominent South Hill family, had been charged with raping a coed in the nearby college town of Cheney. Just before his trial was to begin, police noted a coincidence. The December 29 rape of the daughter of a prominent Spokanite, the last assault of 1979, had happened right across the street from Mounsey's home. The proximity factor became more intriguing when the babyfaced college dropout volunteered for a polygraph test and sent the needles skittering.

Detectives armed with a search warrant carried off half of Mounsey's wardrobe. But before charges could be brought, his family produced a half-dozen highly respectable holiday guests who swore that Blake, a black-haired, blockily built non-jogger with no police record prior to the Cheney rape charge, had been inside the house at the time of the rape.

Temporarily frustrated, police tried to connect Mounsey with the next attempted South Hill rape. Early on the evening of January 2 a sixteen-year-old schoolgirl had been dragged into a rain-drenched yard, threatened with a knife and hit in the stomach by a man in a jogging outfit. She'd broken loose and crawled into the street where a car had almost run her down. The rapist had escaped in night and fog.

After medical treatment the child said that she wouldn't be able to identify her attacker; all she knew was that he'd been of average height and weight. As the investigating officer noted, "Suspect kept her from looking back at his face. She did not see his face clearly and stated she would not be able to recognize him."

The day after the assault a detective interviewed the child and reported, "She stated that she could not remember too well what the suspect looked like. She said that she was not very good on description, but I noted in her report that she thought that he was a jogger, so must have noticed something."

A detective hypnotized the schoolgirl to refresh her memory. A report to the county prosecutor's office noted, "After the hypnosis session, it was felt by the victim... that she did have a good image of her assailant and may be able to identify him.... The lineup was laid in front of her with all names covered. The victim looked at all five pictures and immediately extracted from the lineup the pictures of JONES, EBNER and MOUNSEY. She would periodically close her eyes, as if she were attempting to get a clear picture of the subject in her mind. She then stated that the subject JOHN MOUNSEY was the man who had assaulted her; however, she could not recall the double chin. In the photo showing MOUNSEY, he does appear to have somewhat of a double chin, however, it could be that his head was down at the time the picture was taken. She was asked again if she was sure. She stated, 'Yes, I just don't recall the double chin.'"

On the second day of his trial for the campus rape in Cheney, Mounsey was arrested for the latest attack and jailed. The *Spokesman-Review* made a public connection to the South Hill rapes by reporting that the incident "was one of a series of attacks on women in southwestern Spokane this winter." Only three days had passed since the newspaper had prodded the police into action with its article headlined "Sex Assaults Alert Police."

The courtroom was packed for Mounsey's trial on the earlier charge. Observers from the Spokane Rape Crisis Center and the National Organization for Women occupied seats near the front. Citizens waited in lines and jostled each other for a peep. There was talk that relatives of victims were on hand to ensure that justice was done.

On January 14, Mounsey was found guilty of entering the twenty-one-year-old coed's room through a window and having sexual relations against her will. Under Washington law third-degree rape was the least violent, involving no physical force. Sentencing was deferred while the prisoner was sent to Western State Hospital, three hundred miles west in Tacoma, for psychiatric evaluation and his own protection.

A deputy prosecutor took an anonymous call from a man who said, "Mounsey's dead, I'm gonna kill him." Another telephoner told Mounsey's twenty-two-year-old sister, "I'm gonna rape you like you've never been raped before." Garbage was thrown on the lawn of the Mounsey home. Detectives advised family lawyers that five other rape charges were pending against the suspected South Hill rapist in addition to the January 2 incident with the sixteen-year-old.

The police department drew rare praise. Grateful husbands stopped shadowing their wives; tear-gas canisters were laid aside; handguns were oiled and stored where little hands couldn't reach. Female joggers reappeared, shaping up for the "Bloomsday" race in May. The lovely old South Hill was safe again.

Blake Mounsey's upset mother Patsy had never stopped insisting that the incriminating December 29 rape—the one that had first brought her son to the attention of the Spokane PD—had been planned by the real South Hill rapist to incriminate her notorious son. The victim had stepped off a bus and walked three or four blocks before the rapist jumped her across the street from the Mounseys'—far too great a coincidence, Patsy Mounsey maintained, to be unplanned. Blake's upcoming trial for the Cheney rape had been widely publicized; he'd been the perfect rabbit to send the police galloping off in the wrong direction. She even insisted that she might have seen the real South Hill rapist herself—a young man with a squarish chin like Blake's, wearing gray sweatpants and a hooded yellowish top. The stranger had jogged slowly past the Mounsey house one icy morning and acted so interested that he'd turned and jogged past again.

Police and journalists paid polite attention as Mrs. Mounsey tried to interest them in her theory. But the idea that the real South Hill rapist had deliberately tried to transfer his guilt to another man was just too farfetched. Only a mother would believe a crazy story like that.

36

THE TRUTH—I have never had much interest in masturbation. I consider it second rate sex, at best.—Fred Coe, April 5, 1982

Is Coe the world's greatest lover? This persistent rumor in and about L.A.-Vegas is possibly somewhat exaggerated. On the other hand....
—Fred Coe, Sept. 15, 1982

By the time of Gini Perham's birthday in February, 1980, she and Kevin had known each other for over a year, but it was almost as though they were new lovers. They were together almost daily and in constant touch by phone. With spring a few weeks ahead and Jenifer Coe gone for good, Gini sometimes slept overnight in Fred's little mustard-yellow house. The lovers drove around town looking at properties. When the old Bing Crosby home was put up for sale in northeast Spokane, they were among the first visitors. Gini told Kevin how her grandfather used to play guitar and harmonica at Crosby family music sessions on Sunday afternoons, and Kevin told her that Bing used to be a newsboy for the Cowles publishing company. She said it was a shame that the city didn't turn the old house into a museum, and Kevin promised that Spokane Metro Growth would promote the idea.

He took her to see *Deep Throat* at a downtown theater. When she confessed afterward that she'd been bored, he seemed surprised. "It didn't turn you on?" he asked. She said that love turned her on, not acrobatics. He kidded her about being a typical Spokane woman. They went to a few other movies, but usually he shied away from public places. Whenever he picked her up at her apartment he parked his Toronado down the street or around the corner. The Grand Prix had been repossessed, and he was far behind on the Toronado payments. Gini wondered how long it would take him to get out of the hole.

She noticed that he kept a freshly laundered sweatsuit and tennis shoes on the back seat and often wore a track outfit, although she hadn't seen him jog. Sometimes the inside of his white Toronado was untidy, but more often it had just been vacuumed out. Before he would allow her to get in, he would move things around and check under the seats. He was the most meticulous man she'd ever met.

He often spoke of his admiration for women and openly stared at passing females, especially ones with dark hair. Sometimes the two of them would be having a sprightly conversation in the car when he would stop and gawk out the window at a woman. He told her he was attracted to "Mexican-looking dark-complected girls," and one night he almost drove the Toronado over a curb while staring at one. Another time he told her he liked tall, slender women with short hair and small busts. "It sounds like you're describing a man," she kidded him.

He made no secret of his uneasiness around men. At parties he sought out females, and if a male joined in he would find an excuse to slip away. In face-to-face meetings with men he spoke in an unnaturally low register and conveyed through words and actions that his time was limited. He went out of his way to avoid old classmates. One night he pulled Gini into a doorway while three men passed. "I graduated from high school with those turkeys," he said. "Can you believe it? Potbellies! Don't I look young compared to them?" The only man he seemed completely relaxed around was D. Jay Williams; their meetings always seemed to turn into reminiscences about childhood on the South Hill.

The few times Kevin talked to Gini about his upbringing he stressed that he'd been a happy child in a happy home. "Every Sunday when I was growing up my mother would take me and Kathy to open houses to see the things other people had," he told her. "She called me 'Freddiecoe' and she said when I grew up I could buy her the things she'd always wanted. I said, 'Yeah, Mom, I'm gonna buy you a big fur coat and a car!'"

His mother never hit him, he said, except when he put his feet on the furniture or dirtied his clothes. He said he couldn't understand why Ruth was so concerned about his cleanliness and so lax about her own. "She wasn't a good housekeeper," he said. "God, I hate dirty houses!" He said that his mother constantly hassled Gordon Coe about his low income. "But that's just her way," Kevin said. "Gordo understands. We're a very tight family."

Gini learned more about the tight family on a drive to Seattle with Kevin and his mother, delivering a black collie pup to his sister Kathleen. As long as Gini sat in back with the dog, the cross-state drive was uneventful, but when they switched around so that Gini sat in front alongside Kevin, Mrs. Coe's tone changed.

"I don't see how anybody can work for that awful James S. Black outfit," she began. Gini started to defend her employer, but a colloquy wasn't what Mrs. Coe had in mind. She went on about "those jerks at Black" and the unjust way they'd treated Son. She had special words for the man who'd fired Kevin, called him "an utter incompetent who wouldn't know talent if he fell over it." Her face turned red and Kevin tried to mollify her.

Atop icy Snoqualmie Pass, he pulled off the Interstate for gas. "Don't be upset, V.K.," he whispered. "She just gets like that." After the stop Mrs. Coe reclaimed her position next to Kevin and spoke pleasantly for the last hour of the run to Seattle. To Gini it seemed that the woman had been intensely jealous and unable to control it. The lesson of the incident was clear enough. Don't sit in front with Kevin; that's *Mom's* spot.

Gini found the scene at the house in Seattle similarly disconcerting. After everyone finished admiring the puppy, Gordon Coe arrived in another car, and he and his son-in-law settled in front of the TV while Ruth engaged in a warm conversation with Kathy, the "great children." It was easy to see that mother and daughter idolized each other. Kathleen Suellen Coe Cockburn, a former star swimmer, was a handsome young woman of charm and intelligence.

Kevin seemed to stand just outside the family warmth. Gini watched as he bragged to his sister that he intended to give her his car. "Thanks, but mine runs fine," Kathy told him.

Kevin persisted. He told her that it wouldn't be long before his Toronado was paid off (Gini knew that it was far more likely to be repossessed) and he was going to replace it with a Cadillac El Dorado. He seemed to be assuring his sister that he wouldn't be a failure all his life. As he spoke enthusiastically about his future generosity, Kathy stood with crossed arms, head tilted, looking as though she might have heard the words before.

At dinner, Mrs. Coe seemed to be trying on a new manner of speech, a lilting tone that made her sound like a Hollywood ingenue. After a while Gini realized that the woman was doing a Carol Channing impression, not just bits and pieces but the whole package: the same pliant mouth that stretched and expanded for vowels, the same wide smile while talking, the same open-mouthed response to comments. When Mrs. Coe got up from the table and pranced around in the tippytoe Channing manner, hands arched out sideways and a broad smile on her face, Gini remembered seeing that same dance-walk at their first meeting. The resemblance to the actress was uncanny, even to the five large silver rings set with diamonds and the jangly bracelets and heavy earrings and face-hugging hair-do. Gini couldn't decide if the imitation was intentional camp. It seemed an odd performance for a family gathering.

Over coffee Mrs. Coe switched to a style of speech that she called "the King's English" but which might have been described as "piss-elegant" by an Englishman. Her word of the moment seemed to be "supercilious," which she squeezed into the conversation several times. Peering over the tops of the half glasses that hung from her neck on a lanyard, she threw out Britishisms like "I rather think not," and airy locutions like "as it were" and "so to speak." When Gini asked politely if she'd been on the stage, Mrs. Coe snapped, "Hardly!"

Watching Kevin, Gini began to realize how overpowering the influence of his mother must have been, far stronger than Mr. Coe's or anyone else's. Ruth Coe towered over this group like an empress. Every remark related to her, and if it didn't she turned it around till it did. Kevin sat next to her and seemed to mock her mannerisms; each had a feminine way of putting the left elbow on the table, arm upraised, fingers facing outward and curled lightly with the pinky extended. Now and then Gordon would say a word and Kevin would lower his arm self-consciously, as though in deference to his father, but eventually it would return to the more graceful position. Gini remembered reading somewhere that female-dominated households sometimes produced homosexual men, the theory being that the male infants imprinted on the bold, intimidating mothers as a matter of simple self-defense. Well, this is one time the theory didn't pan out, she told herself.

She couldn't help recalling Kevin's nylon underwear and how he took care of his face and his hair with a woman's fastidiousness, but that was a long way from being gay. Sexually he was all male, give or take a problem or two.

Late that night they fell into bed after a nonstop five-hour drive home. The pattern of nearly a year repeated itself. He couldn't get hard, and manipulated himself under the covers. He entered her with his fingers and told her, as usual, how much he admired her "cunt"—hated word!

When he finally was able to insert his penis he quickly went limp and pulled away, apologizing. "It's that big dinner," he said. "I've got to get back on my diet and stay on it. No more exceptions!"

"No problem, Kevin," she said as she always did. "It's okay."

"No, it's not okay. It's...embarrassing. Please, Baby Bunny, let me try something else."

She felt sorry for him. For weeks she'd been trying to give him confidence, but he still had problems. He didn't seem to understand that she didn't mind. Everything except their love was insignificant. In the end he always tried to please her, an attitude that endeared him to her. Now and then he asked her to play an active role in oral sex, but he didn't make an issue of the fact that she couldn't bring herself to do it. She knew she was acting like the women he'd discussed the first time they'd met: the typical Spokane prudes. Maybe she would improve with age.

By the time the lilacs appeared in the unusually warm spring she knew he was the man she wanted to marry. The others had been prologue. Until this twenty-ninth year of her life she'd known she was capable of deep devotion, but it hadn't quite surfaced. She'd been close to two men: One had turned out to be married and the other hadn't been able to shake the effects of a bad divorce. Neither romance had lasted long. She'd been told by her friends that her standards were impossibly high, and now suddenly they seemed to have been met and exceeded. She thought of how Kevin had entered her life just when her mother was leaving. She wondered, Was it God's own celestial balancing act? Or a coincidence? Whatever the answer, she was deeply grateful.

37

Truthfully, I have no particular proclivity to any type or coloring or race of women. I like them all—if I am attracted to them....In my enormous experience with women, my favorites probably have been the several dozen Jewish girls I have known intimately. But I like blonds, brunettes and redheads equally. I have had countless affairs with black women and orientals—as well as American Indians. Of the five best lovers I have known in my life...three were Jewish, one goy and one black....Gini was absolutely fascinated with my vast sexual experience. She said to me one night..."God, I bet you've been to bed with a thousand women!" I laughed. The figure seemed stupendous— but I had never really stopped to think about it before. I began doing some mental arithmetic and decided that, in fact, it probably was closer to three thousand!...Hell, I had bedded down more than 100 females by the time I left high school!—Fred Coe, April 5, 1982

As summer approached, D. Jay Williams worried about his good friend Fred and the state of their venerable friendship. For twenty-four years Williams had always had a rough idea of where his eccentric buddy was coming from, but lately Coe seemed to be slipping off the edge of the planet.

Jay considered all the Fred Coes he'd known: the charmer and good companion, the short-term streetfighter who showed up at his biggest fight wearing a boxer's mouthpiece to protect his teeth, the smoothie who lined up women for his friends, the would-be tycoon, the vitamin freak, the "Ayn Rand objectivist," the pie-in-the-sky visionary.... The list was endless. Knowing Fred Coe was like having a platoon of friends, some leaving, some just coming on-scene, and all of them, as far as Williams was concerned, well worth the trouble. The two pals had agreed when Jay went away to Vietnam that it would be *Semper Fideles* forever. As kids they'd sworn a blood oath on it. Brothers couldn't be tighter.

But now Williams was afraid he might have given his friend poor counsel. He had encouraged Coe to go into the real estate business and it was turning out to be a mistake. By the late spring of 1980 Coe had been a realtor for a year and a half and as far as Jay could tell had sold only two properties: one when he'd been back at James S. Black and another just recently, to his parents—a ninety-eight-thousand-dollar split-level in the Spokane Valley.

At Jay's suggestion the two old friends had taken adjoining desks at Main Realtors, and for the first time he was seeing Fred as a functioning businessman. The biggest problem was that he was seldom around. He claimed that he preferred working in the evenings when other staffers couldn't listen in on his conversations. That, of course, was the old Coe problem of shyness, but should an essentially shy person have been encouraged to go into real estate in the first place? Jay blamed himself. Fred's anxiety about close contact with men created another problem. Rather than knock on a prospect's door he would sit up half the night typing sales pitches—model letters that could have come from a real estate textbook. Long after midnight he would drop the letters in the post office slot.

As always he spent much of his time dreaming and scheming. He made up a phony questionnaire that included the question, "Do you plan to buy or sell real estate in the next six months?" His mother would dial numbers at random and turn over hot prospects to her son. Fred told Jay that every realtor in town would be eager to buy names and gave a few to Jay for a 20 percent finder's fee. Williams found them useless. He wasn't surprised to learn later that Fred and Mrs. Coe had duded up their business with the name Intermountain Research Systems. To Jay it was just another in a long line of scams.

He remembered a time in high school when he and Fred had talked about buying an abandoned army base and turning it into a hotel. The idea was ludicrous, but when Mrs. Coe found out, she insisted on inspecting the property herself. Jay remembered her saying, "Why, boys, what a wonderful opportunity for y'all!" They were eighteen and she was in her mid-forties; he wondered now why she'd encouraged them in their pipe dreams.

Ruth Coe had stood squarely behind her son for as long as Jay could remember, going to school to fight his battles and sticking up for him in the neighborhood. Once the two companions had thrown ice balls at a car, and the driver had hustled them to the Coe doorway by their collars. Mrs. Coe said, "I suppose you never threw snowballs at cars?" She lectured the man till he drove away. Williams remembered many incidents like that. He wondered how such blind fidelity could have helped Fred develop a morality of his own.

And now it was he himself who had steered Fred wrong. Not that the idea of going into real estate was new to either of them. For years they'd talked about making a killing in the stock market, the real estate market, gold and silver, precious stones, self-help books and novels, music promotion and boxing promotion and dozens of other fields. As far back as 1969 the two friends had all but memorized John Nickerson's book *How I Turned $1,000 into Three Million in Real Estate in My Spare Time.* Fred made deep studies of metropolitan areas to see where he and Jay should go to get rich—he studied average income and growth, climates, population curves, real estate values. He could recite the mean summer temperature in Phoenix, the population of Atlanta, the zoning laws of San Antonio. When a subject engaged his interest his learning powers were frightening.

But none of his plans and schemes had a basis in reality. For as long as Jay had known him he'd been impervious to the everyday lessons of life. One day he would suffer a financial setback like the repossession of a car and the next day he would be pricing small planes to fly from town to town to set up a sales empire that would knock Century 21 and Main Realtors out of business.

Every night when Williams came home from work, he heard similar stories from his son. "Daddy, next month I'm gonna be president." But Donny was five.

Coe often leaned across his desk and announced the starting date of another achievement program. The two friends had had the same conversation hundreds of times, dating back to Jay's return from Vietnam in 1970. Fred would say, "Because of my health regimen, I'll be outselling this entire office in six months." Caught up in his friend's enthusiasm, Jay would leave the office to make a sales pitch while Coe stayed behind and drew up projections and wrote letters. Later Fred would complain that his daily schedule, broken into fifteen-minute intervals, had been upset by his mother or Jeni or some other aggravation, and he would have to start all over again at a later date. "Jay," he would say, "only you can understand how things like this happen. But if you can't do something right, you shouldn't do it at all." Most of the time, Jay realized, Fred wasn't doing it at all.

He was, however, juggling his usual collection of women, seeing Gini Perham daily, sneaking off to "matinees" with another real estate agent, and trying to get something started with the office secretary. One sexually liberated woman blurted out to Williams what a lousy lover his friend was—"He can't get it up!" Jay had been hearing that complaint about Coe since high school. In those days their lives had consisted of a steady succession of females, ranging from a rare upper-class and largely untouchable South Hill girl (called "soshes" for "social") to ten-dollar hookers. Jay and the third member of their in-group, John Nyberg, had passed through that stage and gone on to normal married life, but at thirty-four Fred still seemed to be a predator.

His dealings with women always ended badly and Jay thought he knew one reason why. Fred would make the most outrageous remarks without seeming to have any idea what he was saying. One day the two friends ran into an old classmate, a woman with slightly protruding teeth. Coe said, "I've always meant to ask you. What's wrong with your mouth?"

"My—mouth?" the woman said, her hand flying up.

"Yeah. It looks like there's something wrong with it."

After the woman hurried away, Jay said, "Why'd you ask her a thing like that?"

"There was something wrong with her mouth."

"Didn't you know she'd be embarrassed?"

Coe asked, "Was she embarrassed?"

"Well, yes!" Jay told him. "You can't say things like that. You hurt people's feelings."

A few days later a fellow realtor was describing a great new listing when Coe cut her off. "I only show my own properties," he said.

Jay grabbed Fred and said, "Why did you say something so absurd? Didn't you see how you squelched her?"

"How?"

"Fred, *everybody* shows other properties. You do it yourself. Don't you see how abrupt you sounded?"

"Oh?" He seemed genuinely puzzled.

A week later he acted again like a visitor from outer space. This time the subject was pens. Coe's desktop was always a *tabula rasa* and his top drawer empty except for a small tray with four colored pens. Now and then Williams would reach across and borrow one, returning it exactly where he'd found it. Invariably Fred would return and say quietly, "You've been in my desk."

"How do you know?"

Fred would resurrect a spooky voice from his radio days and make both of them laugh by saying, "The great Coe knows—EVERYTHING!"

One day Jay found that the pens had been removed. He asked Fred why. "Because you keep getting in there," Coe answered.

"How can you tell?"

"I'll show you. You're *so* untidy." He shut the drawer in the normal way— Jay's way—and then demonstrated the "proper" way. With one finger he pressed the pen tray against the front lip of the drawer and eased it shut so that nothing moved. He stepped back like a master showman. "That," he said, "is *neatness.*"

Yes, Jay thought, but isn't it also compulsiveness? He wished he knew more about human behavior. Coe always had to be so outrageously perfect. Jay had heard Gordon Coe tell his son, "You know, Fred, if I added up all the time in my life that I've spent primping in front of a mirror it wouldn't amount to fifteen minutes. You just spent that much time right now!"

Williams was looking at cars at Becker Buick one day when Fred sauntered through the door like a celebrity. Jay thought, Isn't it great to be associated with a guy who looks like that! He introduced Coe to a car salesman but before the two men could shake hands Coe glimpsed himself in a wall plaque and began fussing with his hair. Then he turned and acknowledged the salesman's welcome. Jay thought, What a peacock! There can't be another like him in the world!

Neither Williams nor Sue Williams was displeased that they'd begun to see less of Fred socially. Most of their free time was taken up with the Seventh Day Adventist Church. Jay was now a lay preacher. Coe, on the other hand, had described himself since high school as one who believed exclusively in "biology." They didn't argue that subject or any other. Their friendship had been free of open controversy for twenty-four years and remained so even as Fred's behavior became more quixotic. But they no longer sat and talked about going into business together and becoming multimillionaires by the time they were forty. Jay remembered a scripture about "being unequally yoked together." Sad, he thought, but applicable—like all scripture.

Sometimes he thought he might be taking the whole subject too seriously—no one else seemed to be sitting around worrying about Fred. And anyway, the real estate biz was full of surprises and upsets, not all of them caused by Fred Coe. Someone was still using a lockbox key to steal from homes. Just the other day a woman had called to say that the realtor who had previewed her place that afternoon had gone through her underwear drawer; she hadn't caught his name. One morning Jay went to work at the Main office and saw the women giggling around a desk. A secretary had found something in the copying machine. She seemed reluctant to show it to Jay, but he leaned over and caught a glimpse. It was a photocopy of a penis at least a foot long and three or four inches wide. One of the women asked shyly, "Do you suppose it's—a dildo?"

Jay said he certainly hoped so.

38

One time there was a police decoy. If I'm the rapist, how come I didn't jump the decoy? Sure, I hid behind a lot of bushes and trees. I was looking for the guy and stalking him.—Fred Coe, May 28, 1982

By the end of May a one-man rape epidemic raged on the South Hill. A special police squad was formed so quietly that newspapers didn't get wind of it till months later (and when they did, police officials repeated their earlier explanation that they hadn't wanted to alarm residents). Detectives rousted known sex criminals, staked out likely locations in unmarked cars and sent decoys along the darkest streets.

At the corner of Fifth and Adams, locus of many rapes, they watched a narrowly built young man with collar-length hair pad along after a decoy. He stepped behind a tree and removed his jacket, changing his look. When he took a shortcut through a yard one of the undercover cops gave chase, but the man was gone.

Later at the same corner a man who fit the description of the rapist parked his car under a tree. A woman came into sight and the man stepped out, but before he could make a move a police decoy appeared and the woman ran up to her and asked, "May I walk with you?" The suspect sped away. When the detail returned to headquarters that night a sergeant asked, "What happened?"

"Our decoy fucked it up," one of the detectives explained. From then on every member of the detail, including the decoys, was assigned a two-way radio.

Two weeks later a rookie policewoman named Sandy Brewer watched a suspicious young man a few blocks from the same hot corner. He appeared to be in his late twenties, with dark brown bangs and hair that spilled over his ears. He looked athletic and about five-ten, with a very distinct nose and a firm jawline. He was wearing jeans and a blue sleeveless vest. A decoy had just strolled by, and the man stepped out of the darkness alongside a building and watched her from behind a tree. A car passed and the suspect slid into the shadows, then resumed his observations. When the decoy disappeared from sight, Patrolwoman Brewer saw the man jump into a parked silver-gray Chevrolet Citation with yellowish plates and drive south on Madison at high speed. A check of the license number showed that the car was registered to Gordon H. Coe, fifty-nine years old.

That was the end of it. Plenty of men followed women; if the police were to arrest every randy male in Spokane the county-city jail would be overflowing. Besides, the rookie cop had produced a poor description. The man she'd described was nowhere near fifty-nine. The secret rape squad passed on to other activities, including a close watch on a list of known and suspected rapists. Then the unit was disbanded.

After eighty-seven days of evaluation in Western State Hospital near Tacoma, Blake Mounsey was adjudged not to be a sexual psychopath and returned to Spokane for sentencing on his third-degree rape conviction. On July 2 Superior Court Judge Donald N. Olson took note of a pre-sentencing report that described Mounsey as a first offender, "a charming, assured, highly intelligent young man," and gave him eight months in jail, with half commuted for time served, plus three years' probation.

The Spokane Police Department did nothing to disabuse the public of the idea that Mounsey had been the South Hill rapist. Nor did the local press. The result was that citizens were outraged by the light sentence. The NOW members who had celebrated Mounsey's conviction with a victory party were reported to be after Judge Olson's scalp. "It's upsetting to us," said Susan Fabrikant, acting director of the Spokane Rape Crisis Network. "What has to happen before the community realizes what it's dealing with? Time and time again we tell women to report rape, that something will come of it. Three years' probation and eight months of jail with four commuted is nothing." The husbands and boyfriends of several South Hill victims let it be known that they would be around when Mounsey was freed.

In all the tumult, no one seemed to notice that during the first five months of 1980, while Blake Mounsey had been behind bars, the rape rate in Spokane had risen 300 percent.

39

It is estimated that for each rape that is reported, there are anywhere from 3 to 10 others that are not reported.—James C. Coleman, James N. Butcher, Robert C. Carson, *Abnormal Psychology and Modern Life*

Lynn Barkley was feeling better about everything. She'd been raped almost four months ago in a snowy South Hill yard, and the bad dreams and black moods were just about over. It wasn't easy to stay upset on these summer days when the lilacs and Ponderosas scented the whole city and Spokane was alive with young people like herself having a good time. The place had hard winters, no doubt about that—temperatures to twenty below and snow that sometimes hung around till April—but the summers were perfect.

It was Saturday night, July 5, and she didn't have a date. She did her exercises and worked on the homemaking files that she kept in neat stacks on her living-room floor. Just when she thought she was going to make it through the whole evening without putting on an ounce, she got hungry. She pulled on a top and a pair of shorts and strode off toward Wendy's on Third Avenue. The fast-food restaurant was a mile from her apartment—a short stroll for a young woman raised in Montana—and the calories she added would be burned off by the walk. A stroke of weight-watching genius! After a Tab and a salad, she tried to decide which route to take home, and ended up walking on Fourth Avenue parallel to the freeway. There was a string of hospitals there, and the area was well lighted and busy. Ever since the rape she'd been selective about routes.

When she reached the thick trees along Maple Street, she turned uphill and thought fleetingly about ancient history. Six blocks farther up, a youngish man had poked her in the back with a foot-long dildo, raped her, masturbated over her body while asking a string of personal questions, and robbed her of $40. She willed herself not to think about it.

As she stepped into the intersection of Sixth and Elm, three blocks from her apartment, a jogger came out of a bushy area above her line of sight and began running down the hill toward her. She stopped. "Hi!" he said, continuing past. She saw him clearly. He wore sweats and appeared thin. His light hair was windblown. He was good-looking in a cold sort of way, with sloping eyes. He was the man who had raped her.

She panicked and sprinted up Elm. When she had gone twenty or thirty yards she looked around. He was right behind. She veered toward a brick house and screamed. He caught her on the front lawn and applied a choke hold. She started to black out.

"Be quiet," he said, "and you won't get hurt."

She dropped her purse and he made her pick it up, then forced her to walk toward a deserted school. She couldn't stop trembling. She remembered shaking during the first rape. She'd thought it had been from cold, but tonight the air was warm.

When they reached the steps leading up to the schoolyard she said, "I wiped out my back yesterday, so be nice, will you?" He told her to shut up. She asked, "Are you going to rape me?" and realized it was a stupid question.

He led her to a secluded grassy area and made her strip. She noticed that he was trying to stay behind her. She remembered how violent he'd been the first time, how she'd been certain she was going to die. This time he seemed a little calmer.

The hard ground hurt her bruised hip. "You have a nice body," he said. "How do you keep in shape?"

"Exercise," she managed to say. "I—I bicycle a lot."

"Nice tan." She wasn't sure if she should thank him for the compliment. He went right on in his well-modulated voice, asking her name and where she worked. She answered honestly. He said, "When was the last time you were with a man?"

"You mean—?"

"Yeah."

He had asked something like that the first time. "It's been...a while," she answered. She added quickly, "I broke up with my boyfriend, but I keep hoping we'll get back together."

"He'd be a fool not to."

He slid down her body and begin licking. It felt oddly passionless, mechanical. Then he was back at her side, holding both her hands. "Don't be afraid," he said. "Think of me as your boyfriend. Try to enjoy it."

He told her that he'd once known a woman who worked in a chiropractor's office and that the chiropractor was always chasing her around the table. "That doesn't happen where I work," she said, thinking of her straitlaced boss.

"If I was in an office with you," he said, "I'd sure be after you for it."

After a while, he stripped and rolled on her body. She felt him trying to penetrate but couldn't be sure if he succeeded. Every motion was gentle; it wasn't lovemaking but it didn't feel like rape either. Still she couldn't forget his capacity for violence, or his strength. "Like it?" he asked.

He had asked the same question the last time. "It's great," she lied.

He kissed her hard. Something about his kisses assured her she was going to survive, but why couldn't she stop shaking? She asked him if he'd done this to her before. He stopped abruptly. "When do you mean?" he asked.

"Last February."

"Not me," he said. "That's too cold for me."

His motion slowed and stopped, but the weight of his body still hurt. God, she thought, when will he get off? She shut her eyes tight. His bulk eased; she couldn't tell what he was doing. "Are you in me?" she asked.

"You mean to say you can't tell, for God's sake?" She opened her eyes a slit. He was standing over her jerking at himself. "Jesus," he snarled, "you really *haven't* been with anybody in a long time, have you?" She told herself not to say anything else that could be construed as a comment on his masculinity.

He climaxed in his hand and flopped alongside her, chatting away about nothing. After ten or fifteen minutes he said, "Make sure you don't tell anybody, okay?"

"I w-w-won't," she said, still shaking. "I've gone through that before and it wasn't worth it." She began to feel pity for him. He hadn't hurt her, he'd been willing to negotiate a little, and as silly as it might sound there'd been moments when she'd almost enjoyed him—the talk, not the rape.

He dropped her hands and began pulling on his clothes. "Listen," she said, wishing she could stop trembling. "The next time you plan something like this, bring a b-blanket, will you? This was *really* uncomfortable."

He nodded and told her he would watch as she walked away. She dressed, gave him a sisterly kiss on the cheek, and left. As she hurried toward her apartment, she wondered why she'd kissed him. Put it down as human kindness, she told herself. It surely wasn't a romantic impulse, and it surely wasn't sex.

At home she started to call the police, then flashed on her first rape: the long reports, the swabs and smears, the cops asking questions and writing in their notebooks, the trips to police headquarters for more interviews and line-ups and interrogations without the least confidence that anything would ever get done—the whole trip an exercise in futility.

She put the receiver back on its cradle. Rape was bad enough without its aftermath. This one would go unreported.

40

For a while Gini Perham had suspected that Kevin was seeing other women—a gorgeous realtor for one—but he convinced her that he wasn't. "You must think I'm Superman," he commented. She had to admit he had a point. Their relationship had progressed to the point where she spent most nights at his house. Now that he seemed more sure of her, their sex life was improving.

But other aspects of their romance weren't. She still found him secretive, especially about family matters. Like a typical young lover, she was interested in his late forebears: Gordon's father Harlan, once Spokane's superintendent of refuse; Ruth's father Fred Enfield, a dry goods merchant, Ruth's mother Edna Turnley Enfield, praised by other family members as a saint.

Kevin seldom discussed his childhood, but he seized on any excuse to return to the old neighborhood atop the South Hill and wax nostalgic with Jay Williams or Kathy Coe and her husband. Whenever Gini asked personal questions he acted put off and often complained that she was nosy. She wondered what he had to hide.

One early summer day he showed her a fresh injury to his left hand, a cut in the shape of an arc, with a flap of skin folded over it. "How'd you do that?" she asked.

"I fell on gravel while I was running."

She looked closer. "Why don't you have a scrape mark?" she asked. "That's circular and deep. Gravel wouldn't do that."

He didn't answer. She was no longer offended by his abrupt silences. She knew he didn't mean to be rude.

When he showed up with another wound—a deep scratch on his neck—she asked about it. "V.K.," he said, "you should mind your own business." She was happy to drop the subject. He often jogged in darkness and encountered vicious dogs and low-hanging branches—she remembered his explanation ages ago. He must be accident-prone, she thought. Some men draw lightning.

They often talked about jogging or playing tennis together, but it never worked out. He loved to run and almost lived in his sweats, but she saw him jog only twice, a few casual laps around an athletic field. Several times at his house she awoke after midnight and found that he was out running.

In late summer he told her, "You're as close to perfect as any woman I've ever met."

"What's lacking?" she asked, hating herself for being coy.

"Nothing. Well, uh—you know what would improve your look? Cut your hair."

She'd been entertaining the idea lately. Ever since her sophomore year of high school her auburn hair had fallen to her waist in waves. The real estate business called for a more conservative hairstyle and she'd had to keep it pinned with fifty or sixty bobby pins that gave her headaches.

She slashed her hair to her shoulders. The next day she went to "Sherry's, *the* Salon," Kevin's own hairstylist, for a professional finish. Kevin was ecstatic. He made her spin around. "That's perfect!" he raved. "Come on, we've got to show Barefax!"

They sped to his parents' new house, a multilevel Japanese-style home his mother had dubbed Five Pines. Ruth Coe clapped her hands and said, "Why, Gini, you're a new *woman!*" Gini wondered if all the approbation came from the simple fact that she now looked more like Ruth, but she dismissed the idea as overthink.

There were times lately when she wondered how Kevin had developed his taste. *Not* by emulating his mother. Standing in front of the new house, Ruth had shocked her by saying, "You know, it wouldn't take much to turn this place into a Colonial." Gini couldn't imagine why anyone would bother. The stylish house was surrounded by a rock-strewn field with ponderosa pines. It seemed lifted intact from the Japanese countryside, a perfect setting for Gordon's retirement in a year or two. How on earth could it be turned into a Colonial? By adding floors, porticoes, wooden shutters? But then it wouldn't fit the setting. If Ruth felt that way, why had they bought the place? Surely not just to boost Kevin's anemic sales record.

After Gini came to know the house better, she thought she saw Ruth's real objection. Down the hill was a cluster of low-priced houses. Ruth spoke disparagingly of the residents, just as she'd bad-mouthed the "white trash" near the condo. Gini put it down as another harmless idiosyncrasy. She had almost reached the point of enjoying the woman's company, if only for the entertainment value. Now and then Ruth even showed a touch of sentimentality. On her sixtieth birthday in June, Gini handed her a bouquet of roses accented by a few bell-shaped purple flowers from her own garden. For a second she thought Ruth was going to cry. "Oh, Gini!" she said. "Somebody gave my mother a bouquet like that the day I was born. Why, they mean more to me than diamonds. Gini, how *very* thoughtful of you!"

Underneath her bold exterior Ruth Coe began to come across as a lonely and anxious woman. She could be engaging at times, but she had few female friends and seldom had visitors other than Gini and the Coe family. When outsiders dropped in, she would babble at them till they left. Her closest friend was a pleasant old woman named Rae Shepard whom she chauffeured around in the yellow Cadillac as though to cement their friendship.

The fiction about her southern childhood was soon abandoned, though she sometimes slipped into a grits accent to rave about *Gone With the Wind*. She had her own ideas about the book's authorship. "I know it says Margaret

Mitchell on the cover," she insisted, "but God in heaven wrote that book." She had a table of values that she would defend at the slightest disagreement: Women were superior to men, whites to blacks, Southerners to Northerners, conservatives to liberals, and almost any city in America to Spokane. Her fiery religious speeches came out of nowhere. "Jesus Lord God in Heaven!" she would begin in the middle of a conversation about the price of beef or the latest style in hemlines, and soon she would be expatiating on how the world sorely needed God and millions of people deserved to burn in hell, especially the ones who had affronted the Coes.

When Gini pointed out that some of her own ancestors had helped raise the money for St. John's Cathedral, Ruth went into a tirade about the Church for "refusing to marry Gordon and me," and requested that St. John's never be mentioned in her house. Gini joined Kevin in an embarrassed silence till Ruth smiled faintly across the room as though awakening from surgery and began talking about new landscaping. She said she thought Five Pines could be dramatically improved for something between twenty-five and fifty thousand. The light caught one of her diamond rings oddly and Gini wondered if all those clunky gemstones were fakes. Ruth wore them at breakfast, lunch and dinner. If the jewels were real, Gini guessed, they must have put a strain on Gordon's salary. Maybe the family had outside income. Kevin had mentioned wheatlands in the Palouse, but she understood they'd been sold. And once he'd remarked that Ruth had sold her jewels to send Kathy to college. What was the truth? Sometimes mother and son put Gini in mind of fibbing children, savoring their games and deceptions. Ruth had led her to believe that the curly bouffant hair atop her head was natural, but Kevin said that his mother always wore wigs and that her natural hair was a thin mix of black and gray. Gini wondered why she hadn't noticed. The wigs were a glossy ultra-black, far too dark for a woman of sixty. She decided that Ruth was one of those unfortunates born without a sense of style—no more to her discredit than a missing toe. One day she arrived for lunch in a confused blending of styles and shades set off by a necklace of bronzed oversize pearls more suitable for an evening at the Spokane Opera House. She looked like a gypsy queen who'd dressed in the dark. Kevin complimented her on her outfit and nudged Gini to do the same. Gini knew that he sometimes helped his mother pick out her outfits, but surely not this one?

As the threesome drew closer, Gini began to notice that Ruth always showed up in one of two moods: ecstatic and bubbly or downright bilious. If she was in a good mood she would babble about her life, her "career," her disdain for Spokane, her trips to Hawaii and Las Vegas and her desire to return, and above all her daughter. While Kevin squirmed, his mother compared her two offspring—the beautiful, vivacious college graduate Kathy, and the disappointing Son. Once she said, "Well, at least one child of mine came away with common sense, and it surely wasn't you, was it, dear?" Kevin stared expressionlessly at his plate.

She often gave him gratuitous advice, as though he were still a child. "Son," she said with a sideways smile at Gini, "I'm glad you finally decided to take my advice about women."

"What was that, Mother?" he asked politely.

"You mean you don't remember? I always told you, don't get involved with low-life women—women who hang around bars, women who ride buses, white trash like that."

Once at Five Pines her voice took on a note of urgency as she reminded Kevin that she was depending on him for her old age. Apparently the subject was an old one. "Have no fear, Barefax," he said. "I've got a great plan. I'll—"

"Get out and earn a *lot* of money," Ruth interrupted. "You're the only insurance policy I've got." Gini thought, What about Gordon? Isn't he an insurance policy?

Ruth never let up on the mortal sin of Kevin's life: his marriage to Jenifer. Seated at lunch in the quiet St. Regis, she berated him so passionately that diners put down their forks and watched. "*Ssssucker!*" she hissed. He pushed his food around the plate and acted unabashed. "Fool!" she went on, apparently piqued by his silence. "You're a no-good!" The diatribe continued on the way home in the Cadillac.

Now and then Ruth would get Gini alone and run through her bill of particulars against the missing ex-wife. "Gordon and I knew what she was from the beginning," she said in the unadorned accent of Spokane. "She ruined Son. He met her ten years ago and that's when he started to change. He was a fine boy till then! Handsome, good. *Clean.* Now look at him."

One night in the family room at Five Pines, Ruth seemed even more dyspeptic than usual. Gini supposed she'd forgotten to take her thyroid pills— Kevin had explained that most of her thyroid gland had been removed and that when she screwed up her pill schedule her whole personality changed. Now she was stomping up and down the floor raging about Kevin's inadequacies, his inability to earn a living, his constant borrowing. "By the way, what did you do with that three thousand we gave you last Christmas?" she asked, her lower lip jutting out and her teeth showing. Gini had seen that animal look before on both mother and son.

Kevin hung his head. Gordon stared at the floor. Gini studied a print on the wall.

"And that woman!" Ruth went on. "That—awful—*thing!*" She didn't have to specify. "Listen to me, Son. You and Jay Williams sneaked her back and got away with it. But *don't* try again!" Her dark blue eyes narrowed and her forehead wrinkled. "If you bring her back, I swear to God I'll, I'll—*kill* her!"

"Now, Ruth," Gordon said.

"You'll have to keep me away from her," Mrs. Coe said, her voice subdued now, as though to emphasize that this was more than an intemperate outburst. "Because—I don't want to be charged with murder."

On a hot midafternoon not long after, Gini and Kevin walked out of his little house to preview a property together. "Wait!" Kevin said, clutching her arm. A yellow Cadillac spurted from a parking spot a half block away and sped toward them. "She must've been waiting," Kevin said. "I wonder what it is this time."

The car braked to a halt and Ruth Coe stepped out with arms flying. Her words came so fast that Gini could hardly understand her. Kevin put his arm around his mother's shoulder but she spun away. "I want those clothes!" she yelled. "I know they're inside. That bitch left a rack full. *Now let me in!*"

"Mother," Kevin asked gently, "what would you do with Jeni's clothes?"

"It doesn't *matter* what I'd do with them. I don't want them in your house, understand?"

"You wouldn't wear them, would you?"

Ruth looked horrified. "Hardly! Do you think I'd wear anything that ever touched her skin?"

"Well, what—?"

"I'll *trample* them. I'll *burn* them. I rather think I have that right, don't you? After what she did to your life?"

Kevin talked to her for two or three minutes and then turned to Gini. "Get lost for a while," he whispered. "I've got to take her to lunch. She'll never calm down if I don't."

A few nights later the two lovers were at a Peter Sellers movie when Kevin stood up abruptly and walked four rows back. Gini turned and saw Ruth. She appeared to be in a rage. When the threesome joined up, Ruth was still fuming. Gini was left with the feeling that she was following them everywhere.

41

Even at a hundred pounds overweight, *Cassandra Bates*, a housewife in her early thirties, made a striking appearance. She had long chestnut hair, warm brown eyes, skin like china, and a delicate face reminiscent of the late Merle Oberon's. Cassandra had paid thousands of dollars to psychoanalysts to find out why she had allowed herself to become so fat. "When I was slender," she explained, "I got more attention than I wanted. I was always busty and seemed to excite men. And I couldn't handle it, especially when the attention changed to harassment." The harassment had included three rapes. "And if I wasn't being raped, I was being brutalized," she recalled. "Men wouldn't take no from me. They got rough. Why me? Because I was vulnerable, trusting, outgoing—and dumb."

She armed herself. One night in Browne's Addition, an old section of Spokane marked by apartment buildings and chopped-up mansions full of young people, a stranger became abusive as she walked down the street. "Whattaya think of this?" he asked, pulling out his penis.

"Whattaya think of *this*?" she said, brandishing a hunting knife. She went home and called the police. She remembered the results. "A detective showed up and kept asking me, 'Did you lead him on? Are you sure you didn't lead him on?' He grilled me as though I were a criminal."

As an experienced rape victim, she'd picked up knowledge on the subject. "I learned that legally you have to fight, scream and struggle or no jury will accept that you were raped, but fighting excites rapists and makes them beat on your head and body. That's exactly what one of them did when I struggled, and I had scars and marks for months."

She resolved that she would never be raped again. "I said to myself, 'Dunce, what are you doing wrong?' I read everything I could find on the subject. I learned that it isn't a crime of lust; it's a crime of power and rage. Rapists are excited by your struggling—it makes them feel powerful, makes them mean and mad. Most of them need this feeling to get it up—if the victim is passive, they lose the erection."

She learned that rapists were bored by consenting females. She decided that in any future confrontation—and she was convinced there would be one—she would try her best to stall the beast off, but if it came to the act of rape she would become the most consenting female in history. "I told my husband, 'Gregor, if the guy gets me down and starts raping me, I'm not gonna reject him and I'm not gonna show disgust. I'll even *press* him; I'll even offer to do things for him if it'll make him feel better about himself, so he won't beat me and claw me and sodomize me. That way I'm gonna survive and I'm not gonna get hurt. Because if I'm raped again, Greg, I'm finished. There's not enough psychoanalysis in the world to get me through that.'"

Her husband said he understood. She told what happened soon after that conversation. "It was a hot night late in August, 1980, and I was out for a walk on the South Hill. I don't like the sun on my face, and I don't like to sweat, and I don't like to be seen in public, because I'm too fat—that's why I was walking at night. My bad knee was acting up and I carried a steel cane. I wasn't worried. The South Hill rapist wasn't gonna bother a fat lady.

"I was up near High Drive when I saw him coming out of some bushes next to a driveway. I looked at his face and I knew I was in trouble. People talk about how handsome he is. I thought he had the coldest eyes I've ever seen. His face was blank, but his eyeballs were intent. I've seen that same look on guys getting ready to shoot a rabbit or bird. He wore a gray jogging suit and running shoes and he looked like Mr. Clean. He came straight for me.

"I said, 'Stop!' He mumbled something, raised his arm and kept coming. I waved my cane and said, 'I'm gonna knock your nuts off if you don't stop right now! *Back off!*' That was one thing I'd read—be forceful before they can lay a hand on you because they'll often stop and look for somebody that's less trouble.

"He stopped and started again. I raised my cane and said, 'What the hell were you doing in that bush?'

"His face changed. Mr. Nice Guy. He said, 'Oh, I was just taking a piss.' I thought, how gross! But I figured it was my own fault because I'd used obscene language myself. I told myself to get out of this nice and gently.

"I said, 'Well, back off and leave me alone. I just want to be left alone.'

"He said, 'What're you doing walking at night? You must be looking for a man.'

"I said, 'I'm walking at night because I'm fat, can't you see? It's cooler at night, and heat is hard on fat people. Now that's that!' He kept insisting that I must be looking for a man. I started to walk off and he followed. I turned to face him the way you'd face a dog and I said, 'Get the fuck away from me!'

"He began rattling on in this resonant voice, with real good enunciation. Kept telling me how pretty I was. I said to myself, Okay, Cassie, what're you gonna do? Go up to one of these fancy houses and knock on the door and say, 'This man is accosting me'? He'll have you flat on your back before you get ten feet, and besides, he's probably from this neighborhood, and these people probably wouldn't even answer the door. I thought, All right, Cookie, you are on—your—*own*! Just stay cool and keep control.

"He fell in alongside me. I kept the cane ready. He said, 'What do you think of how I look?' When I didn't answer he asked, 'Are you married? What's your husband's name?' He babbled about everything under the sun. Sometimes he used a deep voice, but when he got excited it went way up. He talked about philosophy, politics. He said he was into *The Fountainhead* and Ayn Rand, but I wasn't paying much attention. I knew he wanted to rape me and he was just looking for an opening.

"We were reaching the western edge of Manito Park, and that's *dark*.

Every once in a while he'd stare over at me. He said, 'Your face is really attractive. When I first saw you from a couple blocks away I thought you were a fat old lady.'

"I thought, He was *stalking* me! We walked past a grove of Douglas firs, black on black. He kept buttering me up. He told me he was into women's liberation and handed me some other psychological nonsense to try to get me to relax. Then he asked me again, 'Do you like the way I look? Do you think I'm handsome? How old do you think I am?'

"I said, 'Oh, about twenty-four. You look young. Your body looks great.'

"He pulled his top up to show his stomach. He seemed excited, and then he would calm down again and start trying to impress me with what he knew. Everything about him spelled psycho. My house was just a few blocks away, but that was the last place I could go—if he ever saw where I lived I'd never sleep another night. He led me into the park to some stone benches. I said to myself, This is dumb, but nowhere near as dumb as letting him find out where I live. He said, 'Do you think I'm sexy?' He said, 'I take real good care of myself. Can you tell?'

"He grabbed me and stuck his tongue in my mouth and started feeling my breasts. I smelled something and couldn't figure out what it was. Then I realized it was a deodorant soap, and I thought, Oh, my God, joggers take showers *after* they run! I started to twist away from him and then I realized that's exactly what he wanted, so I didn't struggle. And I'd already picked up that his ego was low and I thought, If I push him away, he's gonna feel rejected and get mad and that'll give him the excuse he needs to start beating me and dragging me into the bushes for sodomy. It's funny how your mind works when you're in a dangerous spot. All this thinking took about a fifth of a second.

"As soon as he pulled his tongue out, I kept on talking as though nothing had happened, so he would see I wasn't scared and I wasn't shocked. I tried to deny him a reaction. A puzzled look came over his face. I thought, Great! You did the right thing! Keep it up! And then I prayed, God, please help me know what the right thing is. I told myself, Cass, use your brains. Use your brains!

"He kissed me again. When he stopped, I got up from the bench. I figured this is the flash point—either he'll let me go home or he'll rape me right now. I thought maybe I should scream, but kids were always yelling around this fountain at night. The neighbors wouldn't pay any attention. Then I realized he'd spoken. 'Huh?' I said.

"He said, 'I want to take you into the bushes and lick your pussy.'

"I thought, Oh, brother, what am I gonna do now? He came close and said he'd make me feel great. I thought, He wants to get me in the bushes so he can sodomize me. I fear that more than anything else. I remembered what I'd read: Try to control these guys and don't let them control you. Power's what they're after.

"He pulled his pants down and told me to look at his flat stomach. His erection stuck out. I said, 'Isn't that nice!'

"He looked puzzled, and covered up, but then he took it out again. This time I said, 'You sure have a big one!' He pulled his pants back up.

"He said it was time we went into the bushes where he could lick me. I tried to think of how to turn him off, how to beat him at his power game. I said, 'Okay. You can lick me if I can do one thing first.'

" 'What's that?' he asked.

"I took a deep breath and said, 'Suck your cock.' I figured if he was just hitting on me, he would say, 'Sure, go ahead,' and then I'd know he wasn't a rapist and walk home. But if he acted reluctant, he was a rapist for sure.

"He acted reluctant. He got that weird look again and he said, 'No, no, let me do you first.' *He was into control!*

"We batted it back and forth about who would do who. He kept saying, 'Come on, come on, let me lick it and treat you real good.' And I'd say, 'No, no, let me suck you first.' It was an insane argument. Insane! But I could see he didn't know how to handle this situation.

"I headed home. As we were walking along the street I got a good look at his hands. His fingers were kind of short, soft-looking. I thought, You poor thing, I feel sorry for you.

"We reached the sidewalk across the street from my place. There was a moon and a little light from the neighborhood houses. He started kissing me again. Then he pointed to a vacant lot across the street—three or four skinny trees and a little grass. Light from the adjoining houses was falling on it. He said, 'Hey, let's go over there. Please, *please*, I want to treat you good. You deserve it,' and da dah, da dah, da dah....

"I thought, What a poor unstable ding-dong he is! And I felt even sorrier for him.

"He grabbed my hand and put it on his male appendage. I didn't look, but it felt erect. I gritted my teeth and thought, Don't reject him!

"He said, 'What do you think about that?'

"I said, 'Oh, this turns me on so much I don't know what I'm gonna do!' He looked puzzled again. I thought, Anything to get across the street to my front door. He started talking about his girlfriend Gini, how much he loved her. I said, 'I better be getting in now.'

"He said, 'Wait!' and pulled up his top again. I noticed something tucked in his waistband. It looked like an oven mitt. That scared me more than anything else. It was so off the wall. I decided I was still in trouble, so I figured out another power game. Have you ever noticed that when a woman starts getting amorous it sometimes turns a man off? I used that principle. I started telling him I *had* to see him again. 'My husband doesn't pay enough attention to me. I *need* somebody like you.'

"He kissed me and lowered my hand to his penis again. I pulled it away and said, 'Look, I'm gonna get so excited I won't be responsible for what I do. But I want to see you again!'

"I think he decided that this fat woman was gonna follow him to the ends of the earth. He started babbling about how I could be his friend, I could borrow money from him, I could use his car, stuff like that. I flashed that he didn't want me to report him to the cops, so he was coming on about all the great things he would do for me. 'You're wonderful,' he said. 'A person like you should never be lonely. I think you're one of the most wonderful women I've ever met.'

"I thought: Don't anger him now. You've come this far without getting hurt. If you annoy him now, he knows where you live, and he'll come back.

We wonderfulled each other to death. I'd switched in his eyes from a potential power-rape victim to a potential future sex partner, and that wasn't what he wanted.

"He handed me a yellow business card. Under a little picture of him it said 'Kevin Coe' in capital letters and 'Main Realtors.' He kept babbling. 'You can phone me day or night. Phone me up, *please*! I want to be your friend. I want to do anything I can to help you. I think you're *great*!'

"And I thought, This poor guy, he's trying to buy my silence now. My heart just went out to him. I walked straight across the street toward my house. When I got to the front door I turned and looked and he was gone."

A few days passed and Cassandra Bates resumed her exercise program, carrying her hunting knife in an open purse and walking only by day. Her husband convinced her that the man had played her for a fool, that there was no way he could have had rape in mind. Damn me, she said to herself, I made an ass of myself. I acted like a slut. *Dumbo*!

A week or so later she spotted Kevin Coe in daylight standing in a tulip bed forty yards from where he'd first appeared. He took one look at her and sprinted out of sight toward the east. When she saw how fast he ran she was thankful that she hadn't tried to outrun him in the park. She laughed out loud. He didn't want to be seen with a fatty like her! God, she thought, if men only knew how transparent they were.

42

Many people have asked—with all the beautiful women I have dated over the years (including innumerable Vegas showgirls and Hollywood starlets) what I was doing with the relatively plain Gini Perham. Mainly what I was doing was <u>coaching</u>. I was sort of doing a Henry Higgins number, I guess.—Fred Coe, April 18, 1982

Every day it became harder for Gini Perham to maintain a charitable feeling toward her unseen rival Jenifer Coe. One problem was the long-distance phone calls that came in almost every night Gini slept over at Kevin's. "Why do you allow it?" she asked. "Why don't you change your number?"

He always claimed that he felt a responsibility. Gini didn't believe him. She felt, in fact, that one part of him shared his mother's aversion to Jenifer. There were signs: the tightening of his facial muscles when the calls came in, the angry way he discussed her, the diatribes about other men in her life and her wanderings. When he told Gini in August that Jenifer would be coming back to Spokane any day now, he seemed edgy. "She's got something on you, doesn't she, Kevin?" Gini charged.

"Hardly."

"Then why don't you put her out of your life? Are you through with her or not?"

"As a wife, yes. But not...as a human being."

"I never noticed this compassion in you."

"Really? I'm one of the most compassionate men on earth."

After listening in on more calls at his invitation, Gini discarded her theory. If Jeni had something on him, he certainly wouldn't have risked letting her hear about it from the woman herself. Night after night the poor alcoholic sobbed out her love, demanded money and cursed him for not providing it, and then swore eternal love again. She continually blamed Kevin and his mother for her troubles with the law and warned him that he'd damned well better fix things up. Warrants were out for her arrest for vandalizing the yellow Cadillac, walking away from the alcoholism program and misuse of telephone credit.

When Gini insisted to Kevin that he still must have feelings for Jeni or he wouldn't put up with her, he insisted that he loved only Gini and intended to marry her. "Oh, Kevin," she said, "you've told me that before." Almost a year ago, as she recalled.

The arguments persisted, and several times she told him she was finished. She wouldn't see him for three or four days, and then he would call and pour out his rationalizations and his seductive reasoning. He played on her guilt—she realized later that he was a master of the technique. Somehow she always wound up as the offending party forgiven by the kindly male. She wondered what was wrong with her own character that she could keep falling for the same line over and over.

Around midnight on a warm night they were asleep in his bedroom when there was a knock on the back door. Gini awoke but Kevin slept on. The knock came again, louder this time.

"Kevin," she whispered. "Somebody's here!"

A female voice rang out, "Fred! Open the door! It's me!"

Kevin said, "It's Jenifer," and leaped from bed. Gini thought he would turn her away, but instead she heard the unmistakable sounds of a happy reunion. She thought, My God, he jumps out of bed and licks her hand!

She slid the covers over her head as she heard Jeni start to cry. "I'm not sad," she heard the woman say. "I'm just—oh, Fred, I'm *so* glad to see you." Kevin said he was so excited he could hardly talk.

After a few minutes Gini began to wonder when he was going to make his move, maybe offer to take Jenifer to a bar or for a drive—anything but a bedroom confrontation. But the two of them kept talking as though they were alone at last. Gini thought, He's forgotten I'm here!

Kevin used the bathroom as Jeni waited in the hall. When she took a step toward the bedroom Gini called out, "Hi, Jenifer."

The woman gasped and started yelling. Gini could see her tall figure stomping about the hall in silhouette. "If *you* don't throw her out of there," she yelled at Kevin, "I *will!* This is *my* house!"

Kevin barred the bedroom door with his body. Jeni tried to get past him and he said, "No, please! Let me take care of this." Gini thought, Why the hell didn't you take care of it by not letting her in?

She got out of bed to dress. She felt embarrassed and ashamed, and yet she didn't know what she'd done wrong. Hadn't Kevin sworn a hundred times that his marriage was dead and could never be revived, that he was only acting from humanitarian principles? This wasn't the 1950s; there was nothing shocking about committed couples sleeping together anymore. But Jeni Coe didn't see it that way. "Get that bitch out of this house right now!" she ordered.

"Take it easy, take it easy," Kevin said, and in an aside to Gini, "You'd better dress and go. I'll calm her down."

"Sure," Gini said, thoroughly disgusted.

Jeni wandered into the living room. She was alternating between tears and recriminations. Once she said, "It's Vegas again, isn't it, Fred? The night you went out to be a gigolo? You'll never change, will you?" The discussion was still going on when Gini slipped out the back door. She made up her mind: The romance was over. Nothing he could say or do would change her mind. She hardly slept.

The next day he arrived at noon, driving the silver-gray Chevrolet Citation that his father had leased for him after the Toronado was repossessed. He was a study in contrition.

"Don't bother," Gini told him coldly. "You'll never end your relationship with her. So I've ended mine with you."

"Baby—"

"You made me feel rotten last night. You still love her, don't you? Why don't you admit it?"

"I *told* you! I feel a responsibility toward her."

Gini thought, Oh, God, the same old crap. "How about me?" she said. "Do you feel any responsibility toward me?"

"Well, I—"

"Forget it! You showed me all I need to know last night."

The argument sputtered on for an hour. Finally Gini said, "Okay, that's it! Leave—*now*! I never want to see you again."

"You don't believe I love you?"

"You're a manipulator and a liar. Now please leave!"

He left, grumbling about how unreasonable she was. She thought, You're a fine one to talk about what's reasonable. He had deceived her from the start. She wondered how long she would feel like a fool. It would be years, yes, but how many years?

43

Beneath his outwardly gracious manner toward women and his general suavity and social charms, the male psychopath (or part psychopath) nearly always shows an underlying predilection for obscenity, an astonishingly ambivalent attitude in which the amorous and excretory functions seem to be confused.—Hervey Cleckley, M.D., *The Mask of Sanity*

Two or three days after Gini Perham had thrown Kevin Coe out of her life, a dentist's wife was jogging high on the South Hill at daybreak. Mrs. John T. Little III was aware of past rapes in the area, but she'd heard nothing to suggest a pattern. The homes in the neighborhood were among the most expensive in town—a solid mile of houses along High Drive priced at $175,000 and up—and police cars were never far.

Still, the red-haired Liz Little breathed easier when the sun appeared. The rays made her blink as a car drove slowly toward her on Thirty-third Ave. heading toward High Drive. She noticed yellow license plates in a standard format: three letters and three numbers. She wondered why anyone would bother to pay extra for vanity plates that weren't even personalized.

She crossed Bernard St. and remembered that a high-school girl had been raped just two blocks to the north, but that was last winter and thank God police had made an arrest—a man named Mounsey. She ran to High Drive and loped along the top of the south rim. The South Hill rose from the Spokane River valley in a series of steep pitches and flat landings and smoothed out into a gradual slope that extended to High Drive, then fell off to the south so abruptly that no homes or buildings could cling to its side. A thousand feet down, the farm dwellings looked like play houses.

After a few more blocks of easy striding Liz spotted a small car parked on an access street next to a large vacant lot. In the hundreds of mornings she had run this route this was the first time she had ever seen a car in that spot. There were no houses for several hundred yards and nothing on the south side of High Drive but the drop-off and some straggly brush.

As she approached she thought, How strange; it's the car with the funny plates. I wonder if somebody's checking out that vacant lot at six-thirty in the morning. But why? No one was in sight. She peeped into the car; it was empty. She stepped up her pace and headed for home.

A few blocks away, on one of the most scenic stretches of High Drive, the day was beginning for Liz's good friend *Margot Terry*. She slipped into a Day-Glo yellow T-shirt and a pair of running shorts with a blue print, then decided to throw on her blue zippered sweatshirt. Even though it was still August and there'd been a dozen days in the eighties this month, the early mornings had turned crisp. She checked the outdoor thermometer: forty-three. In Spokane, nature didn't go by the book.

She tiptoed around, not wanting to wake up her two little boys. She left a note on the kitchen counter—"Mama's gone running, will be home soon"— and embellished it with a stick drawing of a woman with clumpy tennis shoes, grass, and a flower. The children would see it and laugh. Later that day she planned to take them to the Walk in the Wild Zoo.

She stepped through the back door of her quarter-million-dollar ranch house and squeezed it shut so it wouldn't click. Down the slope toward Hangman Creek a marmot emitted a shrill whistle. She glanced at her watch— 6:45. She decided to run her six-mile course, a meandering route that would take her within sight of the white colonial house of her childhood, back up to High Drive and the rim of the South Hill, and home in time to serve breakfast to two sleepyheads. She'd walked and run these streets for most of her forty years. A college graduate and skilled artist, she'd lived all over the United States, visited every part of the world except South America, climbed Kilimanjaro and Fuji.

She came from a family of achievers. Her father had been a top executive at the Cowles newspapers. Her sister had been Spokane's Lilac Queen, an honor that could have gone as easily to Margot. She was a reed-slender brunette of five-six, with big green eyes and a turned-up nose. She spoke in an educated but unaffected manner. She was social but not snobbish. She ran for health, both mental and physical, and as she ran she administered self-therapy that seemed to be helping. Margot, she would say to herself as she jogged, you are a very worthwhile person. *You are not a wimp!* Her pep talks and affirmations seemed to be helping with her old problem of low self-esteem.

This morning she loped along admiring the flowers and the scenery. The air was just beginning to warm. On the steep slope below High Drive she saw mock orange, juniper, a hawthorn or two, the pale purplish red of fireweed. The traffic far down on Rte. 195 looked like a matchbox car collection, and a tiny train snaked toward the Palouse and rang its tiny bell.

Poking along, breathing easy, she saw something out of the corner of her eye. A man in dark glasses was walking west on Thirty-third Avenue, approaching High Drive. He was wearing gray sweats and a blue quilted vest. She thought, That guy's sure bundled up for a summer day.

In a few more strides she reached a sharp drop-off, broken only by minor escarpments and hillocks. Hang-gliding was popular in this stretch. She ran along a crest on a well-worn trail just inside a cap log that served as a warning fence for drivers. She was thinking that she hadn't eaten breakfast and she was hungry. The man popped up ahead of her on the path, running straight toward her now, his brown hair bouncing the way her young sons' hair bounced when they ran.

As he drew closer, she smiled. In this neighborhood joggers always smiled or said hello. The man came abreast. She thought he was smiling back but she realized it was a grimace.

His arm snaked under her chin and jerked her off her feet. She landed on her back and stared at the sky. She realized she was being dragged down the hillside and he was talking to her. "Don't turn your head! I have a knife. One look and you're dead."

He stopped behind an outcropping, invisible from the path above, and she closed her eyes tight. Just imagine, she warned herself, if you make *one* little mistake and flick *one* glance at him, he'll stick you! She pressed a hand hard against her eyes. My goodness, she thought, what a dutiful little drone I am.

"Strip!"

She couldn't obey, because he was holding her by one arm and her other covered her eyes. "I don't have a free hand," she said, surprised at her calmness.

He yanked down her shorts and underpants and made her take off her zippered sweatshirt. She was naked except for her New Balance jogging shoes. "Don't look," he repeated. "Do you know what it feels like to have a knife in your chest?" As he shoved her downhill, she almost fell. The brushy hill was so steep she had to dig in her heels. He flung her to the ground thirty or forty yards from the trail above. She thought, I wonder if he's Mounsey. I remember reading something about him. Why am I thinking so clearly? It's like my whole body's in muck but my head's in the open. But... I'm scared.

Behind the dark screen of her hand she could tell that he was removing his pants. He pulled her legs apart and rubbed against her. The rocky ground scraped her skin; she could feel the scratches. He began talking. "Do you like sex?"

"I—uh, yes."

"How much?" She felt his probing fingers and didn't answer.

"You're pretty tight, aren't you?" he said. His voice was calm, ordinary. "It's been a long time since you had any, hasn't it?" She didn't answer. He squeezed her breasts and said they were lovely. He tried to enter her and couldn't. His chatter resumed. She decided he must be trying to arouse himself. From the grunting noises she thought he might be masturbating, but she couldn't be sure. Then he ordered her to stand up and guided her downhill to another location. She kept her hand pressed hard against her eyelids. He dumped her on her back and went through the same futile routine again. She thought, Isn't this odd? I always imagined that rape would be a slam-bam thing, over in seconds. And here I'm stuck with a weirdo on the side of a mountain and he can't get himself hard and he's asking me about my sex life.

He lifted her up and shoved her onward. She felt the beginnings of panic. She thought, I'll end up as one of those bodies that some hiker finds. They'll be walking through the bushes down by Hangman Creek and they'll spot this decomposed nude body in New Balance jogging shoes. *I never thought I'd die like this.*

"We've got to go back now," she said, still pressing her hand against her eyes. "I've been gone a long time. You better let me go because somebody's gonna come looking for me." She didn't mention that her husband was at his office, her two older children were visiting in California, and her two little sons were asleep or watching television. "My oldest son," she said, "he'll be down here looking for me. He goes to Lewis and Clark and he's eighteen and. . . ."

She was babbling, overstating her case. Boy, she said to herself, you're sure Chatty Kathy. "Shut up, goddamn it!" he said. "You're keeping me from getting a hard-on." He took her to still another spot, diagonally down the hill. Red spots flashed in a field of black before her eyes, but she didn't relax her grip. One glance, she was convinced, and she would be dead.

He tried to enter her again, this time accompanied by a flood of words about her looks, how she was far too young to have an eighteen-year-old son, how beautiful her breasts were. When he ordered her to urinate, she pretended that she hadn't heard. "Do it!" he insisted. "*Piss!*"

She told him that even in a doctor's office it was hard for her to urinate on command. He cursed and rolled her on her stomach. Her skin tore on the rocks. She thought, Now he's going to kill me. He pressed against her, turned her on her back and managed to penetrate an inch or two. Good, she thought, maybe it's over. But he softened and pulled out again.

He dragged her downhill on his persistent search for the right spot. Her cheek scraped hard against a rock. She was so shocked by the pain that her grip loosened across her eyes and she caught a glimpse of his hand. It wasn't effeminate but it wasn't strongly masculine, either. It was the hand of someone who worked indoors, and not very hard. There were no rings on the rather small fingers. The nails were well-shaped. It was a hairless, androgynous hand.

She saw a foot. She thought: That's sure a raunchy shoe—not like the shoes real runners wear. It looked like a supermarket special: white with blue stripes. Serious joggers used their running shoes strictly for running, but this one looked as though it was worn for everything. Just before she renewed the grip across her eyes, she saw that he was wearing a pair of gray sweatpants with a rip near the knee.

"Get on your knees!" he said. She raised herself to a kneeling position. "No, *no!*" he barked. "Head down, ass out. That's it!" He took her buttocks in both hands and spread them. "Now do it for me!"

She thought, How disgusting. She also thought, I couldn't do that if my life depended on it. But she could pretend to try.

After a few minutes he told her that he would have to get tough. She wondered what had happened to the seductive talk about her looks. They had been together for almost an hour; he must be tiring of her. "Stand up!" he said. She dragged herself to her feet. "Look straight down the hill and take your hand away from your eyes." The light was blinding. She felt his body squarely upslope behind her. "See those pine trees?" She blinked and saw three or four ponderosas and some scrub. "Go down there. And don't look back."

She thought, He's going to shoot me in the back or throw that knife. She stumbled toward the trees, reached the grove and ducked behind a tree, caught her breath and waited.

After five or ten minutes she turned and looked. He was gone. She scrabbled upward in the dirt, found her clothes and had a hard time putting them on. Her limbs were trembling; she wondered why she was so cold. Then she realized that she was in shock. She tried to remember how dangerous shock was, but her mind wasn't working right.

High Drive was empty. She knew that shock was a medical problem, so she walked two hundred yards to the home of a doctor friend. No one was home. She stood on the porch, her ponytail askew and matted with dirt and blood, her lacerated skin on fire, weeds sticking out of her hair. A police car cruised by. It was gone before she remembered to yell. She stumbled back to the sidewalk and walked east. I'll just go home, she said to herself. I don't want to bother anybody. Then she realized that she was up to her old trick of discounting herself and her needs. She staggered to another front door and pushed the bell. She rang three times more and a sleepy-looking woman appeared in her bathrobe. "I've just b-b-been raped," Margot said, trembling. "Can you take me home?"

The woman drove her to her door. The boys were still asleep. Her note lay undisturbed on the kitchen counter. She heated water for instant coffee. She tried to stop shivering and figure out what to do. Call the police? Call her husband? She didn't want to bother Matt; he was under a lot of pressure these days. But he might not like it if she called police first.

She dialed him and said, "Mattie, I've just got home and I was raped. I've got the phone book open in front of me but I can't find the police. What do I look under? 'Spokane' or what?" Just then she found the police number. "Forget it," she said. "I just found it."

A tall policeman responded in five minutes and said he'd been cruising the neighborhood. Matt arrived a few minutes later, drove her to Deaconess Hospital and returned to work. After several hours of interviews and tests, she was escorted home. The day had turned warm, the temperature in the eighties again. Nature needed a new scenarist, she decided. This weather didn't fit.

That night she put together a dinner of toasted cheese sandwiches. No one spoke at the table. The two little boys seemed to sense that something was wrong. After they'd been tucked in for the night, Matt took her by the arm and said, "Don't worry, I won't tell anybody what happened."

She said, "I already told the Griffins next door, 'cause Sissy's home from college this summer and she knew something was up. Besides, I'm so mad!"

"Do you think that was wise? Talking about it?"

"Wise? Matt, this is 1980. You're not telling me you're embarrassed about this, are you?"

The discussion waned. Later in the evening he peeped around his *Chronicle* and said, "I always told you not to run on that side of the street."

She didn't respond. She thought, My God, Matt, it was beyond my control. Don't make me feel guilty. She remembered a word from her Swedish grandparents: *styrka*: "strength." Okay, Margot, she told herself, reach back and grab some *styrka*. The way to fight something like this is to bring it out in the open. She was glad she'd told the Griffins. She would tell anybody who would listen. Maybe it would help to catch that awful creep.

No matter which way she turned in bed that night, her neck and back throbbed, and the cuts and scrapes kept bleeding into the sheets. *Styrka* took care of the physical pain. The mental turmoil bothered her more. She couldn't stop thinking about the instant his arm had gone around her neck and thrown her to the ground. She thought, There are moments in life when you're scared; you park your car in a dark alley, or you get out in a dark garage. Moments of fear. *But this wasn't one of them!*

This was a moment of trust, two joggers passing on the trail, smiling. She knew she wouldn't take another step in public without fear and suspicion. I'll never be able to go out at night, she told herself. I'll never be able to run again. That creature, how could he *do* a thing like that to me?

The world was different now.

All the next morning the phone rang in Liz Little's white frame home on the South Hill. Everybody wanted to talk about Margot. Liz had spoken to the poor woman herself, learned that she was "okay"—as okay as anyone can be after an experience like that.

At breakfast Liz told her husband John about the strange car she had seen just before the time of the rape. "You don't suppose there's a connection, do you?" she asked.

"Could be. Are you sure you don't remember what kind it was?"

"You know me. Cars are cars."

After John left for his office, Liz got into her Volkswagen Dasher and took a drive, first making sure that the car doors were locked. A police car idled at Thirty-third and High Drive, a uniformed officer at the wheel. She parked and got out, suddenly nervous. She told the cop about the car with the mysterious plates, and he seemed interested. "What kind was it?"

"Oh, God," she said, "that's where I'm just hopeless."

"Well, was it big or little?"

"It was a compact. Maybe like a Volvo or a Saab or something. It wasn't a Dasher. That's all I can be sure of."

She asked, "Is this where...it happened?"

He waved toward the south. "Over the rim and down the side," he said. "Do you remember the license number?"

"No. I'm sorry."

"Listen, lady, if I was you gals up here, I wouldn't be jogging by myself. There's weird things going on."

"Weird—?"

"There's rapes you don't even know about. A lady got off the bus at Thirty-fifth and Grand the other day and a guy beat her up real bad. High noon!"

That night a detective phoned and Liz repeated what she'd told the policeman. A few days later she underwent hypnosis at police headquarters and reported that the car was gray or close to gray. That was the best she could do.

Detective Joan Schmick, who had worked long hours to develop evidence against Blake Mounsey, turned up another citizen who had noticed a small silver-gray or bluish-gray car parked near the scene of the Terry rape. The man remembered seeing out-of-state license plates, yellow or orange, maybe New York or Oregon; Washington's were white, except vanity plates which were yellow. The car, he guessed, was a BMW or a Subaru.

*   *   *

Four days after Margot Terry's ordeal, fifteen-year-old *Sue Ellen Wilber* was raped on the South Hill while coming home from a rock concert. Detectives noted the telltale signs: the resonant voice, the hand down the throat, the chattering about her body, the masturbation, the warning that she would be stuck with a knife if she talked. But the police department took no steps to inform the public that the rapist was still in business.

44

On September 7, nearly two weeks after the Margot Terry rape, the case of the South Hill rapist entered the public domain for good. Chris Peck, popular columnist for the morning *Spokesman-Review*, wrote, "A horrible specter is back on the South Hill. In jogging clothes, threatening with a knife, it has begun again to strike at women in one of Spokane's classiest neighborhoods."

Peck quoted a police lieutenant: "He's got everything in his favor on the South Hill. There are older homes, many converted to apartments. They are filled with young women working downtown, walking at all hours, and a lot of them are jogging. And there is 50 years of brush accumulated."

Peck, a serious jogger who lived on the South Hill with his librarian wife, advised women to change their patterns, run with friends, carry sprays. He recounted Margot Terry's story and noted that she was furious. "Women on the South Hill," Peck concluded, "be furious together. Look for clues, find the courage to open your eyes, press charges if you can. Otherwise, creeps will prevail."

His column hit the prosaic old town like a bomb. Telephone lines hummed late into the night as frightened women drew up plans for protection. Deluged with calls, workers at the city's Rape Crisis Center and the local NOW chapter scheduled emergency meetings to discuss the "specter" Peck had described— not that it was anything new to them. Police wires were tied up for days with tips and clues.

Readers who looked for a similar article in Gordon Coe's afternoon *Chronicle* found nothing.

"Listen to this!" Cassandra Bates told her husband. She read aloud from the Peck column: "'His hands were feminine and unkempt.... He had a modulated, sort of loving voice when he called me beautiful.' Gregor, it's him. I know it's *him*!"

"You've gotta have more than that to go on," her husband said.

"More than what? Look, he raped this woman at Thirty-third and High Drive. That's near where I first saw him."

"How could it be the same guy?" her husband asked. "Coe gave you his card, told you to phone him, said he'd lend you money. Besides, what if it *is* him? Are you gonna phone the cops and tell them what happened? They'll say, 'Get outa here! You led him on!'"

Cassandra thought of the police detective who'd interviewed her when she'd been raped as a young woman and how he'd treated her like the guilty party. Greg did have a way of cutting through the BS. She turned back to the column and read, "His sordid sexual desires fit a pattern of other South Hill rapes." To her, that line meant only one thing: that the rapist had been a pederast. She'd guessed right that night by the fountain. She would have died before submitting.

She realized that she was locked into a hopeless position. No matter what that sick Coe did, no matter how many women he attacked and sodomized, she would never be able to report him.

45

[The psychopath] refuses to delay gratification; he will not yield to the rules of any game but his own. The good of society doesn't interest him much if at all. According to Dr. Robert Lindner, he has "a completely defective sense of property." Characteristically, he may steal... blithely or coldly take what he wants.—Alan Harrington, *Psychopaths*

The young guy with the feathered haircut was back for another rip. Jeffrey Hall was sure of it. Assistant manager of a South Hill supermarket, Hall had already been hit twice by this same shoplifter. The first time, he'd been filling in at a checkstand when he saw the young man slip past the deli and out the front door. He caught up and said, "Hey, you're gonna have to pay for that stuff."

The man flashed a pleasant grin. "Oh, gee," he said, "I just made a phone call and I forgot all about paying."

"Well, whatever," the assistant manager said. "You can't leave the store without paying. The next time, I'm gonna nail you for shoplifting."

The smile vanished. "Oh, you're a big deal, aren't you?"

"Don't push me," Hall said.

The man paid for a carton of Minute Maid orange juice and a sack of doughnuts. Strange sense of values, Jeff thought. Why risk a police record for juice and doughnuts?

Three or four Saturday mornings later, the shoplifter had shown up again in the same jogging suit. This time the big Rosauer's store was jammed and there was a line at the checkstand where Hall was working. He watched as the man passed the store's bakery and strolled to the magazine stand. In his arms were a small bag of groceries and a half gallon of milk. Jeff lost sight of him for a minute or so while ringing up an order. By the time he checked again, the thief was driving off in a silver Citation with a yellow license plate.

The twenty-three-year-old Hall was annoyed at himself both for letting the man get away and for not knowing who he was. Front-end managers were paid to be on top of such things; that's what set them apart from checkers and marked them for promotion. He was fairly sure the shoplifter was a prominent citizen or the son of one. Ever since the supermarket had opened a few years earlier, one of its best customers had been a flashy middle-aged woman who drove a yellow Cadillac, and Jeff remembered seeing the young man lunching with her in the store's restaurant. There'd been good reason to take notice. Hall had been sitting with his voluptuous wife and the young man had stared at her so brazenly that she'd finally stuck her tongue out at him. I should have gone over and said something, Jeff told himself. Then I'd have learned his name.

Now it was noon on Tuesday, September 8, and Hall was watching the same shoplifter march into the store again as though he owned it. In a way, he did. Rosauer's claimed to operate on a 1 percent profit margin. Every time a dollar's worth of juice was stolen, the store had to move a hundred dollars' worth of merchandise to pull even. A few energetic thieves could turn a good week into a loser. And assistant managers weren't paid to preside over losers. Hall called the manager in his office. "That guy's back," he said.

"I'll be right down," Bill Haraldson answered.

The two employes stationed themselves by the main doors and watched. The young man appeared near the checkstands with a package of meat and some bottled water. "Watch," Hall whispered.

The man sauntered over to the magazine rack and stayed about ten seconds. Then he made his move. "Let's go!" Haraldson said, and the two men rushed outside.

The thief looked over his shoulder as they caught up. "Oh, gee," he volunteered, "I forgot to pay for these. I was thinking about something else."

Haraldson, a former Marine who classified shoplifters with ax murderers, said, "You're gonna have to come back inside."

"What for?"

"For shoplifting."

"Me, shoplifting?" The man's right eyebrow arched. "Hardly! It's not shoplifting when you forget to pay. What's the problem with you guys?"

"You've been seen twice before," Haraldson said.

"Really? By whom?"

"By me," Jeff Hall said.

The man looked unimpressed. "Of course you've seen me before. I'm a regular customer. So's my whole family. We could buy and sell you guys." His stern expression melted into a smile. "Hey, I'll just pay for these things. It was an oversight, that's all. I would *never* steal."

"You left the store," Haraldson insisted. "It's too late to pay. Now it's a matter of shoplifting."

"You gotta be kidding." The man's eyes rolled back in his head, and he turned toward his car.

Haraldson grabbed his arm and said, "If you run, I'll break your legs."

Back at the checkstand the man demanded to be allowed to pay. He opened his wallet and Jeff peeked in: there appeared to be three or four dollar bills. "Come on," Haraldson said. "We're going upstairs to the office."

"Maybe *you* are," the shoplifter said.

Haraldson squeezed his arm tightly. "Upstairs!" he repeated. "Now!"

They went into the manager's office and Haraldson slammed the door. "Got I.D.?" he asked.

"I'm not giving you any fucking I.D."

"Fine. What's your name?" The man didn't answer. Hall checked the evidence. There was a $5.47 tenderloin steak and a $2.61 four-pack of Perrier. Haraldson asked again, "You gonna tell us your name?"

"No."

The manager phoned the police, then pulled an apprehension report from his desk and filled it out. When a young officer named Benavides arrived, the suspect spoke rapidly. "This is a complete misunderstanding. I offered to pay and they wouldn't let me. Now it's getting out of hand. Just let me pay. This is no big deal."

Haraldson interrupted. "I gotta sell eight hundred bucks' worth of stuff to make up for what you stole. Maybe that's no big deal to you."

"You're fulla shit," the man snapped, then smiled at the policeman and resumed his explanation.

Benavides interrupted. "Name, please?"

"Kevin Coe."

"Is that your full name?"

"My legal name is Frederick Harlan Coe. My name of preference is Kevin."

The officer led Hall outside to take his statement, leaving Coe and Haraldson in the manager's office. In a few minutes Haraldson burst out of the door, his face the color of cooked shrimp. "I've had it with this guy!" he told the policeman. "If he calls me a motherfucker once more I'm gonna put him through the wall."

Benavides filled out a citation and said, "Okay, Mr. Coe, you're charged with third degree theft, a misdemeanor. You'll have to go to court."

Still protesting, Coe was led out the doors. "I don't agree with your strong-arm tactics," he said to Haraldson. "Frankly, I don't understand what you're doing in management."

Hall went back upstairs and read the arrest report. The thief had given his age as thirty-three, height six-two, weight 190, hair brown and eyes blue, address 1418 S. Dyer. Hall knew that part of the Spokane Valley. Nice houses, affluent people. He wondered why anyone from there would stoop to shoplifting. A New York–cut steak and a four-pack of Perrier. Well, at least he knew quality.

46

I prefer total honesty ... always!—Fred Coe, April 5, 1982

Almost two weeks had passed since the night Jenifer Coe had walked in on her and Kevin, and Gini Perham was feeling low. The recession was squeezing the life out of Spokane's real estate market, and just when she needed to be at her professional best she could hardly concentrate. As usual the problem was Kevin.

She told herself that she was feeling guilty and apologetic toward someone who should have felt guilty and apologetic toward her. But the insight didn't keep her from missing the man she loved. She convinced herself that she had overreacted. He'd only been making the best of a bad situation the night Jeni barged in. It was certainly true that he'd welcomed her, but what else could he have done? Let her stand outside and yell till she woke up the neighborhood? Was it right to punish him for trying to help a disturbed woman?

She reflected on the sixteen months she'd been seeing him. Sometimes it seemed they'd spent half their time not speaking to each other. What a bafflement he was! Even when he acted like a jerk, he made her want to throw her arms around him and protect him from—what? Himself? His mother? Life? It saddened her that she couldn't remember hearing him laugh. Sometimes when they watched sitcoms at his place he would emit a short cackle, but that only made him seem more joyless—and lovable. She asked herself if her feelings were healthy. She was afraid she knew the answer but phoned him anyway.

He sounded thrilled to hear her voice and drove right over. As soon as he sat down she could see that he was upset. "What's the matter, Kevin?" she asked. "Is it—me?"

"No, no, V.K., never you."

"Well, tell me then. I *know* you, Kevin. Something's happened." She reached out and squeezed his hand. When he didn't respond she made a guess. "Jeni?"

"She's no problem now." He explained that the ex-Mrs. Coe had gone out on the town the night after finding them in bed and had been injured in a motorcycle accident. She'd suffered a deep cut on her scalp and left town after refusing treatment.

He invited Gini to spend the night at his place. When they arrived he kissed her as though nothing had come between them or ever would. They talked till 3 a.m. He said he had a new plan: Why didn't she quit James S. Black and join him at Main? The two of them would be the most successful team in Spokane real estate. "Another thing, Baby Bunny," he said, hugging her. "I think we should talk about living together."

She decided she was hearing things. For months she'd argued that sharing expenses made perfect sense, but he'd insisted it would never work out. Talk about mercurial! She wondered what had caused this great sea-change.

By mid-September matters progressed to the point where her clothes and some of her furniture were in the yellow house at Twenty-ninth and Rebecca. Then he told her that he'd been arrested as a shoplifter. She didn't doubt for a second that it was all a mistake. Talk about miscasting: He was the last person on earth who would steal. More than once he'd told her that his objectivist beliefs prevented him from even accepting gifts—and he proved it by rejecting several of hers. How could he be a thief? "It happened back when we weren't seeing each other," he explained. "I just couldn't bring myself to tell you about it. It's on my mind night and day."

He talked nonstop for hours, starting with a detailed explanation of his relationship with the men who had brought the charges. "Haraldson and Hall, that's their names," he said. "I've been fighting them for a long time. Robin Rosauer, too, the owner. They framed me and I was too stupid to see it coming."

Gini listened sympathetically. Even if he was dishonest, she told herself, he wouldn't have had any reason to shoplift grocery items. He could always eat with his parents, and often did. Gini couldn't comprehend the venality of "those two glorifed bagboys," as Kevin called them. "When that store opened," he said, "Barefax and I were just about the first customers, and as long as we kept spending a lot of money we were treated fine. Then I criticized some of their displays. You know, like the toilet paper at the front? You walk in the store thinking about juicy steaks and pastries and you see a bunch of toilet paper. Disgusting! You know me, V.K. With my marketing background I'm not afraid to speak out. So I started putting suggestions on the comment cards they keep in the restaurant. I wrote one about how Haraldson mismanaged the store. I wrote one about how Hall put displays in the worst places. I wrote quite a few more—not to be mean, but just hoping that the store would improve and become a big asset to the city. You know, like my Spokane Metro Growth suggestions?"

Gini said she understood, though she wondered why he'd never mentioned the subject before. The two of them had shopped often at Rosauer's Lincoln Heights store; he'd always seemed pleased with the food and the service.

"One day," he went on, "I saw Robin Rosauer sitting at another table. So I wrote out a suggestion and gave it to a waiter to hand to him. Mr. Rosauer looked over and saw me, and then Haraldson came in and talked to him and I could see the two of them turning my way and gesturing. It looked like Mr. Rosauer was bawling him out, because Haraldson kept glaring at me as though I'd gotten him in trouble. That's how it started. Hall and Haraldson knew right then that they had to get me. So they did. The day it happened I was thinking about something as I walked out of the store and I remembered that I hadn't gone through the checkstand. So I turned to go back and there they were. Haraldson threatened to break my legs. But Gini, I had a hundred dollars in my wallet! That was one thing they couldn't explain to the cop—why a man with a hundred dollars in his wallet would shoplift."

She was puzzled. "Well, surely, Kevin, they must have understood what happened?"

"No! I can quote you all sorts of cases where someone has forgotten to pay for something and walked back inside and still was arrested." He reeled off court cases and she realized that he'd done his research.

"I still don't see what's the big deal," she insisted. "Go to court and explain to the judge. Nobody in his right mind would find a person like you guilty. Just say—"

"I can't!" He sounded exasperated. "Those two guys'll lie their heads off. They're out to get me, Gini! There's bad blood between us." She knew he was overreacting, that he was capable of flights of exaggeration. She couldn't imagine a pair of Rosauer employees engineering a frame-up, but she was equally positive that Kevin would never shoplift.

"Have you really thought this through?" she asked. "What if you *were* found guilty? Isn't it about like getting a traffic ticket? They wouldn't send you to jail or anything."

He rolled his eyes as though dealing with a half-wit. "You just don't get it, do you?" he said. "My career would be ruined! I'd rather be convicted of embezzlement, fraud, *anything* but shoplifting." He was quiet for a moment and then apologized for raising his voice. "I hate to lay all this on you, V.K., but there's nobody else."

"Ruth? Gordon?"

"They haven't heard. I used their address when I was arrested, but I went to the clerk afterward and ordered all communications sent to my post office box. My parents would never understand. Not the way you do." He paused. "Thanks for believing in me. Thanks for... standing behind me."

She was glad she'd helped. "Look, if you're that worried," she offered, "why don't you hire a lawyer?"

He said he could do a better job defending himself. Also, he couldn't afford a lawyer and wouldn't hire one anyway; it was against his principles. "I want you to testify for me," he said, draping his arm across her shoulders. "Say you drove with me to Rosauer's that day but you waited in the Citation while I went in. Okay?" She withheld comment as he went on. "Say you got out to have a cigarette and while you were leaning against the car I walked up with a steak and a pack of Perrier in my hand. The steak was against my chest and the Perrier was in my right hand. Little details are convincing." She remained silent.

"Then you saw me stop and put my hand to my head and say, 'Oh, God, I forgot to pay for these; I'll be right back!' And just as I got to the entrance, you saw these two guys come out." He paused and stared hard at her. "How's that sound?"

She shook her head. "Awful!" she said. "Horrible!"

"But you'll testify?"

"Of *course* I won't. Why would you even ask me to do something like that?"

He jumped up. "So you think I'm guilty?"

"It was all a mistake, Kevin. Just tell the judge what happened."

He insisted that no one would believe him in the face of the two plotters from Rosauer's. "I need you to back me up, Gin. There's no other way I can beat this thing."

"Leave me out of it."

"I can't!"

"No!"

Day after day he worked on her. He said she didn't love him and called her a hypocrite when she swore she did. He told her his career would be ruined and it would be her fault. No one with a record as a shoplifter could possibly become a success on the scale he intended. His father would have to run a news item about the conviction because the Cowles newspapers never shielded staffers or their relatives. The whole family would be disgraced over a little steak and Perrier. *And all because of Gini Perham's betrayal of an innocent man—the man she claimed to love.*

She got tired of arguing with him and let him rave. One night he said, "V.K., we've talked about marriage. If you love me enough to marry me, why can't you do this one little thing?" She wished she could see it as one little thing. That would solve the whole problem.

A few days later he said, "Why should we keep on living together when you won't even back me up in court?" He added, "For that matter, why should we even see each other anymore?"

She said, "For God's sake, Kevin, I'll do it. *I'll do it!* Just drop the subject."

"Great!" he said. "That's terrific, Gin! You'll never regret it. Hey, let's run over a few things."

"No," she said morosely. "I know what to say."

He insisted on taking her to Rosauer's parking lot at midnight and walking her through her part. For days he drilled her on details: what they'd both been wearing, the weather, the exact time sequence, the look of the parking lot that day, how far he'd been from the Citation when she'd spotted him, what the two grocerymen had worn. "That's so the prosecutor can't trip you up," he explained. When she was letter perfect, he told her how much he loved her. She wished it didn't sound so much like a payoff.

He helped her carry in her furniture. As fast as one of her pieces was deposited in the little yellow house, he hauled one of his own out. He explained that he owed money to his parents and would repay some of it by giving Ruth a few things she'd admired. Gini looked at items earmarked for Five Pines: a white lamp with a metal stand, a burnt-orange velour sofa, a beanbag chair in Kelly green, a nearly life-size ceramic collie named Rob Roy. She realized that in effect she was helping him pay off his parents, but it didn't matter.

A row of Jenifer's outfits hung in the closet. "I picked most of those out," Kevin said nostalgically. "She always depended on my taste. Poor Jeni. I wonder what she's doing." His ex-wife never seemed far from his thoughts.

After the furniture was installed and they were housemates, he raised the subject of finances. They'd already agreed to split living expenses fifty-fifty and he'd insisted that she pay two months of her share of the rent in advance. Now he wanted an additional $60 for an old phone bill. "Which old phone bill?" she asked. In a corner of her mind she thought that he might be using her, but she dismissed the idea as farfetched even for Kevin.

He said, "It's an unpaid balance left over from Jeni's collect calls." Jeni again. That problem was supposed to be settled. How could he possibly expect her to pay for phone calls made by his ex-wife? The idea was in the worst possible taste. His request for two months' rent—well, that was excusable, given the state of his finances. Hundreds for rent, she decided, but not one cent for Jeni's phone bills. When she explained how she felt, he demanded the $60 "or you can move the hell out." She said she'd already moved the hell in and wasn't budging. He drove away and returned after midnight.

Her anger soon dissipated, but his didn't. He refused to talk to her either at home or at the Main office where they both worked. After five days of silence she drove to the telephone office and paid his balance. When she handed him a receipt, he blew up again. "I don't need you or anybody else to pay my bills! You'll never have to pay another one. I've got all the money I need." He thumbed a thick bankroll; she saw a couple of fifties and several twenties.

"Where'd that come from?" she asked.

"That's my business."

"You didn't make it in commissions and Ruth told me they cut off the handouts. So where'd—"

"Why're you always so goddamned nosy?"

The argument raged. She'd started out expecting to be thanked for paying his phone bill and ended up hearing herself called six kinds of ingrate. The man was impossible! She stalked into the bedroom to pack. Summer, her favorite season, was almost over; it would be a long and lonely time till the next one. She was crying when he walked in. He begged her forgiveness. Each tear, he said, was a knife in his heart. She agreed to forgive him once again.

Three or four days later a bank teller gave her an extra $20 by mistake and she handed it back. When she told Kevin that night he flew into a rage. "I can't believe it!" he said. "That's like stealing twenty dollars right out of my wallet. Tell me you didn't do a stupid thing like that."

"I did."

He fumed for a while and then spoke to her in the voice of a stern parent. "At the point in time when the teller gave you the extra twenty, the mistake was hers, not yours. Got that?"

"Yeah, I got that," Gini answered dryly.

"Therefore the money was essentially given to us, and there was *nothing* epistemologically wrong in taking it."

"Yes there was. It was somebody else's money."

"Oh, shit, how naïve can you get! Do you mean to tell me you've never heard about situational ethics?"

"Situational ethics? No." She could see he was itching to play the pedagogue.

"Under situational ethics, the situation governs your morals and your ethics. Situations can change, and so can morals and ethics. There's no constant morality or system of ethics."

"In my book there is."

The argument expanded. After a while she demanded to know why he always gave in to his mother and his ex-wife. "I have to," he answered. "You wouldn't understand. I have no choice."

"Of course you have a choice!" she cried out. "You make your own choices in life. You can't go around blaming other people all the time."

"As usual you miss the point," he said airily. "There are things that happen that can cause a person to do things he has no control over. No control whatsoever."

"Name one."

He gave her the blank look she knew so well and walked into the bedroom. It was almost eleven p.m. When he came out he was dressed in his gray sweatsuit. He pulled away in his silver-gray Citation and she went to bed. So this was "living together." She hoped it improved with age.

47

By the end of summer, tens of thousands of Spokanites remained unaware that a systematic rapist was at work. Despite the brief publicity about Margot Terry, most citizens seemed unaware of the continuing problem or still assumed that the jailing of John Blake Mounsey had cleared the books.

The young convicted third-degree rapist was free now after serving six and a half months, and public pressure resumed against him and his family. Callers threatened castration. Men drove by the Mounsey home shouting, "Kill the South Hill rapist!" The house was entered and damaged. Cars full of war-whooping teenagers followed the family car like groupies and gave the finger to whoever was inside, even Mounsey's parents. "There he goes!" they would squeal if they spotted one of his brothers.

A janitor at an office building told Blake that the restrooms were kept locked "because there's so many kooks around. Like that guy Mounsey." A young woman at a party loudly advised a friend not to talk to him because "he's the guy that raped all those women." A man approached him in the Viking Bar downtown and said, "I'm gonna kill you any day now."

"Why?" Mounsey asked.

"Because you're the South Hill rapist."

Mounsey and his friends repaired to another bar, and he was lining up a pool shot when a man knocked him to the floor. "You son of a bitch!" the attacker shouted. "You raped my best friend's girlfriend. You're not getting out of here till you pay for it."

"You're all wrong, man," Mounsey said, scrambling to his feet.

"I'm right and I got seven guys to back me up. Enjoy your game. We'll be waiting."

The owner rushed over and Mounsey said, "You've gotta help me get to my car. These guys are gonna do a number on me."

The proprietor said, "Take care of it yourself."

Mounsey called the police from a pay phone. Thirty minutes later no help had arrived. "Okay, asshole, it's *go* time!" a voice came from across the room. He ducked out the exit and ran.

* * *

Mounsey's alibis for the long string of South Hill rapes had been thoroughly checked by a few detectives, notably Tom Scott, and all charges had been dropped. Patsy Mounsey importuned police officials and the media to clear her son's name now that he had served his sentence for a third-degree rape far from the South Hill. "Otherwise," she told one police official, "there'll be a lynch mob up here some night." Her requests were ignored, and in her frustration she concluded that the Spokane authorities found it easier to let the public blame her son than to admit the truth: that a brazen rapist had eluded police for over a year.

The family sold its house on the South Hill, quietly moved to the fringes of town and got an unlisted phone number. The South Hill rapes continued, and Mounsey soon learned that he would be a prime suspect in every rape, if not in the eyes of the police then in the eyes of the public. He resisted the idea of leaving his family but finally moved to another city.

48

In October police administrators doubled the manpower working on the South Hill rapes by assigning the veteran William A. Beeman Jr. to work with Joan Schmick. A few grumbles emanated from the other detectives. The rape-wave had become an embarrassment to the whole department, and everybody knew that no single team was going to solve it.

Bill Beeman was a craggy-faced homicide detective with heavy eyebrows, light-blue eyes and the weathered look of a tireless golfer. He was highly respected by his fellow officers, but as one colleague complained, "Bill's only a coupla months away from retirement, and you can't expect him to go balls-to-the-wall on something like this. And that's what it's gonna take. This raper's made us look sick for a year now. How's Bill supposed to turn things around in two months?"

Within a few days the laments about Beeman had ceased. He was meeting Schmick each morning at 4:30 to cruise bus routes and jogging tracks, working all day checking out leads, then hitting likely rape sites again in the evening. It was discouraging work. The South Hill rapist had struck in schoolyards, between houses, in parks, on hillsides, on front lawns. He never worked a specific neighborhood for long. He would strike in the old dark streets behind hospital row on Fifth Ave. and then a mile or two away in the Lincoln Heights area and then far to the southwest on High Drive. Eight or ten unsolved South Hill—type rapes had happened on the north side of town and several in the Spokane Valley. More and more, "South Hill rapist" was becoming a convenient catch-phrase.

Seeking a strategy, Schmick and Beeman agreed that flooding a single area with decoys was a waste of time and manpower, even if they could get their superiors to approve a method that had failed last winter. It was equally unrewarding to try to anticipate when the rapist would strike. He seemed to average one rape or attack every two weeks or so, but his times were as inconsistent as his locations. The detectives wished they could get the public's cooperation, but all that came in were useless tips. Many of the South Hill women were still surprisingly blasé, as though they didn't understand the situation or connect it to the scare of last winter. Chris Peck's startling column

about the rape of Margot Terry had advised female joggers to protect themselves: "Change your jogging patterns, carry Mace, run with a friend." But
the runners, creatures of healthful habit, soon returned to their old ways.

Early on a dark morning the two detectives spotted a woman jogging on
Manito Blvd., scene of many rapes and attempts. With each stride the woman's
large breasts flopped up and down under her sweatshirt. They pulled closer
and saw an inscription on her sweatshirt. It read "Bouncy bouncy." Schmick
looked at Beeman and Beeman looked at Schmick. They could see the trouble
that lay ahead.

49

Gini Perham awoke in turmoil on the morning of Monday, October 20. In a few hours she was going to lie under oath for the man she loved, an act that would be unarguably wrong no matter what Kevin Coe or anybody else said about "situational ethics." She reminded herself of what would happen if she backed down: Kevin would be found guilty of a crime he didn't commit; his name would appear in his father's newspaper; his career would end and his family would be disgraced. And all because she wouldn't tell a little white lie that was clearly in the interests of justice.

She'd recited this rationalization over and over and never come close to convincing herself. She was going to lie for fear of losing the man she loved; that was the simple truth. She'd waited years for someone like Kevin. He was a worthwhile person beset by troubles not of his own making; he deserved a break, and if nobody else would give him one, she would, even if it meant spending the rest of her life feeling ashamed.

They drove to the courthouse in his Citation. On the way he practiced his opening statement. The veins on his hands stood out as he gripped the steering wheel. He stalled the car three times while fitting into a parking space near the courthouse.

"Don't worry, sweetheart," she said as they walked through the big front doors.

She was surprised at Judge Murphy's age. He had a shock of black hair and couldn't be much older than Kevin. It seemed a good sign. Then Coe nudged her and pointed out the witnesses for the prosecution: Haraldson and Hall. They didn't look like a couple of frame-up artists, but who could tell by looks?

Kevin seemed to calm a little when his name was read. As he took his place on the other side of the bar in his three-piece suit, he looked like a lawyer. He opened by telling the judge that he was forced to represent himself because his personal attorney was involved in a sex-discrimination suit against Rosauer's and one of the prosecution witnesses. This was news to Gini; Kevin had never mentioned the case. The judge said, "Nevertheless, Mr. Coe, you're entitled to legal counsel."

"I'm aware of that, Your Honor," Kevin answered. He was in good voice and sounded sure of himself.

The judge made a few remarks about the folly of representing oneself. "I'm well prepared, Judge," Kevin insisted. He asked if the court was ready for his opening statement, and Murphy explained that the format of misdemeanor trials called for testimony only. Kevin seemed shaken. For days he'd been rehearsing an impassioned opener about his morality and reputation.

The first prosecution witness, Jeff Hall, seemed self-assured for a man so young. He testified that Kevin had shoplifted twice before and that clerks had been on the lookout for him. He drew a diagram of the store and the parking lot on a chalkboard and traced Kevin's movements. When he said that Kevin had kept looking back over his shoulder as he crossed the parking lot toward his car, Gini felt a shock of recognition. That paranoid walk was pure Kevin! She thought, What if Hall's telling the truth?

She looked toward Kevin for assurance. He was seated at the defense table, his body shifted sideways, nose tilted up, his face a study in insouciance. He looked exactly the same when he drove his car: Mr. Cool, Mr. Imperturbable. As he questioned Hall he held a gold pen in his right hand. Gini felt like shouting, Show your emotions! Don't just say that you're innocent. Show it!

As the questioning went on, his broadcast voice began to crack. He would start a question, then stop and rephrase, then ask that it be stricken. He showed contempt for Hall; once he stepped close to the assistant manager and said in a voice pitched higher than usual, "Mr. Hall, I think you're lying." The prosecutor objected, and Judge Murphy ordered Kevin to refrain from such remarks.

Soon it was obvious that Hall was in full control of the situation. At the end of a hot exchange, he said, "Mr. Coe, *you* know you did it, *I* know you did it, and *God* knows—"

"No further questions," Kevin interrupted.

Gini felt weak. She thought, Hall was *so* believable. Unless Kevin does something dramatic to turn things around, it won't make any difference whether he shoplifted or not; he'll be found guilty, and I'll be up there lying for nothing. She thought of slipping out the door. But then she thought: Kevin will never speak to me again. I *have* to go through with it.

Store manager William Haraldson testified as devastatingly as Hall. Several times the judge had to warn Kevin that his cross-examination was improper. "Now please tell us, Mr. Haraldson," Kevin asked, pacing back and forth with his hands joined behind him, "did you threaten me?"

The supermarket manager looked at the prosecutor and then at the judge. "Answer the question, please," Kevin insisted. "*Did you threaten me in any way?*"

"Yeah, I did," Haraldson admitted. "You called me a motherfucker and I told you if you kept it up I'd throw you through the wall."

"Thank you, Mr. Haraldson!" Kevin said as though he'd scored a point. Gini thought she must have missed something. To her, the testimony made Kevin look worse. But he seemed to know what he was doing. He'd been studying law books for weeks.

At last he took the stand in his own behalf. His voice was high and tight;

he didn't sound like the man who ate sardines to lubricate his vocal cords. He sounded like a guilty man, a criminal. When he claimed that Robin Rosauer had helped to frame him, the prosecutor objected and the judge said, "Mr. Rosauer isn't on trial here." Kevin looked bewildered. Gini knew that his whole defense was based on the argument that Rosauer's was out to get him. He began attacking Haraldson and Hall. After a while the judge told him that he was straying from the point.

"Judge, it's all one package," he replied, sounding like a child pleading with a parent. "These two guys *hate* me."

After fifteen or twenty minutes of rambling he got down from the witness stand. "Gini?" he said, nodding toward her.

The option of flight was gone. She knew that he'd already lost the case by his bumbling, stumbling, *guilty* performance. In a way she felt relieved. Now her lies would be immaterial.

She told her story in a monotone, unwilling to add posturing and phony sincerity. Her throat was dry and she kept licking her lips. She was afraid she was about as convincing as Kevin had been.

The prosecutor quickly showed what he thought of her testimony. Twice he ran her through the timetable, and at each answer he shook his head disbelievingly. She wondered what had given her away. Perhaps the over-abundance of detail: Kevin's idea. She'd argued that it would be more convincing if they came into court with something less than total recall, but that wasn't the perfectionist's method.

She was the last witness. The judge reviewed the testimony and said, "Mr. Coe, I see no reason why Mr. Haraldson and Mr. Hall should have lied about what happened. I think it was your intent to shoplift. I find you guilty as charged."

Gini looked at Kevin and wondered, Why the self-satisfied look? He continued to stare unblinkingly as the judge passed sentence: thirty days in jail, twenty-seven suspended, three days of community service. Gini rejoiced inside. Just as she'd predicted, it was like a speeding ticket.

But Kevin disagreed. On the way home in the Citation, he was a study in outraged innocence. "He didn't believe you," he said in a loud voice. "*He didn't believe you!* Can you imagine? That stupid goddamn judge didn't buy a word of your story. Did he think *you* would lie? A person of your background? How could he be that goddamn stupid?"

Gini was confused. He was acting as though her testimony had been true and the judge had mistakenly doubted her, when in fact the judge apparently had sized up the situation perfectly. Wasn't that one of his jobs? Had Kevin already forgotten the truth? He wouldn't shut up. He railed so loudly about the injustice of the verdict and the judge's participation in the Rosauer frame-up that she had to ask him to quiet down; his voice was giving her a headache.

At home he went from room to room slamming his fist into his hand and kicking furniture. He said he would sue everyone involved. "I'll own that goddamned Rosauer's before I'm through. And I'll get that shyster judge impeached, too. I'll put Spokane Metro Growth on his ass. We'll have him impeached, disbarred. How'd a slug like him become a judge anyway? *Only in Spokane!*"

He told her he was going to handle Haraldson and Hall personally; he knew where they lived; they'd given their addresses in the courtroom, and he'd watched Hall shop on South Regal and followed him home. "Don't do it, Kevin," Gini said. "You'll end up in more trouble."

"Changed sides, have you? Where's your sense of outrage, for God's sake?"

She'd heard enough. For an hour he'd been yelling at her as though she were a party to his railroading. "*Where's my sense of outrage?*" she shot back. "You took it away with your overkill. All by yourself you convinced the court that you're a thief. Why don't you stop before you convince me?"

"What?" His jaw dropped. "You think *I* shoplifted?"

"I'm getting there," she said. "Just keep talking."

A day or two later, the normal course of their relationship resumed. It was a well-established pattern by now: a fight, a silence, a reconcilation, then another fight. It may have been a cute plot line for a TV movie about love, but it made for a harrowing life. She wondered where they could go from here. More fights, more silences, more reconcilations? It was as though something in him thrived on disorder.

A few nights after the courtroom debacle, he dropped a typical petulant thunderbolt: "The only reason you want to be with me is sex."

She was stunned. The last reason she wanted to be with him was sex. It had never been crucial in her life, and their sex life together had usually left her feeling a little squirmy. She still wasn't relaxed about his oral techniques, and it bothered her that he had to masturbate under the covers to attain an erection. "Kevin," she said, "get one thing straight, will you? I do *not* consider you a sex object. I'm with you because I love you. Do you understand that? I'm *happy* to be with you. I *want* to be with you."

"I wish you meant that," he said.

She stared into his eyes. "Do I have to take an ad?"

He seemed baffled. The idea that someone could love him deeply—not for his looks or his accomplishments or his penis but for *himself*—was clearly hard for him to accept. It was after midnight and she was half asleep when she heard him murmur, "Do you *really*, V.K.?"

"Huh? Do I really what?"

"Love me."

"Oh, Kevin. . . ."

In the next few days he seemed to relax sexually. His erection problem diminished, and he was able to enter her with less self-stimulation. Word came back to her after their first month together that he'd referred to her at the office as "the perfect woman." Some nights when they were drifting off to sleep he would surprise her by saying, "I love you, Gini." She was pleased, but she couldn't help noticing an artificiality in his voice, as though he were imitating someone trying to be tender, or wanted to be passionate but didn't have it in him. She'd been close to him for over a year now, and she figured she had about 5 percent of him figured out.

A few weeks after the latest reconciliation she waited till they were in bed and asked, "Kevin, why don't you marry me?" She wanted an inkling of his intentions. She hadn't stopped to consider what she would say if he answered that he would, because she definitely did *not* want to marry him—not at the moment, anyway. Her love was total, but what kind of fool would marry a man who was having his own affair with chaos?

He said he would give her question some thought. A few nights later he told her they were already married in spirit.

50

The more affluent residents of the upper South Hill were the first to recognize that the rapist was still active, and they took steps to protect themselves. "After Margot we began hearing of all kinds of attacks," said Mrs. John Little, the woman who had spotted a small car near the site of the Terry rape. "Once in a while the papers would carry a little item, but most of our news came by telephone—rapes, indecent exposures, obscene calls, *sick* things. At first some of us figured it was hysteria, but then we realized: Somebody's out there."

The realization might have saved several women. Shortly after the Terry rape a doctor's wife named Marilyn Klock was jogging on High Drive with her tear gas canister and her dog. "As I rounded a bend I saw a man come out of a wooded area and run toward me. He wore gray sweats and a blue down vest. I thought, Joggers don't wear down vests! I couldn't believe that he'd be wearing exactly the same clothes that Margot had been raped in, but he was. I'd just talked to her a few days before.

"I ran downhill as fast as I could. When I looked over my shoulder he was gone. I told the police I'd seen the South Hill rapist. They sent a cop in uniform but the man was gone. My friends and I kept up on the rapes after that and noticed that he never wore that same outfit again. He must have changed because of the way I ran from him. He knew we had him spotted."

Not long after, Joanne Schneider was delivering a misaddressed letter to a friend a few doors away from her own house near Cannon Hill Park, halfway up the South Hill. It was just after nightfall, and a runner emerged from the shadows a half block away in a black jogging outfit. Her first thought was that it was highly unsafe to run at night in a dark outfit. Her second thought was that it was odd that he'd left the jogging path and headed her way. She put the letter in her friend's mailbox and turned to step off the porch. The jogger was standing below her on the sidewalk. She was trapped.

The man stared silently, a six-footer with layered brown hair and a thick jaw. His face was a blank and his eyes unblinking.

She was anxious but not panicky; nearby houses were flooded with light. The stare-down continued for minutes. Then the man headed westward and disappeared in a patch of bushes. If she continued in her original direction, she would walk right past him. She ran back home, considered calling the police and decided not to bother; the undermanned SPD was notorious for showing up late or not at all, and what, after all, had happened? Nothing that a male cop would understand.

A few days later a woman was raped in nearby Cannon Hill Park by a jogger using the same familiar style.

Marie Oldham, a twenty-seven-year-old gamine with long black hair and brown eyes, walked rapidly toward her new home and thought about decor and furniture arrangements. She had just married and moved to Spokane from Juneau, Alaska. A real estate agent had mentioned that a rapist was loose on the South Hill but her life was far too full to dwell on downers like that.

The late-afternoon sunlight had just faded. After a mid-October warm spell the air had cooled; she was glad she'd worn her new camel-colored wool coat with the dark-brown piping. A jogger crossed the narrow street under a streetlight fifty feet ahead of her. He looked like a college student. Exactly the way the realtor had described the rapist. After he dropped from sight she passed a parked camper truck and noticed a man in a sweatsuit crouched at the rear. She thought he must be waiting to play a trick on a friend—maybe jump out and say, "Boo!"

Instead he grabbed her around the neck. "I've got a knife," he said as he grappled with her. "Don't scream. *Don't scream!*" He poked at her mouth with a gloved hand and she clenched her teeth. He pried her jaws apart and stuck in his thumb. She bit hard. "Don't bite!" he said as he nudged her into a vacant lot. "Relax your mouth!"

She bit again and felt flesh. Blood trickled into her throat. He locked his arm around her ribcage and shoved her ahead of him in a series of jerky motions. "Don't yell, don't scream, keep quiet!" he repeated.

He pried her mouth open again and this time shoved his hand deep into her throat, immobilizing her jaws. Her first thought was that she wouldn't be able to breathe. She'd had asthma all her life; it wouldn't be much of a job to asphyxiate her.

The ground was spongy and damp, floored with a thick mulch of yard trimmings. In lockstep they maneuvered deeper into the shadows. She'd lost a shoe and stumbled. Several times they fell together and he wrenched her to her feet again. Her black slacks and stockings ripped on something sharp. When a car came by he threw her facedown on the soft ground and flopped on top.

He felt surprisingly light; she realized that it was the way he carried his weight, even when he was horizontal—like a cat, lithe and balanced, evenly distributed. She turned her engagement ring around so he wouldn't see the stone and prayed he was a robber. After the car had passed he dragged her on. One of his hands was so far down her throat that his glovetips brushed her tonsils. She tried to shake loose but he only pushed the hand deeper. Blood filled her mouth and she realized it was her own.

She studied his face in the glow of a mercury-vapor lamp from across the street. He had a pronounced jaw, dark almond-shaped eyes that gave him a Castilian look, and loosely curly hair with disheveled bangs. He was wearing dark zippered pants, a polo-type shirt, a waist-length leather jacket and a battered pair of tennis shoes. In the bluish glare of the streetlight he was a study in gray.

When he saw her staring he snapped, "Don't look at me!" He yanked her hair over her eyes and hit her on the side of the face with a fist that felt like steel. When he punched her again she let herself go limp. It must have scared him. He relaxed his hand and retracted his fingers an inch or two, giving her a chance to curl her tongue between the glove and her sore tonsils. He shoved his hand in again. Lord, she prayed, let me breathe! Is that asking too much? I just want to get home and do my new house.

He flipped her on her back and deftly changed hands. The glove he now inserted was covered with weeds and dirt. He tried to undress her one-handed. She was almost deaf in her left ear from childhood mumps but she could hear him mumbling, "You like to masturbate, don't you? Are you married? When was the last time you did it?" Distantly she heard him say, "I'm gonna fuck your cunt." How odd, she thought, he uses awful words but he sounds so educated, so urbane.

He wrenched off her pants and flung her new coat in the weeds, fumbled with her ruined pantyhose and her underwear, then ordered her to remove them herself. She waited for the rape to begin; she had no intention of resisting. Her face and her left temple throbbed, and she was barely getting air.

His fingers shoved at her vagina, probing and tearing. He pulled them out, licked them and rammed them in again. Then he unzipped his pants and began masturbating. As though the two of them were high-school pals he said, "You know, I beat off all the time." He asked her when she'd last had intercourse, and when she couldn't answer he resumed his chatter. He rubbed his penis against her bare skin and she was surprised that it wasn't erect. "Like to be fucked?" he gasped. He finished so fast that she wasn't even sure he'd been inside. The penetration—if that was the word for it—hadn't lasted a minute.

He rolled her over on her stomach, still keeping his hand in her throat. Another car passed, but she couldn't signal. He patted her bottom and she thought, *Oh, God, not that!* "You haven't been hurt," he said. "All things considered, you've come out of this very lucky. I'm gonna take my hand out of your mouth and I want you to count ten before you make a move. When you get home just say that you slipped and fell."

He slid his hand from her throat and added, "I know where you live. If you go to the police I'll come back and kill you. They can't protect you twenty-four hours a day. I'll kill you if you say one word about this."

She kept her eyes shut, counted slowly to five, then sat up and looked around. When she saw that he was gone, she lost her temper. That rotten bastard, she said to herself, I'll kick him so hard in the *cojones* he'll never pull that thing out again! I know exactly what he looks like. That sick cowardly son of a bitch, he picked the wrong party this time! She finished dressing but couldn't find her other shoe. She limped toward home, a block away. As she crossed Myrtle she thought of her new house and started to cry. It was ruined for her now.

Dr. Craig Olson, chief of the Deaconess Hospital emergency room, had examined South Hill rape victims before, but this victim represented a distinct escalation. The woman had a badly battered face. Her lower lip was cut and her mouth was a mass of scratches. The rapist's glove had cut stitch marks into her tongue. Her throat looked as though someone had taken heavy-gauge sandpaper to it. He couldn't recall a throat as raw. Her ribs were bruised and there was a six-inch abrasion along the front of her right leg. The outside of her genital area was scraped. A half-inch tear still bled in her vagina and the cervix was abraded. Seminal fluid was present, containing nonmotile sperm.

Olson tried to concentrate on the treatment and tests, but his mind couldn't stop sifting what he already knew about the South Hill rapist. All doubts were now swept away. The rapist was one man, not the two or three that some had guessed. His MO was unmistakably individual, and he was losing control.

51

It is also characteristic for the real psychopath to resent punishment and protest indignantly against all efforts to curtail his activities....He is much less willing than the ordinary person to accept such penalties.—Hervey Cleckley, M.D., *The Mask of Sanity*

Gini couldn't get Kevin to stop rehashing the shoplifting case. He talked about it in the shower in the morning and in bed at night. He chewed over the subject till she almost wished she were as deaf as her poor mother had been. "Kevin," she said a few days after the hearing, "what good is all this talk? Maybe everybody charged with shoplifting is found guilty. Why can't we get on with our life?"

"I was framed!" he insisted. "And who by? Robin Rosauer, his two flunkies, a cop, and a *judge*, for God's sake! Do you realize the significance of that, Gin? Do you realize what that says about justice in Spokane, when they can railroad somebody like me? Just because I made a few people mad with my constructive criticism?"

"Yes," she said. "I realize it." By dint of thousands of words, most of them at close range, he had cajoled her back to the belief that he was innocent. No guilty man would go on and on the way he had; no guilty man would throw the tantrums he had thrown about the verdict. But he was in danger of letting rage and hatred cost him his job. He'd never spent much time at Main Realtors; now he spent none. Bill Main, the proprietor, asked Gini, "What the hell's wrong with Kevin? He's been with us almost a year and all he's done is sell a house to his mother and father. He doesn't even come in anymore. I like the guy personally, but you tell me, Gini—why shouldn't I fire him?"

She mumbled something about how he had some businesses on the side but planned to concentrate on real estate any day now.

"Yeah," Main said. "I've been hearing that for a year."

She recounted the conversation to Kevin, but he was on another wavelength. He'd moved his electric typewriter out to Five Pines and was busy composing an open letter to Judge Murphy "that'll blow the lid off this town." He read her an occasional passage and she found it to be the same old stuff. She'd never known anyone to waste so much energy beating a dead horse.

What did he think Judge Murphy would do when he got the letter? Recant? Make a public apology? The whole idea was naïve.

When he showed her his finished product on Spokane Metro Growth stationery, her eyes popped. It was a book! She did a quick scan. There were fifteen pages totaling around ten thousand words. She read the opening, "Dear Judge Murphy, I sincerely hope you will take the time to read this entire letter and will respond promptly in letter to me, answering the questions I will ask herein." She skipped down and read:

> I DID NOT SHOPLIFT! I had no intent of committing a crime. I am not a thief. I have never stolen anything in my life. Beyond that, I am morally and philosophically opposed to crime of any kind. I have practiced for years a rigorous philosophy that epistemologically is in opposition to any crime or malicious conduct against individuals or organizations....

She couldn't read another word. The same old arguments! She shook her head sadly. "Kevin, this is a waste—"

"You don't care anymore, do you?" he interrupted.

"I care about you, Kevin," she said softly. "But I'm up to here with the subject."

He stormed out of the house. She was just as glad. If he'd argued from the beginning that the shoplifting incident was a misunderstanding, she never would have doubted him. But the claims about railroading bordered on the irrational. She could only conclude that he was trying to cover his guilt. It sickened her to think that she'd let herself be talked into lying for him. She glanced at the calendar. It was October 31; he'd spent eleven days working on his masterpiece. A guilty man! She wished she understood.

Judge Murphy read the first page of the letter and felt a faint unease about his verdict. He recognized an eloquent plea when he saw one, and in terms of poundage the package represented an extraordinary investment in time and energy, exactly the sort an innocent man might make in justified outrage.

But as he read on the earnest young judge relaxed. The letter shifted to the same polemics Coe had used in the courtroom—the quintessence of irrelevance. He complained again that he wasn't allowed an opening statement and "was immediately thrown out of my 'game plan.'" He admitted he had made a mistake by showing contempt for assistant manager Jeffrey Hall. "When I started off... my voice was its usual deep, clear and resonant broadcaster's voice," he wrote, but "my voice had become tight with anger. And it was breaking badly."

The judge wondered what voice texture had to do with guilt or innocence, but he read on:

> Though I had heard many ugly stories of courtroom inequities, I was such a babe in the woods in criminal legal matters I believed the truth was a simple and adequate defense—and that American jurisprudence would be upheld.
>
> What I found instead, much to my shock and sadness, was that—

at least in cases where the charge is shoplifting—it was just the opposite. The defendant is presumed guilty unless—somehow—he can 'prove' his innocence.

This is wrong. And this is ugly, to say the least. It is a hideous spectre.

The judge ruminated about the case. The testimony had been overwhelmingly against the well-dressed young man, even from his own mouth. He had received the mildest of sentences—seventy-two hours of community service. Some "inequity"!

The tone of the letter soon darkened and the charges turned personal.

My partner and I are very seriously thinking of employing a private detective agency to scrutinize the matter of whether any of Spokane's district court judges are on the take from irate merchants seeking a crackdown on shoplifting. The results of any such investigation, by the way, would be released to the media and thereby to the public. I think that would be the very least of our civic duty. It is a sad thing, of course, to see a judge go crooked. . . . I want to believe you are not foolish and are honest. I had hoped you wanted to believe the same of me. Unfortunately, you showed just the opposite mind-set, right from the start, displaying a hostile attitude toward my presentation, my questioning and my case in general.

Judge Murphy remembered that Coe, against strong advice, had insisted on representing himself. Under those conditions most judges bent over backward to assure a fair hearing. That was how it had been with Coe. And still his guilt had been indisputable.

The long letter closed, "I was able to get a one week extension, until November 7th, of when I have to either appeal this case or accept the erroneous guilty verdict. Thus, I need—and deserve—a prompt reply to this letter." At the bottom Coe noted that he was sending copies to the "Spokesman-Review, Spokane Chronicle, Rosauers, Prosecutor's Office, Corrections Department."

The judge picked up an enclosure entitled "Coe vs Rosauers—a history." It told how Coe had always admired the Rosauer chain and wished it success. "This was especially the case because they are the only major Spokane-owned grocery chain. I do not care for Albertsons or Safeway because—as a part of Spokane Metro Growth—I do not approve of a capital in-flow to Boise or Oakland from Spokane."

He wrote of critical suggestions he'd made about manager Bill Haraldson and how assistant manager Jeffrey Hall had once called him a "son of a bitch" and an "asshole" and shouted, "I'll be watching you, mister! So when you come in here—even if it's just for a Coke—you better make sure you get a receipt and have it on ya. Or else I'll say you were shoplifting." He told of avoiding Rosauer's and then returning, only to be made ill. "I submit I was indeed poisoned that night in Rosauers Family Restaurant. Sound absolutely incredible? I think not."

In an enclosure called "My Version of What Happened—the truth," the judge read, "My very stringent anti-allergy/anti-hypoglycemic diet calls for copious quantities of beef and so... I habitually shopped at least once a day in Rosauers meat department." On the date of the arrest, Coe wrote, he stopped by the book rack; then:

> Holding the steak and Perrier water in my left hand, nestling those items against my ribs, I picked up Robert Ringer's paperback best-seller "Restoring the American Dream." I have all of Ringer's books and I found this newest one fascinating—so much so I lost track of time as I thumbed through his latest hit. Perhaps ten minutes passed as I perused the book, having decided now for sure to buy it. But suddenly I remembered my girlfriend waiting—and the fact I had a 1 PM appointment I had previously forgotten all about! I put Ringer's book back on the rack and walked out of the store—leaving, as I had entered, through the restaurant doors.

Why hadn't he paid?

> I practice a specific application of psycho-cybernetics and mental discipline called Laserlife. This is a system of mental control which allows near-perfect concentration on any given subject. I go in and out of Laserlife states throughout any given day. This heightens mental awareness and allows for extraordinary achievement—but it also makes easy the forgetting of things other than the subject of concentration. My mind was lasering in on my day's crowded schedule and I forgot all about the groceries I was carrying cradled in my left arm.

He wrote of being stopped and cursed by Haraldson and Hall. "I could have just slapped the merchandise on the counter and walked out of the store. As a former boxer of some accomplishment I certainly was not physically intimidated."

Judge Murphy read on in fascination. "Closing Argument" asked, "Is it likely a man dressed in an expensive 3-piece suit... a man well known to be a good and frequent Rosauers customer... a man with $110 in his pocket... a man whose girlfriend was waiting outside in the car for him... would suddenly become a shoplifter? Hardly!"

As for the hearing:

> Even the court clerk seemed stunned at the awful verdict. And my girlfriend—a very classy young lady with the utmost in integrity—was absolutely devastated that the judge would call her a liar. This was a gross insult! Such untoward behavior from the bench demands an apology be made to this decent citizen. The judge sees so much human trash he evidently cannot recognize good citizens when he sees them in his court. In the very near future I plan on having a staffer of mine write a very pointed letter to the editors of area periodicals, citing the disturbing and disgusting conditions poisoning our local courts and stifling justice.

Judge Murphy tried to recall his own reaction to Virginia Perham's testimony. He was sure that he hadn't called her or anyone else "a liar." The final enclosure, "The Injustice in This Case," pointed out that it was hardly worthwhile for a man of Coe's importance to take the time to appeal. "I am the owner or co-owner of four companies. . . . I am an extremely busy man. I work between 70 and 100 hours a week. Considering the kind of money I am able to make 72 hours of community service represents a great deal of money lost. . . ."

Coe suggested that the hearing be declared a mistrial or he be given a period of one year—instead of the customary ten days—to file an appeal. If the sentence were waived, he would be "receptive" to dropping the matter provided he could file a statement that he did not accept or recognize the verdict. Otherwise he would have to "seek vindication through some sort of available courtroom procedure and, then, sue for a reasonable amount of money."

Judge Murphy laid the thick package down and shook his head. Coe seemed to have so much to offer; why waste it on a bloviated exercise in self-importance? The letter only confirmed what he'd suspected all along: that the young man in the three-piece suit hadn't come to court to assert his innocence but to use the courtroom as a stage.

Coe didn't appeal the decision or ask for expunction of the record, and Judge Murphy wound up sharing the letter with a few friends, including a journalist or two. They found it revealing.

52

He seems often charming, intelligent, gallant, brave; where the timid or conventional fear to tread he plunges; even his obvious faults often seem to be only virtues disguised—restlessness, unreliability, eccentricity, egocentricity.—William Krasner, *The Psychopath in Our Society, Neurotica II,* 1948

Once again Gini and Kevin patched up their quarrel, and she even agreed to help with his community service. His sentence called for visits to merchants to wangle contributions for children's social programs. He threw himself into the job with surprising energy for someone who just a few days before had been fulminating about injustice, and Gini wondered if he'd decided to accept the verdict. He worked up a cute fund-raising letter and had her add a cartoon of a child holding balloons. He went from store to store handing out copies of the letter and introducing himself as a city employee. She was with him when he solicited the owner of the Manito Pharmacy on the South Hill. Here on his own turf Kevin identified himself as an aide to the governor.

The pharmacist said, "Coe? Don't I know that name from somewhere?" Before Kevin could comment the man said, "Is Kathleen your sister? What a nice person!"

Outside, Kevin said, "Whenever anybody sees the name Coe, they remember Kathleen and never me." There was a woebegone sound to his voice.

Driving along Twenty-ninth Avenue, they got into a rare discussion about the South Hill rapist. There'd been a savage rape a few weeks before—a young newlywed from Alaska. Gini couldn't discuss the subject calmly. Chris Peck had written a column about a woman named Margot, and insiders said he'd omitted the fact that her nipples had been bitten off. Soon after, according to the same rumor mill, the rapist had attacked a nun in the courtyard of a Catholic grade school. "Something ought to be done about that nut," Gini said. "Have you been reading the letters to the editor in the *Spokesman-Review*?"

"Hardly."

"What do you mean 'hardly'?"

"The only thing duller than the *Review* is the letters to the editor."

"Women are getting *mad* about the rapes," she said. Several correspondents had called for the death penalty, and a few had suggested castration. Gini understood. All her life the quiet green streets of the South Hill had meant home, even when she'd been halfway around the world. Now the homey atmosphere was being destroyed by a coward who terrorized women—and mostly smaller women at that. "When they catch him," she said, "they ought to put him in a room with the husbands and mothers of his victims and let them do whatever they want to him."

"I rather prefer due process."

"He ought to be strung up by the balls."

"*Gini!*" She waited for him to lecture her on her grossness. She had no intention of backing down. There were some points that couldn't be made in ladylike language. As they continued on the drive toward home he didn't pursue the subject. He seemed almost morose. She began to be sorry she'd brought up the rapist. It was always so hard to guess how he would react to anything, but this time she should have known better. He'd always described himself as a believer in the women's movement; his sister was a feminist who continued to use her maiden name after her marriage; his mother boasted that women were superior and were held down only by male tradition and power; his father—well, Gordon didn't say much, but he seemed content to live in a matriarchy. Given a family like that, how could Kevin not be disturbed about the South Hill rapist?

They'd been living together for nearly two months now, and every day she made discoveries. She learned that he wasn't a puffed-up egoist but the opposite. He seemed surprised whenever she complimented him on his appearance, as though he didn't believe her. Once he told her in the most childlike tones that he worked hard on his appearance because he could never measure up to men like his friend D. Jay Williams. Her love was deepened by compassion.

In a hallway place of honor he'd nailed a calendar of musclemen, and he often stopped to admire the gleaming oiled body of the hunk of the month. His own body tended toward the lean and sinewy, but she found out he had surprising strength. One night she grabbed him playfully and tried to tickle him. In an instant he pinned her, ripping an earring from her pierced ear.

She was surprised at his reaction. He got up and said, "Don't do that! I don't like it."

He talked constantly about muscle-building. Often he flopped to the floor for sets of sit-ups, push-ups, isometrics. Still he never looked half as strong as he really was, never looked robust, perhaps because of his paleness. He admitted that he was afraid of water and told her that sunshine would make him old before his time—a particular terror for him and his mother. Gini realized that she'd never seen him take part in a daytime sport. Even his jogging was done in the dark.

It took him longer to prepare for work than anyone she'd ever known. His morning ritual started with a sit-down urination, a puzzlement to her until she decided it was his neatness compulsion again. If she approached the bathroom he would say, "I'll be out in a minute. *Don't come in!*" He was somewhat less modest about his lengthy showers. He would step out and dry himself, carefully patting his armpits, genitals and toes with Kleenex. He applied facial creams for wrinkles and a pink lotion to mask the scar near his eye. He spent ten or fifteen minutes on his hair, combing, spraying, re-combing, picking and choosing among several expensive medicaments to stave off baldness. His blow-dry haircuts were usually spaced six to eight weeks apart, so that the length and style of his hair varied distinctly from one month to the next. He had long discussions with his stylist in Lincoln Heights, telling her exactly what he wanted done, and she always ended up granting him extra time.

Sometimes Ruth accompanied him and paid his bill. "Mrs. Coe's as particular about his hair as he is," the receptionist said one day. "They're so sweet together, the way they hold hands and touch. We were noticing the last time they were in—if Kevin hesitated in the middle of a sentence Mrs. Coe would fill in the word. They're *that* close!"

Gini decided that his neatness came from his mother's influence. Apparently he'd been able to get away with just about anything as a child, but a spot on his clothes had brought punishment. Now that he was grown, he kept his suits and shirts on hangers spaced exactly two inches apart. His shoes were arrayed in a line. He wore nylon underwear and admitted that he'd always wondered what it felt like to be a woman. She wasn't put off; she knew that men were partly women and vice versa, but only the most honest would admit it.

He insisted that the house be kept spotless. Even though he claimed to be a feminist, he seemed to expect her to do the housework—another of his inconsistencies. No matter how well she cleaned, he always found something to touch up. His junk drawer in the kitchen was laid out like a surgeon's tray. He washed and dried dishes as soon as he used them, and his clothes went straight from his back to the washing machine. How fitting, she thought, that we met in a laundromat.

He sneezed often and suffered from a runny nose, but he claimed he'd been far worse before he began the Newbold diet. He blamed his mother for his allergies: "She thought more of her figure than she thought of her son, and she wouldn't breast-feed me." At the office he asked his colleagues to lick his stamps and envelopes, claiming "The contaminants activate my allergies." He seemed to enjoy making others aware of his needs.

At Five Pines one night he shoved his plate away and said, "There's sugar in this!" When his mother admitted there was a pinch, he griped that her lack of consideration had set his diet back weeks. She told him to quit being such a prima donna. He cursed loudly and Ruth leaned across the small table and yelled, "You bum, you never amounted to anything in your life—*and you never will!*"

Gordon said, "Hey, let's knock it off!" It was one of the few times Gini saw him intervene forcefully.

Annoyed by Kevin's pickiness, she almost looked forward to his fasts. At least they were simple. For a week he would live on water and vitamins, growing skinnier with each day. Then he would "flood," gobbling up popcorn, Idaho Spud candies, Mountain Bars, chocolate turtles, potato chips and other junk foods. After a few days he would bloat, break out in an occasional pimple, and stop shaving and showering, as though he had given up on himself. He would leave things lying around and wear dirty clothes, and his hair would grow nearly to his shoulders. Then he would fast again, get a haircut, and change back into the neat young man she had known.

Whatever phase he was in, he had great vitality. He slept only five or six hours a night and was often returning from his morning jog when she got up at 6:30 or 7. Sometimes he came to bed after midnight and explained that he'd been out running, and she would touch him and find that his skin was dry. He never started his distance runs at the house; he would don his sweatsuit with the drawstring bottoms, the blue down vest and black gloves that he almost always wore, and disappear in his silver-gray Citation.

"Why do you spend money on gas to go jogging?" she asked him once. "We hardly have money for food." He didn't answer.

"Is it because you have to run on a track?"

"Yeah," he mumbled.

Now and then she became aware of contradictions concerning his whereabouts; he would say he'd been at Five Pines and then Ruth would call and complain that she hadn't seen him in days, or he would head for a house showing and fail to arrive. She wondered what he was up to. Was it—a woman? She knew that he'd had a fling with at least one other realtor, but that was history. Months ago he'd complained that someone had scolded him for hurting the woman's feelings. He couldn't understand what he'd done wrong. "Well, didn't you lead her on and then kind of dump her?" Gini asked.

He looked mystified and asked, "Who'd be hurt about something like that?" She wondered why it was so hard for him to understand feelings. His constant bad-mouthing of Spokane grated on her, but he never seemed to realize it. For him and his mother, Hawaii was the ultimate playland and Las Vegas the center of the universe. Periodically he renewed his Nevada driver's license through the mail, using a false address.

He had an active telephone life and refused to let Gini in on it. Sometimes she would try to reach him from the office and get a constant busy signal. Later he would claim he hadn't used the phone. Often when she came home unexpectedly, he would hang up or step inside his den to finish his conversation. "What are you doing here?" he whispered one November day when she walked in. He was wearing jeans and tennis shoes and his hand was cupped over the mouthpiece of the phone.

"Kevin, I *live* here."

He finished his conversation behind the closed door of his den and came into the kitchen. "I don't like snoops," he said.

"Snoops?"

"Why don't you announce yourself, for God's sake? You, you—surprised me."

She tried to keep it light. "Who were you talking to, Hamilton Jordan?"

"You don't give me a *second's* privacy."

"Kevin, I didn't even expect you to be here. When I left this morning you were dressed for work."

"Yeah, well—I've got something going."

"In that outfit?" He turned away without answering. She decided there was no use pressing for an explanation. Maybe he'd been arguing with his mother and didn't want to talk about it. Or cadging money from his father—

that went on constantly. She started to tell him she was sorry she'd disturbed him, but he was on his way to the basement. That seemed to be his refuge.

Sometimes she kidded herself that he had a woman down there. It was a full basement with a furnace, laundry room, two bedrooms and dark corners that she'd never examined. She'd seen Jeni's clothes and makeup kit in one of the bedrooms, but little else. When he came home at night from work he would rush to the basement before saying hello. Sometimes he did laundry; other times she couldn't imagine what he was doing. When she followed him down he would spin on the stairs and say, "What do you want?" If he was already in the basement when she headed down, he would yell, "Don't come down! I'll be right up!" He would bound up the stairs and slam the door behind him, as though protecting her from a dangerous beast.

As far as she could tell, he made little effort to succeed at real estate, but he was always griping about bills and hinting that she wasn't carrying her load. She lent him more money, and he made occasional repayments by topping the tank of her Monte Carlo and paying with his father's credit card. He had the same arrangement with his old friend Jay Williams. She also learned that he owed the landlord four months' back rent. She didn't understand; from the first day, they'd split all expenses. When he brought home steaks and other expensive foods, she paid her share in cash. In a moment of doubt she wondered if he was shoplifting groceries and using her payments as pocket money. But she decided she was being unfair. He wasn't the only Spokane realtor in financial trouble.

He continued to play the role of the well-heeled businessman. He test-drove the latest automobiles. He thumbed through real estate listings and circled fancy houses he considered buying. For a while he was excited about the vacant lot next door to his parents' new home in the Spokane Valley. "We'll build a house there!" he told Gini. Then he learned that the $100,000 house on the other side of the Coes' was vacant and wrote the owners suggesting a lease with option to buy. At the time he was borrowing lunch money daily.

Sometimes she wondered if his basic problem was a simple inability to concentrate. He would work on a good sales prospect and suddenly lose interest. He developed clever schemes for making money and abandoned them to compose useless letters from Spokane Metro Growth. He dipped into books but never seemed to finish one; maybe that was why he was so confused about the Newbold diet. He claimed to be a proponent of Ayn Rand "objectivism" but continually misstated her ideas. He didn't always seem to understand his own history. He rhapsodized about his glory days on Spokane and Las Vegas radio, and constantly critiqued the local announcers. One day he insisted that they drive to Buchanan Chevrolet to see a showing of the new 1981 models, and when they got there she couldn't stop him from ogling the mistress of ceremonies. "That's Sunshine Shelly of KJRB," he whispered to her. "Isn't she the greatest?"

He practiced his own broadcast delivery an hour a day, as though expecting an emergency call from the networks. He would switch around for hours trying on different personalities and voices. Gini was reminded of Ruth Coe's varying modes of speech. She began to wonder if he might be harboring a mild psychosis, perhaps schizophrenia. She remembered how the disease had affected her mother and how old friends had drifted away as though being around a disturbed person was too much trouble. Gini would never treat Kevin that way. He loved her, needed her, and showed it—a guarantee of her loyalty.

One night in late October she came home from work to find him pacing the floor, his face the color of scrapbook paste. "Ruth found out," he said in a shaky voice. "Oh, shit, this is awful. She called me every name in the book."

"Found out what?" Gini asked.

"About the shoplifting. The court clerk sent something out to Five Pines and she opened it. I told her I was framed. She said she'll never go back to Rosauer's."

"She believes you?"

"Well, I would certainly hope so. But I have a feeling she'll have more to say on the subject."

Yes, Gini thought, so do I.

53

Tom Dolan detected new signs of discord in the little yellow house across the street. One fall afternoon he heard a shriek and saw a woman he recognized as Kevin Coe's mother burst out of the house and head for her yellow Cadillac. "She was talking at the top of her lungs," Dolan told a friend, "and she was so mad her voice was... I don't know how to describe it. Kinda low and kinda high, like two different people talking at once. I never saw one human being so pissed."

One day Dolan got into a conversation with John Evans, a neighbor and fellow welder who lived closer to the Coe house. "What the hell's going on over there?" Dolan asked.

"It's the mother and son," Evans said. "Usually she'll come for a late-morning or early-afternoon visit, while the girlfriend's gone. The dad's never with her. She'll stay twenty, thirty minutes and you can hear 'em screaming inside the house. A couple, three times I was in my yard and she came outside and they were cursing each other. Not the kind of language you'd expect: a son telling his mother to fuck off. Right in public, with our children around. If they're talking like that outside, you gotta wonder what they're saying inside. Seems like they'll fight about anything. Once it was over a lawn mower. He wasn't doing something right. She called him a little bastard and he called her a fucking bitch. They'll yell like that in the driveway, sometimes at the back door. She's over here two, three times a week and it always ends the same."

"He doesn't fight with the girlfriend?" Dolan asked.

"Who'd fight with her? She's little Miss Perfect. I've never seen her with a hair out of place. My wife says her clothes are expensive. She seems like a nice, quiet person."

"Too bad we can't say the same for the others," Dolan said.

"It'd be a lot quieter around here."

54

With interest rates climbing, Spokane real estate agencies began to go out of business. Kevin Coe returned from his shoplifting trauma to a tense atmosphere at Main Realtors. His peculiarities, once mildly entertaining, now only seemed to aggravate his fellow agents. He busied himself at the computer, summoning up information about vacant houses. One day Bill Main took Gini Perham aside and said in a tight voice, "Look, he's at it again! Does he find buyers at that machine? He's *always* at that computer!"

Now and then word got back that Coe had shown up at a house without an appointment. One listee complained about an impromptu nighttime visit from a man in a gray jogging suit who said he was from Main. She didn't catch the name, but he hung around for ten minutes before she persuaded him to leave. Once Coe was found inside a home when the owners arrived unexpectedly. He explained that he was taking measurements.

Main Realtors had tolerated the young eccentric for almost a year with hardly any return. Coe's record consisted of the sale of the Dyer Rd. house to his parents and a few petty deals and listings. He continued to explain that he was operating three or four businesses but eventually planned to go into real estate full-time.

In November a saddened Bill Main gathered Kevin Coe, Gini Perham, Jay Williams and his other agents together for an announcement. He had sold the firm to the Tomlinson agency. Coe told Williams he would rather quit real estate than join Tomlinson. "Why?" Jay asked. "They're a great outfit."

"I'd *never* work for classmates," said Coe. Tomlinson's president and its top broker had attended Lewis and Clark High School with Coe and Williams. "It's belittling."

"That's ridiculous," Williams argued. "They're great guys. They're not gonna belittle you."

"They already did," Coe said. "When they dropped in after the meeting? They called me Fred instead of Kevin."

"Well, that's what they've always known you by. That's what *I* call you, for goodness' sake!"

"You're different, Jay. If they want me to go to work for them they should use my name of preference."

Gini Perham was also disturbed by her roommate's reaction to the sale of Main Realtors. She wanted to return to James S. Black and he didn't; she remembered good times at the Black agency and would never have left if he hadn't influenced her.

Kevin was furious. "We're supposed to be real estate partners!" he shouted at her. "If you want to break it up, go ahead. You can start by moving out of my house. I'm not going to Black—I'm going with the most exciting guy in the business."

"Who's that?"

"Roger Crane."

Kevin had often spoken admiringly about Roger E. Crane & Associates, but Gini had heard about the valley firm's stringent requirements and knew he would soon have another failure to live down. She waited till a relaxed setting in a Third Ave. steakhouse to discuss the subject. This time he became so angry that he stuck out his lower teeth in the look she had seen before on mother and son. "Move out, Gini," he said, his cheek muscles throbbing. "Just leave! If you don't want to go to Crane with me, let's forget the whole thing."

After an embarrassing scene, she agreed to go wherever he went. He calmed down and told her how he intended to get himself hired. He would meet with Roger Crane personally, then follow up with a letter and a phone call. "That's the dynamic approach," he explained. Later she found out what actually happened:

At first Crane had turned him down on the grounds that he had no sales record. Kevin explained that he'd been working part-time and was ready to make the big jump into real estate "along with my sales partner, Gini Perham." While Crane personnel were checking out Gini's record a letter arrived on Spokane Metro Growth stationery. It sang the praises of a fine young man named Kevin Coe who had unlimited potential as a businessman and "high end" realty specialist. The letter was signed "X. Drew Butler." The real estate partners were hired.

55

[The psychopath] is pleasant and affable during his normal phases, which make up the greater part of his time. One gets the impression, however, that ordinary life is not very full or rich, that strange gods are ever calling him, and that the call is far dearer to his heart than anything else.—Hervey Cleckley, M.D., *The Mask of Sanity*

Emily Sykes, a slender twenty-six-year-old woman with dark-brown hair and smoky green eyes, barely listened as the man on the phone identified himself as a real estate agent. "I'll be in your neighborhood tomorrow," the mellow voice said, "and I wondered if you'd like your home appraised."

"No, thanks," she said. Every day there were more of these unsolicited calls. It wasn't as though she had a lot of free time on her hands. She and her husband both worked, and they were raising two small children. In their small South Hill home leisure time was too rare an item to be wasted on rug cleaners and real estate appraisers.

"Well, listen," the man said, his voice jumping from low to an urgent high as though he were afraid she might hang up, "you really ought to think about this. Our service is free, and—"

"We just bought this place. Why would we want to have it appraised?"

"Lots of reasons. Why don't you talk to your husband about it? Uh—is he there?"

"Yes."

"Well, mention it to him, would you? I'll call you back tomorrow."

He called the next evening. This time he sounded out of breath. "Well, did you ask your husband?"

"Yes, and he said no."

"Come on! Can't you work your husband better than that?"

"What do you mean?"

"Don't you have some female tricks to get what you want? Like when you're...hot?"

She hung up. She'd known all along there was something dingy about the guy. Just about every woman in the neighborhood had been receiving obscene calls lately. Hers had been mild compared to some she'd heard about.

A few evenings later, she was cooking chili when she heard a noise outside the house. She looked through the window but it was too dark to see, and the noise didn't repeat. Later that night she returned home from exercise class, and when she stepped from her sister's car she did a couple of jumping jacks to get a laugh. Suddenly she had a feeling she was being watched. Her sister stayed till she got inside safely.

Harper was home and she told him about her feeling. "ESP, huh?" her husband said, laughing. He went into the bathroom to brush his teeth and Emily switched on the TV. As she walked across the room she glanced at the tiny window in the front door. A man was staring at her. His hair was covered with a stocking cap, but she got a good look at his face. It was blocky and large, and the eyes sloped down toward the bridge of his nose.

She yelled, "Harper!" and snapped on the light, illuminating the porch and the carport. No one was there.

Her husband stepped outside in his bathrobe and looked around. "All quiet," he said.

Early the next morning a neighbor phoned. "Say, I didn't want to wake you, but did you hear my dog barking last night?"

"Yes," Emily said.

"It was some guy in your maple tree." Emily covered her mouth with her hand. The tree stood next to the children's swing set in a back yard encircled by a four-foot chain-link fence. A man in that tree could see into the bedroom window. "He was wearing a bluish jacket," the neighbor went on. "I guess he saw me, 'cause he jumped down and ran off."

That afternoon Emily's phone rang and a male voice asked, "Is Mr. Sykes there?" His voice shook so badly she thought he must be drunk or sick. Harper had been a social worker; maybe this was one of his people. They still called.

"He's not home right now. Can I help you?"

"Emily?"

"Yes?"

The voice lowered, just above a whisper. "I saw your cunt last night. Your tits, too. I'd like to lick them. I want to fuck you. Do you like to be fingerbanged? I'm masturbating now. I'm playing—"

"You sickie!" she said. "You...degenerate!" She slammed the phone down. It rang again.

"Hey, don't hang up!" His voice was louder now, more assured. "You made me mad when you hung up like that. Listen, I'm coming right over to fuck you." She lifted the phone from her ear and shook her head. When she listened again he was saying, "Do you like it top or bottom? I'm jacking off. I'm gonna come all over you. Oooh, suck me off! I'm gonna shoot my load all over you. I'm gonna come over and eat your cunt!"

"You just do that," she said. "I'll shoot your balls off and we'll end your problem."

She dialed the police. As she waited, her disgust turned to fear. Maybe she shouldn't have challenged the guy. Obscene callers could be dangerous. *I'm gonna come all over you.* Yuck! She reported, "A degenerate's called me twice and threatened to come over. If he shows up, I swear to God I'm gonna kill him."

"Don't shoot anybody, ma'am," the officer said calmly.

"Then send somebody to watch my house!" She loaded her pistol, a cheap plastic-grip .22 automatic that Harper had taken from a suicidal woman, and sat down to watch Merv Griffin with her children.

The calls continued for a week, the same shaky voice and fetid patter. A policeman told her that her aggressive reaction was exactly what the man had wanted. A detective visited the house and asked, "Have you heard about our jogging rapist?"

"The South Hill rapist?" she asked. Of course she'd heard about him. He'd struck six or eight times in this eastern part of the South Hill. "Yes. Sure."

"I think he's your boy. He likes small women with brown or auburn hair and pretty eyes. He's telling you the same things he's been telling the others."

Emily was shaken. She stopped answering the phone. She suffered from lupus, a serious disease, and she had enough trouble. She was on a strict diet to begin with, and now she couldn't eat a thing. She lost ten pounds in a week, and then the police asked her if she would mind leading the man on so they could trace the calls.

As soon as the taps were in place, the calls stopped. Then they resumed at the office where she worked—someone would ask the switchboard for Emily Sykes and breathe at her when she came on the line. After a few more days there was a call at home. Harper, listening in on the other phone, lost his temper and yelled, "I'm gonna get you for this, you motherfucker!" The connection died.

A detective told Emily, "He's setting you up. Keep your eyes open."

Emily and Harper worked out a system. She would pick him up at his office at the end of each day and let him off a block from the house so that he would be approaching as she drove up in the darkness. If anyone made a move toward her Harper intended to shoot him. In case his Saturday Night Special misfired, he carried a heavy oak staff to break the man's kneecaps.

No one showed up. The calls became sporadic. Twice the man made short calls in the middle of the night. The first time, Harper cursed him out. A few nights later the caller told Emily, "I'm gonna get you," and she snapped, "No you're not!"

Early on a dark November evening she was in the bathroom getting ready to go to a baby shower. At the kitchen table the children were painting themselves with Spaghetti-O's. Harper wasn't due home for a half hour. It had been snowing all afternoon, and she wasn't surprised when snowballs began thudding against the back door. It's kids, she thought, and turned on the outside light. Her yellow 1971 Capri was in the carport and nothing seemed disturbed. She had just returned to the bathroom when she heard a whiny noise. It sounded as though someone were rubbing a nylon ski jacket against the side of the house. She thought, I'm not going out to look this time. Harper'll be home in a few minutes.

The noise stopped and the gate behind the car began to rattle. Then her garbage cans clanked and there was a knock just under the bathroom window. She called police, grabbed the pistol and sat in total darkness with her two children, wishing to God that Harper would hurry. Police arrived but the intruder was gone. There were tracks in the snow under the bathroom window and a plank positioned against the chain-link fence for easy access to the yard.

The next day Emily was asked to go to police headquarters for an interview. A detective told her she was being stalked by the South Hill rapist. "That's the way he operates."

"Well, do something!" the frightened woman said.

For three or four days she was escorted to and from work by a police team. They staked out her house at night; she could spot the plainclothesmen herself, sitting down the block in an unmarked car. She decided that someone else must have spotted them, too. The harassment stopped.

56

Throughout the blustery November, panic built on the South Hill. There were rapes and attempted rapes, some unreported to police. The worst day of the month was the last: At 5:45 a.m. a woman was attacked as she walked toward her car on the lower part of the South Hill. She broke loose, jumped inside and locked the doors, and her assailant fled after exposing himself. Twelve hours later, in temperatures just above freezing, a sixteen-year-old girl stepped from a bus and was dragged into the yard of a vacant house. The child told police that her rapist wore jogging clothes and was a slender six-footer about twenty-eight years old.

In her new Chinese-red home Marie Oldham read a sentence from a brief newspaper article about the latest attack: "The incident is similar to several other rapes that have occurred over the past several months at different locations on the South Hill involving suspects wearing jogging clothes, police said."

Marie murmured to herself, So he's still out there. This was the third or fourth South Hill rape she'd heard about since her own, and only one had ended well. A woman had caught the rapist full in the face with a chemical spray. But he was back in action a few days later.

Marie had recovered from her injuries of five weeks before, but her peace of mind hadn't returned. For a few nights after the rape Tim had sat up with her; she would cry out with fear if he went out of the room. For a month since then, she'd been protected by helpful neighbors. She would get a ride home from work—buses were out of the question now—and stay with her friends till Tim got home. He postponed a business trip to Alaska and bought her a .38, but she knew she would never use it. In the five weeks since the rape, she'd lost sixteen pounds and all her self-confidence. I wonder, she asked herself, if I'll ever stop being so skitchety. She couldn't stop thinking, *He said he'd come back.*

Cassandra Bates slid the newspaper across the kitchen table to her husband Gregor and said, "Him again. Look! Thirty-seventh and Manito. That's up where he hit on me."

Greg read the item without comment. She asked herself, What can he say? We both know who this guy is and we can't tell a soul. Greg was right from the beginning. The cops would laugh me out of the building. And if they took me seriously they'd want to know why I didn't tell them about Coe a long time ago. All I can do is sit here and keep my mouth shut and hope the poor sick son of a bitch gets caught before he kills somebody.

After Gregor went to bed she sat up looking out the front window of the house on Twenty-third Ave., a few steps from Manito Park. The man on the business card had already been back in the neighborhood, driving a small gray car past her house in the predawn when she couldn't sleep. Once he'd peered straight at her window and smiled. Then the weird phone calls had started.

Cassie, she berated herself, you're a dumb helpless jerk. And *he* knows it too.

Spokane police officers felt disgraced by what was going on. At the Police Guild north of headquarters, they commiserated over bourbon and beer. On the street word flew from cop to cop and car to car: "Another one. Lincoln Heights"; "The bus route again"; "Behind Deaconess, a kid this time." Rape reports were copied and passed around. Officers read them and cursed. Morale had never been high on this top-heavy police force, and now it was at its lowest.

A few optimistic beatmen maintained the hope that they would somehow catch the rapist in the act, but everybody knew that a decoy exercise had failed a year before and the department was so shorthanded that most of the South Hill went unpatrolled in the hours of darkness.

Plainclothesman Steve Christian lived halfway up the hill, and his neighbors wouldn't let him forget that the police weren't doing their job. "We're doing every goddamned thing we can," the blunt-spoken Christian would say, but he didn't believe it himself. Almost a year had passed since the article "Sex Assaults Alert Police." Now a couple of overworked detectives were on the case and the South Hill was hotter than ever.

Christian, a forty-year-old Lee Marvin look-alike and sound-alike, was an odd man out on the Spokane PD. Injured in a fight with a prisoner, the fourteen-year veteran was on light duty. Every cop in town had heard him gripe about it. Along with his uniformed colleagues on the 3-to-11 swing shift, he also griped about the rapes. One day he went to his boss, Roscoe "Rock" Walker, and said, "Hey, why not let me help out on these rapes instead of what I'm doing?"

"You don't like chasing whores?" the lieutenant asked.

"Not when a psycho's running loose."

Walker smiled. Every harness bull fancied himself a Kojak. It wasn't a bad sign in a cop. He arranged for Christian to help out on the rapes. Bill Beeman gave the new hand a list of suspects. After some tailing, Christian said, "Hey, I can't watch ten guys. Why doesn't the chief set something up?"

"I don't know," Beeman said. "Probably because we're shorthanded, as usual."

Christian had an idea. He went back to his lieutenant and said, "Hey, how about a rape squad of our own? Just the guys from swing-shift patrol."

Rock Walker's face showed his surprise. Forty officers were assigned to the shift and on any given night about half that many were on duty. Pull off six or eight for a special squad and the city of Spokane would have about as much police protection as the average crossroads in the Palouse. "Look, Lieutenant, I know the strain on the roster," Christian said, "but these rapes are a strain, too. Jesus, you ought to hear my neighbors."

Walker promised to discuss the idea with the front office and his sergeants. A few days later he asked for volunteers. "You'll hate it," he told his men. "You'll work hard, and you probably won't turn up a damned thing."

Thirty-seven men applied. Christian took Walker aside and said, "We need about six guys to do this right, Lieutenant. Let me pick 'em. I don't want a bunch of fuck-offs. I'm as big a fuck-off as anybody, but this is different."

"Let's give 'em all a whack," the experienced Walker said.

So after a twenty-month siege on the South Hill, another special rape squad was formed at the suggestion of a bored patrolman. Christian's South Hill home was set up as a base station and manned around the clock. Sophisticated radios were brought in from out of state so the rapist couldn't monitor the squad's calls. After a struggle with the front office, the men were authorized to use their own cars instead of the department's easily spotted Chevrolets, another improvement on earlier techniques. Morale improved. At last the PD was doing something.

As a first step the special squad formed up in teams and began the tedious task of checking out likely suspects. Worksheets showed the men putting in sixty and seventy hours per week, and Christian and Lt. Walker knew that much of their time wasn't being logged. It was police work at its most frustrating.

There were fourteen suspects on the first hot list, none named Coe.

57

Eighteen-year-old *Patsy McCoy* was one of the few women in Spokane blithely unconcerned about the rapist. She was a straight-A freshman at Gonzaga University and had little time for newspapers or news shows or gossip with her mother's neighbors on the South Hill. She'd learned about self-defense from a book her mother owned, advising women to knee assailants in the crotch. When the advice was repeated aloud at home, her father and three brothers looked sick and went "Ooooooh!"

After school on a cold Friday, December 12, she shopped downtown and boarded the Lincoln Park bus for home. She got off around 8 p.m. and walked toward the family home in the tree-shaded southeast corner of the South Hill. She stood five feet four and weighed 100 pounds and she was bent over with gift-wrapped boxes, a backpack, her red purse and a brainload of doctrines and theories. She was taking eighteen heavy credits—"to get my money's worth," she explained to friends—and finals were coming up in the next few days in history, political science, economics and psychology.

The area around Thirty-fifth and Regal seemed darker tonight than usual. Thin patches of snow and ice forced her to slow down. She intended to stash the Christmas gifts at home and return to the Gonzaga dorm for an all-night study session. She was trying to remember a quote about economics when a man walked up behind her. She decided he must be a friend playing a joke.

Then she heard, "I have a knife. Do what I say. Don't scream."

She screamed. An arm looped around her neck and a gloved hand slid down her throat. There were houses nearby, but she couldn't force a sound through the heavy leather. As the man dragged her into a front yard she caught a glimpse of him in the light from a window. He wore a dark stocking cap and a bulky ski coat. She couldn't see his face; he was taking pains to stay behind her.

He released his strange grip on her throat and said, "Put down your pack!" She clutched it like a security blanket and screamed again. He grabbed her by the back of the head and rammed her face in the snowy dirt. My God, she thought, what'll I do now? I'll pretend I'm dead and when he lets go I'll scream again. He relaxed his pressure and she kicked him in the crotch. He rammed his glove back down her throat. "Drop the goddamn pack!" he said hoarsely. She broke loose and aimed another kick, and he hit her with a wild swing and then shoved his hand so far down that he sealed off her windpipe. Just before she started to black out, she punched him in the crotch as hard as she could.

He said "Ooooooh!" just like her father and brothers, then yanked at her long winter coat and tried to roll her over. She kicked him and tore at his face and his clothes. He punched her in the upper arm and her coat came off as she broke loose and ran. He brought her down with a tackle and stuck his hand in her throat again. The struggle went on for five or six minutes, with pine needles and bark flying and the night air rent by her screams and his low mutterings and curses. She warned herself that her life was at stake. Rape didn't enter her mind. She was convinced he was a killer. When he removed his hand she let loose a banshee scream. He limped away like a wounded animal.

Gini Perham didn't get home from work till after nine. She wasn't surprised that Kevin wasn't there. These days he came and went as he pleased and offered no explanation. She decided to prepare her dinner and let him make his own when he came home—*if* he came home. She hated to believe he was with another woman, but where else could he be night after night?

She had just opened a package of frozen corn when she heard a noise on the back porch. She looked up and saw Kevin standing in the bitter cold in his gray jogging suit, the top halfway open as though the zipper had jammed. His bare chest showed, and he was trembling. She opened the door and said, "Kevin! Why are you dressed like that? It's below freezing!"

"I've been j-j-jogging." Cloudlets of frost puffed from his mouth and his nostrils.

She pointed to a rip in his pants. "What happened?"

"I fell. Listen, the Citation quit." He rushed his words. "You've got to drive me there. Where the hell have you been?"

"I just got home."

He bumped past her into the kitchen and said, "I ran all the way to the pay phone in Lincoln Heights and you didn't answer. You told me you'd be home early."

"I had to show a house."

"You'd think I could depend on you just once."

She decided not to argue. He was in one of his moods. They got into her blue Monte Carlo and he ordered her to drive south on Regal. As they approached the intersection at Thirty-fifth, he kept jerking his head around as though on the lookout. She said, "Don't you think we should have called a tow truck?"

He ignored her remark and directed her a block west and then a block south. When they came to a quiet residential street he said, "Park at the end."

The Citation was against the curb but facing the wrong way. "How'd you manage to end up like that?" she asked.

"Go home," he said. He jumped from her car and scanned the area.

She said, "I'll wait and make sure it starts."

"It'll start." He sounded tense, but he was holding his voice to a stage whisper. "You go—*home!*"

She insisted on waiting. She had no intention of leaving him stranded again to repeat the same scenario. He got in the Citation and the engine caught on the first try. After fifteen or twenty minutes he arrived home with a sack of groceries.

The next morning the usually placid Bill Beeman suppressed an urge to slam his fist into the wall. An overnight report lay open in front of him. The night before, a surveillance team from the newly formed special squad had been sitting on a hot suspect, a known kink whose description matched the South Hill rapist's. While the plainclothesmen had been watching the suspect talking on the phone, an attempted rape had gone down near Thirty-fifth and Regal. The MO was unmistakable.

Beeman scratched the suspect's name from a list that was diminishing fast. It was becoming more and more likely that the South Hill rapist was someone totally unknown to the Spokane PD, a man with no police record and no overt criminal tendencies. If so, it might take years to catch him. Beeman was due to retire in two months. *Not* catching the South Hill rapist wasn't his idea of the perfect way to go out. The veteran homicide detective looked at his calendar. It was Saturday, December 13, 1980. The attempted rape of the night before had failed. If the rapist followed his pattern, he wouldn't wait long to strike again.

Four days later, on a dark Wednesday afternoon, brown-haired *Stephanie Gibbs* waited at a bus stop in the eastern part of the South Hill. A man threw her to the snow, shoved two gloved fingers down her throat and told her he had a knife. She saw a down jacket, jeans and running shoes but not his face.

When he asked if she masturbated she noticed that he spoke pleasantly, barely above a whisper. He forced his penis into her, but she told the police she wasn't sure he had an orgasm because she wasn't sure what an orgasm was. She was fourteen.

58

Two nights after the Gibbs rape, realtor Anne Munroe Wilson gave a holiday party for fifty friends and invited her colleagues Kevin Coe and Gini Perham. Coe arrived alone, oddly dressed for someone who usually appeared in public in three-piece suits and color-coordinates. He was wearing a brown suede-cloth suit and disco shirt with no tie, and carrying an expensive-looking brown leather coat. His hair was combed, but he looked as though he hadn't shaved for a few days.

The hostess greeted him at the door. "Say, uh, Ann," Coe said, "I'm trying to sell this." He held out the leather coat for her to touch. "Pass the word, will you? Sixty, seventy bucks. And I've got two more just like it, one in evergreen and one in black."

"Kevin, this is a three-hundred-dollar jacket!"

"I need the bucks."

Ann asked him what he would like to drink. "You know I don't drink," he said. "Besides, I'm on a fast."

"What about some orange juice?"

"Reconstituted?"

"Well, yes, but it's pure."

"Don't you mix it with tapwater?"

"Sure."

"Then it isn't pure. I only drink bottled water." She remembered his diet from one of their talks. The whole routine had the earmarks of an attention-getting device. He would fast down to nothing, and all the women in the office would beg him to eat before he collapsed. She found him some Perrier and led him through air layered with cigarette smoke to a table where she'd set out eighteen or twenty trays of food. "Are you sure you won't have a snack?" she asked.

He looked at the table and said, "You don't have anything that meets my standards."

The hostess laughed. She was thinking what a tactless remark that would have been from anyone else. But she knew Kevin—it was just his way. "Come on," she said. "Bend a little. How many times do you get to come to my place?"

"There's nothing pure here," he repeated, an eyebrow arching.

"The turkey's absolutely pure," she lied. She'd cooked the bird with wine and seasonings, but she wanted the poor man to eat. With his stubble and his skinniness he was beginning to look like a derelict. She left him to greet a new arrival. When she glanced his way again, he was gobbling turkey and the serving plate was almost empty. After a while a drunk jostled him and spilled juice on the coat. Kevin stalked out the door without comment.

A few days later a Crane realtor named Lyle Hatcher was offered the leather jacket for fifty dollars. "It's a steal," Coe told him, handing the coat over for examination.

Hatcher was a short, handsome fashion plate. "Kevin," he said, "this is glove leather. This coat's valuable."

"I need cash, man."

"I'm not in the market for a coat, but I'll tell you what. Here's the fifty. I'll just keep the coat for you and when you make a big commission you can have it for the same price. Fair?"

"Fair," Coe agreed.

Back at his desk, Hatcher examined his buy. It was in excellent shape except for scratches above an elbow and a few dark stains on the chest panels. He tried the coat on and was pleased to see that it fit perfectly. He was five seven and Coe was six feet. He wondered if he had inadvertently purchased hot goods, but he'd never known Kevin to be dishonest.

59

At his home in the Spokane Valley, D. Jay Williams started a rape file to send to his congressman. He also considered patrolling his childhood haunts on the South Hill the way he'd once patrolled Vietnam as a Marine—with a loaded M-16. "Honey, we're *different* now," Sue told the newly appointed elder of their church.

"Well, I'm sorry," Williams said, "but the last girl he raped was fourteen. The one before that weighed a hundred pounds. He's going after children now. If it comes to protecting you and the kids, I'll do what I have to do. I'll—"

"Jay!"

"—blow him away."

Williams's morning *Spokesman-Review* began arriving at the breakfast table with cut-out holes and missing pages. His wife was deleting items about rape. "It isn't worth watching you have a heart attack," she explained. One December afternoon he came to an abrupt stop on the sidewalk in front of a grocery store in his neighborhood. Someone had stenciled a scarlet silhouette of a prone female form and the inscription: "A Woman Was Raped Here." A few days later the same message appeared on the walkway in front of his church.

As Christmas approached Williams found himself worrying about Fred Coe. It looked as though his old friend might be passing beyond eccentricity. Telephone calls to his house elicited a charged silence or a bass voice saying, "*Metro.*"

Real estate friends asked what was wrong with Coe—they called him and he answered but he wouldn't talk. Sometimes he made strange guttural noises, as though something were wrong with the phone line, and sometimes the caller could hear him set the phone on the floor and walk across the room. Jay tried a special approach. He would call and say, "Fred! *Fred!* I know you're there." Usually Coe would respond.

Williams took him aside. "Everybody's talking about the way you answer your telephone lately. You don't seem to understand. When you pick up the phone you're supposed to say hello. What's going on?"

"Jeni's charging calls to my number and the phone company's bugging my line. I'm keeping a low profile."

Fred's telephone manners enhanced his growing reputation as a harmless flake. But Jay knew more alarming examples of his friend's irrationality. He'd heard one story from his own father, a prominent Spokane businessman. Fred had opened an account at a bank so far north on Division Street that it was barely in the city limits. Day after day he would show up to perform petty banking tasks—cashing a check for five dollars that could have been cashed anywhere in Spokane, or demanding change for a small bill. One day a teller watched Coe stand in a corner and stare at Jay's father for fifteen minutes. Later the teller told Mr. Williams, "His name is Kevin Coe. He shows up on one pretext or another, but his address is on the South Hill and he works in the valley. Do you suppose he's casing the place?"

"He's no bank robber," said Don Williams. "He's my son's oldest friend."

"Why would he be staring at you?"

"He's *always* stared at people. He's a little odd."

More than a little, Jay Williams decided when he heard the story. He confided his fears to John Nyberg, the third member of their old triumvirate. "There's something wrong, Humpy," Jay said. "I've never known him to be so weird and uptight. It's like he's daydreaming all the time." Williams lowered his voice. "I honestly think he's insane."

"You're exaggerating!"

"I wish I were. Look, he's always been eccentric, right?"

"Yeah, but don't tell *him* that."

Jay laughed. Coe detested the word. Just a few days earlier he'd said emphatically, "I'm not eccentric, Jay; *you're* eccentric. I have a few peccadilloes, that's all. Hey, we're supposed to promote each other! *Semper fideles. Esprit de corps!* If people say I'm unusual or eccentric, just tell them I'm, uh—a colorful individualist."

Williams brought Nyberg up to date on Fred's latest activities. "It's as though he's become so weird he can't hide it."

"Maybe we should talk to his father," Nyberg suggested.

"We sure couldn't talk to his mother—she'd call *us* crazy."

"What do you think's bothering him?" Nyberg asked.

Jay pondered the question. "I don't know," he said. "There's an undercurrent in his life that we don't know anything about."

The next morning Williams woke up wishing he could take back his words. By daylight things looked different. Fred would be upset. He'd always been sensitive about how he was perceived by others. Jay was ashamed of himself. He decided to tell Coe about the conversation and pass it off as a joke. If he didn't the ebullient Nyberg might spill the secret. He told Fred, "I talked to Humpy last night. I told him you were, uh—insane."

"You told him *what*?"

"I told him you ought to be put away."

"And he *believed* you?" Coe looked aghast.

"Of course. I gave him evidence."

Fred's voice took on an edge of anger. Jay was afraid that for the first time in twenty-five years one of them was going to yell at the other. "What the hell'd you tell him *that* for?"

Jay answered with a code expression from their F. Scott Fitzgerald days. "Just a spot of humor, old sport. No harm, surely." In the past that would have been the end of the matter.

Coe said, "Humpy'll *believe* you, for God's sake!"

"Of course he'll believe me." Williams was beginning to lose confidence in his ability to finesse the situation. "That's why it's, uh—such a great joke."

"You've got to retract! Tell him you didn't mean it."

"How can I retract a joke? He'll know you put me up to it and then he'll be *more* convinced you're crazy."

"I'll straighten it out myself."

Later Jay learned that Coe had called Nyberg, then followed up with a letter reaffirming his sanity. When Jay heard about the double disclaimer, he was more convinced of his friend's imbalance.

Gini Perham found herself wishing that Jay Williams had never opened his mouth. For days Kevin raved and stomped about the apartment. "He told Nyberg I'm insane!" he said over and over. "He actually said that!" Then he would ask her, "Do you think I'm crazy?"

"No, Kevin."

"Do I act crazy?"

"No. Sometimes a little eccentric, that's all."

"Goddamn it, Gini, I'm not eccentric!"

After his letter to Nyberg he showed her a note he was about to mail to Williams. She glanced at the words. His main point was that he, Kevin, wasn't the one who was crazy. He enclosed one of Jay's pictures on a business card. The teeth were erased and there was a scar across the face.

60

Psychopathy, possibly more than other mental disorders, threatens the safety, the serenity, and the security of American life.—William and Joan McCord, *The Psychopath*

Fear took over the South Hill after the attack on little Patsy McCoy and the rape of Stephanie Gibbs. The red-stenciled message seemed to pop up on every street corner. The Rape Crisis Center began classes in self-defense; many women were afraid to leave home to attend. Landlords were stuck with the apartments of women who forfeited their deposits and moved to a safer part of town. Some left Spokane for good.

As the holidays approached, subtle changes of life-style began in the shadows of the tall ponderosas and the flickering light from manger displays and Christmas trees. Doors were chained and triple-locked. Women were rarely seen without escorts. "People who used to walk a block or two to the store drive their cars now," said a nurse at Deaconess Hospital. "Some wait till daylight to walk the dog." Buses were thrown off schedule by females who insisted the drivers watch them to their doors. Therapists' appointment books filled up.

Merchants and businessmen soon began to worry about the financial effect on a city that depended on out-of-town patronage. The president of the chamber of commerce lamented that he was hearing about the rapes at national conventions: "We will be sitting around at coffee-break time in some place like Hartford and somebody says, 'Oh, yeah, Spokane. We heard you really have a problem with rape up there.'"

Said another businessman, "With logging and mining down and Kaiser mechanizing, our economic base has been dwindling in recent years, and we're trying to make up for it by wooing high-tech industries. You do that with quality of life, parks, public safety—amenities. But you don't have any quality of life if your wife has to carry a gun to put out the garbage."

Salesmen peddled chemical sprays from their cars, and big chains like Rosauer's offered them in chic leather holsters. The General Store on North Division Street dispensed almost five hundred cans of immobilizing spray in December alone. Full-page newspaper ads advertised firearms for females, and in gun shops like The Trap House and the Gunatorium the delicate smell of feminine perfumes mingled with the smell of leather and gun oil.

A beery vigilante movement resurfaced. Red-eyed young men patrolled the dark streets in pickups and Jeeps, pegging occasional warning shots at traffic signs and street lights. Supermarket parking lots and school playgrounds were illuminated overnight in response to public demand, and parts of the Lilac City were as bright at 4 a.m. as they were at noon. "When I go home I feel like I'm entering a war zone," complained reporter Rita Hibbard of the *Spokesman-Review*. "People spend half their time comparing notes—'Did you hear that weird noise last night?' 'Look at these tracks under my window.' You pick up the craziest rumors. 'He raped a paraplegic in her wheelchair.' 'He always rapes by moonlight.' 'He was seen in Manito Park totally nude.'"

Letter writers demanded action. The *Chronicle* solicited tips under its Secret Witness program, and callers seeking the thousand-dollar payoff tied up the listed phone number, which doubled as the private line of managing editor Gordon Coe. Friends of Patsy McCoy wrote an irate letter pointing out that one of the finest and smallest of Spokane's citizens had been victimized not only by a rapist but by a police department that had invited the madman to strike by its long record of inefficiency. Citizens phoned open-line radio shows with suggestions for proper punishment of the rapist: castration and stoning were high on the list, and one caller suggested that his eyes be pierced with an icepick.

"This scare is traumatizing the most livable neighborhood on earth," Dr. Craig Olson confided to an out-of-town relative. "It's not only frightening, it's infuriating. The other day Johnny Little and I were trying to figure out what we would do if we caught this guy raping somebody. We decided we'd probably kill him. John Little, a law-abiding dentist, and me, a physician sworn to help humanity. That's how bad things are."

Gini Perham was equally furious, and so were her brothers and sisters-in-law and most of her friends. She was glad she could blow off steam with them, because the subject seemed to be anathema to Kevin and his parents. No Coe ever brought up the rapes, and when Gini mentioned the subject herself they looked at her as though questioning her taste. At home Kevin listened to her rages and her theories noncommittally, or, more often, jumped up and left.

By early December, he was making unplanned trips almost every night. Around 9 or 10 he would speed westward on Twenty-ninth. An hour or two later he would return and refuse to discuss where he'd been. If she insisted he would use his stopper: "Prying again, Gini?"

With every passing day he was becoming more inscrutable. He returned from his jogs with welts and scratches; he seemed to have made jogging a contact sport. She asked, "What makes you fall down so much? You're not that big a klutz, are you?" He didn't answer. His heavy, hand-sewn gloves were ripped and torn.

For several weeks she'd noticed that the morning *Spokesman-Review* hadn't arrived. Sometimes she would come home from her new job at Roger Crane & Associates and find the afternoon *Chronicle* missing too. It took her a while to catch on. Kevin was getting rid of the papers. Why? Another mystery. There were so many.

For a month he drove his mother's Cadillac while the Citation was being repaired again. Gini thought nothing of going under the hood of her Monte Carlo, but Kevin didn't even keep his car's oil and water topped. Frequently the little hatchback would overheat; once they had to sit in a cloud of steam awaiting rescue, and another time the engine froze. Apparently the problem was an old one. Once he'd forgotten to put oil in a car he was driving across the Nevada desert; the engine had been a total loss. Gini wondered what kind of person would spend hours waxing a car and then let the engine burn up. Was it forgetfulness, or was he supremely preoccupied? With what?

In return for the loan of her Cadillac, Ruth Coe made frequent demands on him to drive her around. Through these short, dreary days, mother and son sniped at each other constantly, and Kevin became unusually tense. As Christmas approached, Gini found herself developing a soft spot for Gordon Coe. He was often in the crossfire and yet she never heard him complain. For a long time she'd thought he was indifferent to her, but once Kevin had come back from Five Pines and told her, "Gordo likes you, V.K! I can't believe it. You're the first woman I ever went with that he acknowledged or approved."

One tense evening Gini tried to make conversation by asking Mr. Coe if there was anything new on the South Hill rapes. He looked up from a magazine and smiled at her. "Not that I know of," he said. She couldn't remember ever hearing him discuss an unpleasant subject. When hostilities arose he played the peacemaker. She wondered if he had any idea how Ruth and Kevin discounted him. Just the other day Kevin had mused, "You and I ought to get married and move away to some nice warm place. And we can take Ruth with us!"

Gini longed to discuss the South Hill rapes with the old newsman. She was worried about her safety and angered about what the attacker was doing to her home town. A managing editor would know things. But it was obvious that he didn't want to talk.

She decided not to attend a Christmas dinner at Five Pines. It had been a peculiar holiday season; Kevin had refused to permit a tree, and there was no snow. She missed her own mother and didn't want to be around Ruth Coe. "Come on, V.K.," Kevin had insisted. "Gordo likes to see you."

"Hug him for me." She realized how silly that must sound. In all the times she'd seen the Coes together there'd been a bare minimum of physicality. How cold the family seemed compared to her own.

On the day after Christmas Kevin brought up Five Pines again. "Listen, we've got to go out there. Barefax set a place for you yesterday and you hurt her feelings."

Gini felt bad. Whatever else she thought about Ruth Coe, she knew the woman was lonesome. "Sure, let's go," she said.

She was surprised at what she saw in the house on Dyer Rd. The holiday decor seemed to consist of a white silver bowl filled with Hershey's Kisses in red and green foil, a few Christmas balls in another bowl, and a wreath. When she was alone in the kitchen with Ruth she asked why they'd taken down their tree so soon. "We didn't have one," Ruth explained. "We don't go in for that. It's all so commercialized."

On the way home Gini asked when they'd had their last tree. "Years ago," Kevin said.

"Strange," she said.

"What's strange about it?" His voice had an edge. "What's such a big deal about a Christmas tree?" She decided it would be a waste of time to tell him.

In the bedroom that night she stepped on something round and cold. "My God," she shrieked, "what's that?"

Kevin grabbed it. "Just a joke. A friend of mine sent it from Seattle. It's a dildo."

"A what?"

"A dildo. A replica of a penis." He held it out. The thing was over a foot long, four or five inches thick, made of flesh-colored plastic or rubber. "Hey, Gin," he said, "wouldn't it be funny if somebody pulled up at a stop sign and I was sitting alongside holding this in my lap?" He didn't laugh; he almost never laughed.

She told herself, This situation's getting a little too strange for me. I'd better make my move. Maybe I could live with one of my brothers for a while. At least we'd have a Christmas tree.

61

I hope to one fine day soon be sipping Perrier at the Plaza, holding court with the ghosts of Gatsby and Fitzgerald.... Ah, the glory of it all! The big time! But until that sweet mirage materializes I will, as Gatsby, merely drift on against the current.
—Fred Coe, March 11, 1982

Jenifer Coe was back in Spokane for the holidays, but she was staying as far as possible from the Coe residence in the valley. The ex-Mrs. Fred Coe had interrupted her boozy tour of the United States to make a Christmas visit to her twin sons, her parents and her bedridden sister Sonia.

She found herself uneasy from the second she arrived. She had fled a court-ordered alcoholism program the last time she'd left Spokane, and bench warrants were out for her arrest. But far more disconcerting was the fact that she had to deal with The Great Enigma. She phoned a few days after Christmas and told him she was in town. "Great!" he said. "Can we meet someplace?"

She knew from local sources that Virginia Perham had moved into the yellow house; it no longer bothered her. But she'd left her best clothes there and wanted to make arrangements to pick them up. "We can meet wherever you say, Fred," she told him. He suggested the next day at noon in Riverfront Park.

In the four months since her latest exodus from her home town Jeni Coe had kept up a barrage of phone calls—third-number billings, collect and credit-card, some $3,000 still unpaid—and when she wanted to talk to someone, she meant instantly. She thought nothing of making a half-dozen calls in a row looking for Fred. She had raging battles with operators and was often cut off. When she was asked if she had any message it was always the same. "Tell that son of a bitch to send money—or else!"

She was famous around the *Chronicle* office. If she was told that the managing editor was unavailable, she went off like a Roman candle. Once she said, "If you don't get *Mister* Coe to the phone inside of one minute, I'm gonna take my four iron to *Mister* Coe's house! And you can be the one to explain to *Mister* Coe how it happened."

She talked one day to an editor. "Oh, God," she said, "Gordon's not there? Do you know where Fred is?"

"Fred?"

"His son, for Christ's sake! Don't you know who Gordon's son is?" The conversation went on and on. She kept repeating that she admired the husband but detested the wife. "That bitch! She stole my dog! But Gordon—he's a gentleman. By the way, is he there now?"

"No, ma'am. I just told you. He's not in." The editor left a note on his boss's desk: "Your daughter-in-law called."

Later Mr. Coe advised him, "Hang up the next time. She's a drunk. And she has a vivid imagination."

Jay and Sue Williams took dozens of calls from the angry woman, but one night Sue told her husband that she had dealt with Jeni for the last time. "She curses the operator. She curses Fred. And she says *awful* things about Mrs. Coe. I can't stand that kind of talk about somebody's mom."

From then on Jay fielded the calls. He'd known Jeni as a tragic figure given to bouts of self-pity, but now she seemed almost hallucinatory. "He was violent to me," she raved one night. "Did you know that? He, he—hit me!"

"I can't buy that, Jeni," Jay said. "Fred's never been a violent person."

"I could put that bastard away for a hundred years."

"*You* could put *Fred* away?"

"You're goddamned right." There was a pause as though she were trying to decide whether to reveal more. "Did you know we once walked out on a hundred straight meals? And he put me on the street panhandling? That's how devoted a husband he was."

A few days later Jay asked Fred if the charges were true.

"No," he insisted. "I never walked out on a meal in my life, and I never harmed *any* woman. I *love* women! Jeni's the violent one. She pulled knives on me, golf clubs. She threw things. She's, she's—irrational."

"What about the panhandling?"

Coe smiled. "Oh, yeah, I made her do that. And she was *good* at it!" Jay wondered why he showed so much concern about the charge of wife-beating and so little about the panhandling. Both seemed varieties of wife abuse. It was another example of his insensitivity.

Around Christmastime Williams picked up the phone at 4 a.m. and heard Jenifer demand Fred's whereabouts. When he said he didn't know, she became angry and told him she would see him and Sue in the ground. The next day Jay told Coe, "Listen, Jeni's out of control. If she calls here again somebody's gonna have a lot of problems."

Fred promised to intervene. A maudlin Jeni called that night, swearing that she'd never meant any harm, that she loved Jay and Sue and their children, loved *all* children, loved animals, too. Jay thanked her and asked her not to bother them again. She cried and gave her word.

There were Christmas decorations in the nursing home and a Madonna on the wall over Sonia's head. "Nobody understands," Jenifer said. "I've been on the road for over a year, Sonia, and nobody understands."

"Do you?" Sonia asked gently.

Jeni wiped her eyes. "I didn't have a choice, Sonia. I was afraid! He made me into...something different. I have no business sitting in bars, but they're warm and I can meet people and nobody'll come up and beat hell out of me." Jeni walked to the window. "I just live a day at a time. Sometimes I'll take a job waitressing or babysitting, but then I hit the road again. Portland, Las Vegas, Boise. Brooklyn, Staten Island. New London, Connecticut. I met some nice Irish people in Brooklyn. And I've met some not-so-nice people. I wonder how I survived. Where'd I get the nerve to go out on my own?"

"It's always hard to meet people," Sonia said.

"I ride a lot with truckers. They buy me food. I don't eat right, you know, Sonia? A beer driver in Portland ripped me off for seventy dollars. In Idaho some jerk stole my purse in a bar. One guy drove off with my suitcases when I went to the restroom."

"But why, Jeni? Why put yourself at the mercy of people like that?"

"I wish I knew. I have nightmares where I'm back with Fred and he's getting ready to do another crazy thing. He fooled so many people. I just can't explain. Sometimes I even miss him. Oh, Sonia, it's confusing."

"If he upsets you so much, why keep calling him?"

"I don't know. I lived with him all those years. I wake up in a strange city and I call and he says, 'Come home, Pooky, come home. You're safe here, Sweet Bird.' But I'm not! Nobody's safe near that man! He twists your mind, he steers you one way and jerks you another. I know better than to come home to him. It's easier to go out and be a minstrel."

"Will you be seeing him this trip?"

"Tomorrow. To make arrangements to pick up my clothes."

"Don't let him hurt you again."

"Don't worry, Sonia. I won't."

She saw him standing in the rain by the glassed-in carousel next to the rolling green lawns of Riverfront Park. He had the same look, studiously cool, his hair in bangs almost to his eyes. A mini-dog frisked at his feet. Those Coes, she thought—they're incomplete without their pets. I wonder what his mother did with my collie. She walked up and said, "Hi, Fred."

He said, "Oh, hi, Jeni," and began backing away, the dog at his heels. He disappeared behind a small building as two men in business suits approached in the rain.

They took her by the arms. "Jenifer Coe?" one said.

"Y-yes."

"You're under arrest."

1981

62

On the first night of the new year, a few days after Jeni Coe's arrest, a thirty-two-year-old woman walked under leafless trees in a rape zone on the lower part of the South Hill. The temperature hovered just above freezing, as it often had during this unusually mild winter, and she was wearing a light coat. She knew what had been going on in the neighborhood and she was prepared. In a deep pocket she clutched a pressurized canister of "orthochlorobenzal-malononitrite," also known as "CS spray."

Just after 10 p.m. she noticed a jogger heading toward her. She took out the tube of tear gas and rotated the top to the cocked position. She thought how silly she'd have felt a few months before, but by now her actions were as routine on the South Hill as raising an umbrella.

She relaxed a little when the runner stopped in front of an apartment and leaned over as though to tie his shoe. He looked to be athletically built, of medium height, twenty-five to thirty years old, about 180 pounds. Sandy-colored hair spilled to his shoulders from under a light-colored stocking cap, and he wore a gray jogging outfit. She watched intently as he stood up and resumed his run. When he drew abreast she swerved away, but he clamped a hand over her mouth. He was dragging her toward the bushes when she sprayed him full in the face.

He cried out and ran. The woman called the police. A dog lost the hot trail after following it for a block. It appeared that the man had made his getaway in a car.

Nine hours later a deceptively small but strong young woman left her house on the South Hill and tromped through the morning haze toward the Lincoln Park bus stop. Annie Jaksich matched the rapist's composite favorite target. She was thirty-three and looked like a teen. She was five-three, slender, with dark-brown hair and big green eyes.

The Lincoln Park bus route had played a part in ten or twelve of the South Hill rapes, but Mrs. Jaksich wasn't worried. Beneath her little-girl appearance she was a skilled athlete who trounced most of the men she competed against. Relaxed and assured, she'd made up her mind that if the South Hill rapist ever threatened her with his knife, he would wind up eating it.

She reached the stop ten minutes ahead of time for the 7 a.m. bus that ran north to the YMCA, where this morning she would be teaching children to swim. The sun had just come up when she noticed a man walking in her direction. He was wearing gray sweats and a navy blue down vest. Light-brown hair curled from under his stocking cap. She thought, This is odd. He's dressed like a runner but he's not running. . . .

She reached into her bag, drew out a racquetball racquet and stepped onto the grass strip between the street and the sidewalk. The man approached, fumbling with his crotch. He pulled one hand away to reveal a penis a foot long. As he approached in a prancing walk, she saw that it was an imitation. She wondered why she didn't feel threatened. Did flashers rape? The whole thing was just too damned silly. He looked like anybody else from the neighborhood.

Then he lunged. She leaped into the street and whipped the racquet in a vicious forehand that left her arm cocked and ready for a quick backhand stroke. He raised the penis like a protective shield. "Don't you want to touch it?" he asked.

"Get out of here!" she said.

A car approached and the man ran. She stayed in the street just in case, and when the car passed and the man began to drift her way again, she ran for home. The police didn't seem interested.

63

The next day, Saturday, January 3, turned out to be a long one for Gini Perham. The real estate business had slowed to a dead stop during the holidays, but now a few customers had begun showing up at Roger Crane & Associates, and she welcomed the opportunity to take them around. If you didn't show, you didn't sell. After a grueling day she stumbled home tired and hopeful. Kevin wasn't there. She slumped into her black Mediterranean-style chair and leafed through a copy of the *Spokesman-Review*. Her tired eyes caught a headline: "Woman Foils Rape Attempt." The article told how a woman had Maced a man who attempted to rape her two nights before on the lower South Hill. Reporter John Harris had concluded:

> The assailant's description resembled that of a man who has attacked other women on the South Side during the past year.
> He was white, 25 to 30 years old, about 5-feet-9 and 180 pounds. His shoulder-length hair was sandy-colored. He wore a gray jogging suit and a light-colored stocking cap.

Hey, great! Gini exulted to herself. Somebody gave that creep what he needs. She remembered smelling tear gas while standing on the back porch talking to Kevin. The biting aroma had drifted away in a minute or two and she'd put it out of her mind. That had been a month or two ago. Now she wondered, Could someone have gassed him by mistake? Every woman in town was trigger-happy. She wondered why he hadn't told her about it. But then he hadn't told her much of anything lately.

She returned to her paper. She had just reached the sports pages when her summer-green eyes opened wide and she began to tremble. She reread the description on page 5. Everything except the height fit Kevin.

She walked from room to room trying to calm herself. Then she remembered the basement, the first place he went after his mysterious absences. She stood at the top of the steps, too frightened to go down and look. She decided to turn him in anonymously. But she couldn't call the police; they'd arrive with their sirens and lights, and what would she tell them? "I know it's him because he's *weird*"? She had no evidence, just a packet of information and coincidence.

She thought of the *Chronicle*'s Secret Witness Program. That was the answer! Her tip would direct attention to Kevin and the police would do the rest. There was a reward; she wouldn't dream of claiming it. No one would ever know. She got the phone number from the police operator. She took a deep breath and blew a curl of reddish-brown hair off her forehead. God, she thought, what a *heavy* move! Then she dialed.

The phone rang and rang. She looked at her watch: It was just after 9. Maybe they didn't man the phones on Saturday nights. She would try again in the morning.

An hour passed and Kevin didn't arrive. She wondered if she was acting silly. She'd read somewhere that women were reporting their men by the dozens and police were swamped with tips. She thought, Am I turning in an innocent man just because he's a little different? She slept on the problem.

In the morning she awoke in shock at what she had nearly done. *Thank God no one answered the phone.* She was so chagrined that she considered telling Kevin when he returned from his predawn jog. But she held back. He would think she'd flipped.

64

Jeni Coe spent seven days in the Spokane jail. The judge set a high bond when he heard that she'd ignored two bench warrants.

Kevin arrived in the visiting room the first night, full of his usual optimism. "I'm gonna buy you a house of your own, Pooky. I'll take care of you the rest of your life, don't worry. Next week I'm starting my new real estate program. You'll never have to worry about money again."

"Is that why you got me arrested?" she asked.

"Hey, I was as surprised as you! That's why I took off. I thought those cops were creditors."

She knew he'd set her up, and she told her jailers she didn't want to see him again. The night before she was to go to court she heard an outcry in the corridor and recognized Fred's voice. A jailer told her later that he'd become enraged when he learned that he wasn't welcome.

Jeni saw the whole cast at the hearing: Fred, Ruth, Gordon, even Virginia Perham. She wished she could tell the girlfriend a few things about Fred, but she knew it would be a waste of words. The judge reviewed the case and rebuked her for "grossly irresponsible" behavior. Yes, Your Honor, she thought, I know it was grossly irresponsible. I wish I could explain how it all happened, but it would take days, not hours, and I want to get out of here. I've got to get away from these people!

Ruth stared, her eyes narrowed to slits. One of the charges, malicious mischief, had been brought at her behest. Some justice, Jeni thought. She trashed our car twice and I trashed hers once; now I'm in court and she's a spectator. It was Fred's fault, as usual. He'd refused to report his mother. Twice he'd lied to the insurance company about what had happened to the Oldsmobile.

The judge droned on. Jeni tried to look obsequious. She perked up as he explained that he was suspending sentence provided she complete the alcoholism treatment. She recited, "Thank you, Your Honor." She knew that the second she escaped this courthouse and the Coes, she was leaving Spokane for good.

*　*　*

Gini Perham hadn't looked forward to the hearing. Ever since Kevin's trial, courtrooms had filled her with dread. But he'd insisted the family needed her support. The Coe delegation sat in the front of the small gallery like the wealthiest members of a congregation. When sentence was pronounced, Gini felt that justice had been served. Poor Jeni needed help, not a jail sentence. She wasn't a criminal.

At the doorway to the hall, Ruth turned and stared down at Jeni, seated with her mother. A familiar look came over Ruth's face: lower jaw stuck out, teeth bared, eyes narrowed. It was pure animal hatred. Jenifer moved her lips—it looked as though she mouthed "bitch!" Gordon nudged Ruth and she moved on. All the way home she derided the judge and the system.

At Five Pines, she announced that she was going to call county prosecuting attorney Donald C. Brockett and tell him a thing or two. "You've got a very poor bunch of judges down there," she barked into the phone. "That stupid moron let Jenifer Coe off with a pat on the wrist, and you know what she'll do now? She'll leave again! You people should have *insisted* on jail time. But I rather expect too much of you public lawyers. You'd be working for yourselves if you were competent."

It was impossible not to overhear, and Gini wished she were anywhere else. She wondered why Brockett didn't hang up but realized it would be a rare officeholder who would cut off a managing editor's wife. She wondered how often Ruth wielded her secondhand power this way.

After the phone call, the woman began acting like an excited schoolgirl. She was going to a party at the home of her friend Rae Shepard, and she kept asking Gini's advice on what to wear. She pranced into the living room in a black dress with V-shaped scallops at the bottom. To Gini it looked like something that had barely escaped a shredder. Ruth pointed to a pearl necklace and asked if she should highlight it with a diamond clip. "I wouldn't, Ruth," Gini said.

Five-inch backless "slides" and a fluffy fake-fur coat completed the ensemble. "How do I look?" the woman asked, cantering about the room with her arms outstretched and her rings catching the light from a crystal chandelier.

"Lovely!" said Kevin. Gordon smiled and nodded. Gini hoped her feelings didn't show.

65

The executives of the Spokane Police Department, moving at their usual methodical pace, called in their most impressive physical specimen and asked him to take over the South Hill cases. Bill Beeman was about to retire and Joan Schmick was scheduled for rotation to Burglary. Detective Roy S. Allen, six feet six inches tall, with light blue eyes, reddish-brown curly hair and the musculature of a marathoner, respectfully declined the offer. At 43, Allen had been a policeman for nineteen years and a detective for twelve. He was also a polygraph expert, but he was best known in Spokane for his activities as a distance runner amd record-holding fisherman. He was popular with his fellow officers and considered easygoing—not "badge-heavy." He had put in long hours on the Stephanie Gibbs rape in December and exhausted all leads.

The tall detective's negative attitude about taking on the rape project came as no surprise to his friends. The rapist had defeated the best efforts of Schmick and Beeman, both highly regarded. The feeling among top detectives was that the brass considered rape a minor crime and wouldn't provide time or support for a quality investigation. There had never been a permanent police rape unit (although there were units for homicide, auto theft, bad checks, narcotics and vice), and the South Hill cases had been assigned on a scattershot basis from the beginning. Several North Side rapes involving fingers in the throat and other familiar techniques weren't even carried in the same file. Allen was a proud cop with a good record, but as the father of a teenage daughter and the husband of a young second wife, he couldn't have been pleased by the way the cases had been handled.

After a few days he was told that the assignment was mandatory and the South Hill rapes had been made top priority. Schmick would work with him, and both would report to Det. Lt. Eugene McGougan, nicknamed "God," a tough cop who despised sex offenders. The special squad, already at work, was available to provide extra manpower.

Allen asked dispatchers to summon him to rape scenes whatever the hour; under the old system, detectives took over cases the morning after. His South Hill neighbors became accustomed to seeing his long frame bob past their houses as he jogged the six miles from his home to headquarters. Despite his age he was a respectable finisher in distance races like the annual Bloomsday event, and he had just begun appearing in triathlons, torturous competitions that required swimming, biking and running. Everyone from traffic cops to the blind cashier in the coffeeshop agreed: If the South Hill rapist could be caught by sheer stamina, Roy Allen was the man.

A voluminous statistical study, ordered by Lt. McGougan, suggested that the 1980 rapes had been committed by two men working different parts of the area. One composite was in his twenties, five-seven to six feet, 140 to 160 pounds, with medium brown hair to the collar and five o'clock shadow. The other was a six-footer in his mid-twenties, with medium build and light brown hair over his ears. Both had the very common A-type blood.

Each composite suspect wore jogging shoes, dark ski jacket or vest, and jeans. Under "Weapon" the report on one observed, "Assailant says he has knife, never displays one. When victim screams or fights, puts fingers in mouth and down throat." The other composite suspect "says he has knife, however, none is displayed; grabs victim around the neck." Both men operated under cover of darkness, one in the older neighborhood in the northwest corner of the South Hill, the other along bus route No. 7, "Lincoln Park," and No. 4, "Cable Add."

Roy Allen and Joan Schmick gathered up sex-crime reports and made a study of their own. They found common denominators in rapes going back to 1978. Compulsive chatter didn't lend itself to statistical processing, but it was a hallmark of the South Hill rapist. Cunnilingus, masturbation and personal questioning were his customary methods of self-arousal. *Are you a virgin? Have you ever done this before? Do you have a boyfriend? Do you like sex? Do you masturbate? Would you like to be eaten?* He often threw in the word "cunt." For at least two years he had been having intimate conversations with women he didn't know.

The hand in the throat stood out; neither Allen nor Schmick had ever heard of the technique before. It seemed a sadistic way to enforce silence. Also atypical was the fact that the rapes occurred outdoors and usually in highly populated areas. The veteran Schmick pointed out another odd factor: Many of the victims had noticed that the rapist looked and smelled exceptionally clean. One woman reported, "It was like he'd just stepped out of a beauty shop." After ejaculation he liked to turn his victims over and pat their bare buttocks, convincing a few of them that they were about to be sodomized. And he almost always left with a threat to return, couched in more or less the same words: "Don't tell the police. I'll come back and get you. You don't want somebody chasing you for the rest of your life."

Altogether a singular profile, the detectives realized, and quite possibly a single offender. The main disparity between the two statistical composites was in height, but women being raped in darkness by a man who threatened their lives weren't the best sources of vital statistics. They were far more likely to remember techniques, and these were fairly consistent.

The two detectives took off in different directions, back-checking rapes. Wherever he went Allen carried nylon handcuffs. When he jogged he wore them as a head-band. He told Schmick that if he ever spotted the rapist, he would run him down and cuff him around a treetrunk. He modified his regular morning run to cover the busiest rape sites. Packing a small two-way radio, he would leave his home at 6 a.m., jog straight to Hart Field, double back to High Drive, run past Comstock Park and Manito Park and then on down to headquarters. His normal six-mile route stretched to eight or nine, but as he told a colleague, "I'm just like everybody else on the South Hill. I *want* that son of a bitch!"

While Allen and Schmick were hard at work, another detective showed all available information on the rapes to an FBI expert and came away with a profile of the rapist. According to the specialist, the assailant was an under-achiever who was totally dominated, probably by one parent. He was motivated by rage, not lust, and his main intent was to degrade the victim and thus degrade the person who dominated him. He was a "power rapist" with a special hatred for small to medium-sized dark-haired women. He came from a well-to-do family and didn't work with his hands. He was a mama's boy even though he was in his late twenties or early thirties. And he was becoming increasingly violent from rape to rape and should be considered extremely dangerous. The FBI agent warned that the man might even kill.

Gene McGougan ordered an updated printout of all recent sex offenses from indecent liberties to rape. There were hundreds.

As his last step before retirement, Bill Beeman turned in a list of his best suspects. They ranged from a forty-six-year-old man who "followed a woman in the downtown area and seemed a little hinky" to a young WM who "wears gray jogging suit and blue stocking cap; appears to look into homes as he jogs; possibly a voyeur."

The special squad was out and about twenty-four hours a day. Reports poured in:

> Suspect had coffee at Haymarket Square 29th & Regal; while inside saw ——— ——— WM wearing blk fur cap, blk coat, blue jeans, blk horn rim glasses carrying a Mace & scanner on his belt walk in with ——— ——— wearing multicolored plaid & blue jeans.... He was hustling a cute 17 yr old waitress....

> Proceeded to W. Main and contacted ——— ——— and ——— ——— to ascertain if they possibly knew any suspects that would fit the M.O. They stated that they knew of a suspect who's been in the downtown area and has in the past threatened them with a ice pick. *AN* They further stated that he talks of rape and fanticizes that he's commiting the act.... They state they don't know his name, but he frequently comes around.

When a rape was reported on the police radio, a special-squad member would phone the names on the hot list to verify their whereabouts. Another team would show up at Deaconess Hospital with a long questionnaire. Was there tobacco on his breath? Did he smell like bath soap or cologne? Did he mas-turbate? Did he pat your bottom? Did he use the word c-u-n-t?...

The work was tedious, but no one asked to be relieved. One night Pa-trolman Steve Christian reported to his boss, Rock Walker, "We've used every-body that volunteered. "What now?"

"Use 'em again," the shift boss said.

Before long every suspect had been ruled out. "So who's the South Hill rapist?" Christian asked rhetorically. "He's some asshole with a clean sheet. A Scoutmaster, a preacher maybe. Christ, we'll *never* nail the sucker."

"Why don't you run decoys?" Walker suggested.

The volunteer squad was exclusively male, so the first decoys were plainclothesmen in fur coats and heels. "They're swishing it up pretty good, but nobody's buying," Christian complained. Then a blond-haired woman from the radio office volunteered and was sent out in a black wig, since the South Hill rapist had raped three dozen brunettes' and a few dark redheads but not a single blonde. Other women volunteered, including the wives of special squad members and Roy Allen's daughter Michelle. Their salary was bus fare and all the black coffee they could drink. A decoy would ride the bus while a special squad car followed a block behind. When she got off, she would walk six or eight blocks while plainclothesmen followed her progress with binoculars. It was a tricky business; the South Hill rapist had been known to strike quickly, using his fists to intimidate. A typical report hinted at the frustrations of the first runs in winter chill and murk:

1934 Decoy off at 28th & Freya
1945 Decoy completed route 1 without incident
2030 Decoy boarded bus at 17th & Ray for route #2 which was getting off at 37th & Regal, walking E to Cook, S to Thurston & picked up there. . . .
2146 Decoy completed route 3 without incident
2200 Station for reports; should be noted that it was 29 degrees out, streets freezing & extremely foggy with visability sometimes less than 50 yds. There was NO ONE, male or female except us out on foot tonight.

The tough job got tougher. Temperatures dropped, and Steve Christian kept extra sets of long johns at the base station in his house at Fourteenth and Bernard. Decoys stomped inside blowing through their hands and swearing they were quitting, but the next night they would be back on the street ducking snowflakes and swinging their hips. The rapist stayed home.

66

Chris Peck, a Stanford alumnus and former newspaper executive, had written a handful of angry columns about the South Hill rapes, but otherwise the local papers remained in a state of somnolence. Believers in conspiracy theories thought they detected the traditional Cowles tendency to downplay the negative, all the better to entice customers and new businesses to the Lilac City. Both newspapers had always seemed to live in the past. A popular bit of folklore featured an enthusiastic new editor asking William H. Cowles III how he wanted his paper to look. "Exactly the way it looks now," Cowles answered. The young publisher retained the same conservative attitude toward the priceless red-brick structure in which his papers were produced. The copper-topped building, listed in the National Register of Historic Buildings, dated to 1890. William H. Cowles I had worked in the thin conical tower with its understated necklace of white lights; whenever there was a big land deal participants had climbed up for a view of the surroundings. Every subsequent publisher had seen to it that the floors of the building were hand-scrubbed and the brass hand-polished. The prevailing smell in this newspaper office was of lemon wax and polish rather than printer's ink.

But the grandeur of the old building hadn't kept the Cowles papers from being the butt of constant jokes about their flinty conservatism. A campaigning Harry S. Truman was said to have castigated an aide: "I asked you to buy me a *newspaper*. Damn it, this is the *Spokesman-Review!*" Journalism school students picked up on the one-liners in their freshman year: "The *Spokesman-Review* is written for the ten-year-old mentality by the eight-year-old mentality." "The *Chronicle*'s presses stopped. The donkey died." "The *Review* is the most up-to-date 19th century newspaper in the world."

Under managing editor Donald Gormley, a veteran of Chicago's circulation wars, the *Spokesman-Review* had just begun to change at the time of the South Hill rapes. Bright young reporters were being hired, old retainers pensioned off, modern devices like VDT boxes installed. Fewer such changes were evident at the other Cowles paper, the afternoon *Chronicle*, edited by the sixty-four-year-old Gordon Harlan Coe. The *Spokesman-Review* called itself the "voice of the Inland Empire," but the *Chronicle*'s sights were narrower. It specialized in Spokane, city and county, an emphasis that had varied little in a century. Nor was it expected to change under its veteran managing editor. When racial incidents broke out at Lewis and Clark High School, Mr. Coe could be trusted not to give his native city a black eye by overdoing the coverage. If a teenage publicist for the Cootyettes Drum & Bugle Corps marched into the office with a handout five minutes before deadline, the same friendly executive would see that the news made the edition. His colleagues agreed that Gordon Coe was a good old-fashioned country editor working in a city.

An article about the New Year's Day spraying of a would-be rapist had been the *Chronicle*'s first South Hill rape story of more than a few paragraphs. After twenty-five years as city editor and five in the top job, Gordon Coe seemed content with the policies of the past. Under his stewardship, rapes were written short and buried inside—or ignored. The brutal attack on the socially prominent Margot Terry hadn't been mentioned at all. Nor had dozens of others.

In the two separate editorial offices of the Cowles papers there was constant grousing about the rapes. Newspapermen were paid to be nosy, and no group in the city had as much inside information or was more fearful. Most Spokane journalists lived on the nearby South Hill. Their families were at constant risk, and they knew better than anyone that their own publications weren't covering the news.

Spokesman-Review assistant managing editor Shaun Higgins, an Indiana import known for a robust laugh and a cherubic face, was especially worried about his wife, who insisted on taking long walks in Lincoln Heights. When he read about the latest rape attempt in January, he slammed his hand on his desk and muttered to himself, "This shit's gotta stop!"

Higgins asked permission to form a study team. He and Gormley chose three editors, five reporters, a staff artist and several librarians. At the first briefing, Higgins said, "We've got to find out whether the police are trying. If they're not, we're gonna nail 'em."

Neither editor was surprised when the task force ran into a brass wall at the Public Safety Building. Spokane's ranking cops had always been arrogant toward reporters. "They never had to deal with a vigorous, energetic press," a magazine journalist explained. "They never had a managing editor get on the line and say, 'Goddamn it, if you don't give us a little cooperation I'll put ten reporters on your ass!'"

The *S-R* rape team's first conclusion was that top police officials were more interested in their own reputations than in the South Hill rapist and the crime of rape. The old bureaucratic watchword, "Cover your ass," could have been chipped in stone above the entrance. "We looked real hard but we couldn't find a trace of demonstrated concern or commitment or interest by anybody above the rank of lieutenant," said Rita Hibbard, a prize-winning reporter. "They didn't want us nosing around and they didn't want our help. They used every excuse. They told us the South Hill rapist would read our stories and start raping in another part of town, and their detectives would have to start from scratch. We said, 'Fine, maybe that'll make him easier to catch. Obviously he's right at home on the South Hill. Besides, the women up there can use some relief.'"

"Then they warned us that our stories would force him to change his

Four of the many faces of Fred Coe,
as taken by his wife, Jeni,
1971–72

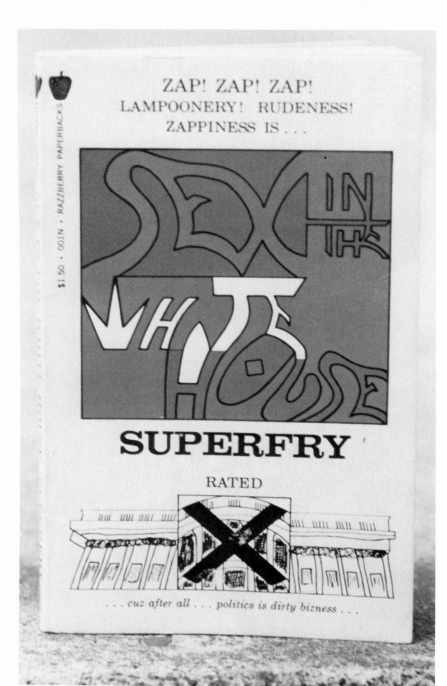

Coe's book Sex in the White House, *and the author in a mail-order ad*

*Fred Coe
at his trial*

Fred Coe with defense attorneys Julie Twyford and Roger Gigler

Lawyer Carl Maxey with Fred and Ruth Coe at Fred's sentencing hearing

Prosecuting attorney Donald Brockett (above) and Judge George Shields (below), targets of Ruth Coe's rage

Gordon Coe waits to visit his wife after her arrest

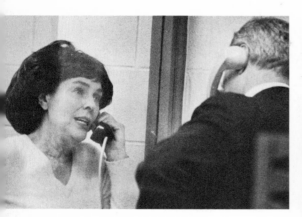

*Ruth and
Gordon Coe
speak in the jail
visiting room*

*Gordon Coe
testifying
at Ruth's trial*

Gordon, Ruth and Kathleen Coe, Carl Maxey in the background

Judge Robert Bibb
listening to
the hitman tapes: "You
want these people..."
"Gone!" "Dead?" "Dead."

Ruth Coe
at her trial

Ruth Coe
assisted by
psychologist
Anna Kuhl

MO," said Shaun Higgins. "We said, 'Maybe that's good, too! He's been doing the same things for two years and you haven't caught him, so maybe if we force him to change he'll make a mistake.'"

Using their own files, the journalists began a study of seventy rapes going back to June, 1979. Higgins's small office soon resembled a war room. There was a large map on the wall with color-coded pushpins for different types of rapes. There were charts and graphs and computer printouts describing typical offenders and typical victims, days and hours of the incidents, locations, moon phases, weather, even barometric pressures. On the third day of the study, Higgins shoved a scarlet pin into the map and bellowed for reporter John Harris, who had been fighting for information at headquarters. "Look up there," said Higgins. "What do you see?"

"A hell of a lot of pins," Harris answered.

Higgins used his gold-rimmed glasses for a pointer. "Look!" he said, jabbing at parallel lines of pins that sliced the South Hill in a north-south direction. "Most of the rapes are along this bus line—and this one—and this one. Now look at *this*." He pointed to the North Side. Similar pins and lines extended north. "These rapes aren't just happening on South Hill bus lines. *They're all over town!*"

Harris, a transplanted Ohioan and University of Oregon graduate, returned to police headquarters and ran the new correlations past a few confidential sources. He learned that the department was still handling North Side rapes routinely. Only the South Hill rapes came in for special attention, and that only recently. When Harris reported back, Higgins decided to ask the police exactly where their investigation stood. "We promised to work with them, to leave out anything that would impede their investigations, and to check our conclusions with them," he said later. "They claimed that their rape files were a shambles. We insisted that our obligation was to provide the public with the information it needed to protect itself. They insisted that the information was private. We went around and around."

The stonewalling continued even after Higgins wrote to police chief Robert Panther, promising, "We will make every effort to assure you that your investigation is not impeded and no undue panic is created in the minds of our Spokane City readers by our reports." Panther countered with a cordial promise of cooperation and said the task force would be hearing from Det. Capt. Richard Olberding—in two months. Higgins rejected the offer on the grounds that six or eight more women might be raped by then. When he sent copies of the finished articles to Panther's office for comment or corrections, there was no response.

The task force's conclusions broke on Sunday, January 11, opening on page 1 with "How the South Hill Rapists Work" and a map of the bus lines captioned "Does Rape Ride the Bus?" The act jumped inside to sidebars on neighborhood reaction to the rape scare, "How to Protect Yourself," composite sketches of the rapist, and a point/counterpoint column entitled "Are Spokane Police Doing Enough?"

Police officialdom was represented by a quote from the chief: "What I want to do is assure the public that, hey, we're working like crazy on these problems, without the bad people realizing that, hey, they're on to us. So far we think they don't know, because there's still a little activity. We will provide information on what the public should be doing. How many reports do you see where the victim was a jogger? Now doggone it, they shouldn't be out there running alone, because they're just exposing themselves to problems. Now they've got to express some personal responsibility if they're going to do these things."

Within hours every available copy of the *Spokesman-Review* was bought up, and the phones in the old newspaper building were ringing with hot tips. City editor Bob Rose, another alumnus of the defunct Chicago *Daily News*, began a file but didn't know quite what to do with it, since police officials had already refused his help.

The day after the big splash the afternoon *Chronicle* soothed jittery residents with an article on page five: "Bus-riding Rapist Theory Doubted." The story included lines like "There could be or there may not be any correlation" and a morose quote from a transit-system official to the effect that the scare stories might cause women to avoid the buses. Managing editor Gordon H. Coe took typewriter in hand to compose one of his rare editorials. It concluded:

> The rape problem is getting a high priority from the police, but other than trying to run down a multitude of tips from citizens, there is not much that can be done beyond some additional patrolling. Obviously available cars and manpower limit the amount of patrolling in the case of a continuing problem. Rape is a continuing problem, flaring up to public prominence every two or three years, but going on at some level all of the time. So Spokane citizens must bear some of the burden of being on the lookout for rapists, although it is hoped that every man out jogging is not hounded off the streets because some rape reports have said the attacker wore jogging clothes. All in all, it amounts to all of us using good sense and keeping our eyes and ears open.

Spokesman-Review staffers scoffed. Spokane rapes had climbed from 49 in 1978 to 69 in 1979 and 127 in 1980; they were more than a "continuing problem" occasionally flaring up. Police Chief Panther didn't seem any more excited about the problem than editor Coe. Panther commented, "In terms of what is happening incident-wise, I don't really see things as out of the ordinary." He noted that crime was down ten percent in Spokane. When a Chicago psychic named Irene Hughes reported that the rapist was of Italian or Greek descent, frequented a new Italian or Greek restaurant, dressed well, had manicured hands, hung out at racquetball courts and health clubs and might be a member of the underworld, the chief promised that her conclusions would be carefully evaluated.

Capt. Dick Olberding had a message of his own for the panicky women of the South Hill, although it wasn't easy for the press to wring it out of him. He told a persistent television reporter named Flo Jonic that there was a simple way to handle the problem of rape: "Just lay back and enjoy it." Then he ordered his deskmen to suppress all rape reports. The next time the rapist struck, only the police and his victim would know.

67

Hysteria set in. It was a panic-type city. I listen to KSPO news radio when I'm on the streets. People would call in on their talk shows offering home remedies of weapons that women could carry, some of 'em ridiculous. How to gouge a man's eye out....I remember one old guy calling in and saying, "Yeah, I'll get that son of a bitch. I've got a hunting rifle. I'm gonna drive around my own neighborhood and if I see anybody suspicious I'll blow his head away....The police aren't doing a goddamn thing."—Fred Coe, Dec. 27, 1981

What was left of Spokane's peace of mind was shattered by the *Spokesman-Review*'s articles. The General Store on North Division, which had sold 500 canisters of chemical spray in a month, now sold 125 overnight. The *S-R* noted, "With all the Mace, tear gas and paralyzer sprays on the market, a male runner on the South Hill feels like a duck on opening day. Some women's purses have become fully stocked arsenals." Prosecuting attorney Donald Brockett bought spray canisters for his wife and four daughters and instructed them not to go out alone at night. So many females were packing weapons that police became alarmed at the possibilities, especially after two women argued about a minor traffic collision and one Maced the other's two daughters, causing the four-month-old to stop breathing for a while.

Once again gun stores sold out of pistols. Karate and kung-fu studios sprang up, and night courses in self-defense turned away applicants. An art gallery did a brisk business in ceramic whistles for female joggers. Up in the airy regions of High Drive, the colorful little tubes were considered the peak of chic hanging on gold chains from their owners' necks. The biggest change was on the city's jogging trails, now often covered with winter fog that gave them a *Hound of the Baskervilles* quality. Traditionally the paths were the scenes of camaraderie and high spirits as thousands of runners began their training for the annual Bloomsday race in May. Spokane had been a running city long before the national jogging craze; it was the home of Olympic marathoners Don Kardong and "Little Jerry" Lindgren, the teenager who had come from behind to beat the Russians. This year Kardong, who had devised the Bloomsday race as a joyous civic event, admitted that he was downright glum about the situation. Male joggers were encountering so much trigger-happiness among the few females still running on the South Hill that they were kept busy rearranging their routes. The president of the Bloomsday Road Runners observed, "It seems like neither men nor women are running up there." The women were afraid of the rapist and the men were afraid of the women.

Columnist and jogger Chris Peck learned to avoid bus stops during his morning work-out. "Whenever I approached one, the women would start groping in their purses." Another runner overtook a woman he'd known for years and hugged her from behind. She slammed him to the ground.

The old South Hill changed fast. "In this friendly neighborhood everyone was uptight," said a dentist whose assistant had been raped. "If you were smart you never waved or said hello to a woman. When you passed one you moved into the center of the street—or she did." Males ran in T-shirts that said "I'm not the South Hill rapist!" Several men were tear-gassed, and a few flirtatious types found themselves looking down the muzzles of cute little pistols, loaded and cocked.

Women improvised imaginative defenses. If a female saw a man approaching, she would smile broadly and wave at a house as though being watched by friends. Some ran with dogs, young sons, husbands. Joggers of both sexes reversed course at sight of another runner. "I might run fifteen miles to finish my seven-mile running route," one complained. The Rape Crisis Center started a buddy system, putting women in touch with other joggers. Females were advised to run in threes and fours; pairs weren't safe. The YWCA staged a "Freedom from Assault" run by several hundred joggers around Riverfront Park. Columnist Rich Landers of the *Spokesman-Review* took note of the supercharged atmosphere: "I pray for the aspiring male runner who, after working up a good sweat for four or five miles, finds he needs to stop and tie a shoelace at Ninth and Madison." Nobody laughed.

68

Gini Perham didn't know what to make of Kevin. He sat in the black chair in the living room and gazed at the walls. Or disappeared for hours. There were scary possibilities. "Kevin," she asked one night, "when you're with your other women, don't you worry about VD?"

"I'm not seeing other women," he said coldly. "If I were, they'd be women with class."

A few days later he muttered that he had "angels" all over town. She wondered if his mother's entreatments about angels and devils had rubbed off on him. She asked, "Angels? What do you mean by that?"

"Uh, nothing."

"Do you mean rich women who give you money? Why don't they give you some now?" She'd just lent him twenty more dollars for gas and a car wash.

"I don't mean that kind of angel," he said.

"What kind do you mean?"

He didn't answer.

Their sex life had turned routine, once or twice a week, with occasional longer intervals at his request. When he told her that he masturbated fairly regularly, she asked herself, What kind of a remark is that? Sometimes at the dinner table he would inquire if she was prepared to make love later, giving her the feeling he was fitting her into his latest schedule.

One morning she was applying makeup when he leaped into the bathroom with the big dildo pressed against his crotch. "Look!" he shouted. She'd asked him to get the thing out of the house and thought he had. She peered into the sink, embarrassed for him and herself. He seemed distressed at her disinterest and repeated the act a few days later, with the same results. That was the last she saw of the dildo, and good riddance.

Lately there seemed to be more and more to argue about. The unseasonal weather was no help. The ski resort at Mount Spokane was closed for lack of snow. Fog sliced off the tops of downtown buildings. Viruses thrived. Spokane, usually fairly dry during the winter, oozed moisture. Money was tighter than ever, especially in real estate. Their rent was eighteen hundred dollars behind even though she had faithfully handed over her share. She was more certain than ever that he'd been using her half for pocket money. He lived on the brink of financial disaster, and now she was approaching the brink herself. If I go under, she told herself, I can call it bankruptcy by association. He owed her a bundle, but it would have been cruel and inhuman—and a waste of time—to press him.

At least she still had a good credit rating. His own was destroyed. One day she went with him to a downtown department store to look at clothes, and an assistant manager warned him in advance that only cash would be acceptable. He fingered some suits and walked out. Sherry's Styling Salon in Lincoln Heights refused his charge card and his check. Only Gordon Coe rated him an acceptable credit risk, but occasionally even that complaisant man turned up with empty pockets, moving Kevin to lengthy perorations about miserly parents.

Now that they argued so often, Gini began to anticipate his debating style. He would lie outrageously and reel off skeins of pseudo-facts and imaginary statistics. He had a good memory for quotes but usually reworked them to make his points. He often contradicted himself. For example, he'd always called himself a male feminist, but when a police captain named Olberding got in trouble for a chauvinistic remark about rape—"Lay back and enjoy it"—his sympathies had been with the cop.

He had trouble following the thread of conversations, rambling and showing anger when she tried to put him on course. He bridled at disagreement and accused her of disloyalty. Sometimes his harangues moved her to tears, and an instant change would come over him. He would follow her from room to room, apologize profusely, take her in his arms and promise never to behave so cruelly again, the original argument now completely forgotten. It occurred to her that this was the way a six-year-old would react to squabbles with Mommy. Childlike, he couldn't handle her tears; they seemed to panic him. After her worst crying scenes he would gulp vitamins as though his health were threatened.

She wondered if he might have brain damage. What else could explain his mental processes? He was constantly drawing wrongheaded conclusions. He thought that Jay Gatsby and the pathetic hero of *American Gigolo* were figures to be emulated, not realizing that their creators had meant them as tragic. He had a surface knowledge of a few aspects of culture, but he was barren otherwise. Sometimes he repeated her observations as his own. It made her realize that she'd been wrong from the beginning; he only *appeared* to be knowledgeable. The difference hadn't shown till she moved in.

As February arrived she was almost moved to tears by the emptiness of his life. He seemed to be losing his last friends. At Christmastime, he'd missed connections with his old pal John Nyberg and lamented, "He doesn't even visit me when he comes to Spokane." Nyberg sent an expensive card on February 2, Kevin's thirty-fourth birthday, and a few days later Gini saw him moving it around as though trying to find the proper setting for such a precious document.

He retreated more and more into the unreality of babytalk. Sometimes he pretended to be an excited little boy unable to get his words out—Red Skelton's mean wittle kid. One day he brought her three roses—yellow, orange and red—and said in a high reedy voice that he'd been inspired by a drive past "the birthplace of our love": the Manito Highlander laundromat. That night in bed he squawked like a duck, "I wub you, Gini." Then he switched to his broadcast voice and told her that they ought to marry and have children. He'd heard of a new diet that would raise his sperm count. Together, he said, they would produce a perfect male child named Chan. The next night he arrived home from his evening jog at 3 a.m. She assumed he'd been with one of his "angels." Her head ached from trying to decide what to do.

There was only one certainty: She wanted out.

69

At 5:30 on a Thursday morning seven weeks after the last reported South Hill rape, the groundskeeper at Sacajawea Junior High School arrived at work in his customary good spirits. Charles Williams's first duty after arriving at school was to check for broken windows. Finding none, he proceeded to pick up papers and candy wrappers on the school lawns across Thirty-third St. from busy Hart Field. The sky was inky and a few dirty patches of snow were scattered around. No parked cars were in sight.

After a while he dropped into the cavernous school cafeteria and sipped coffee with night custodian Doug Gonwick. At about 6:30 the two men drifted into the hall. The sky had just begun to lighten. They spotted a car parked under a streetlight in the school bus zone. It was part of the groundskeeper's job to report such vehicles to the school district headquarters and have them towed if they weren't gone by 8 a.m. The two men stepped outside for a look.

The silver-gray hatchback was parked on narrow Lamont St. under a sign: "No Parking Except School Bus 8 a.m. 5 p.m." It was pointed north, away from Hart Field. Williams wondered what kind of car it was, then noticed an inscription on the side: "Citation." He remembered reading something about Chevolet's latest model, the smallest version of a new line of "X-cars."

He leaned over and admired the sunroof, touched the hood and found it warm. The license plate was yellow, like a personalized plate or an Oregon plate, but it was made up of three letters and three numbers, like standard Washington plates. On the front passenger's seat were a few green and brown folders that looked like schoolbooks, and a bluish nylon jacket.

Custodian Gonwick commented that the car probably belonged to a teacher who'd dropped by to pick something up. "Yeah," Williams said. "I'll check it later." It was too early to summon a tow truck; the school buses wouldn't need the space for an hour. He made a note of the color and model and began giving a haircut to some shrubs.

Irene Pool eased the family car into the Hart Field parking lot and was surprised to see that the running track was vacant. The Bloomsday race was coming up in a few months, and usually there were earlybirds about. She peered the length of the athletic complex, big enough to hold a football field, a baseball diamond and several tennis courts with space left over, and saw no one in any direction. She told herself not to worry; the sun was coming up and someone was bound to arrive in a minute or two. Besides, there'd been nothing in the paper about the rapist for weeks.

At fifty-one Mrs. Pool was older than the typical South Hill victim, but in other ways she met the prototype. Her brown eyes matched her dark-brown hair. She was a businesswoman, partner with her husband Fred in a thriving company, and the mother of grown children. For years she'd been running on Hart Field's quarter-mile track three times a week, and she had a young woman's figure to prove it.

The grass was stiff with frost as she walked toward the gravel track in the early light. She felt a twinge of nervousness as she stepped onto the cinders. She was a block away from the nearest public street. A few mornings before, a car had pulled into the parking area while she jogged, and someone had watched her without getting out.

As she began her regular two-mile run her mind eased. On her seventh lap she realized she wasn't alone. Another jogger had appeared about thirty or forty yards in front of her, running on the grass. From his location, she guessed he must have come from the direction of the junior high, several hundred yards to the north. He was circling the track European-style, in a clockwise direction. How *different*, she said to herself. Nobody runs that way around here.

They closed fast. When he was a few yards away she got a good look and decided he was a stranger. She said, "Good morning." His arm reached out and circled her throat, pressing so tightly she thought her neck bone would snap. "Damn you, damn you!" she grunted. The beating and rape were over in a few minutes.

At 6:40 a.m. Mae Granlund, a cook at the junior high, came to work and noticed a small light-colored car parked in the school bus zone. She mentioned it to the building custodians. They told her they had seen the car earlier. Just after 7, Charles Williams made a final check. The car was gone.

Against her husband's objections, Irene Pool went to work behind a thick layer of makeup. A few of her friends asked what had happened to her face, and she told them she'd fallen down and scraped it while jogging.

A plainclothesman named Steve Christian arrived and took notes. "I swear to God, Irene," he said as he was leaving, "we're gonna catch this creepo. And when we do we're gonna put him away till his thing shrivels up and falls off." She told him he'd expressed her feelings perfectly.

At the Public Safety Building later, a tall detective introduced himself as Roy Allen and interviewed her for an hour. At first he seemed as perturbed as Christian. He said he had jogged through Hart Field minutes after the incident. She gathered that he was upset at missing out on every cop's dream of catching a notorious criminal in the act.

He took her through her story from start to finish and back again. Was she sure his jacket had been red and not blue? Yes, she was sure. Was he wearing a down vest? No, he wasn't. The detective had her hypnotized to see if she could remember more details. She couldn't.

Gini Perham went to the closet to get her red down ski jacket, a men's size forty that she'd bought to fit over heavy sweaters and other clothes. It was hanging in its usual place, but the down was packed into the corners and the panels were flat and damp. She asked Kevin if he'd worn it. He said no. She complained that it had lost its fluffiness, and he told her he knew a trick to solve that problem. He put the jacket in the dryer and tumbled it with a tennis shoe. It came out as good as new.

70

Cheryl Ernst had never been enthusiastic about filling in for police reporter John Harris, and lately the job was even more dispiriting than usual. The cops, even some of the friendlier ones, had turned truculent ever since the *Spokesman-Review*'s big splash on January 11. She knew of no formal retaliatory orders, but there was a definite chill in the air.

On the evening of Thursday, February 5, she was filling in again and wishing she were back on her education beat. It was a slow news night in Spokane and even slower at headquarters. She visited the jail and found no new arrivals of note, checked the reception desk in front, and wandered around the corner to the office of the detective division. She recognized the duty man as a short-timer approaching retirement. "Anything new?" she asked.

"Just a rape," he said, handing over a report. Her article ran the next day:

A 51-year-old South Hill woman was assaulted by a white man who said he had a knife, Thursday morning at Hart Field, just west of Thirty-seventh and Grand, police report. Officers said the attempted rape occurred while the woman jogged on the track at the field.

A white man, 25-27 years, 6-feet, 170 pounds, with long blond hair, grabbed the woman and forced her to a grassy area near the north goalpost, pinned her arms and removed her running pants, the victim told police. She said the man was wearing a dark stocking cap, red ski jacket, jeans and heavy, rough, dark gloves.

When the newswoman ran into Capt. Olberding a few days later, he asked the source of her information. "A report," she told him.

He smiled and asked, "Where'd you get it?" She hesitated; his smile looked pasted on. "There were only two copies," he said. "Who showed it to you?"

"I don't remember. Wasn't I supposed to see rape reports? We've always seen them before." She pulled out her notepad. "Is this a new policy?"

The detective captain said he didn't see why he should answer her questions if she wouldn't answer his, and walked away. Later she learned that he had interrogated everyone in the records unit and threatened to fire the next person who released a rape report. Windowpanes were installed in front of the desk to keep reporters from reaching in to grab papers. She felt apologetic for causing so much trouble.

On Friday, February 6, the day after the Hart Field rape, Charles Williams learned about it from the article in the *Spokesman-Review*. The groundskeeper remembered the silver-gray car with the yellow plates and wondered if there might be a connection. He mentioned the car to school staffers, and an assistant principal suggested that he tell the police. Williams thought about it over the weekend, but he was a shy man and held off. The assistant principal relayed the information for him.

The police sounded grateful.

71

I'm a very sensual person. I'm highly artistic and creative. But I choose to seduce women with charm...good looks... good clothes...material possessions (cars etc.)...and genuine affection for our superiors, females! I doubt if I could even achieve arousal in a rape situation.—
Fred Coe, Oct. 18, 1981

The second week of February blew in cold and windy, a contrast to the earlier days of winter when the temperature had stuck in the high forties and frustrated the city's skiiers. Early on Monday, February 9, four days after the rape of Irene Pool, an intermittent light snowfall began, and by the time *Jeanie Mays* left her South Hill apartment at 6 a.m. to take her infant son Jason to his grandmother's for the day, the wind was whipping about her legs.

Jeanie Mays was a quiet person, soft-voiced, a student at Spokane Community College. She was twenty, an inch over five feet tall, with curly light-brown hair, blue eyes with long lashes, and a petite figure. As she climbed off the bus to carry eighteen-month-old Jason a half block to her mother's, her mind was on school. This peaceful old block of two-story houses, Dutch Colonials and modified Victorians was the essence of middle-class Spokane, solid and unchanging. Most of the residents were respectable professionals who took pride in their lawns, grew arborvitae and blue spruce for decoration, and softened the lines of their squarish old houses with climbing ivy and rock chimneys and wooden shutters. Jeanie had grown up in this safe setting where everyone knew everyone else. She told a friend later, "I'm not a worrier. I knew there was a rapist, but no way he'd be around my mom's."

A few months before, her sister had warned her, "If you and Jason are gonna be waiting for buses before the sun comes up, you ought to have some protection," and bought her a dog-repellent spray. As she hurried down the street with her toddler son, the spray was still in her apartment.

Jeanie gulped a cup of coffee with her mother, then hurried back toward the same corner to catch the downtown bus. She'd been the only passenger coming up the South Hill and she was usually the only one going down. It was the same bus on a turnaround route, and she knew the driver. He'd told her several times that he would wait if she was a little late. Spokane bus-drivers were like that.

The thermometer stood at ten degrees and the wind whined in the bare branches of the maples and sycamores that lined the street. Usually her mother stood on the broad veranda and watched her to the corner, but on this cold morning she stayed inside. Jeanie wondered where the *Spokesman-Review* delivery boy was; he almost always passed her. The weather must have slowed him down. Walking in the glow of a streetlight, she thought she saw a flicker of movement down near the corner. She decided it was a leaf or a speck of paper. The wind was nipping and howling and preening the lawns.

She cupped her hands and lit a cigarette and thought about algebra. At 7:30 she would have a class in office procedures and then a killer test. The binomial theorem kept repeating in her mind; she hoped she had it right. When she was three houses from the bus stop a man emerged from behind a tree. He looked familiar. She thought he must be playing a trick.

He grabbed her from the front. She caught a glimpse of a square jaw and two oven mitts before her face was enveloped in his quilted ski jacket and his arms and the big soft mitts. She could tell that he was saying something, but the jacket muffled his words. She felt one of the mitts start down her throat and screamed. He rammed the padded glove farther down and she bent backward to get away. As she fell, she tasted something salty and realized that her nose was bleeding. The mitt was so far down her throat that she was sure her jaw was going to unhinge. She tried to bite back, but the wad of thick cloth kept her from getting leverage. She started to black out and quit struggling. He removed his hand and she pleaded, "Don't hurt me. I have a little boy."

He raped and robbed her in the cozy shelter of a tall blue spruce tree, a few feet from the uncurtained windows of a Colonial-style house. It took about ten minutes.

A squad car took her to Deaconess Hospital. By the time she arrived she was in shock. A doctor examined her at 7:25 a.m. and found trauma all the way to her tonsils. Her face was smeared with blood. Her genitalia were red. There was a scratch on her forearm and her lip was swollen. Seminal fluid was found in her vagina and more in the cup of her bra. Before she left the hospital a tall curly-haired detective arrived in jogging shorts and asked questions. She told him what she could remember, but her mind was messed up. She asked to be driven to her mother's house to see her infant son.

Roy Allen and members of the special rape squad pounded doors and found several people who'd seen a small light-colored hatchback parked in the neighborhood recently. A seventeen-year-old girl had noticed it near the corner a week before the rape. A man on his way to work had spotted it a few days later. Allen interviewed a woman who lived diagonally across the steet from the rape site. She said she'd noticed the unfamiliar car several times and thought it was a white or silver Monza. The detective perked up. The special squad had been sitting on a suspect who lived a few blocks away and owned a white Monza. He produced a book of automobile pictures and the woman said, "There! It's that Monza right there." Allen cursed to himself. She'd pointed to a Citation.

72

Investigators from the general detective division and the special squad went about their work with surprisingly buoyant spirits under the circumstances. From the beginning there hadn't been one inspiring lead or development; it had been murk and gloom and dark of night and plain old street-pounding and house-sitting. Now there'd been two attacks in a four-day period and both had reinforced the FBI expert's prediction that the rapist's violence might escalate to murder. After thousands of man-hours of work, the cops didn't have a clue.

Every Spokane detective answered to a half dozen bosses, and each desk-bound administrator had his own pet theory on how to catch the rapist. With advice and pressure coming from all directions, word trickled down that the special squad had one more week to produce and then would be disbanded. No longer would the glorified harness bulls have the privilege of staking out in freezing patrol cars for five and six hours at a time, their stomachs growling and their kidneys bursting; no longer would they be permitted to run decoys outdoors in icy weather while their old swing-shift colleagues rode around in warm squad cars. The men were miffed. So they hadn't caught the South Hill rapist. Who had?

Groups like NOW and Rape Crisis added to the heat, demanding action on behalf of the women of Spokane. The media kept asking for progress reports, but under Olberding's orders the subject of rape couldn't be discussed with reporters. It was just as well. There was no progress to report.

On Wednesday afternoon, February 11, two days after the rape of Jeanie Mays, Roy Allen and Joan Schmick dragged themselves off the street and took a look at their desks. Papers of many hues were stacked a foot high. There were tips from citizens, orders and countermands from above, leads from fellow officers, logs and reports from the special squad and dozens of phone slips. There also were several manila envelopes of contributions to the *Chronicle*'s Secret Witness Program, each with a torn corner so that the anonymous informant could match it up with another slip of paper and collect his $1,000 reward.

There were moments when Spokane police officers wished the Secret

Witness Program didn't exist, although it had proved its worth in a few cases, including the sensational hit-murder of a rich grandmother. When the South Hill rape cases were added to the program eager readers produced enough bum steers to choke the PD with paper. One citizen turned in his brother, another his preacher's son—"a goddamn sex fiend if ever I seen one." A reader informed the *Chronicle* that he had been studying the case for two years and it should be obvious to anyone who wasn't deaf, dumb and blind that the chief of police was the rapist and the other cops were protecting him. But it was the more plausible bits of information that consumed the most time. An officer could spend days checking out a promising tip and have it end up as meaningful as the one about the chief—but of course the only way to reach that conclusion was to go out and waste the time.

Roy Allen had toiled an hour or so on his own stack of paperwork when he came across a scribbled note from another officer. It said that a Sacajawea Junior High School assistant principal had called to say that a small car had been parked at the school on the morning of the Pool rape. The eye-weary detective wasn't impressed. Half the vehicles in Spokane were small cars, and Hart Field was in the middle of a residential neighborhood. Why shouldn't there be small cars parked there? He'd already read and rejected hundreds of similar tips, but something told him to put this one aside. There'd been so much talk lately about small cars.

Just before dark that night, he waited in an unmarked Chevrolet across the street from a downtown building. He needed a good look at a hot suspect, a bank clerk who drove an off-white compact. The special squad had sat on him for four nights and would pick him up again later. As Allen watched, the man walked out the front door of the bank and lit a cigarette. Allen broke off the surveillance. Through dozens of rapes not one victim had mentioned tobacco on the man's breath.

On his way down the South Hill on his regular jog the next morning, the elongated detective stopped at Sacajawea Junior High for a word with groundskeeper Charles Williams. He learned that the suspicious car had been parked in a school-bus zone at the time of the rape, and that it had been pointed north, a handy getaway direction that would not require the rapist to drive past his victim. Just across the street from the bus zone was a gate with a chain across it, the only opening along this northern edge of Hart Field. The driver of the gray car had come to run—or rape. But Irene Pool had seen no other joggers at that time of the morning and neither had Allen when he'd crossed the field a while later.

Charles Williams insisted that the car had been a Citation, but Allen still remembered the woman on Twenty-fourth who'd misidentified a Citation as a Monza. There'd been several other false calls; new small-car models were coming out periodically, and only experts could tell them apart. "What makes you so sure it was a Citation?" he asked.

"I saw the upraised letters," the groundskeeper said. "I touched them. C-i-t-a-t-i-o-n." He described the books and jacket on the front seat, the warmth of the hood, the red pinstripe just below the window level, and such minutiae as the plain border on the sunroof and the yellow tint of the license plates. "How come you didn't write the license down?" the detective asked.

"What for?" Williams said. "All I had to do was call the district and tell them there was a car in the bus zone. They don't need the license number to tow a car away."

The detective asked the groundskeeper to undergo hypnosis to see if he could bring back the license number, and they set a date. Allen left the school and finished his long run down the hill to the Public Safety Building. He wrote a report on the interview, and all hands were advised that their quarry might be driving a gray-over-black Citation.

The next day was Friday the thirteenth. On his way to work Allen talked to two other Sacajawea workers who'd seen the silver-gray car. Later he exchanged progress reports with Joan Schmick. She reminded him that a small car with yellow plates had been spotted on High Drive the morning of the Margot Terry rape. They agreed that things might be coming together.

Allen asked the State Department of Licensing for a printout of every personalized license plate in Washington. A clerk promised the information overnight. The detective made arrangements with the men of the special squad to come in Saturday morning on their own time to hand-check the lists for a silver-gray Citation, but after he figured out a shortcut he called the troops off. He and Schmick went to the basement and pulled out a moldy old stack of "call cards," time-stamped slips that were made out whenever an officer radioed in an automobile registration. The collected cards were bound in wire in a corner of the basement and the two detectives spent most of the day unwiring them and going through a thousand or so without turning up a Chevrolet Citation with personalized plates. The persistent Allen tried another approach. He called each of the three local Chevrolet dealers and asked for names of purchasers of gray-over-black Citations with sunroofs. "A lot of people have the sunroof installed privately," a man at Camp Chevrolet told him. "Do you know what kind you're looking for?"

"Hold on." Allen reached for the report of his interview with Charles Williams. "It was tinted dark, and it had a plain border."

"No chrome?"

"Nope."

"Good. That's factory-installed. I can check those out with no trouble." Within a few hours Allen received a list by messenger. Then Buchanan Chevrolet read its names over the phone and promised more, and Appleway's sales manager said he would get right to work on a list. Allen started to dial Chevrolet dealers in nearby Coeur d'Alene and Cheney but decided to see what happened with the locals first.

He ran the first names through the police computer and failed to get a hit. None of the Citation owners had been arrested, even for a traffic offense. It wasn't a good sign. A criminal as impulsive as the South Hill rapist figured to have a record of some kind, if only traffic tickets. Allen and Schmick pondered their next step. The car was somewhere near—at least it had been a few days before. They put out a statewide flier.

A few hours later, a citizen left his house in a silver-gray hatchback and found himself hemmed in by police cars. He stepped out with his hands up and demanded to know why they'd stopped his Fiesta.

73

Among the many lawsuits I'll eventually file, in the multimillions of dollars, will be a suit against the S-R for making the ludicrous accusation that I wrote a series of death threat letters to them last year....I MOST CERTAINLY DID NOT!—Fred Coe, Feb. 7, 1982

On the Saturday after the Jeanie Mays rape, *The Spokesman-Review* received a hand-printed letter in upper and lower case:

DOOMED & THE BleSSeD.

> MOTHER WASHINGTON PLACES
> Pitchforks between her boy
> babies legs, AND her females
> SHE PlACES HARPS.
> THEN SHE LABeLS THEM —
> DEVilS & ANGElS.
> AND Treats them the Same
> THRoughout THeir lives.

Sincerly

THE SOUth Hills RAPist.

City editor Robert Rose remembered a phone call he had taken two days before. A man who identified himself as the South Hills rapist had asked, "Did you get my letter?" Rose had assumed the caller was an impostor; everyone knew it was the South *Hill*, not *Hills*. But a dull holiday weekend was coming up and he played the story on page 1 under the headline "Note Writer Claims He's 'Hill' Rapist." A photograph of the letter ran alongside the story with the word "Washington" deliberately blacked out. The article ended with the news that twenty women had been raped in Spokane in January and quoted Capt. Olberding's recent comment that the local rape problem had been "overre-ported," causing "anxiety and panic."

The next day the S-R carried a front-page appeal to the rapist to turn himself in and verify his identity by providing the missing word. The response was over a week in coming. Then an anonymous intermediary received a call from a man with a medium deep, gravelly voice. He identified himself as the South Hill rapist and said he was going to fill caskets with city editor Rose, Spokane police chief Robert Panther and himself—"We're all going out together."

The caller had spoken calmly and without vulgarity, but he was plainly annoyed at not being taken seriously. "Do me a favor," he told the intermediary. "Get a message to the editor of the *Review*. Tell him I'm billing the caskets to him." Later a man with a similar voice called Woodland Cemetery in nearby Deer Park and reserved thirty-five-dollar plots for "the city editor, the chief of police and the South Hill rapist." Then he ordered caskets. On each call he provided the word that had been deleted from the published letter.

The police department learned of the death threats on a Friday, but didn't notify Bob Rose that he was a target for three days. Asked about the delay, Chief Panther said, "Is he concerned?"

74

By mid-February word spread that the special squad was about to be put out
of its misery. One member called another and asked why.

"The front office says we're not developing anything. Calls are piling up
in the uniformed division and they think we're fucking off."

"Eighty, ninety hours a week? Did they expect overnight results? After
two years of rapes?"

"I guess. Steve Christian called the front office and raised hell. He's about
as popular as a turd in a punchbowl."

"Wonder why."

By Monday, February 23, eighteen days after groundskeeper Williams
first noticed the silver-gray car, most of the Citation owners named by Chevrolet dealers had been cleared. The special squad had eyeballed each car at
the owner's listed address. There wasn't a yellow plate in the lot. Detective
Roy Allen was down to a short list provided by Buchanan Chevrolet. A team
radioed in that they'd spotted one of the Buchanan cars in the owner's driveway
and it had standard plates, green on white. Allen passed along his next-to-last
name, a Citation lessee named Gordon H. Coe who lived in the Spokane Valley.
While he was waiting for results he ran the name through the computer. An
old address came back: Seventh and Maple. If there was an epicenter for lower
South Hill rapes, Seventh and Maple was it. But a quick check showed that
Coe was sixty-four.

The name stuck with the detective overnight. *Gordon H. Coe.* It sounded
familiar. He wondered if the man had a son who sometimes drove the car. It
was unlikely, but no possibility could be ignored. The next day, Tuesday,
February 24, he checked the name with a few of his fellow officers. No one
recognized it. On a hunch he went to the Young People's Bureau and riffled
through the files. On a three-by-five card he found:

Harlan
COE, FREDERICK H.   (16) 2-2-47 ADULT
     1015 W. 29th   SO-PD 29015

#275974 Mentioned in Prop. Damage—Swimming Pool Rpt.
                                         8-21-63

#313146 Mentioned, Carnal Knowledge   6-7-65
#33403 Poss. Assault   5-1-66
#7138159 Indecent Liberties & 1st Degree Burglary
                         5-28-71*   Indent #25015

Once again Allen's hopes soared, but then he realized that the age was still hopelessly off. With a 2-2-47 birthdate, Frederick Harlan Coe would now be thirty-four, and most of the rape victims had described the assailant as younger—"eighteen to twenty" in at least one of the cases. Rape victims were notoriously poor at describing assailants (one reason rape cases were hard to prosecute), but even wishful thinking couldn't convert a man in his mid-thirties to a late teenager. Allen conferred with Det. Sgt. Gary Johnson. SPD mythology held that the burly sergeant could recite the records section from memory. Johnson mentioned that he'd read some reports and was surprised to see that Gordon Coe was being checked out. "Did you know he's editor of the *Chronicle*?" Johnson asked.

"No," Allen said.

"He runs the Secret Witness Program, been around town since the year one. His name's come across my desk a couple times for suspicious automobile or suspicious person. Once it was a gray Citation and once a Cadillac. I think he's got a son."

Allen thanked his memorable colleague and sent for the younger Coe's picture. The 1971 police photograph showed a young man with a sturdy jaw and brownish hair. The picture wasn't nearly as ugly as some mug shots, but the fact that it was ten years old made it almost useless for identification purposes. He had a copy made anyway and turned it over to a couple of hard-chargers from the special squad, Dan Bunn and Eddie Quist. "Drop around and show this to Irene Pool, will you?" he said. "See what she thinks." Mrs. Pool had already viewed some sixty pictures of known sex offenders and other suspects, many of them far likelier candidates than Coe. A few had piqued her interest, but she hadn't come up with a positive ID, and hypnosis had been no help as usual. The businesswoman seemed to know exactly what she was looking for.

Around 4:30 that afternoon Allen had his nose in tips from Gordon Coe's Secret Witness program. He wished he were out in the crisp winter air doing something simple like jogging to Idaho or breaking his state record for walleyed pike. His phong rang; it was Eddie Quist. "She made Coe from the picture," he said.

"*What?*" Allen said.

"Mrs. Pool made a positive ID. Coe's our asshole!"

"How sure was she?"

"She took one look at the mug shot and said, 'That's *him*! His hair is lighter now, but that's *him*.' I asked her if there was any doubt, and she said she'd like to see him in person and hear him talk, because rape's a terrible crime to pin on the wrong person, but then she took another look and said, 'It's definitely him. Look at those eyes; look at that chin. There aren't two faces in the world like that.'"

"Come on in," Allen said. He phoned his wife and told her he would be late.

*   *   *

Early that evening embittered members of the special squad were drowning their sorrows at the Police Guild spa. "We were half shot in the ass," one admitted later. "The brass were putting us out of business and we were sitting there thinking about all the extra hours we hadn't put in for—Steve Christian must have worked five hundred extra hours himself, and there wasn't one of us with less than two hundred. What bothered us the most was that we'd done a good job. We hadn't caught the South Hill rapist, but we'd made a hell of an effort. Wives and girlfriends walking as decoys and all. If the scumbag wasn't gonna be caught that way, how the Christ was he gonna be caught? We were crying in our beers about it. Then Eddie Quist waltzes in with his boyish grin and says, 'Guess what? We're back in the saddle. Here's a picture of our boy.' He waved around a mug shot. We all took our first look at the South Hill rapist and ordered another round. He was beautiful."

75

F H Coe will be a millionaire. It's just a matter of time.—Fred Coe, Sept. 16, 1971

The hard-driving realtors at Roger Crane & Associates were puzzled by Kevin Coe. In his diffident way, the new man seemed full of energy and ideas, but when the talk was over nothing ever got done. Office manager George Korb's patience was almost at its end. Coe spent hours staring at the wall, ripping pieces of paper into small pieces, folding newspapers like an origami artist. He banged at his typewriter in spurts. One day he yelled into his phone, "Why don't you fuck off, bitch!" He repeatedly annoyed one of the secretaries by asking her to perform mysterious chores like calling listees and asking if they would be home that night, or calling to see if anybody answered and then hanging up. No one else in the office worked that way.

Korb figured there was little enough activity in real estate without sending an oddball out to represent the firm. He called in his other new employee, Virginia Perham, and asked about her roommate. "Level with me, Gini. Is he...all right?"

"To tell you the truth, things aren't going well between us," she confided. "I don't understand him anymore."

"I *never* did," Korb said. He hated to fire realtors, but he realized that unless there was a drastic turnaround he would have no choice.

76

If Coe's a rapist—why does he have <u>no police record</u> in any of the cities in which he's lived. NONE!—Fred Coe, Jan. 15, 1982

Roy Allen worried about the photograph Irene Pool had identified. As police pictures went, it wasn't bad, but it was ancient. He needed an up-to-date shot to show the other rape victims.

A real estate show had just opened at the Spokane Interstate Fairgrounds. Allen learned that Roger Crane & Associates had a booth. Steve Christian went to the scene armed with a 35-mm. Minolta and a 400-mm. lens. In the parking lot he found a four-door gray-over-black Chevrolet Citation with real estate books on the back seat. It bore a standard Washington plate, SMX956, covered by a transparent sheet of yellow plastic.

At the Crane booth inside the building, he spotted a young man in a three-piece suit and a layered hair-do. He doubted that it was Fred Coe; the man looked about twenty-five. Christian drifted a safe distance away and peeped through his telescopic lens. A name tag came into focus: "Kevin Coe." A younger brother perhaps? Christian began clicking off pictures. The light was marginal and he moved closer without much improvement. He had a flash unit, but he didn't want to call attention to himself. He phoned headquarters and discussed the problem with Roy Allen. "Don't ask me," Allen said. "You're the photographer."

"Well, goddamn, Roy, I can't just walk up and click the camera in his face."

"We need the pictures, Steve."

When Christian returned to the Crane booth, it was crowded. He attempted several shots at close range, pretending to be shooting an exhibit, but unwanted heads kept getting in the way.

Waiting at headquarters, Allen asked the records division for Frederick Harlan Coe's complete file, including old reports that might have been committed to microfilm. Within minutes a clerk arrived with a teaser: the subject's traffic record.

Allen examined three recent speeding tickets. In October, 1980, Coe had been stopped for speeding at Twenty-second and Ray. He was carrying a

Nevada driver's license and driving a car described as "a gray Chev, Wash. Lic. SMX956." He had told the officer that he was a realtor and was on his way to show a house.

Two weeks later he was stopped again, this time on Freya St., "driving '80 Chev gray Citation" with the same plates. Allen confirmed that the ticket was issued on the date Marie Oldham had been raped after getting off a bus on that same street.

The third ticket had been written on the North Side at 7:15 a.m. on December 17, 1980. Coe, still driving on his Nevada license, was speeding in a '79 yellow Cadillac and explained that he was on his way to a nearby jogging track. The ticketing officer alertly noted that the Cadillac had been heading away from the track at the time. Once again Allen cross-checked the date against his timetables. The Gibbs rape had been on that day. He mused about the coincidence: three tickets, two on rape days.

The microfilmed records of earlier arrests began arriving. The first was for "carnal knowledge of a minor," summer of 1965. File details were skimpy, but detective Bruce Campbell remembered it in detail:

"The girl was a fourteen-year-old we'd seen a lot of. Lived with her grandmother, ran the streets, went from one catastrophe to another. She had plenty of nicknames: 'Nancy the River Rat,' 'Nasty Nancy.' That'll give you the idea. A couple of high school social clubs were sharing a banquet at the Desert Sahara Motel across the street from a joint called the Trophy Tavern. Around seven o'clock the bartender sent word that Nasty Nancy was available in the basement and she was trying to break a record set by her girlfriend.

"She slept with a hundred and some boys. It went on till noon the next day. Mae, the head nurse at the city health clinic, called us up a week later and said, 'What the hell's going on here? I got boys backed up to the elevator waiting for VD shots.' We nailed young Coe and a couple others and got the story. I knew his dad well. I'd been director of a junior-police program for twelve years and Gordon had always given us good ink. We called the parents to pick up their sons, and Gordon rushed over. He had to wait outside the office, and I remember he was upset about that. I expected him to come in breathing fire at his kid like the other fathers. But all he said was, 'What the hell kind of girl is she, anyway?'"

A second yellowing sheet in Frederick Coe's jacket described a "possible assault" on a sixteen-year-old. Late on a Saturday night Fred Coe, a Washington State University freshman, had offered to drive the girl home, then taken her to a quiet spot on High Drive, "kissed her once and held her down on the front seat. He told her she would have to 'hump' or walk back to town. He reached under her blouse and bra, feeling her breasts. . . . When she cried, he let her up, then drove her to 1/2 blk east of the Panda, Third & Division." The young man had refused to tell the girl his name, but as his Chevrolet Nova sped away she memorized the license number.

A follow-up report noted, "Car with license #CCM-758 belongs to a Gordon H. Coe, of W. 1015-29th. Ri. 7-1748. Mr. Coe's son Frederick Harlen Coe 19 yrs. now drives the car. . . . Mrs. Coe was contacted and she said that her son attends WSU at Pullman and he has the car there with him. . . . She also stated that she had visited her son last week at Pullman and was there with him until 10:00 P.M. Saturday night. . . . "

Convenient, Allen thought. Mom produces an instant alibi. He pulled out the report of a follow-up interview with Fred. The young collegian had admitted that much of the girl's story was true but insisted that she'd been more than willing and only left his car when she'd spotted a familiar young man walking nearby. The interview report ended: "FRED doesn't seem to want his father to know about this, but was told to tell him. It may be a good idea to have Mr. COE and his son in the office tomorrow night and have a talk with them. The girl's mother doesn't want to press any charges against this boy." That made two for two for the lucky young man.

The third charge in the file was more serious. The date was May 28, 1971. The case lent itself to a short summary:

> 71-38159 05-28-71 - 5:00 A.M. FIRST DEGREE BURGLARY/INDECENT LIBERTIES S. 518 Maple, Apt. B. Suspect Frederick Coe entered unlocked apartment, climbed on bed with a sleeping WF, unknown to him, unbuttoned her nightwear, rubbed her "private area" and her breasts, stated "Don't you remember me? You invited me up here to fuck?" Victim screamed, Coe ran from apartment but was apprehended by two males after taking evasive action through alleys on foot. At time of apprehension, he told the two "You better watch out. I'm a golden gloves champion." The charges were dismissed 12/4/72. Victim had moved to Texas and failed to reply to letters from Prosecutor's Office.

A *Chronicle* article was clipped to the file. It was dated May 28, 1971, and ended, "Fred H. Coe, 24, W1019 Twenty-ninth, was booked on a second-degree burglary charge alleging he entered an open apartment door and awakened a 20-year-old resident."

Allen read on. The editor's son's next brush with the local police was dated March 18, 1977, six years later. Had he been living elsewhere all that time? The location was Vip's Restaurant in downtown Spokane, the alleged victim a Republic Airlines hostess. The woman said she'd heard a noise in an adjoining booth in the ladies' room, looked up and saw a man peering down at her. "Gee," he said, "you sure have a nice cunt." She screamed, and he ran outside and drove away. Someone noted his license number, and police went to the registered address. The car was parked outside and the hood was warm. An officer talked to the vehicle's middle-aged owner, Gordon H. Coe, who informed them that his son Fred often drove the car but was out at the moment.

The police file showed no disposition of the case. Still waiting for Christian to return with fresh photos, Allen called the city prosecutor's office and asked for a check on Coe in the 1977 files. Nothing turned up. A helpful court clerk went through day-by-day dockets and found that a Fred H. Coe had been charged with violation of a city vagrancy ordinance covering disorderly behavior. On his first court appearance he'd been granted a continuance. That was the last recorded notation. A check in the vault where case files were kept in numerical order turned up another blank. Allen went back to his office wondering who had tampered with the files and why.

The next listed incident was a year and a half later, on November 26, 1978. The offense was "indecent liberties" and the allegation was that Coe had grabbed a woman's breasts while walking on a city street. There were several witnesses, but the case had been inactivated when a detective couldn't locate the suspect. Five cases, Allen said to himself, and five free rides. He glanced at the sixth and last notation in the file. Shoplifting. A routine case with a routine outcome: seventy-two hours of community service.

Steve Christian showed up with film from the real estate show. "There's no vanity plate," Christian explained. "He's put yellow plastic over his tags. The number's SMX nine five six." Another mystery solved.

The lab did a rush job on the film and within fifteen or twenty minutes the two policemen were studying damp prints. There were good shots of the interior and exterior of Coe's Citation, but the pictures of Coe himself were too grainy for photo lineups. Steve Christian cursed himself and the camera. Allen told him to relax; there would be other chances.

The next morning a man with a Texas drawl phoned the valley office of Roger Crane & Associates. He introduced himself as an oilman and said that he'd fallen in love with a house listed in the Sunday *Spokesman-Review*. Could the listing agent, Mr. Coe, show the property today? At the site neither Coe nor his client glanced at a panel truck parked across the street. The Texan seemed especially interested in the front lawn. The inspection of the house took about thirty minutes.

At police headquarters later, the Texan, a civilian employee, said, "I told him I had to have this house, begged him not to show it to anybody else, and he didn't even take my name! That's how interested he is in real estate." The crime lab called with bad news. None of the pictures shot through the one-way glass of the undercover van had turned out. Allen began to wonder if they were dealing with a man or an astral projection.

While the frustrated detectives were plotting another approach, good news blew in from Nevada. An earlier check with the Las Vegas Police Department had turned up no record or picture of Frederick Harlan Coe, but a six-year-old likeness in glorious color arrived. It had been taken under a state law licensing entertainers. Allen and his colleagues gazed at a glossy of a young man with light brown hair to his shoulders, long sideburns, a wispy moustache and a firm chin. "Let me borrow that for a few hours," another detective said. "I want to show it to somebody."

A few hours later the detective phoned in excitedly. A rape victim named Lois Higgins, who'd had a hand rammed down her throat nearly three years before up on Indiana Ave., had made a positive ID.

77

Gini wondered where Kevin would jump next. In less than four months he'd become bored with Roger Crane & Associates. Despite his weakening allegiance, he threw himself into the job of monitoring the Crane booth at the Fairgrounds. Staffers were supposed to take turns, but he was around night and day.

He was having more and more screaming arguments with his mother. One day at the office outcries came from his cubicle: "I'm not a bum. Don't call me that!. . . . Well, *you're* a bitch!" My God, Gini thought, what must the others think?

His face was flushed to the neckline. "That goddamn bitch!" he said in a compressed voice.

"What was it this time?" Gini asked, but he was already stomping out of the office.

On impulse she decided to call Five Pines. Ruth answered lazily, a sign she was upset. Gini explained that she'd heard Kevin's end of the conversation and hoped Ruth wouldn't take it too seriously. He'd been pressured lately—

"He's a liar and a cheat!" Ruth interrupted. She rambled on about her son's irresponsibility, his lying, his failure to earn a living. Gone from her voice were any attempts at an exotic accent. Soon she began sobbing, and then she shrieked, "*You* were a *fool* for getting involved with him! *Stupid!* You're a stupid fool!" Gini had no chance to defend herself. The phone went dead.

Kevin came home late and told her he'd spent the evening at Five Pines. "How'd it go?" she asked.

"I damn near hit her."

Just after midnight, Gini awoke and went to the kitchen for a cigarette. As she was padding through the hallway toward the bedroom she noticed a light and glanced into the bathroom. He was sitting on the toilet. She went back to bed. When he returned he snapped, "What the hell were you doing spying on me like that?" She laughed. Sometimes his accusations were funny.

"Answer me!" he said.

"Oh, Kevin, don't be ridiculous. I couldn't care less what you do in the bathroom."

"Your goddamn spying pisses me off."

She started to respond but didn't. He wasn't angry at her; he was angry at Ruth. He'd never been able to get that straight.

78

Even for reported rapes, the chance of a conviction is small: rape has the lowest conviction rate of any major crime. In one study, 635 rape complaints led to identification of only 167 suspects, of whom 45 were charged and 10 were subsequently convicted—a conviction rate of less than 2 percent (Hotchkiss, 1978).—James C. Coleman, James N. Butcher and Robert C. Carson, *Abnormal Psychology and Modern Life*

From the earliest identifications of Fred Coe by victims of the South Hill rapist, police and prosecutors faced problems never encountered in fiction. Not one of the cases against Coe was solid. Outdoor rapes and stranger-to-stranger rapes were the hardest of all to prove.

Police had known for over a year that they were dealing with an artful practitioner, far more skilled at his craft than they could ever be at theirs. His technique was impeccable. He almost always struck from behind. He almost always worked in the dark. And he almost always threatened to knife his victims if they looked at him. His description varied from rape to rape, a fact that had sometimes led investigators to conclude that he was two men, or even three. He left no fingerprints or tangible evidence, only battered, hysterical victims. Defense lawyers earned six-figure incomes making such women look like sluts and liars in court.

After Irene Pool and Lois Higgins identified Fred Coe from his picture, impatient detectives wanted to make an arrest, but prosecuting attorney Donald Brockett ordered them to seek more evidence. It would be folly to go into a Spokane court against a Cowles managing editor's son with anything less than a solid case, especially on a rape charge. Brockett's conviction record through ten years in office hovered around sixty percent, lowest of any county prosecutor in Washington. He claimed it was because he was reluctant to plea-bargain and tried cases that others would have refused. Whatever the explanation, his professional reputation would never survive a courtroom beating in the South Hill rape case.

Working closely with Brockett, top police decided to try to catch Coe *in flagrante delicto.* Frustrated members of the special squad saw the idea as unworkable. "Too many of our brass watch TV," one member observed later.

"They forget that you can't do a good surveillance on the South Hill. The streets are narrow; the blocks are short. There's a million ways a tail can go wrong."

The first attempts at following the gray Citation were unnerving. "He drives like a stock-car racer," a plainclothesman reported at the end of an evening watch. "It's impossible for one car to follow him. He never goes anywhere in a straight line and his normal speed is fifty."

Another tracker added, "He doesn't recognize stop signs and lights. It's Russian roulette out there. We lost him five or six times. Once we sped up and there he was—staring at us as we drove past. We had to call in another car. We went through four cars like that." Then someone came up with a refinement.

A uniformed patrol team saw two pairs of shoes protruding from under a 1980 Chevrolet Citation in a car dealer's lot. When they tapped the soles, a pair of plainclothesmen wriggled into sight. One of the patrolmen asked, "What the hell are you doing under there?"

"Police business."

The horizontals were from ADVIN, "Administrative Vice, Intelligence and Narcotics," a unit answerable only to a deputy chief. They were trying to find the best place to attach a bug to the underside of a Citation. The transmitter, the size of a cigarette pack, would broadcast a radio tone up to three miles— one tone every three fourths of a second when the target car was in motion, every second and a half when it was stopped. That night undercover cops clamped it on Coe's car.

The next problem was an old one: manpower. Nine men from the special squad and three from ADVIN had been detailed to the surveillance of Fred Coe, but since it would take five or six cars hopscotching and paralleling each other to keep from giving the show away, a round-the-clock tail was impossible. A van with one-way glass was set up a block from Coe's mustard-yellow house, and staffed from sundown to sunup. Undercover cars began following the Citation at the close of each workday and stuck with it till Coe "went down" for the night. That left the daylight hours uncovered—a calculated risk.

On one of the first nights, an ADVIN sergeant named Tom Morris was sitting in the front of an unmarked car listening to tones and watching the warning lights. Coe's car was somewhere ahead and the beeps and lights were strengthening. "Left," Morris told the driver. They sped a block. "Now right." They drove five or six blocks. "Now left."

"Sarge," the driver said after a while. "We're running the bus route!"

After a while they caught sight of a city bus; directly behind it was the Citation. As Morris watched through binoculars, the little gray car darted down a sidestreet. The officers followed in the blind by signal, and when they came into sight of the car ten minutes later it was running behind a different bus on a different line.

79

[The psychopath] hits upon conduct and creates situations so bizarre, so untimely, and so preposterous that their motivation appears inscrutable. Many of his exploits seem directly calculated to place him in a disgraceful or ignominious position.—Hervey Cleckley, M.D., *The Mask of Sanity*

Dr. John Little had to look twice. My God, he said to himself, that guy's running without shorts! The jogger was a hundred yards ahead, his buttocks shining in the bright winter sun. It was 8:45 on the morning of Saturday, February 28, and Little was jogging on High Drive near the slope where his friend Margot Terry had been raped six months before. The South Hill rapes had touched his life three or four times—much too often to suit him and his wife Liz—and he never ran past this point without thinking of Margot's hour of terror and how Liz had spotted a suspicious car that same morning and how Jeanie Mays, whom he'd first met when she was thirteen, had been raped in his own block of Twenty-fourth just a few weeks before.

And now . . . a bottomless jogger.

The dentist tried to judge whether he was gaining on the man and if so whether he should slow to avoid a confrontation or speed up for a better look. He had just lengthened his stride when he spotted two female joggers approaching the runner a block or so ahead. As he watched, the women skipped to the other side of the street. The pantless man jogged past them without breaking stride. Breathing hard, the females reached Dr. Little. One giggled and said, "That must've been the South Hill rapist!" They seemed amused.

When the dentist broke into a sprint, the barebottomed jogger dropped down the slope and ducked behind a tree. The time had come to call police. Little knocked on a door as the other runner peeped over the crest. He was a young man with sandy hair to his ears and dark glasses. Little watched him saunter up on the path in the same red shirt and a matching pair of shorts, then sprint down High Drive. The dentist gave chase but couldn't catch up. He ran home and phoned Crime Check, a police answering service manned by volunteers. He gave his name and address in case they caught the flasher and needed a witness. He waited at home all day. No one called.

* * *

Late that afternoon Patrolman Steve Christian began the day's watch on Fred
Coe, now code-named "Buster." Using established procedure, he followed a
block or two behind the gray-over-black Citation as it sped from the real estate
office to the yellow house on Twenty-ninth. Coe was in and out quickly and
began another evening tour, following buses and slowing at each stop to peer
at those who got off.

Just after dark, the car made a dash for the Lincoln Heights shopping
center and Christian lost sight of it in traffic. When he saw it again, it was
parked unlighted in a driving lane of the shopping center and Coe appeared
to be studying two teenage girls. He stared for five or ten minutes and then
drove off.

Christian wondered when the man was going to make an overt move. It
had been nineteen days since the last rape. Buster was due.

The next day dawned beautiful and bright. Seventeen-year-old Julie Helmbrecht wasn't much of a runner, but a radiant Sunday morning like this was
just too tempting. The high school girl had jogged forty-five minutes at a
blissfully slow pace when she spotted a man stretched out in a beefcake pose
on a bench just above the cliffside on High Drive. He was bareheaded and
his red shorts were around his ankles. She lost her stride momentarily as he
jerked his bare penis in her direction. She ran to the other side of High Drive
and the man stood up, still pulling at himself. She ran home without looking
back. Her father arrived from his own morning workout and called the police,
but no one came to investigate.

Two hours later, at 1:30 in the afternoon, a police sergeant named Charles
Bown was bicycling along the edge of Comstock Park. A silver-gray Chevrolet
Citation passed and Bown noticed the yellow license plate. He was aware that
men from both units had been watching this car for several days, and he
himself had noticed a similar car with similar tags while helping to run rape
decoys a year earlier.

The Citation was moving so slowly that Bown found he could keep up on
his bike. He stayed about a half block behind and watched. The driver was
leaning across the front seat, steering with his left hand and staring intently
out the right window. Bown tried to figure out what he was looking at, but
all he could see were a few joggers and some picnickers, male and female.
The car passed out of the park area and then sped off.

The next day, Monday, March 2, a disc jockey phoned Dr. John Little and
said he'd heard about the Saturday sighting of the barebottomed jogger and
wanted to broadcast details. The DJ had made himself an expert on the South
Hill rapes and considered the dentist's sighting significant; perhaps others
had seen the same man and could identify him. Soon after the information
was aired that afternoon, a detective interviewed Dr. Little over the phone. At
the end of the conversation the dentist asked why it had taken so long to
check out the incident. "Oh, it's no big deal," the officer said.

"But I told you—this neighborhood is where the latest rapes happened."

"Doc, all you got is a lily waver. They're frightened types—shy, recessive. Your lily wavers never rape."

On behalf of his wife and female friends and his own peace of mind, Dr. Little wished he could believe the comforting words. Personality types didn't break down quite so simplistically. Nothing could convince him that he hadn't seen the South Hill rapist.

80

Gini Perham made a few last-ditch attempts to save her relationship with Kevin. She had lived with him for seven months and loved him for two years, but it was porcupine love, full of pain. Moved by guilt and sentiment, she bought him a thin gold necklace. At first he acted surprised that anyone would buy him anything, and tried to hand it back. "You know I don't accept gifts, V.K.," he said sternly, but in the end he did. Then she bought him a spy novel by William F. Buckley. This time he flatly refused the gift and asked how she'd remembered his admiration for Buckley. It seemed a revealing question, an indication of how little understanding he expected from others.

"I remembered it because you mention him every other day," she said.

"I do?" he said. He seemed surprised.

She knew how much he hated to discuss their relationship unless he broached the subject himself, and he hadn't for several weeks, not since he'd idly mentioned that they should marry and have a son named Chan. One night when she was at a low ebb she blurted out, "I don't think you love me, Kevin. You never loved me the way I loved you."

He was broiling a filet mignon. No matter how low their finances, he brought home the best steaks and collected her share in cash. He said, "I'm sorry you feel that way, V.K."

She told him that she couldn't understand what was in their future together. "You'll admit things haven't been going well with us, won't you?" she asked.

He was silent. She walked over and looked straight at him. His face bore the half smirk that he usually wore when she brought up something uncomfortable. She walked away as though leaving the kitchen, then looked back. He was staring at the floor and she was sure he was crying. He lifted his head and saw her, and the old look slid back on his face like a mask. She thought, Why do you always hide the way you feel? If you feel sad, why don't you look sad?

In early March he began watching junk TV for long stretches: sitcoms, game shows, soaps, the same frothy diet that sustained his mother but had always been the object of his scorn. He would stare heavy-lidded, slumped in his chair like a man who weighed three hundred pounds. Sometimes she thought he was only pretending to watch, to keep her out of his space. She felt no desire to intrude. In two years he'd answered all her important questions by answering none.

He became even more hygienic and orderly. He would flop down and rub at a spot for five or ten minutes. She would be using dental floss or Kleenex in the bathroom, and if she stepped out for a minute or two he would throw it away. He even altered his style of showering, leaning forward under the nozzle so that the spray flowed down his back. Then he would hold his buttocks apart for two or three minutes. He confessed that he was thinking of making a radical change in his hairstyle. "I used to bleach it. Maybe I ought to try that again. Or a perm. Maybe grow another moustache."

If there was any improvement in his personality it was in a slight trend toward self-criticism. "I know my main problem," he said one morning when he returned from his early jog. "I haven't been motivated enough. Anger motivates. I need to get angry. I'll capitalize on it and I'll be a hell of a success. Just you wait."

That evening in bed he mused, "You know why I've never succeeded at anything?" Gini had been drifting off, but she came awake when she realized that she'd just heard his first admission that he was a failure. "I was never willing to pay my dues. I never stayed with anything long enough to make it." She remembered saying the same words to him more than once. She was sure that he'd heard them from Ruth, too, and Jeni, and Jay Williams—anyone who'd ever cared about him. But she was equally sure that his new insights were temporary, just as everything else about him was temporary, illusory. Tomorrow he would wake up spouting, "I'm a media man. I have great experience as a *blah blah* and a *blah blah* and a *blah blah.…*" She'd heard it all. In Bob Dylan's words, she had "no faith to lose."

He began a series of revelations about his past. He would be sitting in the living room watching TV or reading the *Chronicle* when he would come out with something new. Much of the information concerned his mother, but the fires burned so hot between those two that Gini could never tell where truth ended or began. He gazed in the distance as he spoke, looks of wonderment and devilment playing across his face, as though he were driven to justify Ruth's history but at the same time to expose her.

He claimed that in both his mother's earlier marriages she had aborted babies. "And she told me she thought about aborting me, too, but she decided that she really loved Gordo and she should bear his children." He said that Ruth had punished him for putting his feet on the furniture. "But her dog could jump all over everything, rip up the comforter on my bed, claw at her clothes, and she'd never do a goddamn thing about it. The dog took precedence." He claimed to have vivid memories of his diaper days and the sensual experience of having his mother touch his penis as she changed him. He spoke of his personal sexuality, a subject he'd avoided earlier. He said he'd had a homosexual experience in grade school. "We lay next to each other and touched each other." There was a note of shame in his voice.

Gini said, "Why, Kevin, that's perfectly normal."

He seemed relieved and surprised. "You really think so?"

"Certainly. Have you been thinking you did something wrong all this time?"

He went on to confess that he sometimes thought about having a homosexual affair but wouldn't get involved with any male of less magnitude than Warren Beatty or Robert Redford or the porn star John Holmes, whose oversize penis he admired. Late one night he brought up his sister. "Sometimes I miss her," he said.

"Were you close when you were kids?"

"I wish we'd been closer. She's a great person. But she had her friends and I had mine. Once when she was here I whispered in her ear, 'I love you, Kathy.' Her eyes filled up." He seemed touched by the memory. Soon he dropped off to sleep. Gini's head was bursting with useless information. He'd been reminiscing compulsively, laying bare selected parts of his life, but what had he really told her? Very little, she realized.

Restless, she looked out a front window. A man was walking past the house. She thought, He could be the South Hill rapist. But she decided he wasn't. He was medium in every respect—height, weight, attire, even manner of walk, looking neither to right nor left. He disappeared in his own medium way, down near Thirtieth, where a van had been parked for three or four days.

81

A few days after police started watching Coe, the overnight men assigned to the camper saw him leave his house in jogging clothes at 5 a.m. An ADVIN car was hurriedly pressed into service and caught up with "Buster" as he drove bus routes in the predawn. The routine surveillance was extended to the early-morning hours, and Det. Lt. Gene McGougan joined his trackers to provide another pair of eyes. There were a few grumbles that the prosecutor should ride too. In the week since Irene Pool had identified a picture of Coe, no one had had a day off.

The tracking wasn't coming easily. Sometimes the Citation stopped suddenly and the homing equipment indicated it was parked. The chase car would creep closer and closer till the red proximity-warning light indicated that the target was at hand, and then the officers would realize that they had just overshot the car, parked under trees or in alleyways where Coe could watch the street without being seen. Sometimes he would follow a bus, then cut across town at dazzling speed and arrive at a corner a minute or two before a bus arrived. Then he would be off to still another bus stop. The policemen decided he had memorized the Metro bus schedule.

He pushed his little car so fast and so unpredictably—the screaming U-turn was one of his standard techniques—that it wasn't always possible to stay on him even with the sophisticated equipment. One night he took the Interstate to Idaho at eighty and ninety miles an hour. The chase car lost him in Coeur d'Alene, but the green light indicated that the target was within two miles. The officers cruised the city streets till the red blinked on. Sergeant Tom Morris turned the sensitivity down; the light still glowed. "Jesus, Rich," he said to his partner Richard Jennings, "we gotta be right on top of him!"

They were. The Citation was tucked between two parked cars just around the corner.

One night the trackers passed Coe head-on four times. Twice he honked his horn as he sped away. "We thought we were made," a detective reported, "but later on we picked him up again and he was watching women at a shopping center." After the first few foggy days of March, the attempt to snare

Buster settled into a frustrating, exhausting routine. Decoys were paraded past his house, but he ignored them. On most mornings he would leave home at 5 or 5:30, follow buses, watch females waiting at bus stops, check out Hart Field, the Ferris High School grounds, city parks and jogging trails. After an hour or two he would return home and reappear at 8 or 8:30 a.m. in his business suit. The trackers would drop him until late in the day when he usually left his office and headed for his parents' home.

At night he followed buses, hung around shopping centers, cruised high-school and college hangouts. He watched jogging trails, especially the one on High Drive. When he encountered young women he stopped and stared. He never ran. By 10:30 or 11 he would be back home, the lights would die in his house, and the surveillance would be secured till dawn. "It's spooky," one of the trackers complained. "He's like an animal hunting prey. And we're sup-posed to stop him from grabbing somebody when half the time we're not even sure where the hell he is."

Questions began to arise. Why no overt acts? Where was the red ski jacket that Irene Pool had seen? Who was the female roommate with auburn hair, the rapist's favorite color? And why did a grown man spend so much time at his parents'? No one doubted that Coe, as the men put it in universal police terminology, was their "asshole." But they wondered more than ever if it made any sense to try to catch a rapist—any rapist—in the act. Misgivings flew back and forth among the trackers, their superiors and the prosecutor's office, but the orders remained in effect. It had been three weeks since the rape of Jeanie Mays on February 9. Timetables had been drawn up, and they showed that Buster was overdue. The watch went on.

82

The *Chronicle* of Wednesday, March 4, carried an article that almost compromised the surveillance right out of business. Under the headline "Rape Inquiry Being Pushed," police chief Robert Panther was quoted as saying that Spokane police were making an all-out effort to catch the South Hill rapist, even donating their off-duty time and their personal cars. To show that his department was working hard to protect the city's females, the chief threw out some figures: "We have expended over 8,600 man hours on this effort. This represents the work of 26 persons giving part or full time to the investigation over the past four months. It also includes approximately 1,600 hours volunteered by persons, not members of the police department, but willing to devote a creative effort of their time to attempt to solve this problem."

Members of the tracking team were outraged. Buster wasn't stupid, and anyone who had ever read police procedurals or watched TV cop shows could tell from the wording that a massive man-watch was under way. Otherwise why so many man-hours? And what except volunteer decoys could possibly explain "persons, not members of the police department... willing to devote a creative effort"?

"Why'd the chief do it?" lamented one of the trackers.

"Because there's a lot of heat on him," a detective said. "He's a politician."

Another plainclothesman held up the newspaper and read, "'The chief said detectives and uniformed officers have devoted their own time and cars to investigate the attacks, but did not elaborate on what exactly is being done.' Jesus H. Christ, why didn't he just give Coe our license numbers?"

The men knew what Buster would do next. He would get rid of incriminating evidence like the gray sweats, the blue down vest and the red jacket. He would leave town, or change his act—keep hands out of victims' throats, clean up his language a little. There were lots of imaginative MOs for rape. Maybe the trackers could resume the hunt after he'd raped a couple dozen more.

Steve Christian had been watching Coe's house from a prize vantage point down the block and sending out an occasional dark-haired decoy. As soon as he read the *Chronicle*'s article he shut down his operation, and the primary job of house-watching reverted to the men in the van. Just after dark on the night the story appeared the van reported that Buster turned in early. Everyone's worst fears were confirmed: They'd been "made." The special squad cars and the ADVIN units were secured.

Around midnight the lights in Coe's house flashed on and off as though he were trying to attract attention. After a while the place went black and Eddie Quist, watching from the van, saw Buster emerge in a dark sweatshirt, gray running pants under dark gym shorts, a dark stocking cap and what appeared to be gloves. He pushed the back gate open and jogged out of sight down the alley. Quist couldn't follow; the van would be too conspicuous on these hushed streets. A walking tail would have been spotted fast and may have been exactly what Coe was trying to encourage. Quist reported what he'd seen and a car was ordered to crisscross the neighborhood. At the tracking team's sub-headquarters in Steve Christian's home, the men dozed in chairs with their clothes on, but the night passed without a rape.

By the light of the next morning everyone tried to agree on the meaning of the bizarre midnight run. Was Coe trying to prove that he was really a jogger? Had he missed the article in his father's paper and gone on the prowl for another woman? The consensus was that Buster was playing games, trying to panic the trackers into giving themselves away with a conspicuous midnight tailing effort. If so, they might as well quit.

The morning surveillance was secured early when Buster didn't make his customary rounds. Later in the day an off-duty sergeant reported seeing him peering at students outside Ferris High School. In the evening all tailing was handled by ADVIN's tracking car, working from three or four blocks behind. But the precautions proved unnecessary. Buster had changed his ways. No running bus routes, no racing across town at fifty miles an hour. The trackers were sure they knew why.

At seven o'clock the next morning Gini Perham awoke to the sloshing of the washing machine in the basement. She wasn't surprised; Kevin washed clothes at all hours. She padded into the kitchen to make coffee. One of the two oven mitts that had been in the house for as long as she could remember had been wedged dripping wet into the refrigerator handle. When Kevin came upstairs she asked, "Why are you washing the oven mitts?"

He looked past her with dull eyes and went back downstairs to his washing. She thought, Oh, God, one more crazy thing, and consoled herself with the knowledge that she wouldn't be living with him much longer.

Sitting at his desk later that Friday morning, Roy Allen realized that something had to be done to ease Fred Coe's suspicions or there would be no possibility of catching him dirty. He studied the latest profile of the South Hill rapist: "manipulative, calculating, bright, middle class and has a perverted courage."

He discussed the problem with his boss, Gene McGougan, and the two detectives decided to manipulate the manipulator. They would plant a newspaper story saying that another man was the prime suspect in the South Hill rapes. With luck, Coe would read it, relax, and revert to his old ways.

Allen broached the idea to Tim Hanson, the *Chronicle*'s young police reporter, without giving away Coe's identity. Hanson told him that any such article would have to be approved by city editor Charles Rehberg and managing editor Gordon Coe. At Allen's request, the reporter took the plan to Rehberg. "It's fine with me," the city editor said. "But every word has to be true. And the story's got to say that there's more than one South Hill rape suspect."

"No problem," Hanson said. To avoid being spotted by other reporters, he met with Allen at the Great Scott Tavern on the South Hill. They drank a few beers and outlined the article.

Gini Perham was surprised to see Kevin at home early that Friday evening. She wondered how soon he was going to do his nightly disappearing act. She tried to remember how long it had been since they'd had an old-fashioned date—dinner, or a movie. Weeks. *Months.* Maybe that was part of their problem together.

"Kevin," she said, "let's go to dinner."

"Huh?" He looked up from the TV as though he'd had no idea she was in the house. "What do you mean?"

"I mean let's go out to eat! Sit down, order, make a little conversation. Like other people."

He grunted "Unh-uh" and turned back to the TV. She was amazed at her anger. What right did this fellow human have to dismiss her with a grunt? She stepped between him and the screen and said, "I'm getting claustrophobia in this damn house, Kevin. We never go anyplace. Come on! We'll be back in an hour."

He didn't respond. When she snapped the set off he said, "Okay, *okay.* We'll take your car."

She wondered why. He'd always avoided driving in her big blue Monte Carlo. "What's wrong with the Citation?"

"Nothing."

"Then why do you want to go in my car? You never did before."

"Well, I do now. C'mon."

She drove them toward the Old Spaghetti Factory on South Monroe, stopping for gas while he sat in the car and watched her operate the self-service pump. She ate a plate of spaghetti as he sat silently, refusing even a sip of water. He reached across the table and helped himself to a spoonful of her ice cream, then pushed back his chair and said, "Let's go."

She paid for the dinner and drove them back home. He was asleep by 10.

By Saturday, March 7, the trackers had been sitting on Buster for almost two weeks and had succeeded in converting him into a stay-at-home. There'd been no rapes in a month. As the sun came up the men in the van watched the house half-heartedly. Tim Hanson's story was still being prepared. Buster and his girlfriend left for work on time. That ended the operation till evening.

The night watch brought new hope. At 7:05, Buster drove to a post-office substation. Word went out, "He's wearing the red jacket!" The trackers watched with binoculars as he opened a P.O. box, scanned his mail and threw it in a trash can. Then he drove south, circumnavigated Hart Field and began following bus routes again.

83

Police broke into my house. On one of the break-ins they spotted a large novelty dildo. It wasn't mine. I don't know whose it was. But the police spotted it. Then they staged a dildo-flashing event with a guy who looked like me. The police never found the dildo later. I got rid of it.—Fred Coe, May 26, 1982, quoted in the Seattle *Post-Intelligencer*

At 7:15 a.m. Sunday two plainclothesmen were sharing a sweet roll in the van when Fred Coe stepped out of his door wearing jeans and a blue jogging top with a white stripe down the sleeve. He backed the Citation from his garage and sped west on Twenty-ninth through cottony clouds of fog. On signal three fresh undercover cars followed, including a red Datsun 240-Z that Roy Allen had borrowed from another detective. The trackers planned to hopscotch and parallel their man and never allow the same car to be in his rear-view mirror for more than a few blocks. Now that Buster was returning to his normal abnormal behavior, they didn't intend to spook him again.

The target car turned south on Ray, sprinting from fog pool to fog pool. A tracker who was out in front sped to Hart Field and arrived just as the Citation whipped around a corner and parked. For several minutes Buster watched a female jogger in her fifties or sixties and then sped off. The chase became unnerving; the paralleling cars not only had to maintain Coe's hot pace but had to drive even faster to catch up when their turn came. The procession sped through foggy residential neighborhoods at forty-five and fifty.

Atop the South Hill, Buster cruised the trail along High Drive, sped down to Twenty-first, made a screeching U and headed back up to Comstock Park and paid a return visit to High Drive. Then the Citation entered a patch of fog and disappeared. The trackers sent units up and down cross streets without success. The ADVIN tracking car had just started a scan with the direction-finding equipment when word came from the van that the target had gone down.

It was a few minutes after 9. Now that the chase was over, the sun quickly burned through the haze. Gene McGougan and Steve Christian were sharing the Sunday paper in Christian's home when word came that Buster had completed his morning rounds.

Christian said, "Shit, he ain't gonna do nothing now." The surveillance was secured for the day.

At almost the same moment, *Leila Hicks*, a track-scholarship student at Spokane Community College, looked out the window of her apartment near the river and decided that it was too lovely a morning to be mad at the world. She decided to be mad anyway. The day before, some nerd had stolen her two-hundred-dollar silver Nishiki bike. She'd thought nothing of riding fifty or sixty miles on it, just as she'd thought nothing of running marathons and other distance races. At eighteen she was a fine-tuned six-footer, lithe and lean, her chestnut hair framing light blue eyes and the face of a high-fashion model.

This morning she intended to run only eight miles before church. Normally she clocked fifteen or twenty miles a day, but she was just coming off a back injury. As she pulled on her sweats she remembered her mother's advice: "Don't always run the same route. There's a rapist around." A few months ago she would have considered herself safe here on the North Side, but the *Spokesman-Review* had reported that the South Hill rapist operated all over Spokane, and now every woman in town was nervous. As she started out the door her roommate Annie called, "Have you got your Mace?"

Leila's mother had bought her the spray can. Sometimes she carried it cocked, but that seemed silly in daylight. She thought, What a hassle, grabbing a can of chemicals every time I leave the house. "Yeah, I've got it," she called back. She stepped through the door and into a crystalline day. Never mind the calendar, she thought. *This* is the first day of spring. If I can't go for a run on a day like this without worrying about some sex maniac, the world sucks.

She reopened the door of the apartment, flipped the Mace canister back inside and took off for a bark-chip jogging trail along the swollen dark-green river. She ran in her easy style past bicyclists, fishermen, other joggers, couples strolling hand in hand. The scene made her wish she were an artist. She settled into full stride as she reached the golf course and the first duffers of spring, circled the course in a few minutes and returned to the four-mile bark trail to head for home. Her mind returned to the stolen Nishiki. Life was getting to be bummer after bummer! The South Hill rapist kept her household in a state of nerves, and just recently she herself had received a total of fourteen obscene phone calls. Now—the stolen bike. She swore she would find it today. She ran on a strip of land between the water and Upriver Drive. Cars droned past on her right. A fisherman sat impassively on a folding canvas chair. She looked at her watch to make sure she had plenty of time to change for church. Her family didn't approve of worshiping God in sweats.

The mausoleumlike bulk of a Washington Water Power building came into sight and so did a young man walking toward her about seventy-five yards ahead. As he strolled through an area of overhanging trees she noticed that he made no attempt to move off the trail. These days most males gave female joggers a wide berth. She told herself not to worry—cars were passing and there were plenty of people within shouting distance.

The man drew near. He was about six feet tall, with a medium build, brown hair and a clean-shaven heavy-jawed face. He wore jean pants, a light-blue jogging top with a white stripe, and very dark sunglasses. When he was eight or ten feet in front of her his hands went to his crotch. She skidded to a stop in the bark. At first she thought he was holding his penis, but then she saw that the thing was too big—over a foot long and as thick as a fist. She said to herself, Yuck! and stepped out on Upriver Drive. The street was empty in both directions.

The man pointed the gross thing at her and said, "Watch me ejaculate now!" His unusual choice of words and his throbbing voice sounded eerie, otherworldly. He called out, "Let me see your cunt. Are you watching me now? *C'mon, watch!*"

She ran for almost a block, trying not to be sick. She felt as though the earth had opened and revealed a huge maggot that stood for all the evil in the world. When she looked over her shoulder she saw that he was still in the same place, a sullen look on his face, as though hoping she would change her mind and join in his puky game. Something about his stance told her he was a mama's boy, a wimp. She turned and ran toward him, screaming, "Catch him! *Catch him!*"

He ran. She chased him for about a hundred yards till he cut across an empty field the size of several city blocks, heading for the railroad tracks below the ridge on the north slope of the river valley. She saw that she would never catch him; she was a distance runner, not a quarter-miler. An old car rumbled out of a nursing-home parking lot and she ran up to the driver. He had pale-blue eyes and a concerned look. A blond woman sat next to him and there was a child of about twelve in the back.

She raised a finger toward the fleeing figure. "He exposed himself," she said, tears of rage flowing down her face. "And he wanted me to expose myself!"

"Go inside the nursing home," the man said firmly. "We'll take care of him."

William Fairfax, a forty-one-year-old born-again Christian and park-maintenance foreman for the city, had just finished a Sunday visit at the Riverview Terrace nursing home with his wife Kathy and daughter Brenda. "That way!" his wife shouted as he gunned their loose-jointed 1967 Chevrolet Caprice in pursuit.

The flasher was running up a long slope littered with dead brush and ground-squirrel diggings. Just across the Burlington Northern tracks near the top, a zigzag staircase led up to busy Illinois Avenue. It looked as though the man was trying to escape that way. Fairfax steered toward him on a rutted old road leading up the slope, the Caprice bumping and bouncing on its old shock absorbers. At the tracks the flasher began running west along the right-of-way. As the Fairfaxes watched he dipped from sight in a depression behind a thicket. The father sped back to the nursing home and told his daughter to go inside and call the police. The view from this far below the slope was so sweeping that it was as though they were on a football field watching someone run around the upper seats of a stadium. When the flasher reappeared, his blue jogging top was gone and he was wearing a white T-shirt. He was carrying his dark glasses and heading for the top of the hill.

Fairfax drove to a cutoff position up above on Illinois Avenue. The man turned and ran back down the hill. The chasers lost sight of him and didn't pick him up again until they saw him climbing into a small silver-gray car parked on a sidestreet off Upriver Drive. As they drove up, the little car squirted into a narrow street behind the big Washington Water Power building.

Fairfax turned into the same street and then braked sharply. The flasher had chosen a dead-end street for his getaway. The two cars idled within a few yards of each other. "What now?" Kathy Fairfax asked.

"Let's wait," her husband said. "He's not going anywhere."

Kathy scribbled the license number, SMX956, on the front of her check register. A young man in a white T-shirt climbed from the gray car and began walking away. "Good morning," Bill Fairfax called out.

"Good morning," the man answered. He strolled around the edge of a ten-foot stone wall and took off running till he was out of sight. Fairfax wondered what to do next. Where were the police? He'd done his job as a citizen; the arrest was a job for experts.

His wife grabbed his arm and said, "Look!" A squad car was passing on Upriver Drive. Fairfax honked and gave chase. The police car sped on; Fairfax caught the officer's attention two miles down the road by speeding past him.

A Pinkerton guard named Louis Leonetti had noticed the Citation and the Caprice racing down the the short street that led only to a loading dock. He thought he might be witnessing the first stages of a Sunday break-in, but by the time he reached the scene one of the cars was already gone. As he approached the gray Citation he saw a man lying facedown in the grass behind the building. The man got up and strolled toward the car. "Just a minute," Leonetti called out. "What are you doing here?"

The man asked excitedly, "Did you see that car that went out of here like a bat out of hell? I'm trying to catch him. Did you notice which way he turned?"

"No."

As the man drove off the guard made a note of his license number. He wondered why anyone would go to the trouble of buying a personalized yellow plate with normal letters and numbers. He checked for signs of forcible entry and found none, then wrote up a 286 security report.

By the time the Fairfaxes led the squad car back to the dead-end street the Citation was gone. The cop thanked Bill for his interest. That's the end of that, Fairfax said to himself. As a city employee, he knew that exposers were a low-priority item. The family headed for home and their Sunday worship. On Upriver Drive they spotted the tall young woman who'd kicked off their adventure. She was jogging on the bark trail along the river and seemed to be back in stride.

That evening Gini Perham came home to a nice surprise. Kevin was there again. She marveled at his timing. Now that she was preparing to leave him for good, he was becoming almost a normal housemate. Except for his attitude. He barely nodded when she said, "Hi!" Social niceties had never seemed to concern him. She thought of Jay Williams' whimsical theory that Kevin was a spy from outer space. Sometimes she halfway believed it.

Head down, Kevin walked from the kitchen to the living room and back again, then repeated the cycle like a caged coyote. She could see that he was suffering and her heart went out to him. Compassion wasn't much to offer, but it was all she had left. She intercepted him in the kitchen and tried to give him a hug. He jerked away. "Kevin, what *is* it?" she asked.

"Nothing," he said, and retreated to his den. The door shut in her face like a slap.

Later that night she made another attempt to comfort him. "Kevin, I *know* something's the matter. Can't I help?"

"It's a few minor problems, that's all."

"Like what?"

"*Nothing!*" He rose up in bed as though to be more emphatic. "I'm thinking, and I can't concentrate with you prying."

"Okay," she said. "I won't pry."

They said the stiff "Thank you" and "You're welcome" of couples in combat and offered each other their backs. It took her a long time to get to sleep. She couldn't escape the feeling that something awful was happening to him — something far worse than shoplifting. She wondered what it could be.

84

In all seriousness we began this year with you far ahead of me. You were taking out 1st-class figs and I was taking out sluts.—Fred Coe, 1965 Lewis and Clark High School yearbook

When Roy Allen jogged into the Public Safety Building on Monday morning, Gene McGougan handed him a disorderly persons report filed the day before. The account was skimpy but included the license number SMX956 and the information that the driver of the car had exposed himself to a young woman. "Jesus," Allen said. "He's going wild, even in the daytime. I think we ought to take him."

While police were laying plans, the Monday *Chronicle* arrived with its planted story aimed at throwing Coe off. The article, "Police Want to Quiz Man About Rapes," said twenty-four-year-old David Monson was "being sought by police for questioning in connection with several South Hill rapes." The page 1 story included some carefully worded deceptions to convince Coe that there'd been no special police activity around Twenty-ninth and Rebecca. It pinpointed the search to "nearby southwest sections of Spokane," miles from Coe's house. An unnamed police official was quoted: "There have been a lot of people searching day and night in an attempt to locate and apprehend David Monson. There have been a lot of hours spent patiently watching all of his acquaintances' houses, last-known addresses, old girlfriends."

Late in the morning Lt. McGougan invited reporter Tim Hanson for coffee. "Thanks for running that story," the detective said as they sat in the courthouse luncheonette. "You've been straight with us and we'll be straight with you. Off the record, the South Hill rapist is the son of—"

He scribbled on a napkin and slid it across the table. The young police reporter blinked as he read the name.

At noon Gini Perham and Kevin Coe and two of their colleagues assembled for lunch at a Mexican restaurant near their office.

Presiding over his customary empty plate, Coe said, "Lyle, how'd you ever land such a gorgeous wife?" The subject had come up often, and Lyle Hatcher had passed out of the stage of being complimented and into the stage of wondering why Coe brought it up.

"Just lucky," Hatcher said.

"It's *not* luck," Coe insisted, sipping a Perrier and taking on a troubled look. "Women fall all over you smaller guys. I don't understand it." He began talking about his friend Jay Williams, a man of Hatcher's approximate height. "It frustrated the hell out of me the way Jay could get women in high school. He had 'em waiting in line! I just couldn't seem to get their attention." He sighed. "Still can't."

Ann Allison, another realtor, thought, What a strange thing to say in front of Gini. What does he mean he can't get women? He's got *her*! Coe's monologue grew louder.

"Hey, don't let it bug you," Hatcher said, touching his officemate on the arm.

"Well, it does bug me!" Coe insisted, pulling away. He kept on for a few more minutes and then fell silent.

By late the same Monday afternoon the prosecutor's office began to unbudge from its position that Coe must be caught in the act. The dildo incident showed that he had to be watched around the clock, and with the chronic manpower shortage he was bound to elude his trackers now and then. Someone pointed out that if he raped while police were on his tail, there wouldn't be enough money in the state of Washington to pay the resulting judgments.

The prosecutorial machinery creaked into motion. Warrants were typed up for approval by a judge. "We've got enough probable cause to grab him right now," Roy Allen told his superiors, but he was ordered to hold off for one more day.

After work, Gini Perham entered the back door of the house and found Kevin there, his mood improved since lunch. She picked up the *Chronicle* and read that a man named David Monson was a prime suspect in the South Hill rapes and that police feared he had fled Spokane. Damn! she said to herself. They'll never catch him now. She repeated her misgivings to Kevin and he listened without comment. Later he told her he was going jogging and left the house.

Police watched anxiously as Buster returned to the bus lines, driving faster than ever. By now the trackers knew his habits and had less trouble keeping up. He checked out his favorite routes and parks and returned home.

85

I set my goal to be total closed volume leader at Crane in 1981. I knew I could do it. 1981 started out well. I set March 10th as the unpostponable date for going full-time—finally—in real estate. Tuesday, March 10th, was a superb start.—Fred Coe, Oct. 18, 1982

On Tuesday, March 10, Roy Allen dragged his six-foot six-inch frame out of bed at 4:50 a.m. and pulled on his running shorts. He felt good about the case. The article in the *Chronicle* had eased Coe's suspicions. With luck he would make his play today in front of an appreciative audience of plainclothesmen. And if he didn't—Buster would be busted anyway.

Allen liked the plan. When their quarry hit the streets, he and Eddie Quist would dog him in the little red 240-Z. If he attempted rape, the two cops would chase him down like hounds on a rabbit. Allen had joked, "But we're not gonna grab him. Oh no! We're gonna run alongside him and I'm gonna say, 'If you make it to the station, I'll buy you a Michelob!'"

Dream on, the detective told himself as he slipped out his front door. We'll take him any way we can. Jogging toward Coe's house, he reached up and touched his forehead. His sweatband, a pair of nylon handcuffs, was in place. In ten or fifteen minutes he reached Ferris High School. He was running along the edge of the big athletic complex when he saw headlights flicker and die at the end of the block. To his left another car turned down a side street. A pickup with a camper shell crawled past. He asked himself what the hell was up. There were too many vehicles out at this hour and they were moving too slowly. Most drivers on their way to work traveled thirty, thirty-five miles an hour.

He ran on. About a hundred yards from the locked main gate of the athletic field, he noticed a small car parked next to the fence in the darkest part of the block. It was the gray Citation, empty. My God, he thought, Buster must be prowling those condos across the street. There'd been an attempted rape in the area recently.

A car eased toward him. He decided it was the trackers; they must have seen him and thought he was Coe. He sprinted off. In the darkness he didn't know whether Coe was a mile or a few feet away, and he didn't want to expose the surveillance just when things were heating up. The car pulled alongside and a voice called in a loud whisper, "Roy? Is that you?"

Allen snapped, "Get your ass outa here!"

"That's Coe's car back there!"

"Go on up and turn. Take off!"

The car went around the nearest corner and stopped. Allen bailed inside, hoping that Coe hadn't caught the whole scene. "Where is he?" he asked.

"We don't know," the tracker answered. "He's out of his car; that's all we're sure of. He got up early and drove straight here."

"Gimme a radio and drop me at the end of the field. I'll sneak up on his car from inside the fence. You guys spread out and keep your eyes open. We'll nail him right now."

It took Allen ten minutes to work his way from one end of the darkened athletic field to the other. The complex was under construction, and he stumbled through an obstacle course of stacked pallets, sod, pipe, boards, mounds of gravel, newly dug ditches and rolls of wire fencing. He was within forty or fifty feet of the parked Citation when it squirted away from the curb. Buster sped to the corner and headed south. Allen turned up his radio and heard someone say, "He's moving!"

He pushed the transmitting button and asked, "What the hell's happening?" There was no response. He squinted at the radio and realized it was a DX-band. He could listen but he couldn't transmit on the right frequency. He looked around for an exit. As far as he could see in both directions the construction work was protected by a ten-foot wire fence. In the distance he heard the throaty roar from the Z's twin pipes. He could make out every upshift and downshift. Damn, he said to himself, it's party time for Eddie Quist, and I'm stuck behind a fence. He picked his way among the boards and ditches and finally exited by scaling the fence at a locked gate. In the distance the pursuit car whined again. God*damn*! he muttered. I'm gonna miss out!

He increased his pace as he ran west on Twenty-ninth, hoping one of the trackers would pick him up. Silence had returned to the peaceful South Hill. He was running toward Manito Park when he heard the 240-Z again. He slowed and tried to position it. The car snapped and growled. It was headed straight toward him. In the dim light the Citation appeared first, piercing the twenty-five-mph zone at the Lincoln Heights shopping center at double the speed limit. Allen tried not to gawk as he ran, but he couldn't help a twitch of his head when he heard three short beeps from the gray car. He saw Fred Coe grinning and waving at him. He couldn't manage a return grin, but he waved back.

The 240-Z came next, running without lights. Good luck, Eddie, Allen thought as it passed. I hope to God you don't meet a truck. An undercover car pulled up and stopped. He jumped in and heard Quist's voice crackling over the radio, "He's gone down. That's our show for today, folks."

"What happened?" Allen asked the driver.

"The usual. He left the house at quarter to six, parked for a while around Ferris, then checked out Hart Field, High Drive, Cannon Hill Park, a few other places. Now he's home."

"I heard. Did he approach any women?"

"Weren't any to approach."

"Lucky son of a bitch!" Allen said. He touched his head. The nylon hand-cuffs were damp with sweat.

A few hours later the Crane realtors assembled for their regular Tuesday morning sales meeting. The discussion turned to the South Hill. With the rapist active, business had become so bad that most felt it was a waste of time for a valley firm like Crane to list South Hill properties. Then Kevin Coe started to speak. Gini slumped in her chair. He had always had trouble hanging onto the thread of a discussion and lately he'd grown worse. People would ask him a question about real estate and he'd answer with a quote from Ayn Rand. She tried not to listen as he spoke. He went on and on, growing more animated, and finally worked up to the idea that Crane "most definitely" should open a South Hill office to grab all the business available up there. Manager George Korb thanked him for his contribution and Kevin smiled vaguely. The poor man, Gini thought. He's lost.

All morning long, representatives of the police department and the prosecuting attorney's office conferred. A tracker reported to Lt. McGougan, "We lost him again this morning. He was out of his car at Ferris—he could've raped by the time we picked him up again."

"Let's hope he doesn't kill somebody," an ADVIN man added.

McGougan didn't have to be convinced. Secretaries were pounding away on the search and arrest warrants that had been roughed out the day before. The plan called for Roy Allen and two other detectives to make the arrest at the realty office. Simultaneously, McGougan would serve a search warrant on the house. There was talk about letting the special squad in on the bust— they'd worked the case longer and harder than anyone—but McGougan said they would talk about that later.

Gini met Kevin for lunch at Denny's Restaurant in the valley; he liked the place because he could sip Perrier from the bar while others downed their various contaminants. She was feeling bad about her financial problems and worse about leaving the man she loved. "Tell me the truth, Kevin," she blurted out. "You've been seeing other women, haven't you?"

He looked hard at her and said, "No, I haven't. And I wish you'd stop accusing me."

He got up to leave, explaining that he had to meet his mother at Mr. Steak—another free meal, she realized. He said he planned to drive to a listing presentation at Newman Lake, over near the Idaho border, and would be home late.

That afternoon the trackers followed the silver-gray Citation eastward at speeds around ninety. They assumed Coe was going to show a house across the border—it wouldn't be the first time. The way he drove, Idaho was a short haul. The spread-out procession approached the state line and Steve Christian peeled off at a pay phone. "How far do you want us to follow him?" he asked McGougan. "Montana?"

"Stay with that son of a bitch. I don't care where he goes. Call back in an hour."

When Christian rejoined the chase he found that Coe was out of his car at Newman Lake. He phoned McGougan again. "I'm busy with paperwork," the lieutenant said. He sounded tense.

"We still gonna pop him today?"

"Yeah. Just keep him under observation at a nice safe distance."

By the time the trackers followed Buster back to Spokane, it was almost dark on the cool winter afternoon. Christian drove his El Camino to headquarters. A secretary was just finishing the last page of the lengthy search warrant.

At the end of the work-day Gini Perham heard laughter from the reception area of the real estate office. She leaned out of her cubicle and saw Kevin in the unaccustomed role of jester. He was sitting behind a desk and talking about his days as a disc jockey, using many voices. George Korb, Ann Allison and several others seemed fascinated. Gini slipped on her coat and kissed him on the cheek. "See you later," she said.

"Yeah," he said, and plunged into another reminiscence about the days when beautiful whores had flocked around his DJ console in Vegas. As she left, she noticed a dark gold car parked across Argonne Rd. and briefly wondered what it was doing there.

The arrest team drove away from headquarters: Roy Allen and two sergeants, Tom Morris and Gary Johnson. Morris would serve the warrant; the Crane office was just outside the city limits and he was the only member of the team with a deputy's commission. Allen and Johnson would pat Coe down, apply the handcuffs and read him his rights. Patrolwoman Judy Carl, a veteran of many icy expeditions as a decoy, would serve as an extra witness. The special squad, kicking and screaming, would be included out.

86

George Korb was a practical man, not given to moods or odd predilections, but something about this darkening evening gave him the whim-whams. He'd been in military intelligence and prided himself on his acuity. He looked around the deserted realty office. The place seemed hollow and strange. Kevin Coe tapped on his door and stepped in. Korb looked at his watch; it was quarter to seven. The office manager said, "Excuse me a second," and went out to lock the door to the street. He couldn't remember ever locking that door while anyone was inside the office and he had no idea why he decided to do it now.

The two realtors talked for five or ten minutes. Korb had never known a real estate salesman with more promise, and the wasted talent baffled him. "You know, Kevin," he said, "you've got it all—the looks, the know-how, everything! All you have to do is go out and—do it!"

"Thanks, George," Coe said. "I really appreciate your telling me that." There was a sharp knock on the outer door.

Korb walked across the office and opened it. A giant of a man stood flanked by two large sidekicks. They looked like enforcers. "Police officers," one said, flipping a badge and walking in. "We want to talk to Frederick Harlan Coe."

Korb knew that Kevin owed everybody money and decided that the trio had come to collect. Then he heard Coe's voice from behind the door. "George, they want to talk to me."

"Frederick Harlan Coe?" one of the men said, stepping inside. "We have a warrant for your arrest. The charge is the first-degree rape of Mrs. Irene Pool."

Coe said, "This must be a mistake. I don't even know this person. You guys are confused."

Korb decided he wanted no part of this action and stepped outside. Behind him someone began intoning, "You have the right to remain silent...." Oh, shit! the office manager said to himself. What an ugly deal!

The front of the little building was crawling with men carrying radios. A red Datsun 240-Z pulled up and two men jumped out. They had "cop" written all over their faces and also "rage." One of them slammed the front door of the car with both hands. They hung around for a few seconds and then sped off.

Korb walked back and forth, wishing he knew what was going on. None of the cops outside would talk to him. He stepped back inside. Kevin was surrounded. He said, "George, I want you to know I'm no common criminal." Korb didn't want to watch him being taken away—he had too much respect for Kevin's sensitivity. He stepped outside again. It's a big goddamn mistake, he said to himself. I'll go down to headquarters and talk to him later.

The men of the special squad had desperately wanted to be in on the big moment, but they lacked an invitation. One by one they parked their cars up the street from the Crane office and got out to watch. Some were sad and some were angry; it had been a point of honor with all of them that they deserved to be present, as one put it, "to put the gotchas on that scumbag."

Buster came out of the office escorted by the three detectives. The trackers saw him duck his head and get into an unmarked car for the ride downtown. The party was over. One of the trackers pushed the mike button on his portable radio and said, "Fuck it!"

A singsong dispatcher's voice asked for a repeat, and another tracker cut in, "He said, 'Hook it!'" The special squad went out for drinks.

Gary Johnson drove, Judy Carl sat alongside him, and Allen and Tom Morris flanked the prisoner in back. "What's this all about?" Coe asked. He sounded sincerely puzzled.

"Well, you're charged with raping a woman named Irene Pool," Allen told him again.

"Where?"

"Hart Field. Are you familiar with Hart Field?"

"I jog there. My regular track's under repair. Ferris High School."

"Have you been to Hart Field lately?"

"Uh—no. Not for a couple of weeks. Ten days at least."

The others knew that he'd been at Hart Field that morning, but no one let on. "How about Sunday?" Allen asked. "Were you up at Washington Water Power?"

"Uh—no."

"Wasn't there a little incident—?"

"Oh, yeah! I was in the area looking at properties."

"Did you have a run-in with somebody?"

"I had a problem with some thug, yes. But it didn't amount to anything."

"You're sure?"

"Yes." He paused. "I'd better not say any more till I talk to a lawyer."

At the station Roy Allen took a look at Coe's driver's license. It listed his height as six-two. He weighed and measured the suspect carefully and noted that Coe seemed to be stretching upward. Allen scratched on his notepad: "6' 1/4. 172."

Gini Perham had arrived home tired and gone to bed. The night before she'd been reading about Ted Bundy, the dashing young psychopath who'd murdered some three dozen women, but tonight she was too tired to read. She stepped into a robe and flopped on the bed. Within minutes she was sound asleep.

She heard the phone but ignored it. Her cockapoo barked several times and she ignored him too. Then she heard faraway voices. She sat up in bed, rubbing her eyes in the darkness, and called, "Who is it?"

"Police!"

Her heart jumped. What could the police want? She tied her robe and hurried to the kitchen door. Four men were waiting. "What's going on?" she asked.

One of the men showed a police badge and introduced himself as Lt. McGougan. "You must be a heavy sleeper," he said. "We knocked on the front door and then the back door and we went to a phone to call you." He showed her a piece of paper. "This is a search warrant."

She saw the name "Frederick Harlan Coe" and the words "first-degree rape." There was a two-page single-spaced list of items that she recognized as Kevin's: dark sunglasses, a gray jogging suit, Nike running shoes with a swirl, white ski hat with design, oven mittens, black leather gloves, navy down vest, on and on. She came to "red down jacket with hood" and started to tell them he didn't own a jacket like that. Then she remembered her own red one and the time she'd found it flat and out of shape. It was big enough for Kevin. She blinked at the word "dildo." Then she exclaimed, "He—he—he had one!"

Two of the men stepped into the bedroom to look around. She told McGougan, "This answers a lot of questions."

"We'll talk about it," he promised. She went into the living room and flopped in the black chair, covering her face with her hands. She felt that any second she would start screaming and never stop. The message tumbled through her mind: Kevin is the rapist! *Kevin is the rapist!* God, I should have known. . . .

Every few minutes a detective came in and asked her to identify something. One carried a box up from the basement and showed her an ash-blond wig that she'd seen before. She remembered a composite picture of the rapist; little curls sprouted from the edges of his stocking cap. That was just how this wig would look under a cap. She told herself that there'd been a mistake and then she told herself that there hadn't. Most of the search-warrant items she'd recognized instantly. Recently he'd thrown away the gray jogging suit, the gloves, a few other things. Another incriminating sign. A detective walked in with the oven mitts. "He was washing those just last week," Gini said.

The man said, "He . . . what?"

"I asked him why and he wouldn't tell me."

She remembered the night in December when she'd started to call Secret Witness and changed her mind. She thought, From that day to this I never suspected him! What a fool! She felt like an accomplice: ugly, exposed.

The detectives seemed to sense her turmoil and treated her gently. She showed them where some of the items could be found, but many that had been in the house as recently as a week ago now turned up missing: tan cord pants, gray sweatshirt, two pairs of gloves, prefaded jeans, green ski jacket with arm stripe, blue ski parka, a dozen or so more. Where could he have stashed so many things? At his parents' house? She was lost in thought when the phone rang. "Gini?" Ruth Coe said. "Are the police there?"

Gini hadn't expected a call this fast and didn't know what to say. "Uh—yes," she said. "They're here."

"Are they taking things out of the house?" Before she could respond Ruth asked, "Exactly *what* are they taking?"

Gini felt hostile and didn't know why. How could Ruth sound so calm? "I don't know what they're taking," she answered in a monotone.

"Well, you know this can't be true, don't you?" The voice heated up. "This is just preposterous! This is just terrible! You're on our side, aren't you, Gini?"

"I don't know, Ruth," she said.

The response made her ease the phone away from her ear. "Son is *not* guilty! I can't believe this! It's *terrible* to arrest an innocent man like this!"

Gini kept mumbling, "Yeah, Ruth. Yeah, Ruth...."

The woman's babblings became almost incomprehensible. Gini stopped listening. When she tuned in again Ruth was asking, "Well, *you* don't think he's guilty, do you?"

Gini hesitated. "I don't know, Ruth," she repeated. She felt defenseless against so much rage.

"You're telling me you don't know he's innocent?"

This is too much, Gini told herself, and hung up.

A detective walked into the room carrying red jogging shorts. "Are these his?"

"Uh, yes," she muttered.

He stepped out and the phone rang again. This time it was Kevin. He spoke in such a hushed voice that she could hardly hear him. "Gin?"

"Yes?"

"Are the police there?"

"Yes." A camera flashed behind her, and then another.

"What are they taking?"

She reminded herself that she was talking to the South Hill rapist. "I don't know," she said. "They've got bags of things. They're taking a lot of pictures."

"This whole thing is a frame-up," he whispered. She didn't comment. She hoped he would think she was shocked, incapable of normal conversation—not far from the truth. He said, "I can't talk long. Listen, come down to jail and see me, will you?"

"Yeah, okay." She disconnected before he could become more precise about the visit.

A detective showed her several pairs of Kevin's shoes: silver-gray high-heeled shoes with pointed toes, black rounded-toe high-heeled shoes, black pointed shoes and a brown pair of loafers. "All his?" the man asked.

She nodded. Cameras kept flashing in the other rooms. She huddled with herself, then looked up to see Lt. McGougan ambling into the living room. "Let's talk," he said.

"Sure." She steeled herself. Be nice to me, she said under her breath. Be nice. *I didn't rape anybody.*

"What would you think if I told you Sunshine Shelly was raped?" he started out. She held both hands over her face and couldn't respond. Kevin had been fixated on Sunshine Shelly. He'd insisted they go to see her at Buchanan Chevrolet. He'd even written her fan notes. Gini lowered her hands and began to talk. She told McGougan everything she knew about Coe's fascination for the disc jockey. She told about his strange comings and goings, how he'd recently thrown away some of the clothes on the long search-warrant list. She told about her suspicions in December. When she was finished McGougan asked, "Would you be willing to testify?"

She started to say yes but stopped herself. "I would," she said, "but . . . I don't think I could. I mean, I don't know how good a witness I'd be."

"Why?"

"I, uh—I lied for him once. In court. When he was arrested for shoplifting."

She searched his face for a hint of disgust or reproval. He was deadpan. "We'll see," he said.

The four policemen left her with a list of home phone numbers, their own and those of two other detectives, Schmick and Allen, and told her to call at any hour if she needed help or conversation. They dragged out several large plastic bags of clothes and personal items. She stood in the front door in her robe and booties trying to be charming. "Thanks for coming."

"Thank *you*."

"And thanks for being so nice about everything."

"Thank *you*, Gini." They drove off in a dark sedan. She shut the door feeling as though she'd just attended her own wake.

At 7 p.m., police sealed off the rear of the Public Safety Building. Uniformed patrolmen guarded every door. John Harris of the *Spokesman-Review* stood around the reception desk and thought, It must have been like this when they brought in Lee Harvey Oswald. He watched as a stream of dark-haired women began arriving, some with their husbands and boyfriends, a few alone. They were greeted by Lieutenant Roscoe "Rock" Walker and escorted into the rear of the building.

The bearded police reporter had a good idea what was happening. Someone as prominent as Coe would be bailed out fast, and police had to arrange a lineup while he was still on the premises. Gordon and Ruth Coe appeared in the reception area and conversed with a man in a mod hair-do. After a few minutes the man disengaged himself from the Coes and introduced himself as Roger Crane, owner of the real estate agency where Kevin worked. "Kevin?" Harris asked. "I thought his name was Fred."

"We knew him as Kevin," Crane explained. The realtor said it was no surprise that Coe was the South Hill rapist; he'd shown little interest in his work and seldom visited the office.

After a while Harris overcame a natural reluctance and stuck out his hand to Gordon Coe. "Hi. I'm John Harris. Of the *Review*?"

"Yes, I know who you are," the elder Coe said politely.

"I really wish I could've told you," the reporter said, feeling like a pest. "I've known for two weeks that they were following Fred, but I was sworn to secrecy. I thought about you a lot, Mr. Coe. I mean, you were one floor up from me. I really wanted to tell you. I hope you know that."

"I understand."

Harris pushed his luck. "Uh—would you like to comment on your son's arrest?"

The black-haired Mrs. Coe slid between the two men. She fluttered long lashes above her dark blue eyes and said sweetly, "*What* did you know?"

Something about the woman was unnerving. From the way she'd been prancing about the reception area, it was clear that she considered herself a major figure in the drama. There was no question that she had star quality, with gleaming hair and five-inch heels, jangling bangles and dangling beads, and an imperious stage presence. Harris said, "Well, uh—I knew Fred was gonna be arrested."

"How *nice*," she said sarcastically, and turned away. He wondered how she managed to look so cool.

The victims were herded together in an interrogation room and told not to discuss the rapes. Around 8 p.m. one of the women counted heads. There were eleven—ten with brown or auburn hair and one redhead. They ranged in age from early teens to middle age. Almost without exception they were well dressed, short and slight, attractive, and with the somewhat preppie look that in another era would have been called "classy." Now and then, detectives dropped in to ask for patience. They explained that a lawyer from the public defender's office was en route to represent the defendant. It would take a while. A few more victims checked in, blinking in the bright light.

After hours of waiting, the women were separated from their escorts and led upstairs to the lineup room. When each had finished peeking at the six men and marking her selection on a sheet of paper, she was led outside by a different route so that her comments wouldn't prejudice the others. The police and prosecutor were doing their best to keep from polluting the case.

To Irene Pool, the rapist's next-to-last victim, the lineup proved almost as traumatic as her rape at Hart Field. The knowledge that she would be charging a man with a terrible crime weighed heavily; she might be ruining a life. Every day she made important personal judgments as a business executive, but nothing as unnerving as this. She peered through the one-way mirror and saw her rapist: No. 3. She listened as he read from a card, "Don't look at my face. Do as I say or I'll kill you. Take your clothes off. Don't call the police. How much money do you have?" She wished she had more time to study the faces. No. 3 had the same heavy jaw and slightly slanty eyes. She went home hoping she hadn't made a horrible mistake.

Jeanie Mays, the rapist's final victim, was convinced that she would never be able to make an identification. It had been so dark that morning under the big blue spruce, and she wasn't good at remembering faces anyway. Before she went into the lineup room she asked a female detective, "Do I have to be positive about the ID?" The detective told her to use her own judgment.

Jeanie was amazed when she looked through the mirror. There he stood, and there wasn't a doubt in the world. He was No. 3.

Marie Oldham reminded herself as she waited that police were notoriously fallible. She'd read plenty of stories about miscarriages of justice based on over-eager cops and careless eyewitnesses, and she wasn't going to put some poor helpless man through the agony of a rape charge unless she was 200 percent sure. She watched as the men in the lineup turned full-face and profile. Her eyes went straight to No. 3. She was surprised to see that he appeared to be calm. When he read from the printed card he spoke in a low monotone as though to disguise his voice. He'd worn his hair Jimmy Connors–style at the time of the rape, with bangs that almost covered his eyebrows, but now it was plastered down and combed sideways. She tried to get a good look at his eyes but couldn't because he was squinting. She circled No. 3 and added a note that the hair and eyes were a little off.

Two schoolgirl victims, Sue Ellen Wilber and Stephanie Gibbs, also marked No. 3 on their cards, bringing the total to five. No. 3, Fred Coe, was returned to his cell for the night.

Gini Perham didn't know where to sleep. The house was no longer hers and Kevin's; it was the staging area where the South Hill rapist had kept his dildo and his gloves, his wigs and hats and changes of costume. Each time a car passed she looked up, terrified that he would burst in and start ranting about injustice, working on her the way he'd worked on her in the shoplifting case. Around 10 p.m., she threw a few things into an overnight bag and got ready to leave. The phone rang. She hesitated. Ruth and Gordon hadn't called back and neither had Kevin. What would she say if it was one of them? "Hello?" she said, her finger on the button.

"Gini! It's me. George!" Her boss's voice sounded high and excited; she wondered what was wrong with him. "Roger's with me. Listen, what do you think?"

"What do I...think?"

"About Kevin. I can't believe it, can you? It can't be him. This is crazy!"

She was sure that anything she said would be widely quoted. Should she protect Kevin or tell the truth? She didn't have to ponder the question. "George, it *is* him. I've had a long time to think about it." When Korb expressed mild disagreement she said, "You don't know what I know, George."

"No," he said. "I guess I don't. Well, take care of yourself, Gini. We're all with you."

"You don't know how much that means to me," she said, and hung up to maintain her composure. She told herself not to answer the phone. The next caller might not be as sweet as George.

The door rattled and she thought, Oh, my God, he's come home! How can I sleep in the same bed? She looked out the window and saw that a truck had passed, shaking the house. She breathed again. Now...where to spend the night? She dialed her brothers and they weren't home. It was close to midnight when she reached old friends, a married couple in the valley, and said that she needed help. They agreed to meet her at Denny's, the restaurant where she'd lunched earlier in the day and listened to Kevin swear for the dozenth time that he wasn't seeing other women. She shook her head at the memory. He'd been seeing other women, all right.

After two drinks on an empty stomach her head felt as though it were floating above the table. When the bar closed at 2 a.m. her friends took her home with them. She floundered about the strange bed half the night wondering why she couldn't sleep and couldn't cry. Oh, Kevin, she thought, how could you do that to all those poor women? And to me. And to yourself.

87

Apparently there's a very dark side to the human character. When you're down or someone has accused you of something ugly—the vulchers flock in for the kill!...Obviously all the years I thought we were close friends—esprit de corps and all—and I thought we respected one another, instead you harbored such a low opinion of me! An opinion so low you could actually pick up a morning paper one day—read your friend has been arrested for rape—immediately decide he's guilty and close your mind to the facts!—Fred Coe to Jay Williams, Feb. 5, 1982

Early Tuesday morning Jay Williams tiptoed to the front door for his *Spokesman-Review*. A short article at the bottom of page 1 caught his eye. It said that Frederick Harlan Coe had been arrested for a first-degree rape on the South Hill.

Williams was stunned. He wanted to think that their friend John Nyberg, the infamous practical joker, had paid a printer to make up this fake front page. He wanted to think it was impossible that his closest friend could have committed the unmanly crime of rape. But he knew better. He slumped into a chair and reread the words. He said to himself, That explains *everything*! Why didn't somebody realize what was happening a long time ago?

He went back to bed and tried to collect his thoughts. One second he was enraged at Coe and the next he was wondering how to help. He felt betrayed, sickened. His best friend had committed filthy, indescribable acts. There had been moments when Jay had vowed to kill the South Hill rapist with his bare hands if he ever caught him in the act. Now he had to cope with the news that the rapist he would have killed was the man he'd idolized since grammar school. Lying in bed staring at his ceiling, he sighed and uttered a churchman's expletive, "Oh, my."

His wife stirred alongside him. "What?" she asked.

He wasn't ready to discuss the subject or even acknowledge what had happened. "Oh, nothing," he said. "Hey, it's time to get up."

He was showering twenty minutes later when he heard the bathroom door open. "Jay!" Sue called out. "Have you heard about Fred?"

"Well...yeah."

"What are you gonna *do*?"

He wished he knew. "I can't be concerned about it," he said defensively. "I've got to go out and make a living. You have to cut away the dead wood." He doubted that he'd convinced her. He hadn't convinced himself.

When he was dressed he called the Coes. "I heard what happened," he told Gordon Coe. "I want you to know I'm available for whatever help I can give."

Mr. Coe said thanks and added, "I can only hope it's all a hideous mistake."

"That's exactly the way I feel," Jay said. He was lying, but it was in the cause of compassion. Deep inside, Mr. and Mrs. Coe must know the truth better than anyone.

En route to the office he felt guilty. I should have seen it coming, he thought. I should have reached out to help. My Christianity isn't supposed to end when I turn from the altar. A week ago he'd been in Pilgrim's Nutrition Center with Fred when a boy of about four had stepped between them. Fred had raised his arm as though to backhand the child. "Get outa here!" he'd said in a guttural voice that Jay hadn't heard before. I should have known right then that he was in crisis, he told himself. Fred was always nice to children and dogs.

Music booking agent John Nyberg was awakened in his Seattle home by a long-distance call from Spokane. "Johnny," his father said, "Fred Coe's been arrested as the South Hill rapist. They got witnesses, they got the whole bit."

Nyberg pondered this bombshell for a while and then called Jay Williams. "Is it true?"

"Yeah."

"You had him pegged, didn't you, Jay?"

"No, I didn't. I knew something was wrong, but I didn't know what. I should have done something."

"Like what?" Nyberg asked. It was just like Jay to want to take the blame. "These rapes go back years. Hell, I saw him do things in high school that were borderline."

"Me too."

"Jay, this is no more your fault than it is mine or anybody else's."

"I wish I could believe it."

Rape victim Margot Terry read the news and couldn't place the name. Then she remembered that her younger sister had gone to school with a boy named Coe. "Why, sure I remember him, and you should too!" her sister said when Margot telephoned. "He was at all those newspaper picnics that Dad used to take us to. A skinny little kid? Never talked, always hung back? I beat him in the potato race and he didn't even care. He was such a cute little squeeze. Why? What'd he do?"

A Spokane suburbanite named *Betsy Peters* found herself swamped with memories when she read of the arrest. She was happily married now, but five years of her life had been spent in love with Coe. She'd offered him a physical love that he'd seemed incapable of taking, and she still didn't understand.

She'd met him when she was thirteen and he was three years older. He was polite and reserved, and she trusted him from the beginning. Before long they were parking in his Dodge at a spot called Suicide for its small cliff. Coe would undress her and bounce on her plump body, asking, "Do you feel a difference in my size? Do I feel aroused to you?" He asked the questions over and over. After they'd been seeing each other for seven months he performed oral sex. She was fourteen by then and asked, "Are you crazy?"

For five years they'd seen each other off and on for what she thought of as "kinky" sex. She wouldn't have minded intercourse, but he seemed uninterested. She dated other boys and soon learned that they were preoccupied with intercourse. But Fred was into oral sex and finger sex, which he kept up till she reached an orgasm. As she got older and met more men she realized that he was different. She hadn't known how different till she'd picked up this morning's paper.

Sonia McNeill steered her motorized wheelchair to the end of the hall and encountered nurse Karen Anderson reading the morning paper. The nurse looked up and said, "Sonia! Did you see that they caught the South Hill rapist? His name's—let's see here— Frederick Harlan Coe."

"*Who?*" Sonia said.

"Frederick Harlan Coe."

Sonia could hardly talk. "Karen, do you know who that is? That's the man you threw out! For dumping ice on Olga Hegg!"

The two women agreed that someone should have stopped Coe long before he was able to carry out three or four dozen rapes. "Karen, would you mind dialing a number for me?" Sonia asked. "I want to see if my mother knows yet. She might know where my sister Jeni is, and Jeni ought to be told about this. She was married to him." The phone was answered by Sonia's twelve-year-old son. When she told him what had happened he began to unreel a strange story.

The child had lived with "Coco" and his Aunt Jeni in Las Vegas for almost a year when he was seven. Sonia listened as he described how his uncle had often yanked on his penis till it hurt, then explained, "I just want you to have a big long one." Coe hit the boy with clubs and boards and made him bleed; sometimes he would awaken stuck to the sheets by clotted blood. Once Coco set out to beat him fifty times but quit because the paddle broke. He punched the child under the chin so hard that he had to be kept home from school, then instructed him to tell outsiders that he fell. "Oh, my God," Sonia interrupted. "Why didn't you tell me or your grandmother when we talked to you on the phone?"

"Because Coco always listened on the extension."

"Why didn't you tell us when you came back home?"

"I don't know. I was afraid. And he's been different in Spokane. He... gives me things." The child went on to recite unimaginable indignities. He said that Coco discussed inserting a large screw into his penis and pulling on it. The size of the boy's organ had been a source of unending interest. Coe often tied a washcloth around it and yanked till the child screamed. "I'm trying to make you into a man," the boy quoted him as saying.

Sonia asked, "Where was Aunt Jeni all this time?"

"He never hurt me wnen she was around," he said. "Once he started to hit me in front of her and she made him stop." He described a Coe technique of personal hygiene. "If I didn't wipe myself right he would make me lean over and spread. Then the collie would lick me. When I said I didn't like that, Coco said, 'I'll let my dog lick your ass any time I want!'"

Sonia felt ill. She wondered where Fred had learned such things. Her son wanted to say more. "Not now, baby," Sonia told him, struggling for composure. "Would you repeat this to a policeman if I asked you to?"

The child said, "Coco would come and get me."

"Is that what he told you?" In tears, the anguished woman let the phone slip from her stiffened hands.

At noon reporter John Harris and photographer Chris Anderson drove to the house at Twenty-ninth and Rebecca looking for a second-day story. A yellow Cadillac was parked in the driveway. They knocked on the front door but no one answered. They had just begun a hunt for quotable neighbors when Ruth and Gordon Coe emerged from the back of the house and drove off.

A while later a watchful neighbor named Sue Evans noticed that the Coes had returned and were filling their car with clothes and other items. She strolled over and said, "I'm very sorry that this happened. I just want you to know that I'm praying for you."

Mrs. Coe stood in the driveway with a stack of towels in her arms. She wore oversize dark glasses and seemed calm. In a voice that reminded Mrs. Evans of Bette Davis she said, "He'll get out of it. He isn't a bit guilty, and it's just a matter of time till the whole thing's straightened out." She sounded as though there weren't a doubt in the world.

Gordon Coe appeared with a basket full of clothes. Sue Evans said, "Mr. Coe, I hope everything turns out okay." He thanked her and observed that the local press had already convicted his son.

George Korb made a courtesy phone call and talked to Mrs. Coe. "How're they treating him?" he asked.

"About what you'd expect," she said, her musical voice strong and confident. "He told us that a policeman threatened to pull his pubic hairs out one by one. Frankly, knowing the police as Gordon and I do, we were hardly surprised."

A fellow executive of the *Chronicle* phoned Gordon Coe after lunch and expressed his regrets. "Which lawyer are you using, Gordie?" the man asked.

"I don't have enough money to hire a lawyer," Coe answered. "We're thinking of going with the public defender." The other editor wasn't surprised. Gordon Coe had always rushed his check to the bank on payday. All of his colleagues knew that Mrs. Coe was a lavish spender and that Gordon indulged her to his last dime. Another staffer had once claimed that Gordon also supported his thirty-four-year-old son, but the newsmen had put that down as exaggeration.

A TV reporter asked Mrs. Coe how she'd first learned about her son's arrest. "We were on our way out the door to vote," the woman answered. "The phone rang and it was Son. I said, 'We're just getting ready to leave.' Normally I would've just hung up on him—we've got that kind of relationship where I can hang up and say I don't have time—but he yelled at me, '*Mom!*' I'd never heard such urgency in his voice. I said, 'Son, what's the matter?' He said, 'Mom, Mom, I'm at the police station and I've just been arrested! They think I'm the South Hill rapist!' Gordon and I were sure there was a mistake so we hurried right down to get him out. We looked him right in the eyes and said, 'Son, did you do this thing?' And of course he didn't. But the police won't listen."

The accused rapist made his first court appearance in the afternoon, wearing a brown three-piece suit, a white shirt and a dark tie and looking dignified and self-possessed. Reporters were searched for cameras and tape recorders before being allowed in the courtroom of Superior Court Judge John Madden. Surrounded by his parents and sheriff's deputies, Coe came in through a hidden passageway.

Gordon Coe implored the judge to lower the $100,000 bail or to release Fred on his own recognizance. "We would ensure that our son would present himself for any proceedings," the newsman promised. He added that Fred's long history of asthma and hayfever required a special diet. "He's already suffering because of the time he's been in jail," Mr. Coe said against an obbligato of his son's coughs.

Deputy county prosecutor L. C. "Bud" Kinnie argued that the defendant was a danger to the public and in danger himself from hotheads. "I'm asking for a little time till things settle down," he said. The judge agreed. Bail was maintained at $100,000 and Coe was returned to his cell.

In the afternoon Roy Allen ran into the prisoner in the hall of the jail. The two natural enemies had a brief conversation, Allen towering over the man he had arrested. "It looks like you're gonna be charged with five more rapes," the detective said.

"How come?"

"You were identified. Listen, why don't you tell me what happened?"

Coe looked pensive. "What'll I get if I'm convicted?"

"I don't know. Maybe they'll just send you to the hospital."

Coe stood silently. Allen had the feeling he was about to confess. Then he said, "I don't want to talk about it."

At midnight, Gini Perham parked her car a block from the house and approached through an alley. She had waited twenty-four hours to come back because she didn't want to talk to anybody, especially the press. And she was afraid of running into Ruth and Gordon. The *Spokesman-Review* had already run a false report that she'd accompanied the Coes to court. She was sure that someone had planted the information to show the public that Kevin's loved ones were solidly behind him. She was embarrassed that her name had been used to bolster a rapist's image.

She had returned to the house to pick up some clothes and personal items. Later tonight she would move in with her grandmother on the South Hill and lie low till things quieted.

She tiptoed across the back yard and used a pocket flashlight to find the keyhole. She left the inside lights off. Through a side window she spotted a neighbor staring at the house. On a shelf she saw one of her favorite books, Ayn Rand's *The Fountainhead*. She opened it to the rape of Dominique Francon and glanced at the words:

> It was an act that could be performed in tenderness, as a seal of love, or in contempt, as a symbol of humiliation and conquest. It could be the act of a lover or the act of a soldier violating an enemy woman. He did it as an act of scorn. Not as love, but as defilement.
>
> And this made her lie still and submit. One gesture of tenderness from him—and she would have remained cold, untouched by the thing done to her body. But the act of a master taking shameful, contemptuous possession of her was the kind of rapture she had wanted.

She wondered how much rapture Kevin's victims had enjoyed, lying on the hard earth, terrified of his knife and his fists, their lives darkened forever by his threat to come back and get them.

She opened the living room closet. His tan trenchcoat swayed on a hanger. A sense of pity shook her like a convulsion, revived deep black feelings of separation and loss she hadn't experienced since her mother's suicide two years before. She grabbed blindly for the coat. The empty sleeve felt warm, as though he'd just hung it up. She would never see him again. "We still have to say good-bye, Kevin," she said. "It's not fair!" Everything was so incomplete. His death would have been easier to take. She remembered him that first night at the St. Regis restaurant, his wild brilliance, his big ideas for himself and his city. He had talked to her as an equal, listened to her with respect and understanding—at least for a while. He'd called her "my perfect woman."

The March wind sounded like women crying. She remembered the horror stories that had spread across the South Hill—women forced to defecate and urinate, violated in every possible way, punched and slapped and dragged across rocks by the man she'd lived with. She'd listened to his stories, offered her body, helped pay his bills, cooked for him, cleaned his house, and now...she missed him. The guilt was too much to bear. She put her head in his empty coat and cried and cried.

After a while, she began drifting about the house like a sleepwalker. She fell across the bed and sobbed for an hour. Whatever he was, she knew she still loved him. She wiped her eyes and walked down the alley to her car.

88

There are very definite aspects to our culture pattern which give psychopaths encouragement. In America we put great value on the acquisition of material gain, prestige, power, personal ascendance, and the competitive massing of goods.—William Krasner, *The Psychopath in Our Society, Neurotica II*, 1948

Thursday evening after work Jay Williams joined Ruth and Gordon Coe in a visit to the Spokane county-city jail. He could remember more inspiring settings. The visiting room was in the general shape and size of a railroad car, with sixteen booths through which visitors and inmates conferred by phone as they stared at each other through plateglass. The white tile floor was stained and the wall was done in a scarred institutional yellow.

Fred had the glazed eyes of a man who couldn't stand another night in jail. A cheek muscle kept pulsing. His coloring had gone from its usual pale to downright chalky. He looked like someone wired on amphetamines. Jay tried a smile, but it wasn't returned. The two old friends picked up the handphones simultaneously and Fred said in a tightly compressed voice, "I hope you know I'm innocent."

Jay hadn't expected the ultimate question to be asked up front. He mumbled, "I know. It just doesn't fit." As his words came out he marveled at his own malleability. Everything fit *perfectly*. But how do you tell your best friend that you're convinced he's a rapist?

Coe shook his head and said, "Can't talk! Phone's bugged." Jay was puzzled. Fred had just finished an animated conversation with his parents, now seated over against the wall. Why couldn't he talk now? As he watched, Coe flattened a sheet of paper against the glass. Penciled on it were large printed letters: "GO TO POLICE. DO NOT REFER TO ME AS ECCENTRIC. TELL THEM YOU AND I WERE TRYING TO CATCH SOUTH HILL RAPIST."

Jay looked around. Gordon and Ruth weren't watching. Neither was the guard in the control booth. He read on. "SAY THAT YOU WERE MY DECOY AND I FOLLOWED YOU IN CAR." He realized that Coe was following his eyes as he read down the sheet. When he came to the bottom it was snatched away and another held up. "YOU WERE WEARING A DRESS. SOMETIMES

YOU WERE JOGGING." Jay nodded nervously. "WE USED YOU AS DECOY BECAUSE YOU'RE SLIGHT IN BUILD AND COULD PASS AS A WOMAN."

Jay was so fascinated by the method that he found it hard to concentrate on the messages. He read: "TELL POLICE YOU WERE PART OF MY ANTI-RAPE PROGRAM ALL ALONG. TELL THEM YOU WERE WITH ME ON MORNING OF FEB. 5 AND I COULDN'T BE THE RAPIST." Jay peered at his friend. Every facial muscle was drawn tight. The veins stood out on his hands. The sheet ended, "DO YOU UNDERSTAND?" Jay nodded.

The next page was more closely printed, and he leaned forward to read the words. There was a brief introduction to the effect that the arrest was a frame-up, police hadn't played fair, and there was no reason to play fair in return. "DO YOU AGREE?" Jay had heard this line of reasoning before, greatly amplified. It was "situational ethics." He read on: "I HAVE A DILDO AND A SWEATER THAT HAVE TO BE DISPOSED OF. THE POLICE MIGHT FIND THEM AND CLAIM THEY'RE THE TOOLS OF A RAPIST. HARDLY! BUT THE WHOLE THING'S INNOCUOUS."

The next sheet began with the words: "GET RID OF THEM FOR ME!" Underneath was the address of a vacant house at Third and Altamont. Jay recognized it as a Gini Perham listing that had been on the market for several months. The message continued: "I HID THE DILDO AND SWEATER UNDER THE STAIRWELL. USE YOUR LOCKBOX KEY. GET THEM!"

Jay looked up. Those gray-blue eyes were fixed on his, as though imploring him to read faster. Jay read: "THE SWEATER WON'T FIT YOU. DO NOT KEEP IT. TAKE IT TO THE FIRST GOODWILL DROP YOU FIND. DO NOT TAKE IT HOME!" He wondered how a sweater could be used to frame an innocent man for rape. Was he supposed to take the dildo home? A fine assignment for an elder of the church. Coe spoke for the first time since holding up the messages. In a compressed voice he asked, "Do you understand so far?"

"Sure, but—"

Fred glowered in a warning against further speech. His darting eyes made him look like a man crossing a busy intersection. Jay suppressed an impulse to throw up his hands and say, "Come *on*, man, stop this foolishness!" But he tried not to show his feelings. His friend was in pain.

The last sheet was filled with ultra-black staccato lines:

"TAKE THE DILDO AND CUT IT INTO 100 PIECES!

"SPREAD THE PIECES IN VACANT LOTS!

"ONE PIECE AT A TIME!

"YOU MAY TALK FREELY TO MY PARENTS.

"DO YOU UNDERSTAND?"

Jay picked up the phone and said, "I understand."

Coe's voice sounded stretched and thin. "Well, thanks for coming. I really appreciate it."

Jay looked again at the papers. The guard was only a few feet away behind another set of thick panes. "Aren't you, uh, concerned about what you've got there?" he asked, glancing pointedly at the papers. "You'd better get rid of those fast." Coe nodded.

Jay left the interview room convinced that his friend had lost his mind. On the way home he drove by the house at Third and Altamont to take a look. He hadn't had time to consider Fred's request seriously and he certainly didn't intend to take action one way or the other till he did, but a light in the house encouraged him to stop and knock. When a woman answered he said, "Hi! I'm Jay Williams of the Tomlinson agency. Is your house still for sale?"

"Well, it was," the woman said, "but we decided to take it off the market. We moved back in four or five days ago."

"Thanks," Jay said. "Just thought I'd check." He left feeling relieved. Even Fred would have to admit that the search-and-destroy mission had now become impossible.

That night he couldn't sleep. Something Sue had said over dinner stuck in his mind: "You were around him all those years, but I wonder if you ever really knew him." She hadn't meant the remark as a criticism, but it made Jay wonder about his powers of perception. How well *had* he known Fred? Like a brother, he'd often insisted to others. But that wasn't true. If his brother had been raping women for two years, he'd have known it; there'd have been some indication. If Fred fooled him that way, how else had he fooled him? He thought back on their years together.

Jay had been the new kid in the Comstock Grammar School on the South Hill when a bigger boy got in his way on the playground and they almost came to blows. Within a year they were best friends: Freddie Coe, son of the *Chronicle*'s city editor, and Donald Jay Williams, son of the general manager of a local Ford dealership. For the next ten years, till Coe went off to Washington State University for an abortive fling at college, the two boys were seldom apart.

The Comstock Addition was an upper-middle-class neighborhood of parks and pines and hiding places. Jay remembered his earliest visits to Freddie's white-frame house on Twenty-ninth Ave., a block or two from the slope that led down to Hangman Creek. The Coes were the nicest people. The easygoing father listened patiently to small boys, stayed in the background and served as a solid role model. Mrs. Coe was an enthusiastic, demonstrative woman whose life revolved around "Son." She hovered over him, dabbing at his face with a handkerchief, straightening his shirt and telling him over and over how important it was to look nice. She was the most supportive parent Jay had ever known, and she set the highest standards. When she told Freddie to be home for dinner at six, she didn't mean 6:01, and he would always break away to beat the deadline.

Jay could sit for hours listening to Mrs. Coe as she spoke wistfully of the plantation life of her childhood, the mammy who never left her side, the quaint darkies. She would cup Freddie's face in her hands till his mouth stuck out like a guppy's and say excitedly, "*My* baby, *my* boy!" She talked to children and dogs as though she was on the same level. Sometimes she seemed almost flirtatious, but Jay didn't mind. He found himself soliciting her attention. He would stand when she entered the room, causing her to exclaim, "Oh, Jay, you're *such* a gentleman!"

Every few months he went out of his way to impress her by doing a rank imitation of the toady on the "Leave It to Beaver" TV show. "Gee, Mrs. Coe," he would say, "that's a beautiful ring you're wearing!"

"Oh, *thank* you, Jay darling!" she would respond, and ask if he would like to see her jewelry collection.

"He doesn't want to see your old jewelry," Fred would say.

Minutes later she would return to the room, hands full of jewels. "What do y'all think of *this*?" she would say, modeling a nest of rings, three separate bands of red, white and blue stones that went halfway up her finger. Fred acted bored, but Jay crowed and clucked in the best "Eddie Haskell" tradition. It was like playing grown-up with a real grown-up.

This topmost South Hill neighborhood was a temple of conspicuous consumption. Jay's family lived in one of the biggest houses. A famous cardiologist lived nearby and changed his red Mercedes every two years. A brain surgeon, a Jew, was forced by restrictive covenants to live in a modest house a few blocks away and was said to be richer than all the others put together. It didn't take long for Freddie to convince Jay that power and wealth were what mattered. While their classmates were playing baseball the two boys blended their last names into a business called "Wilco Enterprises," parent corporation of "Wilco Purity League," "Wilco Boys Club," and other Wilco subsidiaries spun from Freddie's brain. The two boys trudged from house to house seeking handouts or selling car washes and greeting cards, explaining to the housewives who smiled on their beatific faces that every cent went to charity.

One day Freddie announced that he confidently expected to become the richest man in the world. Jay wasn't surprised; he'd frequently heard Mrs. Coe tell her son that untold wealth would be his. Fred told Jay, "We'll make it together."

Jay said, "Wouldn't it bother you to be the richest man in the world and read in the paper that people were starving somewhere?" Coe shrugged.

Jay realized that his friend had never been weighed down by sentimentality. Once he'd said, "If we have enough discipline to become the richest men in the world, we'll have to cut ourselves free from all attachments to this earth, from everything that's dear to us. Understand?"

Jay wasn't sure, but he understood that Freddie was a genius. "Yep," he said.

"Well, then, if we have that kind of discipline we should be capable of killing our parents."

Jay was shocked. "I'd rather not!"

"Well, of course I'm only speaking hypothetically."

"I don't even want to do it hypothetically."

Soon after, Fred found a new word in the dictionary. "A me-ga-lo-maniac believes that he can actually swim the ocean," he told Jay. "It takes megalomaniacs to accomplish big things." The boys agreed that megolomania was a useful insanity, a necessary kind. Normal people could never become the richest men in the world.

And he *still* thinks that way, Jay said to himself as he lay in bed reminiscing. He hasn't changed since we were nine! Just a couple of weeks ago he was talking about what it would be like to fly his own jet from city to city making deals and sleeping with beautiful women. Locked in his cell, I'll bet he's *still* figuring out ways to become the richest, most powerful man in the world. I *know* he is!

Jay had noticed early that Fred seemed to lack emotion. He acted unperturbed by the deaths of his pets. One day he showed up with a gold razor and explained, "It's my grandfather's. I'm gonna hock it."

"Won't he need it?" Jay asked. For years Mrs. Coe's father had shared a bedroom with Fred.

"He died two weeks ago."

Jay was aghast. "Fred, I've seen you almost every day. Why didn't you mention it?"

"I didn't think of it."

"Isn't this a little cold? Hocking his things already?"

"They're not gonna do him any good."

A week or so later, John Nyberg learned of the death and asked Coe, "Why didn't you say something? Wasn't there a funeral? Did you bury him in the yard, for Christ's sake?"

Fred said it had slipped his mind. Later he told Jay, "Somebody said you think I'm cold." It was true, but Jay had meant the words as praise. He'd explained to mutual friends that Coe had great self-control and self-discipline and was as cold as snow about such things. "Jay," the young Coe continued, "when I see a picture of a starving child, I'm moved. My eyes actually well with tears. You don't see that side of me; it's private. I'm *very* emotional." Jay thought, He's trying to talk himself into believing it, but he'll never convince me. "Don't tell people I'm cold!" Fred instructed him. "Say I'm a warm person, a loving person."

"Okay, Fred, I will," Jay answered, but he knew he could never tell that big a lie.

Now Jay thought about the brouhaha over his comment to Nyberg that Fred was insane. I wish I could take back the words, he told himself. He's got enough to worry about already. Six counts of rape! How in the world does something like that get started?

He remembered how ill at ease Fred had always been around women of his own social station. Did that have something to do with it? Coe preferred peeping through the bedroom windows of the South Hill "soshes" and raised his voyeurism to the level of a neighborhood art form. Long after the other boys had passed on to more sophisticated sexual practices, Coe continued his habit. He peeped at a doctor's daughter till he was frightened off by a shotgun fired into the air. There were discussions between parents, but nothing came of them because Fred always insisted that there'd been a mistake—he'd been out walking his dog; he was just taking a shortcut through the back yard. . . .

At sixteen he told Jay about his first attempt at intercourse. He'd ejaculated prematurely, a problem that persisted. He and Jay discussed the situation for a few months; then Coe dropped the subject. He was always sensitive about women and what they thought of him. A slattern's insult could bring him down for days. He broke up with one of his girlfriends because he didn't want her to see him with a stubborn pimple. He shared with his mother the fear that the sun was a main cause of aging and complexion problems. When he drove he sometimes held his hand over his forehead as a sunscreen.

He was a legitimate B student but sometimes cheated for A's. In one school year he plagiarized Herbert Hoover's inauguration speech, broke records on a speed-reading test by memorizing a stolen text, jimmied a teacher's desk and forged new report cards for himself and Jay. The report card caper turned out to be disastrous. Mr. and Mrs. Coe were called to the principal's

office, one of the few times that anyone in Spokane dared to ruffle the feathers
of the important editor and his wife. Fred faced his accusers with a terse
comment: "Jay Williams can explain what happened." Both boys were threatened with expulsion, but Fred insisted to the end that "it must have been an
administrative mistake." He flung the implements of the forgery—rubber
stamps, inks, pens—over a cliff and told Jay he never wanted to discuss the
subject again.

From high school on, Jay couldn't remember his friend without a car
provided by his parents, starting at sixteen with a used '59 Dodge. He painted
one of his cars metallic purple even though Jay told him purple was "reserved
for queers and queens," and with his mother's help replaced a medallion to
identify the car as a more powerful model. He had a paper route for a while
and worked as a busboy and bouncer, but he seldom held jobs for long and
looked homeward for his spending money.

He seemed to seek approval and adulation but was unwilling to work for
either. He wrote poetry and called it "Coetry," quitting when classmates kidded
him about being a poor "Coet." He abandoned track after losing a few races.
He dropped out of B-team football when he failed to make first-string quarterback, his parents reinforcing his claim that the coach had played favorites.
(Later he wrote in a yearbook, "That guy screwed us, and believe me I'm
going to live up to my promise and beat the crap out of that fat ass. He stinks.")
He was admitted to a top social club but lost interest after an election defeat.

He doggedly disagreed when his teachers caught him in mistakes, and
offered strident "proofs" of his own. Sometimes he seemed absent-minded,
lightly tapping his teeth with his pen like William F. Buckley. He carried
around a copy of Buckley's *Up from Liberalism*, though he sometimes criticized
the author's casual dress habits. He boasted about the fortune he would earn
and the beauties he would seduce and tried to pass himself off in the mold of
his literary hero Gatsby—mysterious, glamorous, powerful, a man with a past—
an impossible masquerade for a schoolboy. Jay tolerated all the idiosyncrasies.
He understood that geniuses were different. Someday every student at Lewis
and Clark would realize what a giant had walked among them.

Jay remembered how earnestly Fred had tried to fall in love in his senior
year. He insisted that he was going to marry and move next door to his mother's
house. Up to then his romances seemed imitations. He dated "soshes" only to
upgrade his image. He disliked one South Hill beauty intensely but lent her
his car so that other students would bracket them together. He boasted of his
relationships with a long list of easy women, including several known pros-
titutes, and seemed drawn to lost souls like the pathetic "Nasty Nancy." He
took pride in finding disturbed young "nymphomaniacs" and turning them
over to his friends.

And then he fell madly in love—the mooning, swooning kind that had
always passed him by. Tammy McWilliams was one of nine sisters, all regarded
as prudes by their fellow students. Sixteen years later Jay could still see her
clearly in his mind's eye. She was pretty and petite, barely five feet tall with
a good figure, blue-green eyes, a turned-up nose, and lovely auburn hair. Coe
took her to his senior prom, to movies, parties, outings at the lake. He kept
after her for a year, getting his sex elsewhere, keeping her on a pedestal.
Except for Ruth Coe, she was the first female that Jay had ever seen him take

seriously. When they broke up over difficulties with her family, he was inconsolable. For years afterward he talked about her, lamented that they'd never gone beyond kissing, blamed her father for keeping them apart. When he couldn't adjust to college and returned to Spokane he confessed to Jay, "I miss Tammy too much." By then she was unavailable. It was one of the tragedies of his life that he hadn't added her to his list of conquests. For years afterward his wallet bore a picture of the woman with the auburn hair.

Jay lay awake for hours. Sue's breathing was rhythmic and easy beside him. He worked and reworked his remembrances, trying to see if they added up to rape. He carried his memories forward to the night he and Fred had first met Jenifer in her father's bar and the two of them had married even though Fred insisted that he didn't love her. Over and over Jay tried to solve the puzzle and couldn't. What made a man turn to rape? One overattentive mother, one unconsummated romance and one unloved wife? Was deviant behavior that simplistic?

Maybe there's no solution, he told himself. Maybe an electrical impulse arcs the wrong way in the brain and turns a good man into a rapist. Either that, he told himself, or there's a lot I don't know about Fred. He tried to remember what Coe had printed on the sheets of paper in the jail. "Tell cops that you were my decoy and I followed you in a car. Take the dildo and cut it into 100 pieces. Don't keep the sweater...." He thinks we're still in school, Jay said to himself. He thinks that nothing's changed or ever will, that he can still depend on good old Jay. He'll make up an alibi about the rapes and use me to prove it. Well, he'd do the same for me....

He decided he had a lot of praying to do.

89

So many women arrived for the second lineup on Friday morning that they used the elevator in shifts. As they waited on benches, none knew who had been raped and who had been the victims of other sex crimes. At 9 a.m. they began entering the lineup room one by one.

Shelly Monahan was dubious but willing. She hadn't been able to see the face of her rapist that cold black midnight a year and a half ago in the field alongside KJRB. Mainly she remembered his smell—like a hair rinse or a cologne that she'd never encountered. She'd already attended four or five lineups, including Blake Mounsey's, and she was beginning to doubt that her rapist would ever be caught.

There were still times when she thought about his threat to kill her, but she no longer slept in her closet under a pile of clothes. Her dreams had gone through a stage in which she would escape the rapist and laugh at him, then progressed to a stage where she would wrest a gun from his hands and shoot him dead. She still dreamed that one now and then. For a long time she'd felt guilty about not being able to fight him off, not kicking him in the groin or clawing at his eyes. A deputy sheriff named Danny O'Dell had handed her a fistful of rape literature and helped sort out her feelings. "Shelly," he'd said, "don't let your mind do a number on you. The way we deputies see it, if you make it through a rape alive, you did the right thing."

When she'd confided to the deputy that her husband had seen her in a different light after the rape, O'Dell had told her firmly, "You were the victim of an assault, Shelly, a criminal act. Not every husband can come to grips with that. It's not your problem." She thanked God for Danny O'Dell.

Now she peered through the one-way glass and saw six young men of indifferent looks. She had wasted her time again. Not one was familiar.

Margot Terry reminded the detective who called her that she'd obediently held her hand over her eyes during her rape six months earlier on the slope below High Drive, but he insisted that she attend the lineup anyway. It went about as she'd expected. One of the men seemed the approximate size and shape of her rapist, but she seemed to remember seeing darker hair as he'd jogged toward her. She realized she was guessing and left the paper blank.

Leila Hicks's memory was fresh. The man with the big ugly dildo had approached her at Upriver Drive just five days earlier. She wondered if it would be upsetting to rub elbows with the rape victims. It was. One was a child—she looked barely twelve or thirteen—and her pale frightened face blew Leila away. She wondered why so many of the women had auburn hair. When she looked through the glass, she spotted the creep who had bothered her. His face bummed her out for her finals that afternoon.

Lynn Barkley was the last of some eighteen women to enter the little room. She burst into tears when she recognized the man who had shoved her from behind with a big dildo and raped her, then run her down on a dark street and raped her again five months later. After the lineup she told detectives about the unreported second rape and admitted that she'd kissed the man afterward on impulse. She was told that she wouldn't be called as a witness.

After a long and nearly sleepless night, Jay Williams thought he had figured out the only practical approach to his old friend's predicament. Fred was going to have to come clean. Hiding dildos and inventing alibis were exercises in futility; rape wasn't the same as forging report cards, and superior court wasn't Sacajawea Junior High. Maybe there could be some plea-bargaining. His background and family connections would count. Whatever happened, the worst possibility would be a stay in the state hospital for sex offenders, exactly where he belonged. Jay dialed the *Chronicle* and asked for the managing editor. "Mr. Coe," he said, "can we meet someplace?"

"Well, sure, Jay," Gordon Coe said in a friendly voice. "By the way, I'll be seeing Fred tonight. I know he'd like to meet with you again."

The two old acquaintances met outside the *Chronicle* office and strolled toward the Davenport Hotel, three blocks away. Jay decided to tackle the subject of the dildo first, but he had to proceed carefully in case Mr. Coe didn't know anything about it. "Did Fred tell you about the, uh, errand he sent me on?" he asked as they walked.

"Why, no."

"He asked me to dispose of something that could be incriminating. It doesn't have anything to do with the rape charge."

"Oh?"

Jay waited for Mr. Coe to inquire further and wondered why he didn't. When the silence lengthened, Jay said, "If you see Fred before I do, just tell him there are, uh—people back in the house."

"Sure will, Jay."

They found seats in a quiet corner of the cavernous old hotel lobby next to a pair of brightly plumed birds in a wooden cage. Jay decided to be blunt. "Mr. Coe, I don't want to offend you and I don't want to hurt our relationship and I won't let this go beyond us, but—I think Fred's guilty. I think we have to take control of things and convince him that we're aware of his guilt. He has to start negotiating right now so he doesn't end up in prison."

After a pause, the former intelligence officer said softly, "I can understand that you might think that, Jay, but I've seen enough evidence to think he's innocent."

Jay waited for Mr. Coe to cite some of the evidence, but he didn't. Shoot, he thought, there's the ballgame! How much evidence can there be if Mr. Coe doesn't come up with any and Fred sits in jail making up alibis? Mr. Coe went on, "I know Fred's asked you to do some things for him. He's asked Ruth and me to do some things too. I hope that by the time the trial comes he'll agree with us that it can't be done his way. Fred claims that the police are playing dirty with him and we have a right to respond in kind. But I think he'll change his mind."

As Jay drove back to his office he realized that Fred was in great danger. He remembered his friend's stubbornness and how his parents had always stood behind him. If the family ran true to form, Fred could end up a victim himself—in the penitentiary. That couldn't be allowed to happen.

Late Friday afternoon Charles Williams, the groundskeeper at Sacajawea Junior High, had another talk with one of the school officials about applying for the Secret Witness reward. "Go for it," the administrator said. "You solved the case when you spotted his car."

Williams returned to the stuffy maintenance room with its exposed heat pipes and dialed the Secret Witness number. A voice answered, "Gordon Coe."

"Excuse *me!*" Williams said, and hung up.

As Fred Coe's first week in jail approached its end, Spokanites rich and poor were making angry noises. "Folks are mad because it's the Coes," explained a longtime observer. "They're supposed to be old guard standard bearers. And now everybody believes they've produced not only a bad-ass but the very *worst* kind of bad-ass—a guy who victimizes the daughters of the establishment. If Coe was some poor dumb dude from the North Side, the whole thing would blow over. People're saying, 'For years that almighty Cowles family has been telling us how to run Spokane, and then they let a thing like this happen!' It's not fair, but that's how they feel."

Irate citizens spoke of little else. The old Crosby residence near Gonzaga lost its distinction as the city's most visited home. Cars crawled past the yellow house at Twenty-ninth and Rebecca. A few vigilantes proved their manliness by driving back and forth across the lawn; one of them uprooted a tree.

Neighbor John Evans looked across his fence and told a friend, "God, I hope they know which yard to drive in." Coe's old landlord was afraid his place would be torched. He'd already dissociated himself from his notorious tenant by posting a rent-due notice on the front door—Coe was six months behind—but not all the visitors took the time to read.

One night Sonia McNeill heard a loud voice from the hall of the nursing home. She recognized a female visitor who liked an occasional drink. The woman wobbled into the room and said, "Sonia, I hope that no good son of a bitch— I hope he—*I hope they cut off his prick!*" Sonia felt as though she'd been personally attacked.

*   *   *

Later that night Jeni Coe placed a call to her parents' number in Spokane. For six months she'd been living in San Jose, California, with a troubled young man who was running from a life even more disordered than hers. Not long before, the two of them had been Mickey Finned at a party thrown by devil-worshipers, and one of the satanists had held Jeni's inert hand atop a gas heater long enough to burn off most of the skin. While the wound was healing Jeni told herself it was time to dry out and go home. Her mother answered the phone and told her that Fred had been charged with rape. "Rape?" Jeni exclaimed. "Not Fred!"

"He's in jail. He's the South Hill rapist."

Jeni barely knew about the South Hill rapist, but she knew Fred. He would never rape a woman. He'd always insisted that women were his favorite people. She told her mother she was coming home.

90

For a while detectives Roy Allen and Joan Schmick and their colleagues were
tied down at the Public Safety Building working on details of the Coe case.
Of twenty-four women who had viewed the managing editor's son at live
lineups, eight had identified him as the rapist. One more, Lois Higgins, had
identified him from photos. That made nine for twenty-five, a surprising .360
batting average. The detectives were also encouraged by the IDs that came
in spontaneously:

A woman named Millie Lukens wrote from her new home in California
that Coe was the man who'd flashed her in her parking lot in late 1979.

Emily Sykes, the lupus sufferer who had been terrorized by an obscene
caller and a man hanging around her house, reported that Coe's face was the
one that had peered through the window in her front door.

A massage-parlor girl who called herself "Misty" identified Coe as the man
who'd raped and robbed her in 1979. The identification was backed up by
"Louise," who had avoided being raped by telling the intruder she was just
getting over surgery.

A heavy-set woman named Cassandra Bates told detective Joan Schmick
a story about fending off a man's advances on a long late-night walk. The
woman read his name off the business card he had handed her. It was Kevin
Coe.

Mrs. Patricia O'Malley saw a picture of Coe on TV and went to headquarters to report that he had grabbed her by the breasts when she'd been
jogging near her South Hill home in August of 1979.

There were more IDs, a few from obvious cranks and psychos, but most
from women willing to swear in court that Fred Coe had flashed or peeped or
raped them, or made the attempt. When the phones quieted a little, Roy Allen
pulled the files on all sex crimes for two years back and began showing photo
line-ups to victims. Three more IDs developed. Annie Jaksich, a teacher, identified Coe as the man who'd come at her with a dildo as she waited for a bus
on the South Hill on the first day of 1981. Dr. John Little identified Coe as
the pantless jogger of a few weeks ago, and young Julie Helmbrecht said Coe
resembled the man who had flashed her the next morning while she jogged

on High Drive. On a hunch Allen revisited a woman who lived across the street from the wooded spot where a fourteen-year-old girl had been raped. At the time of his original investigation the woman had told the detective about a recent series of obscene phone calls. Now Allen asked her, "Do you know Kevin Coe?"

"No."

"When you were shopping for a house, what real estate agencies did you work with?"

"My brother's. He's with Roger Crane in the valley."

"Have you ever been out there?"

"Many times."

"Have you had any obscene calls since we arrested Coe?"

"That's when they stopped."

Back at the various real estate offices where Coe had worked, other information came in. A couple who had listed a house with Roger Crane reported arriving home around midnight and finding Coe inside studying their drapes. He explained that he'd used his lockbox key. "This is the way I work," he said, fingering the material professionally. "It gives me more time to check out the features of the house." Asked why his car wasn't in the driveway, Coe said, "Oh, I parked four or five blocks down the street. That's how I get my exercise. I jog." The couple had thought the young realtor an odd duck but hadn't mentioned the incident.

A woman came to the Crane office and told how Coe had knocked on her door at 10:30 p.m. a few weeks before his arrest and tried to talk his way in. She was afraid he would return for her teenage daughter.

Another woman whose house had been listed for sale in 1980 called and said, "I used to throw my underpants in a drawer till one night I came home and found them all neatly folded." There were similar calls from others.

A realtor named Lyle Hatcher turned in a leather coat he'd bought from Coe. There were scratches and stains on the sleeves. The state police crime lab was unable to type the stains; the jacket had been cleaned several times since the purchase.

Gini Perham made a complete report on her experiences with Coe and told about some of his gifts—a ceramic cat, a small gilded statue, other oddments—on the theory that they might have been stolen from houses for sale. The detectives listened with half an ear. They could barely keep up with the sex crimes.

91

Psychopaths are very good at flattering people. Others usually believe them, even those (myself included) who know better.—Thomas Steele, M.D., Yale-New Haven Hospital, quoted by Alan Harrington in *Psychopaths*

You seem to think you're carrying some great secret with you as far as this dildo thing goes. Hardly! My parents have known about it and you for months.—Fred Coe to Jay Williams, Feb. 5, 1982

Soon after his talk with Gordon Coe in the lobby of the Davenport Hotel, Jay Williams visited Fred Coe in jail. This time his old friend seemed calmer. Jay picked up the dull-black handphone with the silvered cord and said, "Man, we got a problem. That house is occupied."

Coe stared hard at him through the plateglass window, then began printing rapidly on a small pad. He held it up: "YOU'RE A PROFESSIONAL SALESMAN. YOU CAN GET BACK INTO THAT HOUSE. I <u>KNOW</u> YOU CAN."

Jay mouthed, "How?"

Coe wrote for a while and flattened another page against the window: "GO UP THERE WITH BRIEFCASE. SAY YOU WANT TO LOOK AT HOUSE. GO UNDER STAIRWELL, STICK DILDO AND SWEATER IN BRIEF-CASE—WALK OUT!"

Jay gave him a look of incredulity and said, "How realistic is that, Fred? The owner moved back in and took it off the market. What excuse could I use?"

Fred wrote in large letters, "WE'RE FRIENDS. I LOVE YOU, I LOVE YOUR FAMILY. I WOULD DO <u>ANYTHING</u> FOR YOU. <u>I WOULD DO THIS FOR YOU</u>." Jay averted his eyes. He didn't want his discouragement to rub off on Fred, but it was hard to conceal. A cell door clanged in the distance—steel against steel. He thought of Fred sitting in jail for years, listening to sounds like that. But his demoralizing thoughts didn't make the retrieval of the items any more possible. Coe held up another sheet: "GET IN THAT HOUSE AND GET THOSE THINGS!!! YOU'RE A GREAT SALESMAN, ONE OF THE GREATEST. <u>I KNOW YOU CAN DO IT</u>!"

Jay interpreted the message to suggest an act of burglary. That was a little more *semper fideles* than he was prepared to offer. He said, "I can't! They've got a dog."

"GO RIGHT UP TO THE FRONT DOOR AND TELL THEM YOU WANT TO SEE THE HOUSE!!!"

Oh, I see, Jay thought. He means bluff it out, use my persuasiveness. Well, it might be possible. Risky, but possible.

Driving back to the valley, he warned himself not to move too fast. He wished he had a better idea where the dildo fit into the rape cases. Would its physical existence prove that Fred was the rapist? But that was provable in so many ways. Nothing I can do will change the basic scenario, Jay told himself. He's going to prison with or without my help, with or without the involvement of the dildo. So why not spare him some public embarrassment? Image is all that matters to him anyway.

He stopped in his driveway before going inside to face his family. He wondered if he was deceiving himself to justify an irrational act of honor and obligation—good old *semper fideles* again. He decided to wait a few days to give the police a chance to find the dildo first. If they did, that would be the Lord's will. If they didn't, he would take it as a message. He would go to the house himself and, if the Lord willed it, retrieve the dildo and destroy it. That way the decision would be out of his hands.

A few nights later, after prayer and meditation, he parked at the Circle K market on Altamont and ambled across the street in his easy ex-boxer's stride. As he approached the small house he mumbled, "Lord, it's up to You. When I knock on that door, I'm not gonna give those people any false reasons, any lies. If You intend for the police to have the dildo, then let them have it. Thy will be done." He was empty-handed, wearing a sportcoat. Fred had told him to carry his briefcase, but he'd forgotten it. He didn't even look his part. That was fine. There would be no props, no double dealing, no dishonesty. If the Lord wanted him to destroy the dildo, the Lord would let it happen.

He knocked and the door opened. A small boy looked up at him and a man and woman peered down from the railing above. Jay gulped and said, "Hello! I'm Jay Williams, Tomlinson agency. We talked briefly several days ago. I understand you don't want to sell your house. Is that so?"

"That's right," the woman said.

"Well, would it be okay if I looked at it anyway?"

"Well, sure," the woman said pleasantly. "My husband and I are watching TV. Do you mind if we don't join you?"

"Not at all."

He stepped inside. The woman said, "Would you like Tommy to show you around?"

"Thanks anyway. You just go ahead and do whatever you're doing. I won't be long." The family faded from sight. Jay went into the kitchen, opened and shut a few cabinets, and headed down the stairs. Below the stairwell he found a mound of toys and junk that nearly filled the opening. He wondered how he could dig around without arousing attention. The TV droned above his head.

He began poking. A box fell with a thump, and he cleared his throat loudly. He groped and felt and rearranged, but found neither sweater nor dildo.

He spotted an opening in the rear and reached inside. He felt soft material. He moved several boxes and pulled out a fluff of dark blue with a white stripe. Coe had called it a sweater, but it looked more like a jogging top.

Something long and hard was wrapped inside. He unwrapped the material and found a cylindrical object over a foot long and four inches thick. In the dim light he saw that it was flesh-colored, made of plastic. He wished he'd had the sense to give the Lord a helping hand and bring along his briefcase. He tried to stuff the thing under his sportcoat. It stuck out like a baseball bat. He tried putting it in his belt, but that was worse. His heart beat hard as he tried to figure out what to do. Fred should have warned him that the thing was so big! He'd expected something six or seven inches long, something more realistic.

He spotted a window. He told himself, I'll toss it out and retrieve it after they go to sleep. He tiptoed over and touched the latch. A dog barked a few inches below the sill. Jay pulled back and thought: If I throw the dildo out, the dog'll get it, and even if he doesn't chew it to pieces, how will I ever take it away from him?

Footsteps clomped above; someone was coming. He stuffed the dildo under a mattress against the wall, but a portion stuck out. His adrenaline was flowing and he told himself he would carry out the mission even if he had to revert to his old halfback days and do a broken-field run out the door.

The footsteps died. He took a look at the blue jogging top and wondered how an innocuous item like that could be incriminating or embarrassing. Jogging tops were jogging tops. It was just too much to haul under the unsuspecting noses of the people of the house. He wadded it up and stuffed it back under the stairwell. If the police really need it to make a legitimate case of rape, he told himself, well, it's still here. A touch of justice....

He stuck the dildo under his arm. It ran from his armpit to his waist. His jacket wouldn't button. His arm stuck out at an angle. It was like trying to conceal a loaf of French bread. He climbed the stairs. He knew his deception wouldn't fool anybody. He intended to walk to the front door and make a break for it. He reached the door and grabbed the knob.

The woman leaned over the railing and said, "Did you get a good look?"

"Yeah," he said. "Fine. Thanks a lot!" He stepped out and headed for his car, but then he realized he would have to pass a window of the house. He didn't want the people to get another look at him or the license plate on his car. He turned the opposite way and walked around the block. He was sure that the woman had seen the lump under his jacket. By now they must have put two and two together and concluded that he was a thief who'd talked his way into the house to make a score. And it was true—that was exactly what he was! He could see the headlines: "Lay Minister Held in Burglary." What a way to repay the Lord.

He shoved the dildo under the front seat, pushed the button that locked every door and started the engine. He hadn't felt this apprehensive in Vietnam. He said to himself, I don't want this thing in my car! What if I die of a stroke? What if I get hit by a truck? Another headline jumped out: "Local Realtor Found with Sex Paraphernalia." As he sped out of the parking lot he remembered Coe's instructions, "TAKE THE DILDO AND CUT IT INTO 100 PIECES! SPREAD THE PIECES IN VACANT LOTS! ONE PIECE AT A TIME!"

That would take all night. Where would he do the surgery? At home? Sue or the kids might walk in. A mile or so past the Central Park Racquet Club, he spotted a Dumpster parked alongside the curb. He wrapped the dildo in paper bags and rammed it as deep into the trash as his arm would reach.

The next evening he told Fred, "I did it."

He was surprised at the unemotional response. "Well, uh, that's good," Fred said in a flat voice. "You did good."

Jay looked around before bringing up another unpleasant subject. The cubicles on either side were empty, and the guard in the control room seemed too busy to be bugging telephones. "Fred, about that other thing you asked me?" he said.

"What other thing?"

"Uh—wearing the dress?"

Coe wagged a finger. Quickly, Jay said, "I won't be able to do it." He didn't want Fred to spend one more night thinking he would do anything as silly as claiming he'd tried to vamp the South Hill rapist in a dress while Fred followed in a car. Who above the age of six would believe a story like that?

Coe looked perturbed. "Why not?"

"Well, gee, Fred, I'm . . . a Christian."

"Yeah? What's that mean?"

"It means I can't swear to tell the truth and then lie."

Now Coe looked puzzled. "You *can't*?"

"No."

"I thought we were taught that lies were acceptable if they served a greater good."

It was Jay's turn to be puzzled. "Where were we taught that?" he asked. As boys the two of them had attended St. Stephen's Episcopal Church, and Jay never remembered any such teachings. Maybe Coe was confused.

"Oh, never mind," Fred said. The conversation petered out and Jay left.

92

With Gini...my mistake was in not removing the unstable woman from my life.—Fred Coe, April 20, 1982

A week after she'd hung up on Ruth Coe, Gini Perham still felt guilty about it. She'd enjoyed many moments with Gordon and Ruth, had gone on trips with them, eaten their food, laughed and joked and made up a foursome. It was true that for the last several months she'd avoided Ruth, but she realized now that the poor woman must be suffering terribly.

Everyone who'd had anything to do with Kevin Coe was now busily distancing himself from the accused South Hill rapist and from anyone connected to him, and an upset Roger Crane had asked Gini to take a few weeks off. She was spending the time at her grandmother's house on the South Hill, avoiding the press and the Coes. Only the police and a few friends knew how to reach her.

On an impulse she dialed the old number and was surprised to find that it hadn't been disconnected or changed. Ruth sounded thrilled to hear her voice. "Oh, Gini, darling!" the woman said. "Gini *darling!* Where've you been? Where've you *been?* We've been trying to get in touch with you. How *are* you?"

"I'm fine, fine," Gini stammered. "Uh—how're you guys?"

"We're fine." Gini heard her say, "Gordon? *Gordon!* It's Gini! Get on the other line!" Then, "Gini, what did the police find in the house?"

"Ruth, I don't know. I was in shock. A few bags full of things; that's all I know."

"Did they find any"—her voice dropped—"women's clothing?"

Gini didn't understand. "My stuff was there. Some of Jenifer's things were in the basement."

"No, no. That's not what I meant."

Gordon came on and Ruth dropped the subject. He sounded relieved to hear Gini and launched into a discourse about the injustice done to his son. Clenching the phone in two hands, Gini thought her heart would break. Poor Gordon had always been so quiet, so dignified, and now he sounded like an excited old man who'd begun to lose touch with reality. She could almost feel his pain. His voice was high-pitched as he complained that the *Spokesman-Review* had violated every journalistic canon of ethics, some of which he'd helped draw up himself. "They convicted Fred after the arrest and they've been convicting him ever since," Gordon said. He claimed that the lineups were illegal because Fred hadn't been represented by counsel. He said he knew a thing or two about lineups from his years in military intelligence, and these had been atrociously managed. He rambled on nonstop. For the first time since Gini had met him two years earlier, he sounded like his son.

Ruth threw in an occasional word of agreement, but let Gordon do most of the talking. When he paused for breath Gini jumped in and said, "I want you guys to eat well. Take care of yourselves. This is a very stressful time."

Gordon said, "Fred wants you to come down and see him. You can go with us. We'll—"

Ruth interrupted. "Wait, Gini! We're getting another call. Hang on!" Gini realized that she had nothing more to say to them. She didn't want to hear illogical arguments about Kevin's innocence, and above all else she didn't want to visit him. She realized that she was afraid of Ruth and didn't know why. How, she asked herself, am I going to get out of this?

"Gini?" Ruth said. Static almost drowned her voice. Gini hung up and hoped it would sound accidental. The instant she put the phone down she felt like a traitor. The Coes couldn't call back because they didn't know where she was. How unfair to cut them off again! They were old, helpless, and she was adding to their misery. She started crying and couldn't stop.

That night she began a series of nightmares. Kevin chased her and threatened unspecified tortures. Sometimes Ruth chased her—never Gordon. She would sleep for an hour or two and wake up from a dream and be up till dawn. She couldn't touch food.

In three weeks her weight dropped from 140 to 117. She was afraid to leave her grandmother's house. She was sure that the Coes were looking for her. Friends took her to the Rape Crisis Center. She was treated as another victim of the South Hill rapist. After some therapy a counselor suggested a temporary change of scene. She visited friends in Seattle for a week, then came back to Spokane to house-sit a big South Hill home two blocks from where Kevin had been brought up.

She was still haunted by what she'd done to the Coes and what they might do in return. Every day she called the jail to make sure that Kevin hadn't been released. She spent days doing therapeutic housework—vacuuming and dusting till the four-bedroom house gleamed—and more hours talking to herself and her cockapoo, Mr. Crumpett. Sometimes she tried to kid herself out of her depression, but her guilt went too deep. She could never forgive herself for ignoring so many signs, and especially for the night in December when she'd changed her mind about turning him in. Friends and relatives gave advice. Her father, Colonel Guy Perham, suggested that it might be better for all concerned if she didn't testify; Gini told him she would think about it. One more decision to make. There were so many.

93

_I don't really like being cast in the role of martyr—as a noble Ayn
Rand character from one of her novels. But my only crime is having
wanted Spokane to grow._—Fred Coe, Oct. 18, 1981

F. H. "Kevin" Coe's first public opportunity to speak in his own behalf came
two weeks after his arrest. He walked into court in a tired seaman's shuffle,
his Prince Valiant bangs blending into his eyebrows, his hands cuffed loosely
in front. He seemed to be having difficulty breathing. The occasion was a
combination bail-reduction hearing and arraignment. In addition to the rape
of Irene Pool on the morning of February 5, 1981 (a charge on which he'd
already been arraigned), he was now formally accused of the rapes of five
other women:

Lois Higgins, nineteen years old at the time of her ordeal on Spokane's
North Side in 1978, the first recorded Spokane rape in which the assailant
rammed his hand down the victim's throat; Sue Ellen Wilber, sixteen, raped
just after midnight August 30, 1980, by a man with a "soft and educated"
voice; Marie Oldham, twenty-seven, raped and beaten by a jogger who rammed
his hand down her throat as she walked toward her new home in October,
1980; Stephanie Gibbs, fourteen, attacked and raped as she walked on a foggy
South Hill street a week before Christmas, 1980; Jeanie Mays, twenty, raped
and beaten by a man who shoved an oven mitt down her throat on the icy
morning of February 9, 1981, while she was on her way to catch a bus.

In between hacking coughs, Coe pleaded not guilty to each count. Prosecuting attorney Donald Brockett asked the court to continue the original
hundred-thousand-dollar bond, and public defender Roger Gigler pleaded for
Coe's immediate release on his own recognizance. The distinguished Gordon
Coe, with his sad eyes, his wavy silver hair and his thick eyebrows that arched
upward as he made his points, looked more judicial than the judge as he spoke
firmly and clearly on his son's behalf: "In forty-five years of observing the
criminal justice system in Spokane rather closely, I have seen an awful lot of
defendants on every charge you can name go through these courts, and I have
been struck all this time by the tremendous differences between the stereotype
that I have seen come to court on various crimes, including rape, and this

defendant, who comes from a loving and close family, has lived a normal life here all his life."

The newsman told of heavy community support ever since the arrest two weeks before. "We were unable to get anything done because the phone rang all the time. And we have had a massive amount of letters supporting this young man and saying that it's ridiculous to think that he could have done these things." According to Coe, there had been heartening communications from friends and families of rape victims and even from police officers.

Ruth Coe, peering at the judge over the tops of her half glasses, said that support had come "from old neighbors...from new neighbors...from clergy, from professionals, from the butcher, the baker, the candlestick maker who have watched this boy grow up and into manhood." She reminded the judge that the Coes were an old Spokane family. "Longer ago than I care to tell you, I was born here," she said coyly. She promised that Fred wouldn't jump his bond; he was eager to get out of jail and prove his innocence. "There is no chance that my son is a rapist. He has great love and respect for womanhood. He's been a loving and adoring son to me, and a loving and adoring brother to his sister and he has many, many girls that he's gone with in his past who speak only highly of him."

Jay Williams testified nervously that he and Fred had been best friends for twenty-five years "and in all of that time I have never known Fred to have ever been violent, to the point that I have never even known him to use violent language."

Paula Whitmore, another realtor, told the court that she had known the Coes for thirty years "and I can say nothing but tremendous things about the whole family." She described Fred Coe as "an extreme gentleman. He's always been very chivalrous. He's always conducted himself as a gentleman with me."

The defendant, wearing a three-piece tan suit, spoke with difficulty. "I am having a little trouble talking," he explained, "because I'm suffering from allergies that being in jail exacerbates." After a paroxysm of coughing, he elaborated: "I suffer from an acute allergy and asthma condition, which normally I'm able to control with a very intense diet and lots of fresh air and exercise. That has been severe—this condition has been severely aggravated by being in jail." He sneezed and continued, "I could very possibly become even seriously ill. In the two weeks that I have been in jail my health has gone from an optimum level to where, as you can see, I have a hard time talking. I have had several minor bouts with asthma. The—the—this is because I'm not allowed my usual treatment which is natural, not medicinal. There is no medicine I take for the treatment."

He paused to catch his breath. "Speaking of health, both my parents are over sixty." Seated in the courtroom, Ruth Coe raised her dark blue eyes to the ceiling at this revelation of her age, drawing a chuckle from a few spectators. Coe swore that he was not the South Hill rapist. "My normal life still does not include any criminal activity. It does not include being a rapist. I am no danger to this society. I will be, if released, in the presence of one or both of my parents constantly, the entire time. . . . I have no criminal record. . . . I have a number of witnesses who will testify that they knew that I was involved in an activity to search out the South Hill rapist and this is why my car was seen in a number of places and so forth." He said that he was employed, and "additionally I have my own business and I have exceptionally strong ties to the community." He explained that he was needed for real estate closings and added, "I have financial matters that have to be administered to"—no petty argument in mercantile Spokane.

The judge reduced the bond to thirty-five thousand dollars. For several days news photographers hung around the jail to film the dramatic release, but Coe stayed inside. Jay Williams asked what was going on. "My parents are trying to raise the money," Fred confided. "The bondsman wants thirty-five hundred dollars. My mother tried to hock her jewelry but most of it's fake."

Another week passed, and the accused man remained in jail.

94

In the Chronicle, dad had reported the South Hill rapes as news, in a polite and proper news fashion.—Fred Coe, May 26, 1982

Gordon Coe had absented himself from work in the first days after his son's arrest, but now he was back on the job and emphatic in his complaints about the "railroading" of his son. He lamented the way jailers treated Fred and spoke at length about his need for a special diet, his allergies, his asthma. The news that the young Coe was sickly came as a surprise to the staffers. Gordon charged that Fred's jailers were inhumane.

As more and more allegations came to light, the managing editor shot them down one by one. He buttonholed staffers and made them feel intimidated. They tried to be understanding, but all agreed that it was an unusual stance for a man who'd built a career on being vanilla. Nobody knew exactly what to do about the problem. Coe had worked for the *Chronicle* for forty-two years and had just been put up for Washington State University's Alumnus of the Year award. But for all his popularity he seemed close to no one outside his family. Colleagues who had worked with him for decades had visited him at home exactly once—when Ruth Coe had redone the place and shown it off at an open house. "I've never worked with anyone who said as little about his private life as Gordie," said a retired editor. "In nearly thirty years, I don't think he volunteered five minutes of conversation about his family."

Coe was regarded as a pleasant man with a nice grin, a cautious leader who would never get the paper in trouble, a shy man who hated to criticize or fire anyone, and an unabashed fourth-generation Spokane booster. He was also seen as an overreacher who took on too many petty chores, personally answering every letter he received and handing out the morning mail like an army clerk. His longstanding habit of falling asleep at his desk remained enigmatic to his staffers because he consistently refused to admit that he had a problem. Said a colleague, "I've seen him doze off while interviewing somebody for a job. One afternoon Mr. Cowles himself had to wake him up. Some of us thought it might be hypoglycemia; he ate a big chocolate bar every day. Some of us thought it might be tranquilizers. One of the secretaries asked him if he had narcolepsy and he said no and acted surprised that she'd asked.

Once I suggested that maybe he should see his doctor. He said he couldn't imagine why."

With his son's arrest for rape Gordon Coe showed an entirely new face—the vociferous crusader for justice. He flatly denied a *Spokesman-Review* article about Fred's shoplifting conviction, calling the story "fabricated from whole cloth." The next morning he took two editors aside and apologized; there *had* been a shoplifting incident, he admitted, but Mrs. Coe and Fred hadn't mentioned it to him, and anyway the affair was a frame-up just like the rape charges. After several complaints about his arm-twisting found their way to the publisher, Coe was summoned to the third-floor executive offices. He was told he could remain in his post, but the coverage of his son's case would be handled by others. If the order was intended to silence him, it didn't work. A group of staffers met and agreed that something more drastic would have to be done.

On Saturday, April 4, twelve days after the bond hearing and four weeks after his arrest, Fred Coe was finally freed. His father had sold the family's 1979 Cadillac to raise the thirty-five-hundred-dollar bondsman's fee. Fred went home to his parents' house in the Spokane Valley. The next day his mother was treated for a broken right wrist. She explained to the doctor that she'd tripped over a flower box.

95

The psychopath makes a mockery not only of the truth but also of all authority and institutions.—Arnold Buss, M.D., *Psychopathology*

Jay Williams was showing a house when his pager beeped. He phoned his office and a secretary gave him a number to call. Jay dialed and heard a familiar voice. "Fred!" he said. "Where are you?"

"I'm out of jail. I'm in a phone booth. There's a bug on my parents' phone. Listen, I've got to see you soon." They arranged to meet at Jay's home as soon as he could break away.

Jay called his wife Sue and told her to instruct the two children, aged six and nine, to be courteous to Fred and not to ask him questions about jail.

Fred arrived before Jay, and Sue answered the door. He stood in the entranceway shifting from foot to foot. Three of Sue's friends had just arrived, and Fred whispered, "I don't want to come inside. I don't want to talk to anybody."

"It'll be okay," Sue said in a hushed voice. "Come in and sit down."

Coe went into the living room and stood in a corner. He beckoned Sue over and said, "My parents are outside. I'm in their custody and you have to acknowledge that you're here so they can leave."

Sue stepped out and waved to the Coes, parked in the gray Citation. They gestured back and drove off. In another room the children had started arguing, and one of Sue's visitors told little Donny in an unnaturally loud voice, "You shouldn't be concerned about what other people think. You should only be concerned about what *Jesus* thinks." Sue recognized the words as a moral reminder to Coe—from a woman who hadn't been inside a church in thirty years. She wished her guests would just be themselves.

When Jay arrived Fred asked what people were saying about him. Jay said he hadn't heard many nice comments. Fred said he was preparing a list of lawsuits—for defamation of character, false arrest, illegal imprisonment, slander and libel. He planned to sue the city, the police department, the prosecutor's office, both newspapers and the women who had identified him.

"Listen, Jay," he said, smiling and patting his old friend on the arm, "you can work with me on these lawsuits. We'll have so much money we'll open up a real estate office, selling high-end properties. The primest of the prime!"

Jay winced at the familiar big talk. At the moment, the real estate market was stagnant. He was wondering how to make his own house payments and how to keep his utilities from being cut off. He'd even considered bankruptcy, but he couldn't bear to think of the effect on his family's financial future. And here was Fred, facing the same problem plus far more serious ones, acting as though the two of them were about to find success.

Jay found it hard to concentrate as Fred trumpeted his innocence. He said he'd been out searching for the South Hill rapist himself; that's why police had seen him following buses and studying bus stops and houses. Jay thought, If this whole tragedy didn't involve my best friend, I'd have to laugh. I'd have been the *first* person to know that he was tracking the rapist, and he never said a word about it. "I've got plenty of witnesses," Coe was saying. "My mother and father knew what I was doing. But they're relatives. Jay, it would really cinch things if you'd testify for me."

"Testify to what?" Jay asked.

"What I told you in jail. That we tried to catch the South Hill rapist together. We put you in a dress because you're short and slight and could pose as a woman. I followed you in the car waiting for the rapist to attack."

"But—"

"Listen to me! They're gonna try me in a month. *One month!* If you just go to the police and explain, they'll drop the whole thing. Jay, you can alibi every rape! For starters we'd have a five-million-dollar lawsuit against the city of Spokane. We'll make so much money—"

"Fred, sit down, will you?" Jay asked. He tried to sound calm. "Let me just say a few things, okay?"

Coe said, "Go ahead," but refused to sit.

"You know what our friendship means to me," Jay began. "*Semper fideles, esprit de corps*—it's as real to me now as it was when we were in school."

"That's why I don't understand—"

Jay held up his hand. "Right now you could talk me into anything. I'd even agree to lie, say whatever you asked, whatever would solve your problem. But—how are both of us gonna handle it when the Lord moves me to repent my lies? How are we gonna handle it if I alibi you out of these charges and then get up in court and admit that I was lying? We'd *both* wind up in Walla Walla. Is it worth that risk, Fred?"

"What makes you so sure you might repent?"

"Jesus rules my life, Fred. Jesus *is* my life. I told you in jail—there's no way I could put my hand on a Bible and then betray my oath." Something in Coe's stare made him realize that his message wasn't getting across. "Look," he said, "there must be somebody else you can get to testify for you."

"My family would do it," Fred said. "But I don't know who else. Kathy's husband John lived with my parents for a while when he was looking for a house here. He could help me, but he's—funny. Besides, they're getting a divorce."

"He's 'funny'? What's that mean?"

"He has principles against lying. He says he'll only testify about what he remembers. I don't know if that's enough to help me. I'm still working on him, but I don't think the guy'll lie." Fred's tone suggested that he regarded John Cockburn's honesty as a quirk.

While dinner grew cold in the other room, Coe begged him to listen to reason. "I'm being railroaded by crooked cops and prosecutors. They talked all those women into lying. Not one of them could've honestly identified me as the South Hill rapist, because I'm *not* the South Hill rapist. You know that, Jay. You said yourself, It doesn't fit. Those women are going to get on that witness stand and tell lies, and the cops are gonna back 'em up. How's an innocent man supposed to fight a frame like that? The jury might doubt my parents, Jay, but they'd never doubt a born-again Christian like you. Your testimony can save an innocent man! *Think about it!*"

Jay wanted to say, Look, Fred, I'll always be your friend, but I don't think you're innocent! He found it impossible to be that cruel. The poor guy was going down for the third time and yelling for help.

"You don't know how bad it is," Coe continued. "Listen to this: We found out from the prosecution that a dozen cops are ready to testify they saw me in a gray running suit like the one the rapist wore. A dozen cops are gonna perjure themselves! What these people won't stoop to! I never owned a gray jogging suit in my life, Jay. You know that!" As he spoke, Fred wore a look of sincerity; he seemed convinced by his own words. Jay was baffled. Not only did Fred own a gray jogging suit; it was his favorite. Jay thought, I've seen him in those gray sweats a hundred times. Now suddenly they never existed? Has he started believing his own lies? Surely that's a sign of insanity. Surely that's a sign he needs to be hospitalized, not prosecuted.

Coe spoke faster. He brought up *semper fideles* and *esprit de corps* again. He reminded Jay of a blood oath they'd sworn as boys. He recounted past favors. At last Jay said, "Let me think about it, Fred, okay? Give me some time."

"Time?" Coe said. "There's no time, man. The trial's in a month."

Jay said he was late for a church committee meeting. Fred phoned his parents and told them to pick him up at the church. The hard sell continued until the two old friends said their good-byes in a pew. A church member took Jay aside and said, "It's him, isn't it?"

"Yes," Jay admitted. "It's him."

"He's come to talk to the pastor, has he?"

Jay turned to look at his old friend. Fred was sitting in half-light on the front steps of the church, waiting like a child for his parents. He's sick, Jay thought. The poor guy's as sick as if he had cancer. "Oh Lord," he prayed under his breath, "help me save my poor sick friend."

Gini Perham almost panicked when she heard that Kevin had been released on bond. She called headquarters and learned that Joan Schmick and Gene McGougan had gone to his cell just before he was released and advised him that she would be a witness for the prosecution. "We told him he'd be wise to stay away from you," Schmick informed her. "The judge released him to his parents' custody. So relax, honey. He wouldn't dare approach you now."

Gini wished she believed it. She was still house-sitting on the South Hill and the big place seemed spookier than ever with Kevin free. At night she slept in a locked bedroom with her toxic spray on the side table and her mini-dog on guard in the hall. After a few sleepless nights she gave up and moved in with friends in the Spokane Valley.

Her two weeks of enforced layoff from Roger Crane & Associates were over, but she found it almost impossible to concentrate on business. Kevin sent word through intermediaries that he wanted to see her as soon as possible. Just the thought of running into him or his parents was enough to frighten her.

After lunch on the afternoon of Friday, April 24, she was talking to a client in front of the office when a secretary ran out and said, "Kevin just drove by in his Citation. Didn't you see him, Gini?"

When Coe made a second pass Gini telephoned Schmick. "Stay right where you are," the detective said. "I'll be right there."

By late afternoon everyone was still on watch. At 5 p.m. Gini spotted a familiar female face peering from a gray Citation, her white wing-tipped dark glasses catching the sun as she stared hard at the Crane office. "That's Ruth!" Gini shouted. "Kevin's driving!"

Later office manager George Korb got a call from the public defender's office: "Was our boy out there snooping around?"

"Yeah," Korb answered. "That son of a bitch better keep away from here."

"Well, that does it. We're gonna tie his feet down."

Not long afterward Coe asked Jay Williams to pick him up at his parents' home for another conference. At the house, Ruth Coe started talking about rape. "It's no big deal," she told Jay. "I've known women who were raped and didn't let it bother them. They picked themselves up and dusted themselves off. *Cindy Stafford* has been raped twice. It didn't ruin her life." Mrs. Coe said that she'd seen Irene Pool, the fifty-one-year-old who'd charged Fred with rape at Hart Field, "and she's much too ugly to be a convincing witness." As for Lois Higgins, the young woman who'd been raped three years before on Indiana Avenue, "She's a little nuts. She won't make a good witness." Jay was surprised at Mrs. Coe's insensitivity.

Gini Perham saw that her career in real estate was over. If it wasn't true before, it was true after Kevin started cruising her office. What an irony, she thought. The man who steered me into the business now forces me out. She couldn't attend or hold open houses or advertise her listings for fear Coe would catch up to her. As she explained to Korb, "If you're not advertising and having open houses, you're not in real estate. It's a public profession, and I can't practice it anymore." Korb agreed and said it was a damned shame.

Out of both work and money, Gini drove to northern Idaho to a relative's vacant cabin. She arrived late in the afternoon, drew water, chopped wood and did some cartooning, the profession she hoped to enter someday. After a while she began to relax. The dark waters of the lake lapped at the beach a short stroll from the cabin. Anyone approaching would make a loud *crunch-crunch* with his feet.

Around midnight her cockapoo began to yip. She shushed him. Then she heard someone walking up the gravel path. She jerked the curtains closed. The noises grew louder. She knelt in the dark room clutching the little dog.

Footsteps pounded on the deck. She knew Coe's sound. It was him. She grabbed a butcher knife, ran into the bathroom and locked the door. Too late, she remembered Mr. Crumpett in the main room. He was barking like an attack dog. After fifteen or twenty minutes he fell silent. She wondered if he'd been strangled.

Then she heard him whimpering at the door. She opened it an inch and looked out. No one was around. She sat up till dawn with the knife on her lap.

96

*Mark my words when I tell you flatly that the Space Needle is merely
a cheap imitation of my hard-on (in miniature) and soon the damn
thing will shoot its fucking rocks like a cocksucking volcano and spew
manure, rags, cunt juice, cunt jews, and rotten beever pelts all over.*—
Fred Coe to John Nyberg, Jan. 31, 1974

John Nyberg had just learned of Fred Coe's release on bond when the phone
rang in the office of his Seattle booking agency. Nyberg steeled himself when
he recognized the voice of a friend of the Coe family. He knew that Jay Williams
had already been pressured to give alibi testimony. The booking agent wasn't
averse to helping a friend, but only within limits.

He and the caller exchanged small talk—everyone enjoyed Nyberg because he knew the latest jokes and inside information about comics and rock
stars. Like the other members of the old Lewis and Clark High School trio,
he was now thirty-four years old, but unlike the others he was a successful
businessman in a field that called for charm and chatter, his specialties. He
was short, bright and articulate, a man of a few thousand words, most of them
funny. But at the moment he didn't feel funny. He was afraid he knew what
was coming. "Oh, by the way, John," his caller asked, "do you know what's
going on with Fred?"

"Of course."

"Do you remember when he was over here three years ago?"

"Sure."

"He came to visit you and your wife in April '78, right?"

Nyberg knew that Coe had been accused of a rape in Spokane on April
26, 1978. "Yeah, he came to visit us," he said, picking his words carefully,
"but it wasn't in April."

"Sure it was. Don't you remember?"

"No. Why? Is it important?"

There was a pause; then, "Well, John, we all know that Fred's innocent,
right?"

There it was: the big assumption. Nyberg had heard that Fred and his
parents were acting as though the whole world thought him innocent. He

himself didn't, and he couldn't understand why anyone would try to line up witnesses for a man who obviously needed psychiatric help far more than he needed perjured testimony. Fred was a fascinating guy—talented, bright, funny as hell. He was worth saving. "Fred would never rape anybody, John," the caller went on. "Never!"

Nyberg marveled at the naïveté. "I could tell you things you don't know about Fred," he said.

"Like what?"

He started to respond and thought better of it. "Let's wait and see what happens at the trial."

"That might be too late. C'mon, John, try to remember." The voice took on a pleading tone. "He visited you and your wife, and the three of you went out. April of '78. Remember?"

"That wasn't in April."

"Oh, John, it *was!*" The caller sounded disappointed in him. "Are you telling me you won't help out?"

"Debby and I broke up in February. How could Fred have gone out with us in April?"

"But John, Fred's *innocent*. You're supposed to be his friend. Couldn't you testify? It would be *such* a help."

Nyberg remembered what an alibi artist Fred had always been. But the South Hill rapes were a little different from peeping or cheating or going too far with a girl. "I can't verify a false date," he said. "You're doing something you shouldn't. If you knew what I know about Fred, you'd back off."

"What's that mean?"

He wished he could answer.

"I met Coe when we were high school sophomores," Nyberg told a friend later. "He approached me one day and said, 'You're such a humorous guy. We have a lot in common.' At the time I needed the flattery. I didn't have a lot of friends; I was a shy, frightened kid with an insecurity complex. Jay Williams and Coe and I became our own little in-group. For a few years we tried to be the junior version of the clan—Sinatra, Joey Bishop, Peter Lawford, that crowd. We worked at nice restaurants, wore tuxedoes and cummerbunds, poured coffee, had our nails done, served from the right and cleared from the left, and we knew *all* about women. We bought that silly dream.

"In high school Fred did unusual things, but they didn't seem unusual in the context of what the three of us were doing at the time. Looking back, there were warning signs that something was wrong with his thought processes. He always acted like he admired me and Jay, but he was just egging us on to perform. He was more interested in seeing. He was the complete voyeur.

"All through high school he subordinated everything to sex. We belonged to a social club, but he seemed bored by it except on gang-bang nights. He wasn't good at meeting girls. He'd always stroke me and Jay so we'd operate for him. He'd meet some easy lay and say, 'Humpy, I found a nymph! Let's go!' We'd park somewhere and he'd watch. He'd make up some excuse like, 'I'll look out for the cops.'

"He wanted to be the cocksman extraordinaire, but he couldn't. He studied books on clitoral arousal, foreplay, labia coloration. He asked me, 'Have you ever seen your mother naked?' He had boundless curiosity about sex. It wasn't till years later that I found out he had a secret sex life that I knew nothing about—peeping, entering apartments, kinky things that he kept to himself.

"His big thing was living through others. At prizefights he used to send Jay up to get autographs or shake a fighter's hand. Then he'd question Jay about it. We had a friend who shot up, and Fred kept asking him how it felt, but he wouldn't dream of trying anything that disorderly, not even for the experience. Later he pretended to understand the counterculture, but he really didn't have a clue because he refused to experience any of it, even to take a hit on a joint. He drew all the pictures of his life without color, because he only had a superficial feeling for real living. We'd drink beer and when he thought I wasn't looking he'd pour his out. It was as though a little brew might make him lose control. He wanted an edge on everybody.

"He never revealed himself much—not even to Jay and me. He was the leader of our little group and he treated us the way his mother treated him, with big compliments, backpats—always overdone. 'Jay, you're the greatest!' 'Crunchberg, you're the funniest person alive!' Look what he wrote in my yearbook: 'One day the world should remember you as the king of wit. You got it in your bones, Johnny. Greatness. You come out of the great mold that Crosby Presley Gable did. They weren't academics but they had talent and gifts and now they're rich. Good by, good luck, King.'

"One night he said, 'Humpsickle, we've got to get out of this burg and see what the world looks like.' So we drove all night to Seattle. We saw a few buildings and Coe says, 'See, Crunchturd, this is a *city*!' He says, 'Look at the difference between Seattle and Spokane!'

"I think it was the summer of '64 when he read a biography of one of his heroes, Clark Gable. He says, 'Crunchtoid, you gotta read this book. Gable's the great one, the king. Women loved him and he was incredibly popular, wealthy, powerful. He started out working in the oilfields. That's something we have to do, Humpy—work like real men, be around laborers, build up our masculine image, be *strong*!'

"I said, 'There aren't any oil wells around Spokane to be Clark Gable in.'

"He said, 'No, but there's hard work. Let's find it!'

"He clipped out a help wanted ad: 'Fish for waterdogs.' Those slimy sal-amanders that fishermen use for bait? There's a lot of them in the lakes around Spokane. The ad said, 'Hard work, good pay.' So we called the guy and said we were tough dudes and wanted the job. He said it was hot sweaty work in the open and we said that's exactly what we want. We met this potbellied Okie with his jaw full of chew-tobaccy and tufts of hair sticking out of his unbuttoned shirt—a sewermouth with a second-grade education. He drove us to the lake in his old pickup, put us in hip waders and gave us long poles with nets. He says, 'Now you take this fucking net out there in the water, boys, and pull the cocksucker through the water till you catch them sum-bitches.' Well, those lakes all have mud bottoms. We had to drag the net around, then clear out the crap and the waterdogs, all for a buck fifty an hour. We made our first haul and the old guy looks and says, 'Hey, them fucking sumbitches is green, boys. How kin Ah sell them cocksuckers! Y'all boys go 'round again!'

"After a while Fred says, 'Let's quit! Clark Gable never went through anything like this.' He couldn't comprehend the experience. His mother had filled him full of bullshit about not having to work like the other boys. He'd always been spared hard labor. Mrs. Coe convinced him he was above all that. She was always the vortex of that house. Gordo wrote the checks and handled business things, and she was diamonds on the fingers, talk talk talk, prancing around in her fancy outfits. Sounded like she had a mouth full of pralines. The way to stir her up was to mention the Civil War. I liked to get her going, and Fred would say, 'Crunchturd, would you *please* not goad her like that?'

"I'd say, 'Why? She likes it!'

"'Yeah, but I have to hear about it later. I have to deal with it. Leave her alone; let her think what she wants to think. That's why Dad doesn't argue with her.'

"She raved about Rhett Butler constantly. That's how she and Fred got started on Clark Gable. Gable wasn't a natural hero for Fred—he was really before Fred's time. He just accepted his mother's hero and all her other opinions.

"She hated Spokane—he got that from her. She was spiteful about everybody there, and he was an extension of her spite. He broke out of Spokane for a while, and she broke out of it by pretending to be southern and changing her clothes six times a day. She always called Spokane 'this little town.' She taught Fred to admire places like L.A. and New York for the power and money. She hung on him like a mama lion. I'd go to his house and I'd have to wait till she fed him. She'd say, 'Mah baby boy! Mah Son!' I'd wait while he did his workouts. He was obsessed with his body. Ruth had drilled into him that he was different, he was superior. But there was a razor edge to her affection, too. She demanded reverence. And she could get mean if he didn't measure up. She was always telling him that he had to produce, that she would give him a start but he'd have to do the rest on his own. There was heavy pressure on him to succeed.

"For years she kept her hooks in him. She followed him to San Francisco, to L.A., to Vegas. She'd stay six months at a time, and he'd always act glad. I've never known anyone whose mother had that much control over him. Sometimes she'd tear across the room at him with her nails out—and he'd always back off. Two minutes later, she'd be cupping his face in her hands and talking babytalk. I'm telling you, that house was Ozzie and Harriet visit *Streetcar Named Desire*. But Fred always said his family was the only one he ever wanted.

"Looking back on it, he and I were close, but not as close as we pretended. He concealed his real failures and weaknesses. He had personality and wit, but he never seemed to lighten up and have fun. It wouldn't occur to him to go into an arcade or waste a few hours playing games. He never did anything just for the hell of it. Somebody convinced him that he didn't have time."

A month or so after the abortive attempt to get him to testify, Nyberg drove to Spokane on a vacation trip and visited Fred Coe at Dyer Rd. For a few hours, the clock was rolled back fifteen years. Gordon Coe brought out frosty beers while Mrs. Coe pushed her bridge mix. When the two friends were alone Fred displayed a clump of papers that looked twenty or twenty-five pages thick. "This is my whole case, Crunchberg," he said. "Here's how I'm gonna beat this phony rap." He pulled off several sheets and handed them over. "Read this. It's my opening statement."

Nyberg read the typewritten pages with fascination. The emphasis was on Fred's business achievements and his well-known respect for women. When Nyberg came to the line "I've always supported the Equal Rights Amendment," he stopped reading. He didn't know whether Fred expected him to believe crapola like that or if it was just written to fool a jury. The subject of the disputed 1978 visit to Seattle didn't arise.

97

I do not want sympathy—I want <u>OUTRAGE!</u> I want the public to know the truth and be outraged that such a thing could happen! I want the public to know about the extensive corruption in Spokane's criminal justice system, and I want them to rise up and crush the <u>real</u> criminals!—Fred Coe, Mar. 11, 1981

Legal maneuvering continued through April and May, and the trial was postponed till July. Newspaper coverage changed from extensive to routine as both sides maintained a strategic silence. Jungle drums beat again, and tidbits of rumor and information flew about. It was said that Fred Coe had made the decision to use the public defender because he intended to do the brainwork himself. Later he explained, "We knew that I was picked on just because I was the son of the managing editor, and we knew that Brockett's case was pitifully weak. So we thought, Why in the world spend good money to win a case that any moron could win in court?" He didn't mention an equally pressing reason for the decision: The family was broke.

Courthouse insiders learned that he was second-guessing every stratagem for his defense. He consented to a five-hour diagnostic session with a respected Spokane psychiatrist, Dr. Robert A. Wetzler, and bragged later, "I asked him if he thought I was a sexual psychopath, and he said, 'No, I realized within fifteen minutes that you weren't.'" But there was also a rumor that Dr. Wetzler had concluded just the opposite. When Coe's lawyers mentioned the possibility of plea-bargaining for hospitalization, he said the idea was absurd because "I'm not a sexual psychopath and I'm not guilty."

It was also learned that he was flatly denying the most innocuous claims about him. He insisted that he'd never owned gloves or oven mittens in his life and that his family would back him up. When he was advised that the prosecutor almost certainly would find witnesses to testify otherwise and that there was no point in being called a liar on such unimportant issues, he responded that those witnesses would be perjuring themselves and he would sue them for millions later. He insisted that he'd never owned a gray jogging suit, and when he was informed that Gini Perham had produced recent photographs of him in a gray sweatsuit, he explained, "Sure, I used to wear gray *sweats*. But that's not a gray jogging suit. They're two different things."

He continued to insist that the Upriver Drive dildo incident was staged by police. When he was told that several observers had identified him and reported his license number, he admitted that he'd been in the area with his parents, but only to look at houses and pay his electric bill at a drop-box. All other claims about his behavior that Sunday morning—flashing the dildo, using foul language, fleeing from the Fairfaxes, lying down behind a building—he branded as part of the frame-up.

His lawyers asked him why police and prosecutor would take the trouble to frame him, and he made a rambling explanation about bad blood between his family and the prosecutor's office over the handling of the Jeni Coe cases. The police, he explained, were angry about the publicity on the South Hill rapes and decided to get even with the newspapers by railroading an editor's son. No explanation was offered for the fact that if Coe's explanation was true, the railroaders had picked the wrong editor on the wrong paper. His father's *Chronicle* had underplayed the South Hill rapes to the end.

Over three months after his arrest Coe produced a piece of documentary evidence to show that the police had reason to be annoyed at him. He turned over what he claimed was a copy of a letter to Richard Olberding, dated February 20, censuring the detective captain for his "loose mouth" on the subject of rape. "I want to say your statement offended me greatly!" the letter read. "A statement—thoughtless as it was, to say the least—undoes much of the work I and others have done to upgrade Spokane's image!" The material had been typewritten on a Spokane Metro Growth letterhead and signed "X. Drew Butler." Olberding swore he never received the letter and in any case wouldn't have recognized "X. Drew Butler" as Coe. He suggested that the carbon copy of the note was a fakery designed for the upcoming trial. Coe's lawyers had to decide whether to risk embarrassing their client by trying to introduce it as evidence. They decided against.

"He refuses to take their advice on anything," a courthouse insider said. "He won't allow himself to be put in a bad light, no matter how unimportant it is. If they say he was caught jaywalking, he says it was a case of mistaken identity. He makes up whatever he needs and acts like he believes it himself. The first thing a criminal defendant learns is, Never lie to your lawyer, but he lies to them every day. Apparently his techniques have worked for years and he's not gonna change them now. He's driving the lawyers nuts. They want to give him the best defense, but they don't want to be involved in rigged testimony. He's making their job impossible."

Someone else was being driven nuts by Coe's approach to the case. Jay Williams told a friend later, "He knew that a terrific conflict was going on in my mind. He kept calling and saying, 'I've got to talk to you.' Each session would last three or four hours. He'd try to convince me to lie for him, and I'd tell him I couldn't. He typed out my testimony. I still have it."

In exasperation Jay asked Coe, "What about Gini? Are you sure she won't help you?" Fred said she was listed as a prosecution witness, but he hadn't completely given up on her. He said he planned to write her a letter that would blow her mind.

"I thought you weren't supposed to contact her?"

"I'll send it to one of her brothers. She'll understand."

Guy Perham received the letter in mid-June and immediately turned it over to his sister. It turned out to be an eight-page example of revisionist history. She nearly gagged at the implausible details of his search for the South Hill Rapist "for my dad's 'Secret Witness' service," and how she had fallen into a "police trap." She decided he must think she was a moron. But one paragraph gave her chills because it was something she'd once believed.

> I'd come to love Gini very much. And I still do. We had a very special rapport. I'd never experienced anything like it before. We had so many common interests. I felt closer to her than any woman I'd ever known!

She put down the letter and cried. It was a long time before she could bring herself under control. Then she read more:

> Deep down I knew I wanted to marry Gini, that I had wanted to for a long time. And I still do.

She cried again. Once it had been the dream of her life to become Mrs. F. H. Coe. She remembered how she used to wonder why this soft-spoken hero had chosen her. Her memories distressed her as much as the letter. She'd believed she was over him. God, she thought, one letter and I'm a wreck!

She resumed reading. There were kernels of truth, but certain passages were unexplainable from any standpoint except lunacy or intentional lying. He wrote of the "three occasions" when she'd heard someone prowling their basement and claimed that it had been the police "looking for items with which to frame me." But there'd been only one such occasion, and it had been a false alarm. He wrote that the police were responsible "for all the calls to my house—most of them received by Gini—where the caller just hung up." There'd been no such calls. He wrote about a morning when "I awoke, went running, then breakfasted at my parents' house as usual." She wondered if he was setting up some kind of alibi; he'd never gone to Five Pines early. Ruth Coe was an insomniac and often was just falling asleep when Gordon arose at dawn to make oatmeal, a dish Kevin detested. She usually got up around noon and wouldn't see anyone, including her son, until she'd had time to dress and put on her makeup and jewelry.

One paragraph of the letter was stunning in its audacity.

> I'd planned for Gini and I to marry sometime in March. I felt by no later than June 1st we'd have the money to move into a new house. I had my eyes on the house next to my parents because it'd be convenient, because Gini and I both liked it and because we felt we could lease it with an option to buy.

Oh, Kevin, she thought, you made all those big plans, but you forgot one little thing—*you forgot to mention them to me!* She wondered how he could expect anyone to take him seriously.

At the end she slammed the letter on a table. The only certainty in her mind was that she would testify against him. Nothing could change that, not even a residue of love and sympathy for a highly disturbed man. She picked up the phone and dialed Joan Schmick. "I have a, a—long letter from Kevin," she said. "Do you want it?"

"Oh, yes!" the detective said quickly.

"I'll bring it down."

On the way to the Public Safety Building she stopped at a florist and ordered a yellow rose to be delivered to Kevin at his parents' home. At first she had no idea why she did it—only that it made her feel better and put a smile on her teary face.

As she drove on, she talked to him in her mind. I loved you very much, she said, and I still love a lot of things about the man I lived with. But what you did makes me sick, Kevin. So I'm sending you this rose as a symbol, a period at the end of a sentence. Good-bye, Kevin. A part of me will always love a part of you. . . .

At headquarters Schmick ran off several copies of the letter. "It outlines his whole defense," she said happily.

Gini reread one of the copies and started to cry again. The policewoman gave her a hug and asked what was the matter. "Nothing," she said. "I'll get over it. It's just—he knows how to push the right buttons, doesn't he?"

"That's part of being a psychopath."

Gene McGougan hurried into the office with a mimeographed profile of a typical rapist, drawn up by psychiatrists at Western State Hospital. "Read this, Gini," he said. "It'll help you."

She began reading. After a few minutes she looked up at the two detectives and said, "Why, this . . . this is Kevin!" She paused and smiled. "You showed me this because you thought I might change my mind about testifying, didn't you?"

They didn't answer, but the looks on their faces showed that she was right. She'd long since realized that no one around the Public Safety Building was taking Kevin's conviction for granted. "Don't worry," she said. "I knew I'd testify the night you came in the house with the search warrant. I won't back out. Too many people were hurt."

"We're just getting the whole picture," McGougan said. "When Coe was living with his parents at Seventh and Maple a few years ago, there were so many rapes in the neighborhood that women were moving away."

"Dear God," Gini said. She wished she could take back the rose.

Jay Williams picked up the ringing phone and heard the excited voice of his friend Fred. "I got a yellow rose from Gini! I'm home free, Jay! It means she won't testify against me."

"Couldn't it mean something else?" Jay asked.

"No! You should have read my letter. I turned her. She won't be trying to railroad me anymore."

Jay didn't necessarily agree, but he said he thought the rose was a nice gesture.

A few days later Gini received the thanks of the prosecutor's office. Coe's letter had spelled out defense strategies that had only been guessed at before. She was told that he'd mailed the letter over the objections of his attorneys. Now they were improvising a new defense, with Gordon and Ruth Coe promoted to major roles. Gini wondered what they could possibly testify.

98

On a Sunday afternoon in the middle of the dry hot summer, the masseuse who called herself Louise was earning extra money by kneading male bodies and performing other personal services at the Bath in downtown Spokane. The place wasn't usually open on Sunday, but the owners permitted employes to come in and work if they needed extra money. Louise was dead solid busted. She'd only recently returned to Spokane from her hometown of Kennewick, Washington, where she'd gone to hide from the man who had raped Misty in 1979.

She told a fellow worker that she was going to the drugstore. When she opened the door to the dazzling sunlight on Stevens Street, she saw the silhouette of a man walking up the front steps. My God, she thought, it's him.

She was too frightened to move. She seldom read a newspaper, and she hadn't even known he was out of jail. As her eyes adjusted to the light she saw that he wore jeans and a T-shirt. His hair was shorter and darker than on the day he'd tied her up and gagged her. He pushed his sunglasses up his forehead and lowered them again. "Oh," he said. "You're working here now?" She stepped backward. He said, "Are you open?"

"Uh—no, we're not! I just came in to—to defrost the refrigerator!" Her thin legs shook. Her bladder started to let go and she caught herself just in time. When the man took a step troward her, she ducked inside and slammed the door. "Juanita!" she shouted. "Call Judy!" In the demimonde of the massage parlors, Judy was bookkeeper and boss; when trouble struck, the girls called her, not the police.

The man returned a short time later. Louise called through the door, "We're busy!" She didn't mention that pictures and descriptions of him were posted in every parlor in town. He tried to visit the Bath five more times that Sunday before Louise finally came right out and told him, "I'm sorry. I can't book you in. We have orders." She phoned for a friend to escort her home and didn't work again for weeks.

One by one the whoopee joints of Spokane had to confront their old customer Fred Coe and turn him away. New instructions went out: If he made an issue of being rejected, the police were to be notified. But the parlor girls soon learned that whenever Coe showed up, the cops weren't far behind. It was as though he had a personal escort.

One night a masseuse named Shawna looked up and saw a man who resembled Coe walking into the reception room of the Bath. Another parlor girl yanked her into a side room and said, "He's the one who's been following me home every night after work!" Shawna politely told the visitor to come back later. "We're all booked up." It was the standard excuse when a girl didn't want to do an applicant.

The man had hardly left when a squad of policemen burst in showing badges and photographs. "Was this guy just here?" they demanded. "What did he want? What did he say?" Shawna swore that no business had been transacted.

A week or so later, the public defender's office received an irate phone call from another massage parlor owner. "Listen, you gotta do something," the caller said. "He's killing us."

"Who?"

"Your client. Coe. He's tried every parlor in town. Whenever he shows up the cops wait till he leaves and then make a sweep. He's driving off business!"

A staffer from the defender's office called Coe and asked him if it was true that he was visiting massage parlors at a time when he was supposed to be on his best behavior and in the custody of his parents. "Hardly!" he answered. He was informed that he'd been spotted. "Well, I did go to a few," he admitted, "but—it was strictly on business."

"Business?"

"Yes. I'm checking them out for a friend of mine in Las Vegas. He's interested in them financially."

Everyone looked forward to the trial.

99

Through the long summer Jay Williams battled his conscience. He'd finally convinced Coe that he wouldn't lie under oath, but Fred still wanted him as a character witness. Sue Williams protested. "Jay," she said, "you're an elder of our church. You can't have *anything* to do with this."

He said he wouldn't, but he still wasn't sure. He felt that he could give supportive character testimony that would neither prove nor disprove Coe's innocence. But what if the prosecutor asked him on the witness stand if he thought Fred was guilty? What could he answer but yes?

He made a few stabs at persuading Fred to take another course. "Nyberg and I were talking about your case and we have an angle," Jay said. "If things start going against you at the trial, why don't you plead insanity and try to get into the sexual-psychopath program? That way you'd be out in a year or two. And you wouldn't have to do hard time."

Fred looked disgusted. "I get it," he said. "You're not convinced that I'm innocent, so you're suggesting I lie about my own sanity. I most certainly would not!" Jay told himself that he should have remembered that Coe's pride would never let him admit to a flaw in his mental processes. Ever since they'd met in grammar school, he'd had to be perfect.

Investigator Bill Beeman showed up to interview Jay. In a peculiar flip-flop, the retired homicide detective who had once inactivated a minor sex case against Coe was now working for the public defender, and he made it plain from the outset that he represented Coe and Coe's interests. Jay was impressed with the craggy-faced ex-cop and spoke frankly. "Fred wants me to lie for him and I can't do it."

"We're not looking for anybody to lie," Beeman said. "But if you know something that might help—"

"I don't know anything that would help and a lot that would hurt," Jay said. Beeman looked unhappy as Jay recounted the incident involving the dildo. "So I *know* he's guilty," Jay said at the end of an hour and a half.

"Look," Beeman said, "I'm just trying to find some way to help him. That's my job." Jay felt that they understood each other.

Two weeks before the trial was to open, he rendezvoused with Coe in a small real estate branch office. Fred yanked a couple of typewritten sheets from a briefcase and said, "Do you remember a meeting I mentioned with a Dr. Wetzler?"

"The shrink who said you weren't a sexual psychopath?"

Coe nodded. "He gave me a book to read. It's all about psychopaths. It gives a list of their characteristics: self-assured, superficial, etc. Since you'll be my main character witness, I've written out some words for you to use to describe me, so the jury won't get the idea that I'm a sex psycho." Jay reached for the typewritten pages, but Coe snatched them back and said, "Jay, I want you to get this down pat." He grabbed at the papers again, and again Coe pulled them away. "No no no no *no!* I want to talk about this first."

"Just let me see the thing!"

"Let's do it my way. I want to read each point to you and see if you don't agree that these are legitimate descriptions of my personality. I'm not asking you to violate your Christian conscience. I'm your friend; I'd *never* ask you to lie."

Jay thought, He's talking down to me again. Why does he do that so often? As a Martian he can't see how obvious he is. "C'mon, Fred," he said. "Give me the list!"

With a sigh, Coe handed it over. Jay read that he was to testify that his friend had "*joie de vivre.*" He asked what the phrase meant and why he was supposed to say it. "It means joy of life," Coe said. "Sort of happy-go-lucky. Sexual psychopaths don't have it. You mispronounced it, by the way. It's *zhwah-da-veev.*"

Jay couldn't imagine himself before God and a jury swearing that Fred Coe was happy-go-lucky. Fred had the least *zhwah-da-veev* of anyone he'd ever met. Besides, the phrase was pretentious, exactly the kind of language that would put off a Spokane jury. "Fred," he said softly, "do you really consider yourself happy-go-lucky?"

"Of course. I'm always up."

"You're energetic, but is that the same?"

"Close enough," Coe said impatiently.

Jay read on. He was to testify that Fred was respected and popular with his peers. "Stress that!" Coe insisted.

The truth was that most people shied away from him. Jay said, "I could testify that you're well liked, Fred, but I'd also have to say that a lot of people consider you eccentric."

"For God's sake, don't say I'm eccentric! That's on *every* list describing psychopaths. Use 'individualistic.'"

Jay continued reading. He was to describe Fred as assertive and socially domineering, always eager to get his points across, a natural leader. But that wasn't even close. Jay looked up and said, "A natural leader?"

"Certainly."

"Fred—"

"Look, you can say I'm assertive, can't you? You wouldn't have to lie. You can agree to that, can't you?"

Jay's eyes had caught the next instruction. He was to testify that Coe was very popular with women and sexually active. He said, "You're serious? You want me to say... *this?*"

"Yeah."

"You want me to suggest to a rape jury that you're oversexed? That's gonna be exactly what they expect!"

"Ah, but real rapists aren't like that. It's all in the book. Sexual psychopaths are unsuccessful with women. It's a frustration with them. They're almost never womanizers."

"Fred, that may be true, but there'll be twelve people on that jury who didn't read the book. They're not experts in psychiatry. They're gonna think, 'This guy's oversexed. No *wonder* he went out and raped!'"

Coe tapped a front tooth with his pen. After a while he said, "You're right. Just say I had a normal sex life."

Jay took the typewritten sheets home and dutifully committed them to memory. As the days went by, he wondered how he could ever go through with his role. He said to himself, I could honestly testify that I never knew Fred to be violent, never knew him to use profanity, never knew him to be sexually perverted. But all these other things... how could I describe him as his exact opposite and still answer to the Lord? He decided there was no way. But there was also no way he could tell Fred. He was whipsawed between his God and his friend. He agonized and temporized as the trial drew close.

Police alerted Gini Perham that Kevin was attacking her credibility behind the scenes. By the time the yellow rose had withered, he'd apparently realized that he'd misinterpreted its meaning and informed his lawyers that she was a perjurer. "He's saying that you don't dare testify against him or they'll bring up the shoplifting thing," Gene McGougan warned her.

"But I told you about that the first night you came to the house!"

"I know you did, Gini. Listen, talk to Don Brockett."

The prosecuting attorney, a wisp of a man with a reputation as an unbending law-and-order advocate, told her, "It happens to a lot of people. They commit perjury in court, not realizing that it's a criminal offense."

Gini knew that she'd committed perjury, but this was the first time anyone had made an issue of it. "I'm shocked, Mr. Brockett," she said.

"At... me?"

"No, no. At *me*. At what I did." She didn't intend to play the innocent female, and she wanted no misunderstandings about where she stood in the matter of the people vs. Frederick Harlan Coe. "I'll still be a witness. If they bring it up and embarrass me in front of the world, that's the way it has to be. I chose to lie for him. It's my fault, not his."

Brockett confirmed what she'd already heard, that the prosecution case was tenuous and her testimony was badly needed. He said, "There may be a way to keep them from destroying your effectiveness as a prosecution witness. This perjury thing cuts both ways. It makes you look bad, but it makes Coe look bad, too. For subornation."

"Subornation?"

"Talking somebody into lying under oath. That's what he did, didn't he?"

"Well... yes. He worked on me for weeks. He said we were finished if I didn't lie for him."

"He's so manipulative. I wonder if the defense wants him painted that way in front of a jury. Let me do some checking."

Not long afterward Brockett talked to her again. "I don't know if the defense is gonna bring it up at the trial," he said, "but I kind of doubt it."

She was exhausted from lack of sleep. "Thank you," she said. "Thank you very much."

"That's all we can do."

"I understand."

The top editorial people at the Spokane *Chronicle* were in a sweat as the mid-July trial date approached. All of them had worked with Gordon H. Coe for years and respected him as a journalist. But he had agreed, at the publisher's direction, to keep hands off the coverage of his son's case and not discuss it with his subordinates, and he was in flagrant violation. He'd maintained a steady barrage of comments and complaints. His colleagues resented the implicit interference.

The elder Coe also kept busy stimulating interest in his son's plight among out-of-town newspaper executives whom he'd met in his years as managing editor. One result was a long article that popped up three hundred miles away in the Seattle *Times* of July 5. The story was headlined "A Case of Being in Wrong Place (Spokane) at Wrong Time?" Fred Coe, who had refused all requests for interviews by the *Chronicle* and the *Spokesman-Review*, was quoted at length. "I was in radio and television for 12 years," he began with his customary hyperbole. "I understand the kind of story it is. But what is lost in all the coverage is my denial. I'm innocent." He repeated earlier claims that he had only been trying to catch the South Hill rapist for his father's Secret Witness Program. "I'm not even sure if I was eligible for the reward. But that wasn't important. Catching the rapist was."

Ruth Coe was quoted as saying, "He'd occasionally jog the streets and I'd follow in the car. We were amateur sleuths, trying to break this thing." She added, "Yes, I think they deliberately wanted a son of a media person. We are the only people at the paper with a son the age and description that comes close. So they got my son, and they got a real plum."

Spokane journalists believed that only an uninformed Seattleite could believe that Coe had been arrested because his father worked for the *Chronicle*. And they didn't feel that the rest of the article was accurate, fair to the Spokane press, or within Bench-Bar-Press guidelines. There had been talk about moving the trial to Seattle; the strong pro-Coe slant seemed certain to prejudice potential jurors.

On July 16, a *Chronicle* sub-editor wrote a lengthy memo to a superior. Part of it read:

> Gordon initiated a conversation with me Tuesday afternoon about his son's trial. . . . He came over to the city desk and started talking about how he didn't think the prosecution had much of a case and that the case had a lot of holes in it. . . . It troubles me that I need to write this note, for I can empathize with the situation Gordon finds himself in. But this story is difficult enough to handle without unsolicited assistance from a superior who in a manner is personally involved.

Later that day publisher Bill Cowles heard from John Lemon, the *Chronicle*'s assistant managing editor. Lemon memo'd that Gordon Coe, with whom he'd worked for over three decades, had discussed "the framing of Freddie Coe" with one of the *Chronicle* reporters and had brought the subject up with the associate editor, an assistant city editor, and himself. "Coe endeavored to convince us of his son's innocence, weaknesses in the prosecutor's case and alleged unfair and illegal tactics by police. . . . He seemed convinced that his son is the victim of a sort of vendetta against the *Chronicle* and him."

Gordon Coe had just gone on leave to prepare for the trial. Plans were made to convert his leave to retirement.

100

The trial itself was a cheap circus! Cameras and crowds everywhere! It was treated as a hyped media event ... spectacular entertainment. It was sickening! An innocent man's life was on the line! A lynch mob—fueled by irresponsible media coverage—lusted for blood! A newspaperman's son yet!—Fred Coe, February 5, 1982

The midsummer trial of Fred Coe was the hottest indoor ticket in Spokane history. The magnitude of the event was matched by the splendor of the setting: the rococo Spokane County Court House. The brick building, eighty-six years old, was described in booster literature as "an excellent example of European and Cathedral/Castle architecture," but around Spokane it was known as "Disneyland" for its spires and turrets and general look of a medieval fortress spun in brown sugar.

If the courthouse seemed equal to the process of trying Spokane's most notorious criminal case, the remodeled courtroom seemed overmatched. Superior Court Judge George T. Shields, a lanky Columbia graduate, presided at one end of the building's top floor in a room with three short rows of benches for spectators and a jammed capacity of some five dozen souls, including judge, jury, court officers and press. Lines of spectators bent into lazy S's in the narrow hall. Security was heavy. Half of the fourth floor was sealed off. Spectators with proper yellow tags were forced to negotiate a system of baffles and screens erected to inhibit anyone with plans to storm the courtroom. Windows were covered with cardboard and tape. Five deputy sheriffs roamed about with metal detectors.

Media interest was so intense that a TV monitor and a loudspeaker had to be wired directly from the court to an adjacent press room to accommodate the overflow of journalists. Local television stations broke into regular programming with updates direct from the scene. Soap operas were interrupted for this real-life drama, and for once there were hardly any complaints.

Even before testimony began, skirmishes went on across the conference table in Judge Shields's chambers. Prosecutor Brockett, intent on winning this biggest case of his career, had refused to turn over the complete police files to the defense as required in a discovery law enacted in 1973. Instead he provided summaries of police reports plus the victims' signed statements, claiming that this satisfied the intent of the law. Asked why he was changing his own policy of eight years standing, he said that he'd been "meaning to test the policy for some time." Some felt it was an unusual time for a test.

As the public part of the trial began, a delegation from NOW set up a vigil—"to make certain that the victims in this trial do not become the defendants," as the organization's newsletter pointed out. A courtroom seat was reserved for the Rape Crisis Center, four for relatives of victims, and two for the Coe family. Newsmen and photographers walked softly—Judge Shields allowed them free rein but demanded discretion. The judge asked one hyperactive cameraman to leave, but later allowed him to return.

Fred Coe presented a self-assured exterior through the tedious early days. He sat between his lawyers, Roger Gigler and Julie Twyford, and wore a different three-piece suit each day. He took notes with his gold pen and held it tightly the rest of the time. He produced an occasional bemused smile, nodded in agreement with abstruse points of law, maintained his composure when rulings went against him and in general behaved as though he were just another officer of the court. Spectators arriving for the first time had to do a little studying to figure out who was the defendant.

There were few surprises in the state's opening statement, delivered by assistant prosecutor Patricia Thompson. She told the jury, flown in from Seattle, that six women would describe how the defendant had raped them and medical evidence would back them up. Five of the women would testify that they were threatened with a knife. "Virginia Perham, who was the girlfriend of the defendant Frederick Coe, will relate regarding the relationship that she had with Mr. Coe, his sexual habits, his jogging activities, the clothing that he had, as well as a pair of oven mitts that were taken from the house, that she knew had been worn by him." The assistant prosecutor started to tell the jurors about the dildo incident on Upriver Drive, but she was silenced by the judge on the grounds that he hadn't yet decided whether such testimony would be admissible.

Julie Twyford, assistant public defender, reminded the twelve imported jurors, "As Mr. Coe sits here before you, he is presumed innocent....The defense and Mr. Coe do not have to prove a thing." Reporters' pencils flew as an outline of the defense emerged from Twyford's opening statement. "The evidence will show that Fred, due to some heavy financial problems...spent a great deal of time over at his parents' house, especially ate breakfast and dinner with them...during the hours, also, that some of the rapes occurred." Twyford, a Connecticut Yankee who had come west to take her law degree at Gonzaga University, told the jurors, "Fred, in effect, launched his own investigation, and in fact was looking for clues to lead to the arrest of the person that the police sought....He definitely was in many areas as the police have said they viewed him, but...he was there for a specific purpose." Everyone waited to see how Coe would prove it.

101

The Higgins rape charge was so absurd. It didn't fit even the pattern of any of the other rapes. Mr. Brockett threw in as much garbage as he could, is what it really adds to.—Fred Coe, December 27, 1981

When Lois Higgins had heard that she would be the first witness, her instant reaction was that she just couldn't—she would fall apart from fright and nerves. Her next reaction was that nothing could stop her. She'd never been able to discuss her rape calmly, and she was still in a rage at the sicko who had rammed his hand down her throat and kept on ramming his hand down the throats of innocent women for almost three years. She couldn't imagine how anything so obscene had been allowed to happen in a civilized American city.

Lois's life hadn't been going well, but there were hopeful signs. Her biker husband had disappeared in the weeds with his teenyboppers and left her and two-year-old Becky to fend for themselves. Then along came an all-American boy named Tom who seemed okay at first—till the night he touched her on the upper arms, where the rapist had grabbed her and sensitized her forever. She dived under the sewing machine, and he dragged her out and punched her so hard on her thigh that she thought the bone had snapped. He ripped off the most beautiful nightie she'd ever owned, $12.95 from K-Mart, bit her breasts and nipples, her stomach, her genitals, then forced himself inside. When he was finished he said, "That was the hottest fuck I ever had."

A friend, a grocer named Bill Drecksage, took her in, and after a few months they fell in love and married. The patient Mormon began bringing home every article and book he could find about rape and its after-effects. Whenever he heard of a Phil Donahue show or another TV program on rape, he encouraged her to watch and sat with his arm tightly around her. He talked her into going to the Rape Crisis Center for treatment, paid for the ten-dollar sessions, and stood by when she was at her worst.

The therapist took her through the rape again and again. Lois would say, "No, no! I can't talk about it," and the woman would insist that she *had* to. The therapist kept trying to convince her that she had rights as a woman: rights to her own body, the right to say no to sex, and the right to take her own sexual needs as seriously as the male's. Growing up in poverty, she'd learned that sex was taken like castor oil, at the behest of others. At last she was hearing otherwise. And at home she was learning that not all men were cruel, not all men were rapists. Some were like Bill. She was beginning to heal.

And now she had to risk all her progress and testify. She'd had three years of being ashamed and confused and only ten months of treatment at Rape Crisis. Her therapist told her she was in a critical stage, and Lois explained to the man from the prosecutor's office that she would make a poor witness. "I know I'll cry and block things out and not remember."

"That's all right," he said. "We need you."

As the trial approached, she worked in her garden for strength. When she arrived at the courthouse on the hot Monday morning of July 20, she was flanked by her therapist and her husband, and still her thin legs trembled and she could barely stand. Newly pregnant, she'd had a bout of morning sickness a few hours before. Inside the crowded courtroom, she noticed the TV cameras. The judge asked if she objected to being photographed and she answered, "Yes, I do."

As she was settling into the witness chair she saw him. She knew his name now: Frederick Harlan Coe. He was staring at her, and so were his lawyers, a man and a woman. At first she could barely get her words out, and the prosecutor moved the microphone closer to her mouth. She recounted the details of the night in 1978, how she'd had an argument with Al at a restaurant and decided to walk home and how she'd been jumped by a man who smelled of peppermint and bath soap and dragged her between houses. Once she cried and had to stop, and most of the time she was so confused that she was sure she wasn't making sense.

She thought she would wither and die when the prosecutor insisted that she repeat the exact words the rapist had used. She'd never uttered words like that in her life. She testified, "Then he put me on the ground, and then he told me that..." She stopped and gritted her teeth. Maybe if she just led up to it slowly. "...Then he asked me if I liked that; if I had any children, if I lived around the neighborhood; if I liked..."

She stopped again. She could think the word but she couldn't say it. She looked at the judge. Please, she said under her breath, help me! At times he had seemed stern and cold behind his glasses, but now he looked like a kindly gray-haired grandfather. "Go ahead!" Mr. Brockett insisted. *"How did he say it?"*

"I *can't* say it," she responded. Silence fell over the courtroom. She felt like a willful child defying her elders. She shut her eyes and murmured, "If I liked—fucking." She looked down in embarrassment.

When she'd finished telling her story the prosecutor asked, "Can you identify the person who raped you on April 26, 1978?"

She was confused, and a wave of nausea was coming on. Did he mean when the police brought the pictures to her house? "Where?" she asked, trying to get her bearings.

"In the courtroom," Mr. Brockett answered.

"In the courtroom?" The walls were moving. She hoped she wouldn't throw up. She'd caused so many delays.

"Yes," Mr. Brockett said with a wave of his arm.

"You want me to look around?" she asked. God, she thought, what's the point of that? The guy's sitting right there!

The prosecutor said, "Yes, please."

She followed instructions, her eyes sweeping the courtroom. At last she said, "I think so. . . . Sitting right in front of me."

Mr. Brockett asked Coe to stand up, and she looked away and tried to compose herself. Her hate for him went beyond words. "Is this the individual that you have pointed out?" the prosecutor asked.

"Yes, that is him." She began to cry aloud, and she was relieved when Mr. Brockett said, "That is all the questions I have."

The pretty woman sitting next to Coe stood up. She'd interviewed Lois a week or two before. At the session she'd been polite and soft-spoken. "Miss Higgins," she asked, "do you think you can go on at this point, or do you want to take a break?" Lois asked if she could have five minutes to herself, and the judge said that would be fine.

The defense lawyer ended up keeping her on the stand much longer than Mr. Brockett. Sometimes speaking softly in a little-girl voice like Lois's own, sometimes speaking hoarsely, Julie Twyford bore down on details: earliest descriptions of the rapist, memories of the scene, what kind of car the rapist had stepped from behind, what color his eyes were, what kind of shoes and belt he wore. She dwelled on the subject of the photo lineup for what seemed like hours. The numbers on the backs of the pictures swirled in front of Lois's eyes. Several times she had to admit misstatements and lapses of memory— just as she'd predicted to the prosecutor earlier. Several times she couldn't help showing annoyance at the questioner and herself. How could they expect her to concentrate underwater? She wanted to stand up and scream, I'm doing the best I can! This happened a long time ago!

Toward the end she felt faint again. Miss Twyford asked, "Mrs. Higgins, you said that your ex-husband looked like the picture?"

"No. His eyes only."

"And did he have angry eyes—your ex-husband?"

She thought about the fights with Al. "At times, yes," she said. "Very angry eyes." It wasn't fair to ask about her days with Al. She'd been trying to put him out of her mind for two years now. The question upset her and she showed it. She realized she wasn't making a good impression on the jury.

"Are you okay, Lois?" Miss Twyford asked gently.

"Yes."

"When you looked, or when you see that face, or when you looked at the photograph did you see that face with the mustache and long hair?"

"Yes."

"And sideburns, too?"

"Yes. I saw it all, just like it was, just like it has been. The whole nightmare." The questioning was over. She'd been under pressure for two hours. A bailiff led her from the courtroom. She hoped she hadn't blown the case.

A few hours after the first trial day had ended, viewers watching KXLY-TV, Spokane's ABC outlet, saw the most publicized figure in town coolly discussing his case with black-haired Anamaria Bell, a Spanish-born newcomer to the local news scene. An announcer explained that the four-hour interview had been taped a few days before and portions would be aired each evening during the trial.

Viewers were treated to the sight of the natty defendant sitting under a fern in front of a simulated brick wall. His brownish-blond hair was cut in the sculptured look, every strand in place. He wore a light-blue suit, no vest, a light tie and light shirt, and clutched a gold pen. He talked like a detached analyst, at times sounding as though he hadn't the least connection with the case of the South Hill rapist. He discussed theories about the rapist, how and why the local police failed to protect the women of Spokane, why the authorities went out of their way to frame the innocent son of a newspaperman. He remarked on clues that had been overlooked, sloppy police procedures, criminology, jurisprudence, and made specific suggestions for catching the real rapist. He often stretched and widened his lips, showing strong white teeth. He seldom smiled but sounded relaxed and friendly ("I'm glad you brought that up, Anamaria"). He leaned back in his swivel chair, made relaxed quarter turns, and frequently licked his lips. Occasionally he lingered over his vowels in the manner of William F. Buckley: "I raaaawther think so.... Yes, I waaaaas."

He was also surprisingly incoherent for someone who'd had weeks to plan his responses and whose patient sister had rehearsed him till the tapes started rolling. Sometimes he sounded like a presidential candidate caught without a prepared script. To the question of why he'd granted the interview, he answered, "Well, I would say primarily because the flood of information disseminated especially right after my arrest which in my opinion at least was highly inflammatory and violated every principle of bench-bar-press guidelines, and, uh, I think really only one side of this has been heard." He told the interviewer that he felt "a sadness first of all for the people of Spokane county because they've been deceived, tricked as it were into believing that a series of crimes has been solved when in fact they have not. The South Hill rapist is still out there somewhere. Or he's left town. So sadness for the people of Spokane County and then sadness of course for myself, my family. After that, the natural thing, which is sadness for the rape victims themselves."

He took pains to explain how it happened that he and his mother had found themselves chasing the South Hill rapist: "Let me just say that when I returned to Spokane five years ago I came up here with two major goals in mind: One was strictly a personal goal to be able to be in a position hopefully to invest in real estate here in Spokane in what I considered to be basically an underpriced market. And the second reason was a little less personal and that was simply to be involved positively in what I felt was Spokane's growth... an area that is destined to grow. I just wanted to be a part of that... helping to promote Spokane in my own ways.... I was just concerned about the fact that the papers were suddenly being dominated by a headline referring to the South Hill rapist and suddenly the communities that I'd lived in before—Los Angeles, Las Vegas, San Francisco, which are overrun with crime—suddenly Spokane was taking on that sort of an image perhaps instead of the quiet conservative family town that it is and which is positive to promote...."

Anamaria Bell asked, "Did you and your mother actually *trail* the buses?"

"...My mother and I are business partners primarily. She does a lot of work for me. We spend quite a bit of time together, so when I got interested in looking at clues to the South Hill rapist I mentioned that to her and she's kind of a mystery buff and she was interested and she merely accompanied me on a number of occasions when I was both jogging and following the buses."

Coe ridiculed the identification procedures and the police lineups and gave a prescient description of what his prosecutor was up against in the courtroom: "Remember, their attack took place in the dark, a frenzied situation where the rapist had all the advantage. He was trying to keep them from seeing what his face looked like. For all we know he may have been wearing a mask, he may have been wearing a disguise, he may have been wearing makeup, he may have disguised his voice." He sounded like someone who had made a thorough study of the subject.

The *Spokesman-Review* headlined KXLY's coup "Fred Coe's One-man Media Blitz." Asked for comment, Judge Shields said, "My only concern was that he get a fair trial. I guess now that the jury is sequestered it doesn't matter what the defendant says."

"It's against my advice," commented chief defense counsel Roger Gigler, a mellow Minnesota native with a superlative record in major cases. "It gives the prosecution a hand. If he says something to the TV or the newspapers contradictory to what he says in the stand, then it all could come out in the trial."

Responded Coe, "Having spent eleven years in the media, I know what is appropriate to say and what isn't. My attorney is running my trial. He's not running my life."

No one could remember such an audacious public relations maneuver in the course of a trial. If any of the lawyers had taken to the airwaves like Coe, contempt citations would have been in order. A Spokane criminal lawyer observed that the interviews were "marvelous preparation for cross-examination," adding, "Don Brockett couldn't have asked for a better cram course in handling the witness." The prosecutor said he and his staff were enjoying the show nightly.

102

All six of the rape victims... their testimony was lousy. Each of the six, they were emotional, they were unimpressive witnesses, they were not the highest caliber of women in some cases, and the whole thing was just very unimpressive. When he got done with his six rape victims, Brockett didn't have any convictions. He was a loser.—Fred Coe, December 27, 1981

One by one the rest of the victims told their stories to the jury. Young Sue Ellen Wilber examined a composite sketch of the rapist and explained, "I tried to make him as ugly as I could." The picture resembled Coe only superficially, and the defense happily introduced it into evidence. The child said that she was convinced that she had the right man when she looked at Coe and heard him speak at the lineup. A hush fell over the courtroom as the defendant, at the request of the prosecutor, read the rapist's words in unmodulated tones: "Don't look at my face. Do as I say or I'll kill you. Take off your clothes. Don't say anything and I won't hurt you. Don't call the police. How much money do you have?"

Brockett asked, "Is that the individual that raped you on August 30, Sue Ellen?"

"Yes, sir," the girl answered.

Marie Oldham, the housewife who had been raped by a man who jumped from behind a parked camper, was on the witness stand for almost the entire afternoon of Tuesday, July 21. She told about the rapist's peculiar technique: "He had his fingers so far down my throat I thought I was going to suffocate." She described the man's looks in minute detail, with special emphasis on his hair: "He had loose curly hair, and it was cut so that it came down just over the top of the bottom of his ear lobes, and it was a little bit longer, about to the top of his collar in the back. And he had loose bangs, and his hair was very well cut." The assistant prosecutor asked her how she could be so sure of the details, and she answered, "I used to be a hairdresser."

At times Roger Gigler's cross-examination almost turned into open argument. "When something like this is happening, do you really want to look at the guy's face?" he asked.

"You bet!" the brown-haired woman snapped. "I want to *memorize* his face."

Gigler asked, "Did you also say that he had a little Latin in him, that his eyes looked Latin?"

"Yes," said the witness. "I said he had a little Spanish in him. Spanish is not really—well, it's Latin, but I don't mean Mexican, I mean *European* Spanish."

"Also, did you describe the suspect as looking kind of like a cross between the dark fellow on "CHiPs" and the dark fellow on "Starsky and Hutch"?"

"Yeah, I think I did, but I don't remember. But he does! And he does have dark-brown hair. Just because he has it cut doesn't change anything."

"I am not arguing with you, but there are a lot of people that wouldn't call that dark-brown hair. And I would rather that you didn't argue with me."

Later Gigler questioned her closely about the lighting in the neighborhood. "The lighting couldn't have been too good if you described him as looking Spanish?"

The witness peered across the defense table at Fred Coe. "I still think he looks Spanish," she insisted.

At the conclusion of Oldham's testimony, courtroom handicappers marked the trial even—the Lois Higgins testimony a plus for the defense, Sue Ellen Wilber a draw, and Marie Oldham a probable win for the prosecution. The first witness Wednesday morning improved the odds for Coe. She was fourteen-year-old Stephanie Gibbs, raped by a man who rammed a leather glove down her throat while she waited on a dark South Hill street corner for a friend. She testified that her attacker threatened her with a knife, rubbed her breasts, asked her if she'd ever seen a man naked and if she ever masturbated. Then, "He had oral sex with me." She was asked to define oral sex. She said that the man shoved two fingers into her vagina and then inserted his penis. That, she said, was oral sex.

At the end of the direct examination Brockett asked her if the man was in the courtroom. All eyes turned to Coe. He sat motionless in a gray-blue three-piece suit, one arm draped over a chair as though he didn't have a care in the world. The child pointed to him and said in a shaky voice, "That man right there."

She still appeared to be holding the jury's attention and sympathy. If anything, her confusion about oral sex had strengthened her credibility. Then defense attorney Twyford picked up a police report and asked, "Stephanie, you told the two officers that first arrived, that talked to you the day this happened—do you recall talking to them?"

"Yes."

"And you told them quite a few times that you never saw the man's face. Is that right?"

"Yes."

"And you told Mr. Beeman that also?"

"Yes."

The testimony sent a stir through the courtroom. Surely the prosecution hadn't brought a rape charge on a teenager's voice-identification? Brockett tried to clarify the matter on redirect. He showed the flustered child a picture of the March 10 lineup and asked how she'd made her selection. "It was the way the voice was." she answered. "And he said the comments exactly like he did the night of the rape."

"Were you looking at his size, and other things, in the lineup also?"

"Yes."

"Would you describe what you were looking for?"

"Mostly the voice." A deep gap had opened in the prosecution's case.

Irene Pool looked angry when she took the stand later Wednesday morning, but she was just as angry at herself as she was at her rapist. She still relived the rape. At work she found it hard to concentrate; at night she awoke from bad dreams and couldn't get back to sleep. For six months she'd been admonishing herself that she should have fled when she spotted the man circling the track in the wrong direction. She was still too ashamed to discuss the details with her grown children.

She told the jury how the rapist had tried to stuff his glove in her mouth while she yelled "Damn you, damn you!" She told how she screamed and how he threw her to the ground, raped and "mauled" her—causing cuts on the inside of her mouth, a bruised neck and a big contusion on her arm. "I felt like someone had killed me, for a week," she told the jury. Her voice fell away as she quoted one of her attacker's remarks: "You have a nice cunt."

Gigler asked in his soft, rumbly voice, "Did you also describe him as having acne or pock marks?"

"I said he had a few marks...a few blemishes on his face."

Gigler asked the court's permission for Coe to approach the witness. He walked toward the witness chair till his face was only a foot away. For a few seconds, he stared into her eyes. Then he strolled back to the defense table, his face blank. "Do you see any pock marks or acne?" Gigler asked.

"No. He could have had perhaps—"

"You don't have to explain. *Do you see any pock marks or acne?*"

"He has one blemish. But, no, I don't see any." The defense had scored again.

The last South Hill rape victim, Jeanie Mays, testified in a weak voice. She was frightened and upset; her boyfriend, the father of her son, had been acting lately as though she was more to blame than the rapist, and she knew he would be studying every word about her testimony in the newspapers. She told how the man had thrown her to the ground and shoved an oven mitt down her throat. She remembered saying, "Don't hurt me. I have a little boy," and the rapist's response: "I won't hurt you if you do what I say. I have a knife, and I will use it."

After she testified that he had told her she had a "nice cunt," she was asked to describe his voice. "Not too rough, or low, and not too high," she answered. "Just kind of mild-mannered, or whatever. He didn't use very much slang or anything. And, he didn't talk very mean to me. You know. It was more gentle than I would expect from someone like that."

She told how he masturbated into her underwear and robbed her of $20. She looked at Exhibit 16, the oven mitts taken from Coe's kitchen the night of his arrest, and said they had the same design and flowers as the mitt the rapist had used. When Coe once again read the approximate words used by the rapist, she told the jury, "He is talking a little bit lower, but it's the same voice."

*   *   *

Spectators agreed that the totality of the victims' testimony was damaging to Coe, but certainly not conclusive. The defense had succeeded in suggesting that most of the victims had provided contradictory descriptions of the rapist from time to time and that hypnosis had tainted much of their testimony—a strong appeal point. Veteran observers were reminded once again that street rapes were always the hardest to prove.

103

Up to the day she was scheduled to testify, Gini Perham wasn't sure what she wanted for Kevin Coe, and her head hurt from thinking about it. Certainly she hoped he would be sent where he could harm no more women. But she also had deep yearnings for the man she'd once thought him to be. For months she'd desperately wished there were some way she could believe in his innocence.

She no longer worked for Roger Crane & Associates; Kevin's snooping had made her position untenable. She was now quietly selling mobile homes, earning $1,000 a month, far more than she'd been making in the depressed real estate market. She told her new employers about her role in the affair of the South Hill rapist, and they said they didn't care about her personal life as long as her sales held up. She began to entertain a small hope for the future. After changing addresses five or six times to avoid detection, she was living with her cousin Jane in the Spokane Valley. Driving home from work every night, she circled the block a few times to make sure she wasn't being followed. It wasn't the most relaxed way to live, but it beat running into the Coes.

On the evening of Wednesday, July 22, Donald Brockett phoned and told her that the testimony of the rape victims had gone faster than anticipated and she would be needed in the morning. She felt as though she'd touched a hot wire. She'd always known she would have to tell a courtroom full of strangers the details of her intimate life with Kevin, but she'd expected something more than overnight warning. She caught her breath and said, "What time?"

"Nine," he said. "I'll be putting on some witnesses about an incident on Upriver Drive. Then it's your turn."

She thought of a conversation she'd had with the soft-voiced prosecutor a few weeks before. He'd asked her to speculate on what the Coes might dredge up from her earlier life. She'd told him there was nothing to dredge up, but that she was sure they would repeat the same false charges they'd made about Jeni—that she was dirty, neurotic and whorish. They would claim that Kevin had lifted her from the gutter and cleaned her up. And they would probably try to bring in her mother's suicide.

Brockett said, "We hear from the defense that you're dating a black guy. I couldn't care less, Gini, but—are you?"

"I don't even know any black guys."

"Be on your guard. They might want to prejudice the black woman on the jury."

"They must be desperate."

Brockett said, "This is a big case, Gini. Don't be surprised at anything."

On the way to the courthouse in her cousin's Volkswagen Beetle, she took deep breaths to try to calm herself. In her hand she clutched an Agatha Christie thriller: good diversion. The cousins reported to the Public Safety Building, where Lt. McGougan walked them across the courtyard and up an inside stairwell to the fourth floor of the courthouse. All Gini could see were swarms of people waiting to hear her testimony. Thank God, she thought. They don't know who I am—yet.

A deputy rushed up. "Wait!" he said. "The Coes are in the doorway." Gini felt a jolt of fear. She wondered how the Coes managed to intimidate so many people. It couldn't be because of Gordon. As an editor he had power, but she'd never heard that he used it unfairly. No, it was Ruth—something in those dark blue eyes and the bird-like tilt of her head, something not quite right. She asked the deputy why the Coes weren't inside the courtroom, and he explained that listed witnesses were excluded until their testimony was completed. All through the trial so far, Ruth and Gordon Coe had waited outside, often with their daughter Kathleen.

After the family was steered away from the door, Gini and her cousin were ushered into a side room to wait. It was a few minutes before 9 a.m. The courthouse was beginning to feel like a sauna; someone mentioned that the air-conditioning wasn't working. A deputy came in and said to Gini, "The Coes watched you through the glass door as you passed."

She shuddered again. The Coes were everywhere, always watching, even in her dreams. She was grateful when her two brothers and their wives arrived, and when Joan Schmick and Sergeant Gary Johnson popped in to buck her up. The central problem was that she was just plain scared. She briefed herself: You don't have to put on an act; all you have to do is tell the truth and *don't get mad.*

Five hours went by before Schmick stuck her head in the room and said in her tiny voice, "Gini?" She stood up, her legs uncertain, and walked into the courtroom behind a chubby little bailiff with a sweet smile.

Just before they reached the witness stand the woman turned and whispered, "Now you're gonna be sworn in." Gini held up her hand and faced her. The bailiff said, "No, no. The judge."

Gini looked up at Judge Shields. Oh, God, she thought, does he have to look so grim? He mumbled some words and she mumbled them back and took the stand, carefully avoiding a glance around the courtroom. She knew what she would see: every seat occupied by goggle-eyed gossips and right down in front the man she had loved, taking notes with his gold pen and trying to look like the master of the situation. Don Brockett sat directly in front of her, and she used him as a focal point. She meshed her fingers and squeezed as Brockett said, "Would you state your name for the court and jury, please?"

She was surprised to hear her own voice say that she was Virginia Kay

Perham, and equally surprised when she found herself coolly answering questions about her romance with a man who'd called himself "Coco"—from their first meeting in a laundromat to a live-in arrangement on the South Hill. She told about his injuries, his night and morning jogs, his obsession with his voice. "He was very proud of the fact that he had developed what he called a 'radio voice.' He would speak normally, and the next minute he would lower it, and it would be very deep. And he felt that his diet would also help to better the quality of his radio voice."

She talked about "flooding" and how it changed his appearance and sometimes caused him to break out. She described his various hairstyles: to the collar, curling a bit at the ends; freshly barbered into short neat bangs; unkempt and scruffy after three or four days of flooding. Once, she said, he explained that "he did not want to be recognized."

She quoted him about his trouble dating girls in high school and his opinion that Spokane women were "prudish." She identified the oven mitts and the red ski jacket and told how she'd been surprised to find them washed. She identified some of his clothing and explained that his heavy black leather gloves "progressively became beaten up. I would notice a rip or two. And the last time I saw them they were very scarred, torn, ripped. The fingers were hanging off the end."

She described his yellowish license plates and explained that he "liked the idea of having his car appear as if it were from out of state."

Brockett asked a leading question: Had Coe ever said anything about women's underwear? Chief defense counsel Roger Gigler jumped up and observed, "Mr. Coe's opinion on women's underwear I don't see is relative to—"

Judge Shields interrupted, "If you are making an objection—?"

"Yes."

"—It is overruled."

Gini answered, "There were a number of times when, while he was working, he wanted to do housework and he volunteered to do my laundry. And on one occasion when he did my laundry he was rather disgusted with the condition of my underwear, and said that there were rips and tears and things like that in them. And he said his mother's underwear was in pretty much the same condition."

"Did you ask him about that?"

"He seemed embarrassed, and he turned away from me, and he said, well, he had done his laundry at their home a number of times, and when he was doing the laundry there, he had discovered that."

She told about his dildo, and how he walked naked into the bathroom holding it in front of him. She said that he'd kept it in the bedroom on the floor until she asked him to take it away. "Then it surfaced a month or two later in the bedroom again... and there was one time when it was by the chair in the living room for about two days on the floor."

When Brockett opened the subject of their sex life, Gigler objected again, and Gini was grateful for the interruption. She'd felt controlled so far, but her throat was drying up and she was having trouble breathing. The prosecutor had told her before the trial that he was going to ask about everything they did in the bedroom. *Everything.* It tied in with the rapes. She began to sweat.

It was stifling in the courtroom; the lawyers and the jury seemed to be suffering equally. She looked out over the crowd for the first time and saw a few people in shirtsleeves fanning themselves with papers. She wondered if someone had sold programs. Then she thought: What will they think of me in this town? My relatives, my friends—my dad? She wished she could be back in Spain for the next hour. "The sex life at home," Gigler rumbled, "I don't think has anything to do with this case."

The spectators remained silent. She entwined her fingers to keep her hands from shaking. For an instant she hoped Gigler's objection would be sustained so she could leave with her dignity. After a long pause the judge said, "Subject to the tie-up and relevancy, Mr. Brockett, you may proceed."

The prosecutor rushed ahead. "Would you describe to the members of the jury what Mr. Coe would do preparatory to having intercourse with you?"

The answer refused to form. She wrung her hands, bit her lips, stared at the floor, and when she finally started speaking, it was in a halting voice that was just above a whisper: "More times than not he would, uh, perform oral sex on me, and then—on his knees, in front of me, while I was on my back, while fondling himself, and especially a number of months before he was arrested—for what he claimed to be lubrication purposes, he would, uh—lick his fingers"—she sucked in air and went on—"and place his hand that he had licked in between my legs, and then intercourse would take place, and when it did, almost always he was up and away from me—with his hands on the bed like that."

There! That took care of the first question.

Brockett asked, "Did he refer to any of the parts of your body in a way other than medical terminology?"

"Well, he said 'ass' once in a while."

"Would he use any particular terminology in referring to your vaginal area?"

"Yes." Oh, how she wished he wouldn't pursue this!

"And what words did he use?"

She tried several times to say the word and finally asked if she could spell it. "Yes," Brockett said, and she spelled, "c-u-n-t." The courtroom was so still she could hear her own breathing. She glanced sideways. Every juror seemed to be glowering, arms crossed, sternly sitting in judgment on her and the faulty air-conditioning. Her eyes caught one compassionate black face. Thank you, ma'am, she said to herself, for understanding.

The prosecutor switched to identifications of Coe's clothing and photographs she'd made of him in his gray sweatsuit, and then announced that he was finished. The judge said, "Mr. Gigler, you indicated to me that you thought her cross-examination would be quite extensive, is that not correct?"

"That's correct, your honor," the beefy defense attorney answered.

Judge Shields apologized to the jury for the poor ventilation and announced a break till the next morning. Joan Schmick and assistant prosecutor Patricia Thompson guided Gini past Kevin and into the waiting room with her cousin. Lieutenant McGougan escorted them down the same interior stairs and uniformed policemen walked them to the Volkswagen.

On the way back to her cousin's home, they were driving across the four-lane Monroe Street Bridge when Gini yelped, "Jane! *Look!*" The Citation was in the adjacent lane; Kevin was driving and his mother sat alongside. Gordon wasn't in sight. Gini ducked and said, "Did they see me?"

"No."

"What are they doing?"

"Ruth's hands are flying. It looks like she's yelling. He's trying to calm her." Gini thought, I guess they'll never change. She stayed out of sight till the gray car sped ahead.

In court the next morning, she learned from friends that Coe had spilled his cup of water when she'd walked into the courtroom the day before. She was told that he'd been the picture of unconcern through most of the earlier testimony, but her presence had seemed to agitate him. It was small consolation. This wasn't a game of embarrassments and discomfitures. If it were, she'd have lost a long time ago.

Gigler's cross-examination opened pleasantly enough. "Good morning!" he said after she'd arranged herself in the witness box. He seemed friendly, a personality double for her former hero Gerald Ford. He had large jowls, dark hair cut in a conservative style, and warm brown eyes. He spoke in a naturally resonant voice that was far more pleasing to her ear than Kevin's. She understood that he was second in command in the public defender's office, and that from the beginning he had been outspoken in his claims that his client had been framed.

"Good morning," she responded in her light voice. She wondered how he would start—with the shoplifting? One more public embarrassment. If it came up, she would march straight home and pack.

But the opening questions harked back to the beginning of the romance—Coco's attire, his diet, his hair-do and lack of mustache, his remarks about girlfriends and his ex-wife. The air conditioner seemed in good working order, but the place began to warm up when Gigler asked, "Did he ever tell you about his high-school experiences as far as dating goes?"

Brockett called out, "Object to that, Your Honor. It calls for hearsay."

The judge said, "She is testifying to things he told her. Overruled."

Gigler asked, "Did he ever tell you about his high-school dating?"

Gini said yes and asked, "Would you like to know what he said?"

"I will ask the questions!" Gigler snapped. "*Did he not tell you he had many dates in high school?*"

Gini was caught off guard by the sudden intensity. She hadn't meant to be evasive. "No," she said. "He did *not* tell me that he had many dates in high school."

The questioning turned to their earliest meetings. "Back when you were first together...wasn't it *you* that had a difficult time dating?"

"No. I don't remember talking about my difficulty dating anybody."

"Wasn't it *you* that thought that Spokane was ultra-conservative?"

"I think Spokane is conservative. But I don't think that's necessarily bad."

"Just answer my question."

After some high-pressure interrogation about the oven mitts, she took her first peek at Kevin. Friends had asked her why she'd avoided his eyes the day before, and she didn't want to seem intimidated. There he sat in his three-piece suit, scribbling rapidly on yellow legal paper. He looked more like a lawyer than his own lawyers. She didn't see how a jury could convict him of anything. She looked away as Gigler asked, "Were you in the army?"

"Yes."

"Honorable discharge?"

"Um-hmm."

Brockett called out, "Your Honor, I fail to see the materiality of this question."

Gigler ran a finger down his slightly bulbous nose and started to say, "Well—"

"Go ahead," the judge told him.

Gigler turned back to Gini. He patted his forehead with a handkerchief and looked uncomfortable. He asked, "Did you ever relate to Fred lesbian activities?"

"Your Honor," Brockett interrrupted, "I object to this! I would ask to approach the bench." Gini shouted inside, No, Don, no! *For god's sake, let me answer*! She'd been warned to expect a few cheap shots, but she'd underestimated Kevin's malevolence. She had no doubt whatever that the question had originated with him—probably scribbled on his yellow pad. At that instant she realized that she was free of him once and for all. He was a conscienceless, hateful robot, and she couldn't imagine what she'd ever found to love.

The lawyers mumbled at the bench while she studied the floor. She wondered if the question would be carried in the evening newspapers. How unfair! Would they print the question and not her denial? She would take a lie-detector test! *And demand that Kevin take one!* Then the whole town could see who was telling the truth and who wasn't. When everyone was back in place, Gigler asked, "Isn't it true that you masturbated?" The judge sustained another Brockett objection. Gigler asked, "May we approach the bench? Masturbation was made an issue yesterday by the prosecutor."

"As to the *defendant*, Your Honor," Brockett said.

When the judge sustained the objection, Gigler turned back to Gini. "Isn't it true," he asked, again looking oddly uncomfortable, "that you like oral sex?"

"Objection, Your Honor!" Brockett called out.

"All right," the judge said wearily. "Counsel, approach the bench."

When this second short conference was over, Gini steeled herself for another embarrassment. It came immediately: "Isn't it true that you would ask the defendant to perform oral sex?"

She waited for Brockett to object, but he remained silent. "Occasionally," she answered.

"Did you ever perform oral sex on him?"

"No."

"... I'm sorry, some of these questions are a little hard to phrase. Now, you said at times prior to intercourse he would put his fingers in your vagina, is that correct?"

"Yes."

"Isn't that normal?"

Another objection was sustained. Gigler asked, "As far as his language, I believe you testified he said 'ass' once in a while and 'cunt,' is that correct?"

"Yes."

"Did you ever use those words yourself?"

"When—if I am really mad at somebody, I might use the word 'ass' once in a while, but I did not use the other one."

After a while Gigler wanted to know if Fred had allergies, and she answered, "He *said* he did."

He asked if she had volunteered information to the police. "Many times," she said.

"Many times?"

"Um-hmm."

He asked if she hadn't wanted to marry Coe, and if she felt like a woman scorned. She said that Coe had also mentioned the subject of marriage. She wished she'd brought his letter to Guy to prove it. At last the judge said the words she'd been dying to hear: "Thank you, Miss Perham. You may step down."

She walked slowly toward the waiting room, avoiding Kevin's eyes. She was relieved that no one had brought up the shoplifting trial but distraught about the rest of her testimony. When the door shut behind her, she started crying. "Don't, Gini!" her cousin Jane ordered.

"It's all those things they said about me," she blubbered. "All those things they tried to make me out to be."

Brockett came in and patted her on the shoulder. "You were great," he said. "You answered the questions and you didn't elaborate. I'm proud of you."

"Thanks," she said, but she had no feeling of triumph. She couldn't imagine who would ever speak to her again.

104

We had far more credible witnesses than the prosecution but—unfortunately, many were my family.—Fred Coe, Oct. 18, 1981

The defense of Fred Coe was of a type almost never seen in sophisticated modern courtrooms—the defense of blanket denial. It was a symphony of absolutes, of couldn't-haves: he couldn't have rammed his gloved hand down throats, because he never wore gloves; he couldn't have been seen wearing a stocking cap, because he never wore hats; he couldn't have been the man who'd raped Irene Pool, because he'd never had complexion problems; he couldn't have committed the two early-morning rapes, because he always drove to his parents' house for a long breakfast starting at 6 a.m.; he couldn't have lusted after strange women, because he'd never had trouble finding girlfriends.

The absolutes were reinforced by defense witnesses. The mildest points made by the prosecution were flatly denied, then denied again. The mode of defense was believed to have been drawn up by Coe himself over the objections of his experienced counsel. Courthouse habitués couldn't help recalling the bromide, "A man who is his own lawyer has a fool for a client."

Every morning, attorneys for both sides met in Judge Shields's chambers to sip coffee, exchange small talk and accuse each other of various procedural offenses, especially the unfair withholding of information. Gigler and Twyford would bring up prosecutor Brockett's failure to furnish original police reports, and in turn Brockett would complain, "What's the defense gonna be? Who're your witnesses? We're entitled to know." But before the Saturday-morning session Brockett was unusually quiet. Gigler twitted him, "Aren't you gonna demand discovery this morning, Don?"

"Nope," replied the tight-lipped prosecutor. "I know your case now, Roger. I watched Fred last night on TV."

On the first day of defense testimony Sheriff's Lt. Richard Lovejoy, who was responsible for escorting Coe between jail and courtroom each morning, noticed a change. At the beginning of the trial Coe had seemed to enjoy his notoriety, but gradually he'd become less content. Instead of holding his head up when the cameras began clicking, he shied away or ducked. Now he wanted a favor. "Why can't we come up the private steps in back, so the damned press vultures can't take my picture?"

"No way," Lovejoy said. "It's too isolated. I could get in all kinds of trouble if anything happened back there."

"Other guys are brought up the back way."

"Other guys, yeah. But not you."

The first defense witness was the best friend and former roommate of Coe's sister Kathleen—Carolyn Black, a university student described as "almost like a member of the Coe family." She testified that Fred couldn't have committed the Lois Higgins rape of April 26, 1978, because he'd been visiting Kathy in Seattle. On cross-examination she was asked if she could be thinking of 1979 or 1980, and she said a firm, "No." She testified that at the time of the rape Fred had worn neither mustache nor long hair, as Lois Higgins had testified.

Marsha Albert, another old friend of the Coes, told the jury that she'd called Kathleen Coe in Seattle at the time of the Higgins rape and Kathy had mentioned that Fred was there visiting. She also testified that she'd never seen Fred with pimples or with a heavy growth of beard, or wearing a cap or hat.

The dark-haired Kathleen Coe, first member of the family to take the stand, was equally positive about the April visit and added details. She proudly described her brother as neat and clean. "He was as a child. His things are always in order. If you borrow a magazine, or read a book, he reminds you to be very careful of them." She said that she had never seen him unshaven for three or four days and that he had "never had much of a problem at all with his complexion." When the assistant prosecutor suggested that Kathleen couldn't be positive about her brother's day-to-day appearance since she was seldom with him, the witness snapped, "I am not his Siamese twin, right."

A resident of the Higgins rape neighborhood inflicted more damage on Count 1 by testifying that he'd seen a short man fleeing the scene. Then the defense's first big gun ambled toward the stand. After four decades as a local newsman Gordon Coe had the look and manner of a prominent citizen who was unawed by the judge and the courtroom. When Gigler asked him where he'd gone to school, the managing editor quipped, "You want me to tell how old I am?" He ran down his curriculum vitae, ending with his promotion six years earlier to managing editor of the *Chronicle*. Then he confirmed the testimony that his wife and son had been in Seattle during the Higgins rape. "We ran up one of our big phone bills that week. We talked back and forth. I believe we have the bills here."

"Did you talk to both Mrs. Coe and your son?"

"Yes. I actually talked to my son Fred more often. He seemed to answer the phone when I called more often."

Four prosecution witnesses had testified earlier about Fred Coe's suspicious behavior the morning of the dildo incident; now the Coe family's version was heard for the first time. "Well," said Gordon, "he had come by on the way to work, and that was a Sunday, and about ten o'clock roughly. And we have a habit of going out Sundays and eating these brunches where you eat enough for the week and try not to overeat the rest of the time. And we were going to do that." But instead, the witness continued, Fred suggested that his parents follow him in their Cadillac while he pointed out some real-estate-development sites along Upriver Drive. When they reached the area, all three got out of their cars and looked around, and Fred said, "I got my water bill with me; I think I will go pay it in the drop-in place." He drove off in his Citation and accidentally took a dead-end street. An old Chevy came roaring out of the same street, followed in a minute or two by Fred, who commented, "Did you see that nut come out of there driving like a madman?" Then the family departed.

Coe said he remembered talking to his son about the South Hill rapes and the Secret Witness Program. "I said, 'I don't even know whether you would be able to collect the thousand dollars or not, being related to someone at the *Chronicle*; but in any event, for goodness' sake, if you get something, a tip, don't phone it in, send it in by mail and someone will handle that and not me.'"

Gigler asked, "Did you ever warn Fred of the possibility that the police might get suspicious if he gets too involved?"

"Yes. I did a couple times when we first talked about it, and when we discussed the Secret Witness thing. I am afraid that he didn't understand the full import of my warning, and I didn't make it specific enough because I have had the years of experience with the police, and I know what they are capable of, and what might happen, and so on. And I should have been a good deal more explicit on that point."

The editor testified that he'd never known anyone who wore his clothes as neatly as his son, that Fred hadn't had a mustache in at least three years and had "a heck of a time growing one," and that he'd never suffered from acne or pimples and never wore hats or gloves. "He is one of these people that sort of ignores winter. He figures in another month it will go away, and he wanders around all winter long never with a hat, and never with gloves." Nor had he ever seen Fred with a substantial growth of beard. "I was always on his back to—let's shave every day, and you always try to make someone in your image, I guess."

His son never had problems finding women in high school, Coe testified. "He had more trouble fending them off." He said the liaison with Gini Perham had begun as "an economic thing, someone to share the rent with." But unfortunately the troubled young woman had misunderstood. "All of us had great sympathy and empathy for Gini when we first knew her, and when Fred first knew her. And therefore, when we were introduced to her, it was shortly after her mother committed suicide, and a schizophrenic thing, and so on. And we were very careful to her feelings, careful to be as nice to her as we possibly could. And Fred was trying to bring her out, to get her to dress better, fix her hair, and so forth. And we were all sympathetic towards this. But— tremendous problems with her mood swings...and it was a difficult thing sometimes for us to be as sweet and careful with her because you never knew when you start out—taking her to lunch or something—she would be in a fine mood, and before the afternoon was over, she would be in a totally different mood, very often very depressed, very ugly, or whatever." The distinguished witness summed up, "She was a problem."

Donald Brockett opened the cross-examination with the subject of the family breakfasts. "Mr. Coe, are you saying that between September of 1980 and March 10 of 1981, when your son was arrested, that he ate breakfast with you *every* morning, and dinner with you *every* evening?"

"Yes," Coe answered. "He may have missed one day sometimes. I can't remember it."

"... He was living with Miss Perham at that time, was he not?"

"Yes."

"And yet he came to your home every morning for breakfast?"

"Yes."

"And came to your home every evening for dinner?"

"She was unable to provide the food...."

Coe's testimony kept circling back to Gini Perham, almost as though she were the defendant. Brockett asked, "You didn't say anything to Fred about whether or not he ought to marry her, or shouldn't marry her?"

The editor's forehead squeezed into furrows before he answered. "I think we did express to him the fact that we didn't think it would be a good idea to marry her, because we didn't think they should have children in view of her history."

"And she was just sort of a poor farm girl that he brought—?"

"I object to that," Gigler interrupted.

The prosecutor revised his question. "Didn't you sort of have to teach her how to dress?"

"Well, I didn't teach her anything, Mr. Brockett. But Fred tried to improve her. In the course of her life, I gathered she had gone through periods of being less than well dressed and suave...."

Coe's testimony concluded with a critique of the police lineups. He said that Fred's voice had been high and tense. He said that anyone could tell that No. 1 in the line-up was a policeman and the others "kids out of the jail."

"And you think your son stood out?" he was asked.

"Very obviously."

When Gini Perham read the weekend newspapers, she was angry, then hurt, then embarrassed. She told her cousin, "All those things Gordon said about me—*he was describing his wife!* Ruth's mood swings, Ruth's unreliability."

Her cousin told her to simmer down. "It's gonna get worse—I know it," Gini moaned. "Ruth takes the stand Monday."

By the weekend recess the trial was at least half over, and Jay Williams still hadn't figured out how to tell Fred that he couldn't be a character witness. A few days before, he had prayed, "Lord, I really want to feel a very, *very* strong conviction within this day of what you would have me do. I wouldn't lie, Lord, but I would like to make some kind of gesture for Fred." Before the end of the day, Jay had the reply: an overwhelming no. The feeling was so strong that it wiped out every vestige of *esprit de corps* and *semper fideles*.

But how to break the news? A few days earlier Fred had reminded him, "You're the key, Jay. If you give me a strong character reference, I walk. Otherwise it doesn't look too good."

On Sunday night Fred called and said, "I've just heard a rumor that you're gonna drop out, like Paula Whitmore. Is that true?"

"It's true," Jay admitted. He tried to describe his problem. "Fred, I, uh—

if I testified as a character witness, it would suggest that I think you're innocent, and that would be a lie. So I can't."

"You *can't*?"

"No."

He'd expected more of an argument, but all he heard was Coe's typically subdued voice: "I didn't know that Christians couldn't lie."

Jay ignored the comment. "Fred, can't you see that you invalidated me as a witness when you had me dispose of that dildo? You promised me it was innocuous. I read what you did in the papers and it *wasn't* innocuous. What am I gonna say if they bring that up in court? I'd just incriminate you further."

In the end he had to admit that Fred took the turndown sportingly. In twenty-six years, the two friends had never spoken angrily to each other, and their record remained intact. All Fred said was, "I can't believe that your principle against lying is more important than my going to prison."

"Well, I'm sorry," Jay said. "But it is."

105

At 5:30 a.m. Monday, four hours before the defense was to resume, a line began to form at the courthouse. By the time the front doors were unlocked the hopefuls were backed up to the street—wheat farmers and their wives from the Palouse, silver miners, out-of-work loggers from Coeur d'Alene, aluminum workers and railroaders and just plain folks from Spokane and surrounding towns like Spangle and Opportunity and Medical Lake and Elk.

Just before the day's proceedings began, a stir went through the courtroom. A deputy sheriff led a stylishly dressed woman with black hair and vivid green eyes to a seat in the front row. She was Margot Terry, rape victim and special guest of the Spokane police department. The bailiffs and deputies watched the woman apprehensively. Each had been forewarned: "*No outbursts!*" If she jumped up and said, "That's him!" or something similar, there could be a mistrial.

Mrs. Terry said later that they needn't have worried. "I was well aware of the problem. I wasn't even going to breathe loud. I sat on the aisle and when Coe came into the courtroom he looked at me and didn't blink or acknowledge."

The other Coes made their way down the crowded corridor. To some they resembled the characters in a '50s movie—well-chiseled faces, straight noses, full lips, darkly gleaming eyes, careful coiffures. Camelots old and new had never produced a more alluringly matched set. Ruth Coe, the day's big attraction, wore reddish-purple lipstick, a raven-black medium-length wig, a conservative white suit, and a black and white floral print blouse with a plunging neckline. A pair of half glasses hung from her neck by a chain. She took the stand in what appeared to be a jaunty mood, carrying on the family theme of grace under pressure.

When the judge wanted to know if she objected to having her picture taken, she smiled and said pleasantly, "I don't mind in the least, Your Honor." Asked her age, she said, "I was born in Spokane over sixty-one years ago. I won't be coy." From the outset of the direct examination she gave the impression that the limelight was old stuff to her. She spoke of her professional experience. "I was coordinator of fashion shows, and then I went into teaching at the college level, teaching fashions, working always with women in personal grooming, wardrobe clothing, fashion all the way.... I did my lecturing on campuses at the college level, all three states: Washington, Oregon, Idaho. I did many color lectures all over those three states, and also taught at high school, and at the junior high school levels, the same thing—grooming."

She confirmed earlier testimony that her son had been in Seattle at the time of the Lois Higgins rape. She was asked if she remembered August 30, 1980, the night of the rape of Sue Ellen Wilber. "Yes," Mrs. Coe replied. "I remember that. That was the evening that we, his father, Fred and I, were watching television. We were watching *The Best of Carson* that night, but for me they would flip over so I could see an Errol Flynn movie. I had not seen it. It was *Virginia City,* filmed in Virginia City, Montana. I had been reading a book, actually two books, on Errol Flynn. I am not a fan of his, but I was reading those. They had mentioned in the book *Virginia City* that he was beginning to break in his career, and that if you saw that film, you would see certain indications of his stardom slipping, places where he was under the influence of dope, or something like that. So I badly wanted to see that, to see if I could pick them up; so we would turn back and forth to see that. Miriam Hopkins was playing opposite him."

Julie Twyford asked, "Do you recall what date that was?"

"Well, that was the twenty-ninth, coming on at eleven-thirty. So it went into the thirtieth. That would make it the twenty-ninth and the thirtieth." The rape of Sue Ellen Wilber had been just after midnight.

The witness emphatically backed up her husband's account of Fred's visits at mealtimes. A depression had hit the real estate field and "I said it takes no longer to cook for three than two, and it wouldn't be much more costly. So he ate every breakfast with us. He arrived usually at six, usually five or ten minutes before, but definitely by six o'clock every morning, and breakfast hour went on at the home until about seven-thirty. He seldom left before seven-thirty." Irene Pool and Jeanie Mays had been raped between 6:30 and 7:30 a.m.

"...Then he ate our dinners with us," Mrs. Coe went on, "which the dinner hour is five to seven-thirty." Stephanie Gibbs and Marie Oldham had been raped between 6:30 and 7 p.m. The communal eating pattern continued "until roughly the fifteenth or twentieth of February." Surveillance of Coe had begun on February 25, and police reports hadn't shown a single morning trip to the parents' home. Mrs. Coe's testimony neatly explained the discrepancy.

The questioning got around to "dildo day," March 8. Did the witness see Fred that morning, too? "Yes, I certainly did. And I shall never forget March eighth, ninth or tenth. They are very vividly etched in my memory. March eighth was a Sunday, and Son had called us too, and then had come by...." The threesome had set off in two cars to look at some property. "We went down—" She interrupted herself and swung toward the jury. "Since you are from Seattle, I won't bore you with the details how we went down...." Her description of the subsequent events tallied with her husband's.

She was asked if she and Fred had ever discussed the South Hill rape situation. "Yes," she said. "We not only had discussions, but after many discussions we decided to see if we could find any clues. We both felt—one reason he came back to Spokane is that it's a very sweet, homey town, a lovely place to raise children. This is the image that we wanted to help protect.... We had always lived on the South Hill, and we saw it, you know, as kind of hitting at home too. So we decided we would go out in the hours that the rapist was, as we would get them from the paper.... Son would jog, and I would follow in the car at a very slow pace. We did give up, though. You said spring, summer of 1980. And by fall we had been very unsuccessful, so we did give it up."

But they resumed the chase once more, after the *Chronicle* included the South Hill rapes in its Secret Witness Program and the *Spokesman-Review* ran its January splash about rape riding the buses. "Now that gives the idea, good, we will follow the buses, which we did, looking for clues," said Mrs. Coe. "We were looking to see if we could find a known lady getting off the bus where a man would get off behind her, or a block or two away, so that we had a clue, something to go on. However, we never did find any. And by, oh, the middle of February, I was tired of it and said I didn't think I would like to continue, and Son said he would like to quit too because, of course, the spring real estate season was coming on; so, we were both into that."

"How many times do you think you went out with Fred?"

"Oh, I would say a good ten or twelve, maybe more times."

Mrs. Coe testified that her son hadn't worn a mustache in years, was always very neat and clean, kept his hair short, never had complexion problems worse than an occasional pimple, never wore gloves or a hat as an adult, and got along so well with the Lewis and Clark high school girls that "we were thinking about putting in a second phone for him because each of us—I being freelancing, I was being contacted constantly by phone, and I needed to get on it and usually couldn't."

She was asked about his eating habits and went into a vivid description of his allergies. Around weeds and grass, she testified, "He explodes. His whole body explodes, and the water is running, and the nose is running. When he would mow that lawn, he was in bed for two days afterwards."

Defense attorney Twyford asked for a description of the relationship between Fred and Gini Perham. Ruth Coe cleared her throat and said, "I have a feeling, when he first met Gini, I think he felt the compassion we all felt." Assistant prosecutor Patricia Thompson objected on the grounds that the answer was unresponsive. The witness said, "Would you ask me the question again, please, Julie?"

"Would you just describe the relationship with Fred and Gini?"

"Well, I feel, I think it was—"

"Your Honor," Thompson broke in, "I object. She is stating her feelings."

The judge said, "Well, let her answer the question. Go ahead, Mrs. Coe."

"Thank you, Your Honor," she said. "I saw it as an economic relationship for both of them. She had admired the real estate field, and it was through Fred that she went into it. I mean, he helped teach her.... And she was quite insistent for a long time, wanting to move in with him, and when he—he had not wanted that at all, and had resisted for a long time...."

"Would you tell us what Gini's attitude towards Fred was?"

"Well, she told me many, many times, through my amazement, that she had waited ten years to find him, that he was just the greatest thing that ever was, that she just thought he was fantastic. It rather shocked me because I am his mother, and I know him pretty well, and I didn't think he is fantastic."

She smiled down at her son. "But she emulated in him, in his beliefs; hers seemed very contrary in the beginning, but he introduced her to authors he liked, and she accepted them very much, and she seemed to feel he was very, very—she accepted what he offered, and help. And she thought he was *marvelous.*"

"Mrs. Coe," Julie Twyford asked, "was there anything unusual in the relationship between Gini and Fred?"

"It was a little bit like Henry Higgins and Eliza Doolittle in *My Fair Lady.* He was helping her. When she entered his life, and she was—she had just gone through quite a trauma. Her mother had committed suicide. I felt that her experience, and perhaps her attitudes, and her own violent mood swings were, perhaps, the offshoot of having gone through this traumatic thing. And I thought that Fred was doing as I had often done with people in my classes who would be sent in from mental institutions, to get them to care once again how they looked, how their hair was, how their weight was, how their clothes were, and we would be back on track to getting them to normality.... He was very kind to her, always very understanding of her, and through him she did lose weight, considerable weight. She did improve her dress habits. She improved her cleanliness habits, changed from the hippie look that she had, and really made quite an improvement."

At first, assistant prosecutor Pat Thompson was unable to shake a word of the woman's testimony on cross-examination. Mrs. Coe even managed to buttress her negative characterization of Gini Perham. "Gini was not a cook; she is not even a dishwasher—big piles of dishes—but she didn't want to cook, seemingly...."

"Couldn't Fred do the dishes?"

"If they were done, he did them."

"But I thought you said he was a very neat and fastidious person. Why would he let the dishes pile up?"

Mrs. Coe sounded emphatic. "Because *Miss* Perham didn't wash her own dishes. He did *not* eat at home."

The questioning turned to the events of April 24, the day Fred Coe cruised the Roger Crane office and returned later with his mother. "Mrs. Coe," the deputy prosecutor asked, "isn't it true that you've covered for Fred, saying he was with you at one time when he wasn't with you?"

The witness looked over the top of her half glasses. "Miss Thompson, if you are asking me would I lie for my son—"

"I didn't, Mrs. Coe. I didn't ask you that. I asked you whether or not it was true that you had covered for your son, saying he was with you at one time when he was not. Yes or no?"

"You would have to be more clear." She paused and added, "No, I rather think not."

"Do you remember back on April 24 of this year you went to the hairdresser at The Crescent at University City?"

"Yes?"

"And you indicated to Mr. Beeman, the investigator...you talked with Mr. Beeman and indicated that you had gone to have your nails done, and that your son was with you the entire period of time?"

"Yes, I do. And he was. And I had a broken wrist—"

"Mrs. Coe, thank you. Do you remember, though, it being checked out, and the fact that he was not with you the entire time—he came in the last fifteen minutes?"

Twyford objected again. "I don't believe this witness can even testify to that."

"I'll withdraw the question," Thompson said. "Didn't you say your son was with you for that entire period of time when he in fact was not?"

Mrs. Coe said, "I had a broken wrist and could not do my own nails."

"Mrs. Coe," Thompson snapped, "answer the question!"

"He was there, Miss Thompson. I will give you the logistics."

"He was there the whole period of time?"

"He was not sitting right next to me the entire period. The magazine section is there, and I said to him so that people could hear—he was reading magazines earlier; when we finally did discuss it, he came right into where we were, and the girl did my nails, and said it wouldn't be too much longer."

Thompson refused to drop the subject. "Didn't you say he was with you the entire time, and he was not?"

"And he *was* with me. If you mean sitting right next to me—"

"Mrs. Coe, thank you! That is all."

The first witness after lunch was a young banker, John Cockburn, recently deposed as Kathleen Coe's mate. There was tension as he took the oath. Word was out that he'd warned Fred Coe he wouldn't lie. He testified about moving to Spokane from Seattle about six weeks before Coe's arrest and living temporarily with Gordon and Ruth on Dyer Rd. Gigler asked him, "During these times did you see Fred Coe often?"

"Yes," Cockburn answered.

"And did you see him there at breakfast time?"

Cockburn asked, "You are speaking about prior to the—"

"Yes, prior to the arrest."

"Okay. A few times."

The trio at the prosecution table—Brockett and Patricia Thompson and Detective Roy Allen—leaned forward. The words seemed to contradict earlier testimony that Fred had breakfasted with his parents every morning.

Gigler quickly asked, "And would you see him there at dinnertime?"

This time Cockburn answered unhesitatingly. "Yes. On a regular basis."

"Would that be every day?"

"Yes."

"And at the times that you did not see him at breakfast, it's possible that he could have been there also, is it not?"

"Yes. It is possible."

After testifying, Cockburn walked stonefaced past the Coe family, seated in the back row. Kathleen Coe smiled up at him but he left without returning the smile.

Next up was Fred Coe.

106

I want it understood. I'll never admit to anything.—Fred Coe, May
26, 1982

Everyone except the defendant seemed tired and drawn as Coe walked briskly
to the front of the muggy little courtroom and took the oath in his resonant
"broadcaster's voice." The trial was almost two weeks old, and the outside
temperature had climbed well into the eighties every day. But as Coe stood
in front of the judge and agreed to tell the truth and nothing but, he looked
as though he'd just stepped from the front window at the Bon Marché. His
father had testified that he'd never known anyone who wore his clothes as
well as Fred. The proof was on display.

He took his seat in the witness box, shot his cuffs, gripped his gold pen
and looked expectantly at Roger Gigler. "Fred," the defense lawyer said softly,
"would you tell the court your name and where you live, please."

Coe answered, "Frederick Harlan Coe, and at 1418 South Dyer, Spokane,
99206."

After he had answered a few more questions, spectators began to mumble
to each other. This wasn't the Fred Coe who'd repeatedly read on command,
"Take off your clothes. Do as I say or I'll kill you," etc. That voice had sounded
ordinary. This one was mellifluous and cool.

For almost an hour, he spoke of his career: leaving college early, attending
radio school in San Francisco, taking his first broadcasting job in a small town
in western Washington, returning to radio school in California, then coming
back to Spokane to work for KJRB (later Shelly Monahan's employer) before
moving to Los Angeles in 1970. He made his job descriptions sound like a
steady upward spiral toward success. Of his days as movie usher and popcorn-
maker he said, "I was in Los Angeles working in the theater business for about
a year.... I was working for the National General Corporation, which was a
multinational conglomerate. They both own theaters and motion production
companies. My long-range interest at the time was hopefully to get into screenwriting, so I worked for the theater in the corporation with the hope of getting
into screenwriting. The theater I worked at was within about a mile's drive of
Universal Studios, where National General did a lot of their filming. So I was
close to where I was trying to break into it."

As he testified he gestured with his pen and made disarming head movements toward the jurors. From time to time, he nodded at his words, confirming his own veracity. He sipped water and frequently rested his arm on the rail in front of him, as though completely at home. He answered unhesitatingly and at length.

Donald Brockett had confided before the trial that the prosecution's biggest problem would be convincing the jurors that a man like Coe could be capable of rape. As the testimony proceeded the jury seemed to be following him closely. He was coming across like a teacher, a patient lecturer to a somewhat slow class, a young Mr. Chips. He told how he'd written a novel, but "the agent's effort to sell the book, especially in the European market, had kind of bogged down. He was very high on the manuscript and tried to sell it as hard as he could, and after six or eight months he was getting somewhat discouraged, and told me I should probably write a little bit different type of novel." Another defendant might have testified simply that the work had been rejected, but that wasn't Coe's way. His mother, seated in the back of the tiny courtroom, smiled and nodded as he made his points and occasionally emitted a loud sigh or muffled comment when the prosecutor registered objections.

Coe spoke of his job in Las Vegas as a disc jockey. "I started off as the midnight-to-six-a.m. man, which midnight to six is not a very preferred shift in a city as big as Las Vegas. Actually it's a tremendous shift because you have the biggest audience of the day, really...." From KENO in Las Vegas he was lured into the discotheque business "because I had a great deal of experience with disco music and black music." But the job had presented problems for his wife Jenifer. "She was not able to handle the strain of the constant attention from women that a disco DJ—just naturally you are going to get. The groupies and all that kind of thing. It just blew her mind, to coin a phrase." He testified that she'd been an alcoholic for ten years—"but I did not know that."

Gigler asked, "Did this drinking eventually lead your marriage to dissolving?"

"I would say that that was it, yeah," Coe began. "The constant strain of the other-women problems. She was a very jealous woman anyway, and the disco scene in Las Vegas is a very unusual site." He leaned into the mike and said, "And, you know, it would take an hour probably to describe it, but suffice it to say that some of the most beautiful women in the world live in Las Vegas, and the attention that somebody in the DJ's position gets from these incredibly beautiful women, showgirls and so forth—Jenifer is, herself, a very attractive woman, but she felt intimidated by it, and began to suggest that I was having affairs of all kinds, and so forth. That led to the drinking."

A bailiff noticed that some of the jurors were straining to hear. The microphone was designed to pick up voices from a foot or two away, but Coe was caressing it with his lips and distorting the sound. The judge had reached over and fiddled with the dials several times. The bailiff didn't help much.

The life story went on for over an hour, Coe narrating with little prompting from his lawyer. Ruth Coe kept up her coda of approval in the back row, and the other two members of the Coe family showed by their expressions how well they thought the case was going. Most of the testimony seemed irrelevant to the issues, but the prosecution made no objection. Sometimes Roger Gigler looked a little disturbed by the length of the answers. His client was in the middle of explaining how Jeni's drinking had caused him credit problems when Gigler abruptly changed the subject. "Now, Fred," he asked, "how tall are you?"

"Well, I've, since being an adult, and having had full height, I have always measured out at six-one or more." As though mindful that he had also been measured by Roy Allen at a fraction over six feet, he added, "I guess people vary a little bit in their height." He was asked about distinguishing scars or marks. "Yes," he said. "I have a very distinguishing scar under my left cheek here that I got many years ago as a child. I got hit by a snow shovel accidentally."

At Gigler's request, he displayed the scar to the jury, then returned to his seat with a little hop step. Veteran observers couldn't remember a cooler display by a man on trial. Courtroom ghouls had expected a timid, frightened defendant, but that wasn't Fred Coe's way either.

The subject of allergies came up and the rambling resumed. "... It never became a real problem until the spring of 1963. The Soviet Union was doing a lot of testing of some kind, and I remember reading a newspaper way back then that certain scientists in this country feared that the fallout from whatever the Soviets were doing—it was before certain nuclear treaties had been signed that don't allow that kind of thing anymore, but—biologically, the plant life, wildlife, might be affected; and they actually projected that some people who were kind of latent allergy sufferers would suddenly have a bad allergy; and no more sooner than I read that and in fact it was the case with me. I had never had a great noticeable problem with allergies, and suddenly in that same year, 1963, I, for the first time, noticed allergies like to grass, and so forth. We would be doing calisthenics on the ground. I would suddenly start sneezing, and so forth. And so from 1963 on, really, is when it was any problem."

From allergies he turned to the subject of dieting. He spoke of reading a diet book by a Dr. Newbold, "the world's leading allergist." He had just begun to say more when Gigler asked, "Now what is the diet basically? Don't go into—"

"It's a very simple diet, as a matter of fact," Coe broke in. He described the diet in detail and added that it hadn't worked for his sister—"she was not into sardines, radishes and so forth."

It was mid-afternoon before he finally reached the subject of his romance with Virginia Perham. He told of meeting her at the laundromat and maintaining a casual relationship for a while. "But there was a poignancy to her mother's suicide that kind of touched me. And we began seeing each other more."

Donald Brockett had heard enough degrading testimony about his witness and when the subject of her "cleanliness" came up, he registered an objection. Gigler said, "I am sorry, Your Honor, but we are answering certain questions raised by the state's own witnesses. One of them has to do with his personal habits and her personal habits as far as newspapers, clothes, and what have you."

Judge Shields said, "Well, you can direct your attention to specific items, but not in general."

"All right," Gigler said. "When Gini moved in with you, did she have many clothes?"

"...She would bring her baggie full of clothes on any given night that she was going to stay there, and it would just contain the clothing she was going to use the next day. And she eventually got tired of bringing that baggie and started insisting that she move in." Coe told of arguments about his throwing the newspapers away and said he told her, "I am getting tired of the house constantly having papers and all kinds of things all over the place." He said that the subject of the South Hill rapes had come up seldom and that when it did, "I just mainly listened to her, and I dropped the subject."

He had been on the witness stand for almost two hours and seemed more voluble than ever. Brockett made a few objections but mostly listened quietly. The jurors seemed to be paying attention. The judge was seldom called upon to intervene, although when Coe rambled on after twice being informed that he was engaging in hearsay on a particular point, the judge leaned over the bench and asked, "Didn't you hear me?" As Ruth Coe sighed loudly in the back row, Coe rephrased his answer.

Gigler asked him to comment on the testimony about his jogging injuries. Coe replied, "In the entire two-year period that I knew Gini, and was jogging, my usual situation, I would say that happened maybe three or four times. Maybe at the outside most, a half dozen." He explained that he usually ran in darkness on tracks that weren't well maintained. "I remember one time in particular stepping on a rake by the pole vault area at Hart Field."

Asked about the leather gloves that Perham claimed had gone to pieces around the fingers, he said, "To the best of my knowledge, I never owned a pair of gloves, period....I don't like gloves. I don't like the feel of them on my hands...." He admitted that he'd once owned a gray warmup suit but said he usually jogged in a yellow outfit with the words "Gold's Gym" emblazoned on it. He said he'd never owned a stocking cap.

"Did you ever own a dildo?" Gigler asked.

"I never owned a dildo, no."

"Have you ever seen one?"

"I have seen them," he admitted. He backed up previous alibi testimony for the rapes of Lois Higgins and Sue Ellen Wilber but said he didn't remember what he was doing at the time of the rapes of Marie Oldham, Stephanie Gibbs and Jeanie Mays. As for Irene Pool, he said he remembered her because he'd said "Hi!" to her at Hart Field a half dozen or a dozen times over the years. In fact, he said, he jogged past her two-and-a-half weeks after the rape date— "and I was as close to her as I am to you right now."

He corroborated his parents' testimony about his interest in the Secret Witness Program and how he'd gone out with his mother looking for the rapist. "The main problem is that we were neophytes. You know. We weren't real detectives and very sophisticated at it." He spent fifteen minutes refuting the four witnesses who'd testified that he'd flashed a dildo on the Upriver Drive jogging trail and run away. Not only had he not been on the path, he testified, but he hadn't even known of it until after his arrest. Late in the day he began to talk about Spokane's attitude toward the South Hill rapist. "You know, I would listen to KSPO radio here—"

"Objection, Your Honor," Brockett said. The judge informed Coe that he couldn't testify about what he heard on the radio.

Almost abruptly, Gigler asked, "Fred, uh, are you the South Hill rapist?"

"No."

"Have you ever raped anyone?"

"No."

Gigler said, "That is all the questions I have." After the courtroom had cleared for the day, a juror took one of the bailiffs aside and complained that Ruth Coe's behavior was becoming a distraction. Backstage, the delicate matter was discussed privately by courtroom personnel and the judge. There was agreement that the frequent sighs and comments were much too conspicuous. One court official said, "The surprising thing is—we put the family in the back row so they could be anonymous if they wanted to, but it's obvious that they don't want to be just spectators. So much whispering and smiling and nudging."

Judge Shields passed word to the defense.

107

"He's a complete egotist," says Brockett, "and I saw him putting his hands around the mike, like he was an announcer again, looking over to smile at the jury, and I knew then it was going to be an act." Brockett asked one question, got his answer, and looked down at his notes for the next. Coe seized the pause. "Fred said, 'And I might add...,' and he went on for two minutes," recalls Brockett. "I thought, that's how you cross-examine Fred Coe. You ask a simple question, and let him go on and on. He tried to excuse everything. He was like a little kid, trying to explain everything away."—The American Lawyer, December, 1982

The courtroom was stifling. The day before, the thermometer had climbed to ninety-three, highest reading of the year, and this Monday morning didn't start out much cooler. As usual, spectators sat sweat to sweat. When one left, another squeezed in.

The prosecuting attorney opened his cross-examination by asking Fred Coe the titles of the novels he'd written. Over defense objections Coe cited *Shirley*, *Snowy*, *Outrage*, and added, "My company published a book called *Sex in the White House*, which was a lampoon on the Watergate situation."

"What personal experience of yours did that relate to?" Brockett asked.

"Well, it didn't relate to a personal experience. . . . It was basically the type thing that you would read in *National Lampoon*, like you see on 'Saturday Night Live.' We promoted it as a wildly hip, hysterical look at Watergate. It ended up being prophetic, prophetic in the sense that at the time we put it together there hadn't been any major sex scandals in the American politics that I am aware of, at least in recent times, and we satirized the Watergate situation by bringing the vent of what it was to a sex scandal."

This morning Coe was speaking slowly, with many "ummms"and "ahs" and clearings of his throat. "It was a humorous book," he went on, "and I have heard it described since my arrest as obscenity-filled, but I don't think that's accurate. It's a satire. And it's prophetic in the sense that in the next few years America did go through a number of sex scandals—the Fannie Fox thing, and the recent one with John Jenrette. So it was a book kind of ahead of its time."

Brockett asked, "What different types of sexual activities did it detail?"

Gigler interrupted. "Your Honor, I am going to object to this. I see no relevance, no materiality in what he has written. That wasn't the subject of direct."

"Overruled," the judge said. Coe had brought up his attempts at authorship in his lengthy autobiographical statement on Saturday. Under questioning by Brockett, he characterized the sexual activity in *Sex in the White House*: "Full range, I guess you could say. It was a typical, you know, you might say, I suppose, libertine approach. . . . We were trying to tap into a specific audience."

Brockett shot back, "An audience that masturbated a lot?"

"I don't believe that was a big subject in the book."

"Wasn't there a considerable description of masturbation?"

Coe tapped his teeth with his pen and said slowly, "I haven't read the book for so many years I really don't remember." Brockett waited silently. Coe added, "There was some of that, yeah." He explained that he hadn't written the entire book, but that he'd been a major participant. Brockett asked if X. Drew Butler had helped in the writing, and Coe said no.

"Who is X. Drew Butler?"

"That's another pseudonym, a name I have used in connection with Spokane Metro Growth."

"And what is Spokane Metro Growth?"

"Spokane Metro Growth is me. It's a one-man Spokane booster group, interested in the positive growth of the Spokane area, which is the reason why I ever got interested in the South Hill rapist."

"What does 'X. Drew Butler' stand for?"

"It stands for nothing. It's just a name."

In the middle of a skirmish about the origins of the pseudonym, Coe brought in Spokane Metro Growth, the smog in California, the Lilac City's image, and his father's position in the community. Brockett steered him back to the original question, and once again Coe insisted that "X. Drew Butler" stood for nothing. "Doesn't the name 'Butler' stand for 'Rhett Butler' in the movie?" the prosecutor asked.

"It doesn't to me."

"That isn't where you got it from?"

"Certainly not."

"Just pulled that out of a hat somewhere?"

Coe squeezed his pen. Before he could answer, Gigler jumped up and insisted that the question had already been answered. The judge reminded the defense attorney that this was cross-examination. Coe said, "The name could have been John Smith. You know, it really didn't matter. . . ."

"It could have been 'Mr. Coe' but it wasn't; it was 'Butler.' Where did you get the name from?"

"It just came to me, is all," Coe said. "I can touch on that maybe briefly, and it might give you some insight to it." He paused, then said, "I don't really have the answer for you." He hesitated again. "I will try to give you some reason why it might be something like that."

"If you don't have the answer for it," Brockett interrupted, "isn't it better for you not to give me any reason for it?"

Gigler said, "Now *he* is being argumentative." The judge agreed, but

Brockett had made his point: that Coe seemed to be tailoring his answers to his needs.

The prosecutor asked, "Mr. Coe, you in fact used Spokane Metro Growth and the name X. Drew Butler to obtain one of your jobs, did you not, by writing a letter under that signature to a realtor, recommending yourself?"

"No, I don't think so."

"You didn't do that?"

"I don't recall that. If you can show me the letter, I can study it. I don't remember it." Once again the answer seemed evasive.

Brockett turned to the crucial question of Coe's varying physical appearance. "I think you said yesterday that you are one hundred eighty-five pounds, is that correct?"

"I think that's what I weighed two days ago."

"How much do you weigh today?"

"One hundred eighty-two."

"How many different weights have you carried in, say, the last year and a half?"

"I would say that I vary between one hundred seventy and one hundred eighty-five all the time."

"And when you are one hundred seventy do you look much thinner than you do today at one hundred eighty-five?"

"Not to me I don't...."

As the questioning heated up, the other members of the Coe family began to make themselves noticed again. An occasional snicker was heard along with Ruth Coe's stage-whispers. Bailiffs conferred but couldn't decide on what to do about it.

For almost an hour Brockett questioned Coe about his diet, his fasts, "flooding," pimples, allergies, his jogging pace. The defendant retained his composure, but he rambled often and spoke slowly, and Brockett seldom interrupted. At times the judge seemed bored, and a few members of the jury seemed to be having trouble maintaining their interest.

Coe painted a dreary picture of his relationship with Gini Perham. After she moved in, he testified, her finances took a dip. "She was unable to continue to share with the rent, and ended up owing me a great deal of money." She would absent herself from the realty office willy-nilly, once for as long as three months, and then work in spurts. Brockett asked, "Weren't you eating well, though?"

"Well," Coe answered, "I was eating with my parents."

"You were buying the food for them?"

"I was buying the food for my parents?" Coe looked past the prosecutor at the back row, as though to reassure his mother and father. "No, just the opposite."

"Weren't you buying steaks every other day?"

"I would get money from my parents, and I kept food on hand at the house. And I would eat some at home too." Brockett stood silently and Coe went on. "See, I would eat five meals a day. That's part of this diet. By 'meals' I don't mean all of them gigantic meals, but there were five eating sessions, so it was not uncommon for me to keep some food at the house on Twenty-ninth and eat a little bit there, too. But the primary meals were eaten with my parents."

"You had to eat very expensive cuts of meat, didn't you?"

All the lawyers knew that Brockett was trying to bring in the shoplifting, but Coe wouldn't take the bait. "Not necessarily expensive cuts. I would eat expensive cuts if I had a little bit of money. Primarily, it was less expensive cuts of meat. Hamburger, in fact, a huge percentage of the time. Round steak."

"You weren't spending a lot of money on filets?"

"When I had it, occasionally."

"... Didn't you in fact approximately every other day buy filets at Rosauer's Supermarket, which was near your house?"

Coe leaned forward into the microphone. "There was a period of time in the summer of 1980, before Gini moved in, when finances allowed me to purchase better quality steaks, yes."

"... That was being purchased for yourself, but not to take over to your parents' house to eat?"

"It was being purchased for me and for Gini on many occasions. I supplied her with a great deal of food."

"So during that period of time you didn't eat with your parents?"

"No. I was eating with my parents, but I might also eat at home, too." He was nuzzling the microphone again, and some of the jurors leaned forward to hear. "As I say, there were five meals, and I would leave steaks in the refrigerator for Gini on many occasions."

"So you would go to your parents' and eat, and come home and eat breakfast again with her?"

"That happened sometimes, yeah, because sometimes I would only eat a little bit with my parents...."

"So you told her each morning you were eating with your parents?"

"I don't know if she was aware of exactly what I was doing."

"Weren't you telling her that when you were running, it was returning from eating with your parents?"

"Not necessarily."

"In fact, you told her you were returning from jogging?"

"From jogging. Whatever else."

"Why didn't you tell her you were eating with your parents?"

Coe sighed. "There were a great many things I didn't tell Gini. She was a very inquisitive person. She was one of these people that wanted to know every facet of your life. She was very jealous, a possessive woman. She was constantly insinuating I was with other women, and so forth. So for the most part when she asked anything I would be very vague. I didn't think it was any of her business."

"In the evening hours when you were missing, you explained to her that you were eating with your parents?"

"I don't think I was missing. I was just out doing things...."

He told about housekeeping guidelines drawn up when Gini moved in, but "very quickly she, for the most part, ignored that, and the burden of doing the housework almost entirely fell on me.... The dishes would pile up, and she got mad a few times when I went ahead and washed all the dishes. She said, 'Leave them; I will do them,' but I went ahead and did it anyway because it bothered me. And when I would do that, that made her mad, that I would demonstrate that she was not doing her job."

Brockett asked if "you were vague with her when she asked why you were washing the oven mitts?" Coe said that he had never seen oven mitts in his house and suggested that the police might have planted them. Brockett asked, "And they planted the story with Miss Perham?"

"No. I didn't say they planted the story with Miss Perham. Her testimony on that subject is, well, as most of what she said, was not accurate.... It was blatant, blatant lies on a number of things where she has taken a wrong conclusion to maybe something she observed, but I would say at least ninety percent of her testimony was through one reason or another false." Heads bobbed in the Coe delegation in the back row.

Brockett asked softly, "And is that always the way you have known her to be?"

"No. I wouldn't say that I have always known her to be that blatantly false, no.... I wouldn't say that Gini being a liar was a major factor of her personality. I would say Gini being subject to tremendous mood swings was a major part of her personality." As Coe leaned into the mike again, a bailiff slipped in behind the witness chair and tried to adjust the controls on the audio system, but the sound quality remained poor. "Gini is a very impressionable person, very easily swayed by almost anybody who is good at manipulation, or persuasion," Coe went on, "and I have only suggested that the police perhaps were able to manipulate her because she is subject to that kind of thing. One reason I know that is that when I met her, she had certain political views which were directly opposite of mine. And over the period of our two-year relationship she had totally adopted all my views, although I hadn't particularly tried to push them off on her; she had actually become more radical in the area than I was."

The subject of the dildo came up again. Coe admitted that he'd seen one in his house and in his car, though it wasn't his. "So somebody else planted it, then?" the prosecutor asked.

"I wouldn't say planted.... I assumed that it belonged to Gini."

"There would be no reason for you being nervous about it being found in your car, is that correct?"

"Well, there would be no reason.... The episode I think you are referring to was an embarrassment. Maybe not nervous, because I didn't know where it was in the car."

"What episode is that?" Brockett inquired innocently.

"Well, what episode are *you* referring to?"

"I don't know," Brockett said. "What episode do *you* think I am referring to?"

"... Well, I think you are referring to an episode in a car wash where, after the car was washed, a young guy who worked there, one of the attendants, came up to me and said, 'That thing in your car really grossed out the lady that is working here.' They have some women that work at a car wash that I go to frequently. And I said, 'What thing?' He said, 'Well, that deal under the seat.' I looked under the seat, and there was this dildo that I had seen previously in the house. I said, 'Oh, well.' That was it."

After a mid-morning recess a thunderstorm broke across the hot summer skies and the temperature skidded into the low eighties. Everyone breathed easier. Coe took a sip of water, gripped his gold pen and testified that he very seldom jogged farther than three miles at a stretch. Brockett asked, "But didn't Miss Perham testify that you were gone for periods of two to four hours in the evening, and when you returned, you indicated that you were jogging?"

"Miss Perham testified to a lot of things. Also, I have already said, where I told her I was going, where and what I really did were often very different things. I maintained my privacy.... When I told her I was going jogging, that might mean that I was going jogging and maybe a lot of other things. Or it might maybe mean that I wasn't going at all, depending on what I had to do. But if I was gone for the four hours straight, you can be assured that I was doing more than jogging."

"Rather than not giving details, you gave a false detail, did you not?"

"It may have happened a few times, yeah. But I am saying she was a very inquisitive person, and I sometimes would get tired of having to answer in great detail every last minute of where I was, or something. As far as I was concerned, if I told her I went jogging, that sufficed as an explanation for her. She could accept it or reject it."

He was asked how it happened that the Sacajawea Junior High School custodian had seen his car parked across from Hart Field at the time of the Pool rape. "Mr. Williams did not see this car," Coe testified. "Mr. Williams may have seen a car very much like mine. The Citations are extremely common, and silver is the most common color of all automobiles worldwide. I commonly in a given day will see twenty cars, silver Citations, many of them exactly like mine."

He admitted again that he'd been in the neighborhood of Upriver Drive the morning of the Leila Hicks dildo incident but denied involvement. He certainly hadn't run from the Fairfaxes or anyone else, and had never lain behind a little house, as the Pinkerton guard had testified. "I am not calling the man a liar," he said. "I am suggesting that he is inaccurate in what he thinks that he saw."

He testified that he was in contact with his mother every hour or two each day. Sometimes she handled his real estate calls. They both loved Spokane, and the publicity about the South Hill rapist troubled them. They decided to go out and look for clues together.

After lunch Brockett asked point-blank, "Mr. Coe, isn't it a fact that you have rehearsed your testimony for this trial?"

"It's *not* a fact."

"Well, didn't you give extensive press interviews to the television stations here in Spokane, which has been playing during this trial?"

Coe's lips almost touched the microphone. "Well, I gave an interview to one television station, but I don't see that as a rehearsal for this testimony."

"Isn't it a fact that your testimony here in court has followed almost exactly what you said in that interview?"

"... Well, I would hope so. You know, everything I have said has been consistent from the moment of my arrest until now. And so I would assume that the television interview would follow what I have said here, yes."

"And you have talked to one of the reporters in particular for the Spokane daily *Chronicle,* your father's newspaper, by the name of Peck?"

A guffaw came from the back row. Everyone turned and stared at Ruth Coe. She made no effort to conceal her merriment. After a silence the witness corrected the prosecutor's error: "Mr. Peck is with the *Spokesman-Review,* the other paper."

"Okay, the *Review....* Isn't it true that you told him, 'Having spent eleven years in the media, I know what is appropriate to say and what isn't?'"

"... I was not afraid to talk to the media, and everything I said from March 10 on was consistent with every person I had ever talked to.... And I was simply referring to the fact that years and years of being in the media—that I felt that I could handle the situation."

"And you feel that your years in the media would help you to handle *this* situation, too, Mr. Coe?"

"Not particularly," he answered slowly, "because you are just asking the questions. I am just responding....I am not in control of the situation. *You* are." He flicked another glance at his parents.

The prosecutor asked if he had written a letter to Gini Perham's brother Guy suggesting that she not testify against him. "That is not a part of the letter at all," Coe answered, showing a trace of annoyance. He stabbed his pen at the air and said, "There is nothing in there in reference to Gini's testimony one way or the other. I wrote a letter to Guy Perham saying I wanted at least one member of his family to know the truth...."

Brockett read a paragraph from the letter: "I counted heavily on Gini's moral support and her testimony, which would corroborate my whereabouts at the times of the rapes I was falsely accused of having committed."

"Right!" Coe commented. "... I'm referring to the fact that when I was informed, while in jail... that she would be a prosecution witness—and what I'm saying in that paragraph you are referring to is that I was shocked and surprised by that because I had counted heavily on Gini being in my camp and speaking only to the truth as she knew it, which would corroborate my whereabouts as I indicated."

"At the time of the rapes?" Brockett asked.

"Well, because she knew what my basic daily regimen was, yes."

"But Mr. Coe, haven't you told us that she can't corroborate your actions at the times of the rapes because you were with your parents?"

"Yes. But I didn't mean she could specifically, you know, know where I was." The judge reached around and touched the dials on the audio system. "But she knew that I was out jogging, and that I was doing such and such, and she knew that I spent a lot of time with my parents...."

"Even though because it was none of her business, you often misled her as to what in fact you were doing?"

"Well, I didn't really mislead her; I just didn't tell her everything."

"In fact, you told her you were jogging when in fact you were eating with your parents, didn't you?"

"Well, as I said before, if I told her I was going jogging, I probably jogged and did other things, too."

Brockett looked down at his notes, then asked, "Mr. Coe, have you ever been convicted of a crime?"

After long haggling between lawyers, the witness answered, "Of a misdemeanor, yes."

"What was it?"

"Third-degree theft."

"What did it involve?"

Coe rolled his eyes. "What did it involve? It would be a very, *very* long story."

"What did you steal?"

"I didn't steal anything!"

Gigler's request for a recess was denied by the judge. "What were you convicted of stealing?" Brockett demanded.

"Well, Mr. Brockett, this would involve a tremendously long discussion. If you want to get into it, that's fine."

"What particular items were you convicted of stealing?"

"Well, I didn't steal it."

Brockett ran his fingers through his hair. *"What were you convicted of stealing?"*

Coe said, "A steak."

Brockett nodded. "In connection with the steak, did you write a letter to Judge Murphy—"

"I certainly did."

After another Gigler objection the prosecutor asked, "Mr. Coe, in that letter to Judge Murphy didn't you also indicate that because of your unfamiliarity with courtroom procedure, you were immediately thrown out of your game plan?"

"Yeah. By that I meant I had assumed, never having been in court before, at that point in *any* kind of court, district court or anything, that, you know, my knowledge of the courtroom at that time was 'Perry Mason.' I couldn't afford an attorney, so I thought I will be my own attorney, and I thought that would go smoothly, and I thought you were allowed an opening statement. I had the opening statement fairly laid out in my mind as to what I was going to say. And then Judge Murphy threw me kind of a curve because apparently in district court that's not the way things go. At least it didn't in his court that day. And that being the case, it kind of made everything difficult from there on out. . . ."

"Has *this* case been going according to your game plan?"

"I have had no game plan at all in this case. . . ."

"In your letter is it true that you said that your voice was its usual deep, clear and resonant broadcaster's voice, but 'by the time I was able to question the prosecutor's first witness, my clear voice had become tight with anger, and it was breaking badly'?"

"That's a true statement and gets into the matter of voice that I was hoping would be brought up at some point anyway. That relates to the allergy situation, and relates to the lineup situations. My voice was not itself."

"Your voice hadn't had any difficulty as your testimony has gone along here?"

"My voice is not like the deep, clear, resonant, clear voice I am referring to in that paper. I am off the diet, and have been for a considerable length of time, but at the time of the appearance in Judge Murphy's court, on a misdemeanor charge, I was on the diet. The voice was at its full strength, and so forth. But the point I was trying to make to him, the whole thing was such a flustering situation then, then the nerves activate allergies, so experts think that allergies are about forty percent nerves, and my way and my reaction to a nervous situation is the voice going much higher, and so forth."

"But you haven't had that nervous reaction here in testifying?"

"Not particularly."

Brockett noted that the letter to Judge Murphy mentioned Coe's spending $125 a week in Rosauer's, and asked, "You weren't having any difficulty with money then, were you, Mr. Coe?"

"As I say, my food money was primarily borrowed from my parents."

"...You say that yours was a political trial and had nothing whatsoever to do with the actual shoplifting?"

"...If I used the word 'political,' what I meant to say is that there was more to that situation than met the eye."

"...Do you think *this* is a political trial, Mr. Coe?"

"I think this is a much more political trial than that was, for sure."

"Because the police are out to get you?"

"No. I don't think the police were out to get me specifically. I think the police were out to get *somebody*."

"That's what makes it a political trial?"

"I think the police hostilities to the media and the fact that I am related to the media, and I gave them an excellent opportunity to be under suspicion, I think in that sense it's a political question."

"So they could get back at your father and your father's newspaper for criticizing them for not catching the rapist?... But it had to be somebody who looked like you so that he could be identified in court, and somebody that has a father who is involved in the media, is that correct?"

"No....What I've said is, by my own stupidity, similar to the Rosauer's case, I put myself in a position where they could arrest somebody connected with the media, and I am sure the police were salivating over it."

Once again Brockett quoted from the letter to Judge Murphy: "'I am an extremely busy man....I work between seventy and one hundred hours a week. Considering the kind of money I am able to make, seventy-two hours of community service represents a great deal of money loss, money I would otherwise have made.'" The prosecutor asked, "Haven't you just told the members of this jury that you weren't making any money during that period of time?"

"I didn't say I wasn't making any money. But the thing is that obviously a real estate agent is capable in any one period of time of making great money, and I was simply expressing my outrage with the fact that that was the case...."

Brockett read more: "'And my girlfriend, a very classy young lady with the utmost in integrity, was absolutely devastated that the judge would call her a liar.'"

"She was!" Coe interjected.

Gigler called out, "I would like to object. May we approach the bench?"

"Overruled," the judge said, "and you may not approach the bench."

Brockett said, "So you thought that your girlfriend, Virginia Perham, was a person with the utmost integrity?"

"Yes. As I said this morning, I wasn't saying that being a liar was necessarily a part of her personality. I said mood swings was...."

"...But she doesn't have the utmost integrity when she is not in your camp?"

"Well, I don't think she has been of the utmost integrity in this case, no...."

Brockett turned toward the defense table and said, "That is all I have. You may inquire."

Gigler stood directly in front of Coe. In a soft voice, he asked, "During this period of time, what was your approach to your real estate business?"

The answer took seven minutes; it was as though Coe were relieved to be talking to his own counsel. He explained that he'd never really been interested in earning money as a realtor. His first interest had been as an investor and later as a potential broker. "So mainly it was a question of what I could learn more than how much money I could make." At the same time he'd been running his demographics business, he said, and keeping busy with his non-profit work at Spokane Metro Growth.

After a while Gigler picked up Exhibit 8, Gini Perham's red jacket, and asked Coe to try it on for the jury. He wriggled into the jacket and held up his arms to show that the sleeves were too short. Later he began another long explanation—the origin and need for Spokane Metro Growth. Gigler concluded his redirect examination by asking for special permission to introduce a piece of evidence that he had intended to introduce earlier. It was the phone bill referred to in Gordon Coe's testimony—the document that "proved" Fred Coe and his mother were in Seattle at the time of the Lois Higgins rape in 1978. There was no objection.

The state's rebuttal witnesses were brief. A gas-station employee testified that he had seen a dildo under the seat of Coe's car and that it was nine to fifteen inches long. Roy Allen disputed Coe's claims about where he jogged and when. Clerks from Washington Water Power testified that Coe had never used the drop slot on Upriver Drive. Greg Stirns, Coe's former boss at Main Realtors, told about finding a Xerox copy of a dildo in the office trash. Roger Crane said that he had seen Coe wearing a trenchcoat and black gloves. An auto repairman testified that he had seen Coe wearing gloves and once had found two pairs in his Pontiac Grand Prix.

The only high drama in the rebuttal stage of the trial came during the testimony of Irene Pool's husband. Fred Pool looked and walked like a retired welterweight boxer, and as he turned from the oath-taking and arranged himself in the witness box, his eyes locked on Coe's. Throughout his short testimony his gaze never varied. He testified that he and his wife had resumed jogging some weeks after the rape. He said he accompanied Irene to Hart Field "every time." He was asked if they had ever seen Coe while they were running. "No!" the witness snapped.

"You are looking at him now in court?"

"Yes!"

"You never saw that individual there?"

"No!"

Pool continued to stare at the accused rapist as he left the witness stand, and after he had passed beyond Fred Coe he glared at Gordon Coe till he was led from the courtroom.

By the time of Brockett's final remarks to the jury, he'd had a chance to study the Coe family phone receipts belatedly introduced by the defense. Gordon Coe had testified four days earlier that his son couldn't have raped Lois Higgins, because he'd been in Seattle with his mother and the phone records proved it. The receipts seemed to tell a different story, and Brockett saved it for his clincher. "Take a look," he told the jury. "Mr. Gordon Coe said 'I couldn't leave, my family went over, and I called every day. And I ran up one heck of a telephone bill.' The rape was on April 25 going over into April 26—because of the midnight on or about April 26. And, 'they weren't here, they were in Seattle.'"

Brockett waved the receipts. "No telephone call on April 25," he said, pausing for emphasis. "No telephone call on April 26." After another dramatic pause he said, "Telephone calls on April 27! Discounted, class of call 'R.' 'R': *evening.* . . . Mr. Coe was telling the truth! He called every day. He called on Thursday evening. *The rape was on Wednesday night, early Thursday morning!* When they got there, they told him. 'Did you make it all right?' Talked to him for eight dollars and forty-eight cents' worth of time. Then he called them on April 28, and he called them on April 29. . . . *No* calls between April 22 and April 27! There is the evidence. The state has proven to you beyond a reasonable doubt that Frederick Harlan Coe raped six women, and he should be found guilty of all six. Thank you."

108

For ten days and nights the men and women of the jury—three Boeing Co. employees, two clerks, a municipal employee, a kindergarten teacher, a secretary, a medical technologist, a banker, a custodian and a clothing store manager—had lived a life best described by the title of one of the few movies they'd been permitted to watch on TV: *Motel Hell*. Sequestered, they'd been denied most TV and all radio, phone calls and theaters. They were forbidden any sightseeing except an occasional trip with a bailiff. They could talk only among themselves, but not about the subject uppermost in their minds. The big diversions of their days were breakfast, lunch and dinner, with gourmandism discouraged by the court's limit of $3.50 for breakfast, $4.50 for lunch and $7.50 for dinner.

Now the jurors had the case at last, and one of them, an engineer, seemed eager to catch the next plane home to Seattle. He opened the proceedings by proclaiming, "He's guilty of all six! I know it! I just know it! *And I'm not bending!*"

David Barkman, a twenty-five-year-old clothing store manager with a wife and newborn daughter, laughed to himself when he was elected jury foreman. Back in Seattle he'd put up a fight to be excused because of business and personal pressures. Twice Judge Shields had turned him down. As he passed out ballots for the first vote, the young juror was convinced that Coe was guilty on all six counts, but—beyond a reasonable doubt? He wasn't so sure about that. Later he described his thinking:

"By the time the victims had finished testifying, I was wide open to the defense. I'd watched Fred Coe in the courtroom and perceived him as a well-educated, super-fantastic guy. As far as I was concerned, the gentleman was innocent. I couldn't believe a fellow who looked like he did, talked like he did and came from the background he had could be guilty of rape.

"I also felt sorry for Gini Perham. That question about lesbian experiences made me think of the *National Enquirer*. She was put on the spot so many times in her testimony. But nobody except a professional actor could have faked being as nervous and upset as she was. She was choked up, blown away by the questions—telling the whole world about their intimate sex lives, things that are nobody's business. She was believable.

"As soon as the defense began, it was obvious that something was fishy. At first I felt that the father was using his background as an editor and intelligence officer to control the situation. When he began to testify I said to myself, 'They've *practiced* this testimony!' It was too well rehearsed. I mean, all folks believe in their children, but the Coes tried to say that Fred couldn't do *anything* wrong—he was a saint. And I know better than that about people.

"It wasn't enough that they could remember the year and the month that something happened; they could also remember the exact date and the time, and what they'd been doing at that exact time, and what the weather was like. It was all so unreal. Nobody has a memory like that, let alone a whole family. It was too elaborate. If they'd just testified normally—admitting that they couldn't remember everything—Fred would have done better.

"The evidence was foggy on both sides, so I ended up putting a lot of weight on the character of the witnesses. It became a question of who to believe and who to doubt, and I ended up feeling quite comfortable about it. That's how I make my living—judging people. I was impressed by Kathleen Coe. A lovely gal. She came across as the most genuine of the Coes. My first impression of the mother was that she was a little dingy. She was the most obvious about editorializing. She damaged her son more than anybody. She was much less believable than Fred because she's less conniving than he is. Or less skilled at it.

"And he didn't help his own cause as much as he could have. He kept trying to tell us he was lily white. But nobody is lily white. My own mother isn't. He could have been almost believable if he hadn't taken the stand after his parents, with all their editorializing and implausibilities. He carried himself in such a way that if you knew nothing else about the case, you could believe him. He is *good* at manipulating people, so skilled at his pervertedness, his lying. But in the end it was all clear. I've never met any situation in real life that was as absolute as his guilt."

On the first ballot most jurors voted for conviction on all counts. The dissenters insisted there was reasonable doubt on counts 1 and 4. Count 1, the Lois Higgins case, was over three years old, and defense testimony had contradicted the victim's somewhat hysterical account. Count 4 involved a fourteen-year-old victim's identification of Coe by voice alone.

Since most of the jurors understood rape to be an act of sexual hunger and lust, there were also a few doubts about why such a handsome man would need to commit the crime in the first place. A Boeing employee confessed, "Right from the beginning I questioned why he was guilty at all. He had a great availability of sex. Why would he resort to this type of thing? But the defense was so weak. There really wasn't any. The Coes seemed to be saying, 'We're the Coes, and you can't touch us.'"

For almost an hour the jurors rehashed the defendant's own testimony and found it wanting. A female juror said she was reminded of a child caught with ice cream on his face. "His mom says, 'I told you you couldn't have any ice cream.' 'No, you didn't, Mom,' the kid says. 'You told me I couldn't have a *bowl* of ice cream. This is a cup.'" The consensus was that Coe had harmed his own cause by rambling and rationalizing and splitting hairs. One juror said he wondered why it was so hard for him to say a simple yes or no.

Before long, they agreed unanimously that there was a reasonable doubt in the Stephanie Gibbs case. For a few hours they stood at eleven to one for acquittal on Lois Higgins. The holdout was the engineer who'd announced at the outset that he wouldn't bend; he had bent in the Gibbs case but not on the other. The balky juror kept citing evidence and testimony that didn't match the memories of the others. "Don't you see," foreman Barkman said patiently, "if the rest of us don't remember that testimony the way you do—can't you see that alone shows reasonable doubt?" After five hours and fifteen minutes, the unbender bent. Count 1 was the last to be decided.

It took fifty-five minutes to assemble the interested parties and set up security. Extensive plans had been made to protect the defendant and the jury. A platoon of armed deputies patrolled the corridors and the stairways. Three deputies and three extra bailiffs took up positions in the courtroom along with two plainclothesmen. All had been briefed: If Coe were to be acquitted on every count, he would be rushed back to jail for his own protection and the jury would be driven to the motel in a bulletproof van, then flown out of town on the first available plane.

The proceedings were broadcast and televised and began at nine minutes after midnight. Jury foreman Barkman watched Coe as the judge read the slips one by one. "I thought he might finally show some emotion," Barkman said later. "But his face was the same old mask. His father kept shaking his head as though he couldn't believe it. Mrs. Coe and Kathleen hugged each other and cried. But Fred—*nothing*."

After the verdicts were read Donald Brockett handed the judge a prepared order. The prosecutor had a reputation for cockiness, but now he just looked tired. "The court is signing an order jailing the defendant," Judge Shields announced. Four armed deputies entered like centurions through the main entrance and stood in a semicircle behind the convicted man. Coe was hand-cuffed and taken to jail.

The remaining three family members seemed dazed as they stood in the well of the courtroom talking with their lawyers. "We've come to expect the worst," Gordon Coe commented to a reporter. The editor's face was pale, and every once in a while he shut his eyes and pursed his lips like someone who has just witnessed a bad accident. When his daughter started to cry, he said, *sotto voce*, "She's not used to how rotten the world is yet."

A photographer worked in close, and Kathleen Coe asked in an annoyed voice, "Do you have enough?"

Ruth Coe turned and managed a smile. "You know," said the former charm teacher, "you shouldn't take pictures of people when they're down, because people look so much nicer when they're up." The photographer focused for another shot. "We're down," said the woman in the glossy black wig, "but not out."

Waiting for the verdict, Gini Perham had taken refuge in an empty office. A deputy stuck his head in and told her Coe had been found guilty on four counts. She was pleased but couldn't stop crying.

Lois Higgins and her husband Bill had waited up to watch the proceedings on TV. The pregnant woman sat on the bed eating a peanut butter and jelly sandwich. "Hey, it's starting!" she called out, but Bill was asleep. When she heard the finding in her case, she cried out, "No! *No!* He's guilty! I'm positive he's guilty!"

She cried as she grabbed the scrapbook she'd been keeping about the case and tore it up. She didn't hear the other five decisions. She threw the remains of the scrapbook in the garbage can and crawled back to bed.

Columnist Chris Peck quoted Ruth Coe: "They have taken a fine, clean, up-standing young man and ruined him." Mrs. Coe said she had expected justice until she'd begun to notice that Judge Shields was regularly denying defense requests. "From hindsight, in retrospect, I would never try to play fair again," said the upset mother. "Because the law doesn't play fair. I'm telling you, from what I know now, I should have told my son to run. I should have got in my car and driven him over the border." She insisted, "I'm not an overbearing mother. Fred and I have a very normal relationship. And my son has never put me in a position where I had to lie for him. Do you think mothers think their sons are Mr. Perfect? They don't. A mother looks at a son with a very realistic eye."

She said that the matter of guilt had been "the first question" they'd asked themselves the night of the arrest. After Fred had insisted he was innocent, she said, "From the time I would get up in the morning until I went to bed at night, his defense was my life." She regretted that her love for Spokane "will never be the same. For a long time I didn't understand how people in this world could not go out and lend a helping hand. Now I do. My family offered a helping hand and has been slapped in the face." The proud woman didn't want any of her fellow Spokanites to view her as crestfallen or defeated. That frame of mind had never been characteristic of the Coes. "Tell them," she said, "they are not going to run me out of this town."

109

Roy Allen wasn't surprised to hear from a jailer that F. H. "Kevin" Coe had asked for an off-record chat. He'd noticed the same phenomenon with other criminals—they often felt a rapport with those who had brought them to justice and enjoyed rehashing their cases. The tall, curly-haired detective was always willing to listen. In many ways Coe was still an enigma to him and his fellow officers, and probably always would be. "I'll talk to you as long as you want, Kevin," the detective said after they'd exchanged greetings, "but on one condition—don't tell me that you're not the raper because I *know* you are. If you're not the raper, I would quit my job this minute. That's how much I believe you're guilty."

Deputies escorted the prisoner down to police headquarters from the maximum security wing of the second-floor jail. Except for his clothing Coe appeared unchanged. His hair looked as though it had just been washed, combed and blown. His eyes were clear and bright—he didn't look as though he was having trouble sleeping. The word from upstairs was that his mood had been good at the beginning of the trial, sagged a little toward the end, and now was elevated again. Allen was glad to see him adjusting well. "I'll talk to you as long as you want, Kevin," the detective said after they'd exchanged greetings, "but on one condition—don't tell me that you're not the raper because I *know* you are. If you're not the raper, I would quit my job this minute. That's how much I believe you're guilty."

"All right," Coe said pleasantly. "I won't. But I do want you to consider the possibility that I was down there running a lap."

Allen thought, My God, not *that* again! Coe was referring to the predawn before his arrest, when his car had been spotted near the Ferris High School athletic field and Allen himself had stumbled through a tangle of construction material trying to catch up. The detective's own suspicion at the time, shared by his colleagues, was that Coe had been out peeping.

"Kevin," he said, "there is no way. In the first place, I was standing right there. You're not gonna park as far from the entrance as you parked and then come back and run one lap through all that junk. I could barely *walk* through it in the darkness."

Coe said, "I don't know why you insist on considering me the rapist." A touch of petulance had crept into his voice. "I don't know why you can't at least entertain the idea that it was somebody else."

Allen was puzzled—not by Coe's words but by his personality. What kind of stubbornness could account for a denial of such obvious guilt? An impartial jury had convicted him, and the police department was preparing a lengthy presentencing report that implicated him in dozens of other incidents—peeping, indecent exposure, obscene phone calls, indecent liberties, child molestation and more rapes and attempts. He was the undisputed all-time champion of Spokane sex offenders, and here he sat acting as though his guilt were still a matter of opinion.

"Okay," Allen said. "Let's take your car. It was seen by the school groundskeeper and three or four other people. Yet you keep denying it was yours. Who else has got a car like that?"

Coe started to answer, but Allen said, "Please! Let me finish; then you can talk all you want. You're driving a silver-over-black Citation with a factory sunroof and a little magnetic turtle on the side, right? That's exactly what they saw. How many cars like that do you think are driving around Spokane? Your real estate books and your jacket were on the seat, and the yellow plastic was over the license. The car was parked at the Hart Field rape; it was seen at another rape, and it was even seen by our decoys a year ago. It adds up. That was the car, Kevin, and *you* were the driver."

"You might be convinced," Coe said, "but has it ever occurred to you— I've researched this, and there were thousands of silver cars sold in Spokane in the last few years. *Thousands*! Silver's the most popular color, and..." He was off on one of his patented rambles, and Allen sat back and tried to pay attention to a line of irrelevancy he'd heard before. Coe kept acting as though it were crucial that the detective believe in his innocence. Allen thought, I wonder why it's so important to him. Me of all people! The last guy he'll ever convince! What makes him act like this?

When Coe paused, Allen smiled and said, "Kevin, I think I know you by now. If we caught you raping and took your picture, you'd have an alibi. You'd claim she was an old girlfriend—it was her idea. If she said different, you'd call her a liar. Then you'd run around trying to find somebody to back you up and you'd send us a twenty-page letter proving your innocence."

Coe managed a weak smile. "You're blowing this out of proportion," he said. "Let me tell you something else you don't know about silver cars..."

Thirty minutes of the requested "chat" had passed, and Coe was still on the subject of cars. Allen thought, Why doesn't he talk about all those women that identified him? And the way the blood types matched, and the oven mitts, and the hair sample we found that matched his, and the other evidence? Why does he always ignore facts? "Kevin," he said when it appeared that Coe was winding down, "someday when you want to admit what you did, I'd like to sit with you and go over this case. Even if I'm retired. Promise me you'll look me up and do it?"

Allen was surprised at the answer. "Okay," Coe said with a sigh. "I will."

110

I disagree with the United States Supreme Court that the death penalty cannot be applied for the crime of rape. I know some women, women in my own family, who feel that to be raped would be a death sentence for <u>them</u>, that after that they would be dead as women.—Donald C. Brockett in *The American Lawyer*, December, 1982

Fred Coe faced sentences of twenty years to life on each count. With four maximums he would be imprisoned one year less than a half century before becoming eligible for parole. At the other extreme, he could be a free man after serving three years. Still another possibility came up at a hearing a week after the trial.

By this time an old Coe family retainer had come on the scene: Carl Maxey, a fifty-six-year-old lawyer with a broad café-au-lait face and a leonine mane of fluffy white hair. Always controversial, he had built a flourishing practice specializing in divorce cases. Although resented by many local lawyers for a tendency, as one observer put it, "to keep throwing his blackness up to the court for special treatment," the talented Maxey was considered by other Spokanites as an earthly version of St. Jude, the patron saint of impossible causes. The Coe family handed him one: keeping Fred from the penitentiary.

At the first sentencing hearing Judge Shields informed both sides that police had given him a thick packet of information about Coe. The judge's next words were often quoted and misquoted later:

> The Court is also mindful of the fact that had a petition for sexual psychopathy proceedings been filed by the State in the beginning in this case, there would have been an option for treatment, but that petition was not filed, and I can at this point see why it was not because two determinations would have to be made in that case in any event. One would be that the defendant was a sexual psychopath on the one hand, and secondly that he was amenable to treatment.
>
> The defendant's testimony at the trial, and in the presentation of his defense, being a total, flat-out denial of the situation, would indicate that there would be no question that he would not be ame-

nable to treatment, at least in that context. That, nevertheless, is a matter that should be properly addressed by defense counsel in consultation with their client, as it may affect the possibilities of recommendations made by the Court to the Parole Board with respect to the sentencing.

Maxey took the words as an invitation and went to work offstage. He had no dearth of advice; the subject of Fred Coe's future was on every Spokanite's lips. The majority wanted his head; the South Hill rapist had held the Lilac City under siege for far too long, and it was retribution time. A journalist with a reputation for moderation confided, "As a citizen, as a husband, as a father, I'm terrified at the prospect that Fred Coe will be turned loose. I don't think he ever should be."

A few cynics predicted that the managing editor's son would get off lightly, that already the court was scratching around for an excuse to keep from sending him to the penitentiary. The more widespread opinion was that Coe would pay a higher price than if he'd been a nobody. It was said that Judge Shields was plugged into Spokane's moralistic power structure. Besides, he had to run for office, and a judge who didn't throw the book at the South Hill rapist would soon be back in private practice. A letter to the *Spokesman-Review* read:

> As he so aptly demonstrated in court, Mr. Coe is no ordinary criminal. He is, among other things, a pathological liar and a consummate actor whose quickness of mind cannot be disputed. Like most psychopaths... he has spent his entire lifetime outwitting others and his bag of tricks is far from exhausted. We, his potential victims, have reason to worry now that Mr. Coe will be clever enough in the end to outwit even the most intelligent members of our community, persuading them to believe that he is reformable and safe to be at large. It is our fervent hope that Judge Shields will take this into account....

At the final sentencing hearing Donald Brockett reminded the judge that the harshest possible sentence was *not* four consecutive life sentences, as commonly believed. He turned toward Coe and said, "We still have a statute that specifically allows for the castration of the defendant." He quoted Irene Pool's cry as she was being raped—"Damn you! Damn you!"—as though that too might be a reasonable sentence, if available. In the end the prosecutor settled on a more practical demand: life imprisonment on each count. Since Coe had picked his victims one by one, he urged that the sentences run consecutively.

Carl Maxey, a tall man with an ex-athlete's economy of movement, rose for the defense while Coe's two public defenders watched silently, reduced to bit parts. Maxey surprised spectators by calling a witness, Dr. Robert A. Wetzler, an elder statesman of Northwest psychiatry who had helped set up sexual-psychopathy programs. After Coe waived his doctor-patient privilege, Wetzler testified that he had examined the convicted man three times: once back in May for the defender's office and twice recently. Maxey asked him what he had found out.

"First, that he was a psychopath," the doctor answered, "and second, he does come under the heading of a sexual psychopath."

Reporters realized why Coe had withdrawn his permission to allow himself to be photographed. The man who had just been branded a psychopath by his own expert witness sat tight-lipped at the defense table, hands clasped. For the first time since the legal proceedings had begun weeks before, no gold pen protruded from his fingers. Maxey strode back and forth in front of the distinguished witness and asked, "Did the interview include any statement by Mr. Coe with regards to any offense?"

"Yes, sir."

"And what was said with regard to the counts by way of admission or denial?"

"Admission of Count Number Six, sir."

Coe had confessed to the rape of Jeanie Mays! Radio reporters ran from the courtroom, missing the rest of Dr. Wetzler's direct testimony: that the patient had been cooperative and open about his sexual problems and that he was amenable to treatment in the psychopathy program.

Brockett's cross-examination consisted of a single question: "Dr. Wetzler, isn't one of the signs of a psychopath the fact that he or she is manipulative of others?"

"Correct, sir."

Maxey fired follow-up questions. "I asked you if you were satisfied with the candor of Mr. Coe to you. Were you?"

"Yes, sir," the psychiatrist answered.

"And you have been a doctor for a long time, right?"

"Yes, sir."

"And you have no interest in the outcome of this case, do you?"

"No, sir."

"And were you satisfied that he was not being manipulative with you in talking to you?"

"Yes, sir, I was. He was not being manipulative."

"Are you satisfied, sir, that perhaps in a studied environment of a hospital situation, Mr. Coe can discuss his background and circumstances even more fully?"

"That would be very much a part of the program and a very serious part of the program, that he open up fully and discuss in detail his life, his lifestyle, and his behavior patterns. And this does happen in the treatment program. That is the way it works."

"Are admissions difficult to be made by a person in Mr. Coe's present frame of mind?"

"Extremely difficult. Denials of rationality are a part of his personality."

In an emotional appeal to the judge, Maxey summoned up Clarence Darrow, Abraham Lincoln and Frederick Douglass. He threw in a typical ethnic reference: "It's particularly not hard for me to talk about safety and sanctity, because this rape law has been used against blacks so indifferently, so unjustly, that the Supreme Court itself had to stop the carnage." He reminded the court that just two months earlier an innocent man had been sentenced to prison for rape in Seattle. He asked for compassion for the Coe family: "Somewhere along these lines it was portrayed that the Coe family was something that they weren't. A harder, more industrious family personally I have never known. I can see the effect on Gordon's face from the travail of this situation. You can see the retirement that obviously was built towards, and that will be expected to be lived with concern."

He flicked a glance toward Brockett and said, "Nobody has to be reminded, in order to find just treatment, that somebody can be castrated." He submitted affidavits from former prisoners and public officials attesting to what would await Coe at Walla Walla. Rapists came right after informers and child molesters on prison hit lists. Maxey insisted that his client deserved better, that he had "lived for an awful long period of his life with no difficulty." He asked for a sentence that would give Coe a chance at rehabilitation and treatment. "That's the best protection. That's the tribute to the women that you want to give security to." The whole affair, the defense lawyer said in sorrowful tones, had been "a litany of tragedies."

Roger Gigler, looking more wan than at the trial three weeks before, joined in the plea for hospitalization. "I did not know Fred's family prior to this case," he said, "but I have learned to know them. . . . They are fine people, intelligent people, and Fred is an intelligent person—an intelligent person that has now, through the testimony of Dr. Wetzler, admitted that he needs help and wants help."

Sentencing time had arrived. Judge Shields started slowly. A national Episcopal leader, he pointed out that true guilt was "a matter for the judgment of God." He noted that there were two additional victims in the case: "his mother and his father." He mentioned for the second time that the prosecutor had failed to petition the court to send Coe to the hospital, and added, "The sexual-psychopathy statute is generally against a background of a plea bargain in which the defendant enters a plea of guilty." He observed that he was without discretion in the matter. Defense attorneys exchanged glances.

Video cameras began to whir as the lanky judge described rapists and psychopaths as "manipulative personalities in a high level of denial . . . who rationalize their behavior. We know that rape is generally an act of aggression, a violence derived from the need to control other people, through which sexual arousal is enhanced by the abuse of women. We know . . . that rape is a learned behavior, and that it is frequently planned in great detail, that rapists tend to know or scout their victims, that rape is generally an escalation of some other sexually deviant behavior such as exposing, obscene phone calls, peeping and matters of that sort.

"Clinically," he went on, "it is also known of rapists that as their activities continue, so must their control, so that as the escalation of the offense occurs, so does the escalation of control, so that it will start off on a basis of surprise, control through surprise, and then go to intimidation, and then threat, and then physical injury, and eventually unintentional—and yet unfortunately in some cases, intentional—killing." He said, "About those factors, and about this case, I have worried, I have been very concerned, I have thought, I have read, I have researched, and I have prayed." He cleared his throat and said, "Mr. Coe, you may rise."

The convicted man had been sitting straight, expressionless as always, hands still clenched. He stood up as the gray-haired judge asked, "Is there any reason that the court should not proceed at this time to pronounce sentence upon you?"

"No," Coe answered.

"Mr. Coe, do you have anything that you wish to say to the court at this time on your own behalf?"

"No, Your Honor. I think Mr. Maxey and Mr. Gigler have spoken well." Gone was his "broadcast voice." Spectators had to strain to hear.

Judge Shields paused as though surprised. "You have nothing further that you wish to add at this point?"

"No."

There was a sepulchral silence in the courtroom as he read from notes. "It is the order, judgment and decree of the court that the defendant is hereby sentenced to a maximum term of imprisonment of not more than twenty years for Count Two... of not more than twenty-five years for Count Three... of not more than thirty years for Count Five...." He hesitated before the Jeanie Mays count, the rape which Coe had confessed, then said, "And—to life imprisonment for Count Six." The sentences were to be served consecutively.

Ruth Coe started to rise. Her daughter grabbed her shoulder and urged her down. Gordon Coe sagged in his seat. Maxey, Gigler and Twyford looked stunned. No one in the courtroom had ever heard of such a severe sentence in a rape case—life plus seventy-five years. Coe wouldn't be eligible for parole until well into the twenty-first century.

Spectators seemed pleased. "Terrific," said one. Another whispered to assistant prosecutor Patricia Thompson, "We're all very proud of the job you did." NOW's courtroom monitor murmured that the sentence was "precedent-setting." Fred Coe was fingerprinted at the clerk's desk and led from the courtroom by two uniformed deputies. Everyone could see that the defense was puzzled. Something had gone terribly awry.

Investigating reporters soon learned that Roger Gigler and Julie Twyford hadn't been happy about Maxey's entrance into the case. They felt that they'd given their client the best possible defense under the circumstances. The sudden hiring of Maxey had made it look as though the Coes felt otherwise. Nor had the two public defenders felt comfortable about bringing in a psychiatrist to jeopardize what they regarded as a strong appeal by testifying that Coe had confessed. In private discussions Kathleen Coe had tended to side with them. But Ruth and Gordon Coe were afraid of what might happen to their son in the state's penal system and opted for hospitalization.

The outspoken Maxey complained that the judge was the villain. He claimed that Shields had deceived him in court and in chambers by pointedly suggesting that Coe might be eligible for the psychopathy program if he showed contrition. "We accepted his full-blown invitation, and that invitation was never withdrawn," Maxey told a reporter. "I got to work on it right away and gave the judge what he asked for. And then he turns around and gives the longest sentence ever handed down in the state of Washington."

George Shields emphatically denied any backroom agreements and referred questioners to his previous remarks on the record. He said he presumed that Maxey had put Dr. Wetzler on the stand to show that Coe required psychiatric treatment *before* imprisonment, a recommendation incorporated into the sentence. The judge explained that the sequence of increasingly severe sentences "was reflective of the escalation factors in the course of a rapist's career." He viewed the second rape as more serious than the first, the third more serious than the second, etc. But all rapes, he said, were "serious."

Coe himself gave varying explanations of the endplay from time to time. He told *The American Lawyer*, "Behind the scenes, it was conveyed to me that the judge personally offered a lenient sentence if I would cop to one of the charges. So the decision was reached to take out an insurance policy and allow a psychiatrist to take the stand. I paid $1,000 to a doctor to take the stand and say things that were mainly news to me, to satisfy the judge's thirst. Then the judge turned around and said, 'Life.' It was a disaster."

In typically discursive manner he told a reporter from the *Seattle Times*, "It was simply the better part of valor in terms of I was facing four life terms, which would mean the possibility of fifty years in prison as the mandatory minimum versus the good sense of once you have these convictions and how do you handle 'em, which was to say, well, maybe it'd be better to go ahead and admit to one, which would make me perhaps eligible for Western State psychopathy program and be back out on the streets in maybe a couple, three years.... I think it was a mistake in terms of it didn't succeed.... As a strictly legal ploy it makes good sense, but it didn't work. The judge in fact tricked us." He spoke as one who well understood trickery and manipulation.

Later he wrote, "I paid Wetzler $1,000 to testify. I suppose he thinks he did his job; but, frankly, I was appalled by his testimony! So was my family— who consider him a senile old fool anyway! I am most certainly NOT psychopathic or psychotic or even neurotic! I am quite normal—sexually and in every other way!" Reporters who checked with the public defender's office found that neither Coe nor his family had paid the psychiatrist's witness fee. Like all Coe's legal expenses, it had been borne by the taxpayers.

The highly respected Dr. Wetzler, accustomed to the slings and arrows of analysands and patients after four decades of practice, remained aloof from the discussion. Asked if he stood by his testimony, he said calmly, "Of course."

Most of the victims seemed satisfied with the sentence. Sixteen-year-old Sue Ellen Wilber said, "I'm relieved. I had a big, huge sigh."

Marie Oldham said, "I'm really happy. I was edgy because I was afraid they would let him get away on that stupid sexual-psychopath thing.... I feel sorry for his father. And I really feel sorry for his mother because I think she really did feel he was not guilty. I commend her for defending her son the way she did. But—he's guilty."

At first Irene Pool said she was "elated" by the sentence, but withdrew the word because she felt it was wrong to feel elated about helping send someone to prison for life.

Jeanie Mays said she was only sorry that the sentence wouldn't bring back her disapproving boyfriend.

Prosecutor Brockett noted that the South Hill rapes had stopped after Coe's arrest. He maintained his cold-blooded reputation by saying, "I'm not sure castration would have been so inappropriate." A female caller on an open-line radio show said Coe should have been taken to a wooden shack, nailed to the wall by his testicles, and burned to death. In large part, she spoke for Spokane.

111

Jay Williams recognized the telephone voice immediately. He hadn't spoken to any of the Coes for three weeks, and he'd been wondering where he stood with them since backing out of Fred's defense. "Jason *dahling!*" Mrs. Coe said in her musical voice. "How *are* you?"

"I'm very fine, Mrs. Coe," he said. "How are *you?*" It seemed to him that every conversation with Fred's mother opened in the same ritualistic way.

"You know, Jason—Gordon and I will be leaving town soon. You may have heard that." He relaxed a little now that he knew what the call was about. On his early visits to jail, Fred had mentioned that his parents wanted him to handle the sale of their house.

"Yes, Mrs. Coe," he said. "I've heard that. And I'm sorry about it."

In a low purring voice she said, "Jay, I just wanted to get one thing settled in my mind. I just wanted to ask you"—she paused—*"how can you live with your conscience!"* She shrieked, *"You sent my son down the river! How could you—"*

"Mrs. Coe—"

"—turn on him like that?"

"Mrs. Coe, please! It's hard to understand you."

The tirade continued for several minutes. She kept asking if he thought Fred was guilty, but she wouldn't give him a chance to answer. "You were friends for twenty-five years! And now my son's gonna be spending time in a—in a—*penitentiary! And you could have saved him!* Why didn't you testify? *I want to know why you didn't testify!"*

Jay tried to recite the reasons, but he was rattled. He hadn't expected to be called upon to defend himself over the telephone. The main reason he had refused to testify was because he'd been convinced of Fred's guilt, but he couldn't say that; he didn't want to upset the distraught woman any further. If she had a mother's irrational need to believe in her son's innocence, that was fine with him. He felt very sorry for her.

"Mrs. Coe," he said, "if you want to know why I didn't testify, ask Fred." He thought of the affair of the dildo and wondered what Coe had told his parents about it. "He knows why I couldn't testify."

"No he *doesn't!*" the woman insisted. "We're *both* disgusted with you, Jay. We *don't* know why you didn't testify."

Jay was surprised. He and Fred had discussed the reasons in detail. Was his old friend turning on him for the first time? Lying about him? It seemed unfair. Fred was the convicted rapist, not Jay. "Oh, is that right?" he said, trying not to sound disturbed.

"Yes, that's *right!* You're a turncoat! You—you—what kind of Christian are you? I just hope you don't raise your children to be the hypocrite you are. That's exactly what you are, Jay! *A Goddamned hypocrite!*"

"Mrs. Coe, listen—"

"You and your phony religion!"

"Mrs. Coe, please—"

"I'll spread the word about you, Jay Williams!"

"Mrs. Coe—" There was a click in his ear.

Jay knew that his adherence to Christian principles was profoundly imperfect, and this was one of the moments that proved it. As Sue stepped into the room, he dialed the Coes' number. When the familiar "Hal-*lo*-oo!" came on the line, he launched into a tirade of his own: "Since you've opened the subject, Mrs. Coe, let me tell *you* something. I know your son better than you ever will! I know *so* much about him. And he's guilty, Mrs. Coe. He's so guilty it's pathetic! You and Mr. Coe must be the only people in town who don't know it. *And it's because you don't want to!* Your heads are in the sand! It should have been obvious to you a long time ago that something was wrong with Fred. Couldn't you see how crazy he was acting? The six months before his arrest, I thought he was about to have a nervous breakdown."

There was no reply, so he continued. "The main thing that stuns me is your total insensitivity. The women that Fred brutalized, the victims—*you have no concern for them!* You're only concerned about your son. Do you remember the time you told me that one of the witnesses was too crazy to be a cogent witness against Fred? She—"

"She *is!*" the angry voice interrupted. "She's *crazy!*"

"Remember the woman that you said was too ugly for Fred to rape?" Jay went on. "*Remember that?*"

Mrs. Coe said, "That woman *is* ugly. She is *far* too ugly for Son. He would *never* rape a woman like that!"

"Mrs. Coe—"

"You're so *naïve*, Jay! You don't know the first thing about rape. All these women running around saying they've been raped—it's not *that* traumatic." He remembered her saying the same words months before. What a wonder that her son's trial and conviction and the testimony of six pathetic victims hadn't taught her a thing about the nature of the crime he'd committed again and again—some forty times, police now claimed. "It's not *that* big a deal," she went on. "Read your Bible. It's there in your Bible."

Jay wasn't sure he'd heard right. "It's in—*my Bible?*"

"Yes. The Bible states that it's the role of women to be brutalized by men. *That's women's lot in life, Jay!* These women that got up on the witness stand—they're exaggerating, they're making a big deal out of *nothing!*"

"Rape isn't nothing," Jay insisted.

Her voice became shrill again. "Oh, you—you *hypocrite!* Do your friends know what a hypocrite you are? Maybe I should tell a few of them!"

Jay felt his wife reach over and touch his arm. "Mrs. Coe," he said, enunciating each word clearly, "if it ever gets back to me that you've said anything about me to anybody—if I hear *one* word that you've been slandering me or my family or my religion—*I'll have you and your son back on the front pages tomorrow!*" He hung up.

Sue asked, "Aren't you frightened of her?"

"I just hope I don't have to fight her off. I'd hate to have to hurt an old woman."

"Well, I'm worried about the kids." Sue sounded disturbed. "How do we know she's not gonna come over here and—?"

"She wouldn't." But he wasn't as convinced as he sounded. He remembered how Mrs. Coe had trashed Fred's cars, and some of her tirades about blacks and the Civil War and religion. He wondered if she'd turned psychotic, if Fred's tragedy had driven her over the edge. She'd always seemed a little irrational. For the moment he had to worry about his own wife. He put his arms around her and said, "She'd never do a thing like that." It was a long time before they calmed down.

112

In the weeks since the trial Gini Perham had wondered if it wouldn't be better if the earth just swallowed her up. It wasn't a suicidal feeling, just a feeling that her existence meant nothing, even to her. For five months before the trial she'd had something important to think about, something that gave meaning to her disrupted life. But after the conviction and the sentence her spirits sagged.

The folks at the mobile-home company waited till she had testified and then announced that they could no longer afford to pay her salary. She thought of returning to real estate, but the market was still depressed. Who would hire her? She was the girlfriend of the South Hill rapist. After thirty respectable years that was her identity. Thoughtless remarks drifted to her ears. "That Gini, she *must* have known." "How could any woman live with a rapist?" "What kind of a person—?" She put the talk down as ignorance, but it didn't improve her morale.

She read in the *Chronicle* that Kevin was being held in maximum security in the county-city jail. The deputies were afraid other inmates might attack him. She hoped not. She didn't miss him, but she felt compassion. She still avoided the few places they had gone: the St. Regis Cafe, Riverfront Park, the laundromat, two or three theaters. For the first time in her life she found herself crying often. She thought, Gordon and Ruth testified that I was a creature of moods, and now I am. When had fiction turned to fact?

She had nightmares about the two of them. She'd heard that they intended to leave Spokane. Their $98,000 house had been listed by Kevin months before his arrest. Thanks to creative financing, they had next to no equity to lose— "a couple hundred bucks," as he'd once told her. Dear God, she told herself, wouldn't it be great if they moved? I could stop looking behind me all the time.

On a warm Sunday a few weeks after the sentencing she made a snap decision. She packed her bags, kissed her brother and sister-in-law good-bye, grabbed the handful of fur known as Mr. Crumpett and headed east on I-90 in her Monte Carlo. It was an act of fear. The day before, she'd ventured downtown, hoping that no one would recognize her. She'd spotted a black-haired woman a half block away and mistaken her for Ruth Coe. She hadn't experienced such fright since the night at the lake when she'd heard footsteps coming up the path. She had to get away.

She drove nonstop across the Idaho panhandle, past familiar places like Coeur d'Alene, Cataldo, the doomed silver mines of Kellogg. As she crossed the Montana border at Lookout Pass, she realized that she'd been checking every car. Fear was spoiling her fun. Near Saltese she pulled to the shoulder of Rte. 10 and gentled herself down the way she'd once gentled horses. *You're safe now. There's no danger....*

By Missoula she realized that what she'd been seeking wasn't so much security as freedom to do what she wanted without worrying about what people would say, freedom to be anonymous, to laugh and run and do silly things with her dog. Out here in all this Montana space she was beginning to feel free again. As she sat at a drive-in watching a hot dog disappear into Mr. Crumpett, she laughed aloud. My God, she thought, was that frightened person *me?*

That night she stayed at a motel in Butte, "the richest hill on earth," and the next day drove straight through to Wyoming, stopping for the night at a place called Riverton that proudly billed itself as "Uranium Capital of Wyoming." The lilac capital of Washington seemed far away.

On the third day of her trip she turned south toward Denver, where she had friends. Just outside of Laramie, Wyoming, the sun sent orange fingers of light to the base of the clouds hanging over the Rockies. To the east a double rainbow arched over the plains. The sight made her gulp. After dark her car topped a low foothill and Denver appeared, the "mile-high city," its buildings aglow. On the car radio Christopher Cross was singing one of her favorite songs:

Sailing
Takes me away to where I'm going....

Mr. Crumpett caught her new mood and yipped as the moon came into sight atop a tall building. She took it as a sign. She was free of Spokane, free of the Coes, free of worry and fear and embarrassment. She had always believed in omens.

113

During our interviews [a psychopath] repeatedly expressed the strong
conviction that it would be shockingly inappropriate for him to be sent
to the state prison and forced to serve his term there. "Why, that place
is full of criminals, people hardened in crime," he said, as if in a
spectacular unawareness that he, himself, had committed more crimes
than most of the inmates now held there. "That's not the proper place
for me."—Hervey Cleckley, M.D., *The Mask of Sanity*

From the beginning of his incarceration in Spokane, Fred Coe had kept busy.
While others griped and served hard time, he wrote letters, read, and exercised
in his maximum-security cell. When a homosexual forger slipped him a copy
of *Penthouse* and asked how he felt about sex, he replied in a note that he
had experienced first-hand "virtually every sexual thing imaginable except
hard-core S&M and bisexuality." He said he'd been in the "group sex orgy
scene" and had done "three-way scenes both with a man, woman and two
women." He'd been a Las Vegas gigolo for two years, he wrote, catering
occasionally to men "if they were clean, attractive and rich." He signed off
with the disclaimer that he was neither a rapist nor a sex psycho.

He conversed with other prisoners but said nothing to compromise his
courtroom testimony. He said that his mother would do anything for him and
he felt the same about her. He mentioned breaking into a woman's apartment
in Browne's Addition years before and rubbing against her body; he explained
that he'd been drunk on liquor and allergy pills. He took part in the constant
jailhouse chatter about escape and said that he would go transsexual if he
could get away. In occasional playful moods he exchanged black humor about
the South Hill rapist. In a note to an inmate he printed, "SHR Sucks," "The
real SHR is a fucker," and "SHR for president." Another note bore the phrase:
"The real South Hill rapist is a dyke with a dildo."

As always he worked tirelessly on his public relations. He asked a fellow
inmate to "spread the good word about me... see what you can do for the Coe
image." He seemed upset that the other inmates didn't understand that he'd
been railroaded. He got word from the outside that one of his father's old
colleagues at the newspaper office had said, "That Coe kid is guilty as

hell.... Why, his parents have always had nothing but trouble with him!" With a stubby pencil, the only writing tool permitted inmates, he painstakingly printed a reply of over a thousand words, attacking the local press, claiming that he had been framed by the police and the prosecutor, and taking the journalist to task for jumping to conclusions. He wove in some autobiographical information about his school years: "I was socially and academically popular, active in sports and maintained slightly over a 3-point grade average. I was never arrested." In his familiar style he carefully buttered up the journalist, telling her what a "delightful lady" she was, how much he respected her work, how he'd always considered it "gospel, insightful of the Spokane scene." He said she should have checked with his parents before saying anything negative about "Gordie Coe's son."

On Thursday, October 29, three months after the conviction, the chief justice of the Washington State Supreme Court ruled in a cross-state telephone hearing that Coe would have to enter the state prison system. The prisoner was informed that night, and at 4:30 the next morning he was awakened in his cell and told to dress. On the way down a flight of concrete stairs, he slipped in his plastic jail-issue sandals and bumped his head against a wall. He insisted that he wasn't hurt, but a medical technician took his "vitals" at the direction of the shift supervisor. They were normal.

He showered and changed into sportcoat, slacks and a dress shirt open at the neck. In a sally port one floor below street level a sheriff's lieutenant and sergeant, both SWAT members, locked him into travel chains and put him in the back of an undercover car. The chains kept him from raising his hands higher than six or eight inches above his waist. En route to the Corrections Center at Shelton, "Christmas Tree Capital of the World," 330 miles west over the Cascades, the travel party stopped at a holding facility and picked up a convicted burglar. Coe tried to start a conversation, but the older man refused to respond. Just before they reached the diagnostic center at Shelton, Coe asked the other prisoner, "What's this place like?"

"Just like any other prison," the man said.

When Coe persisted, the burglar said out of the corner of his mouth, "You're gonna find out *exactly* what it's like."

Within thirty minutes of his noontime arrival, the new man was placed in protective custody, where he would spend twenty-three hours a day alone and one hour in closely guarded recreation. He had hardly arrived before the taunts began to echo along the tier. As the first days passed, he seemed to maintain the same aplomb that he had maintained during four months in jail in Spokane. He told an interviewer, "Prison life is probably greatly exaggerated as to the hardness of it and so forth.... The experience that I've had so far is one that is not an appreciably horrible lifestyle. I think probably certain aspects of military life are worse, as a matter of fact.... This is a sad comment, but I would expect the average prisoner lives a lifestyle that is appreciably better than twenty to twenty-five percent of the nation's population." He described himself as "pretty much an up person to begin with and pretty generally stay that way." He dismissed the harassment by his fellow prisoners as "pretty typical of prisons anyway. I mean, I'm not the only one who takes a lot of harassment in here."

After three weeks of medical, educational and psychological testing, Coe was assigned to "The Walls"—the last-stop penitentiary in the southeast Washington town of Walla Walla. The decision was a major setback for the Coes and their lawyers. Walla Walla housed hardened criminals, and a federal judge had ruled that any confinement in the overcrowded prison represented cruel and unusual punishment.

The state parole board met to set a minimum number of years on Coe's four sentences. The members considered Brockett's recommendation of forty-two years and Judge Shields's recommendation of thirty-four. They reviewed the case file and the psychological appraisals from Shelton and announced that the prisoner would have to serve seventy-five years. With a maximum of twenty-five years off for good behavior, he would be eligible for parole in the year 2031 at the age of eighty-four.

114

At 10:35 on the morning of Monday, November 2, an anonymous caller phoned the Spokane County prosecutor's office and spoke to L. C. "Bud" Kinnie, veteran chief criminal deputy prosecutor. After the conversation, Kinnie dashed off a memo:

> Received a call from our switchboard directed to me. The caller was male with clear voice, nothing distinctive except he used proper English. He refused to identify himself and stated that Mrs. Coe was contacting members of our underworld and trying to arrange a contract to have somebody killed. The caller did not know who but guessed it was Brockett or [Sheriff] Erickson. He would not meet with me or anyone else.
>
> I asked him how he knew this and he stated one of the parties contacted was a friend and told him. He wanted to know if we couldn't start watching her—I told him we didn't have the manpower to watch her 24 hours per day—he said he understood this. I gave him my home phone and he promised to call if he heard anything else.

Kinnie discussed the call with police and deputies, including Sheriff's Captain Edmond Braune, a friend of Gordon Coe. After their son's conviction the Coes had received a series of threatening calls, and the authorities suspected that the call to Kinnie might be an attempt to cause the family more pain. Braune agreed to phone Gordon and try to find out "who would be calling the prosecutor's office to say anything to direct heat or attention to the family," as he memo'd later. The sheriff's captain tried repeatedly but got no answer. A week and a half later, he was still trying, off and on, when suddenly he was instructed to stop. Confirmation had arrived. The anonymous tip had been substantiated.

That afternoon a lawyer named Thomas H. Brown had paid a call on the prosecutor's office and repeated information provided him by a former massage parlor operator named Violet Cooper. Ruth Coe and her elderly friend Rae Shepard had visited Cooper on a business matter a few months back, and in the course of the conversation Cooper had spoken jokingly about having to borrow Mafia money to pay her debts. Mrs. Coe took her aside, asked if she knew anybody in the Mafia and said she was in the market for a hit man. When Mrs. Coe said, "You know who I want hit, don't you?" Vi Cooper fobbed her off. Before Mrs. Coe left she called out, "Thank you, *thank you*! I know the Lord led me here to you today."

The former massage-parlor operator had sat on the information for a month before mentioning it to a family friend, Don Tuttle. It was Tuttle who had made the anonymous call to Kinnie on November 2. Attorney Brown said he heard full details from Cooper and believed her to be honest.

Gini Perham, back in Spokane after two months of R&R with old friends in Denver, picked up the phone at her brother Tom's house and heard a familiar voice ask for him. Gini asked, "Is this... Joan?"

A small female voice replied, "Gini?"

"Hi, Joan!"

"Oh, my God, Gini. Are you in town?"

"Yes! Why? What's wrong?"

Joan Schmick said that she had been calling to get Gini's number in Denver—"so I could tell you to stay there a while. Gini, something's, uh—happened." She had never heard the policewoman sound so flustered. "Something serious. Wait a minute. Gary wants to talk to you."

The deep voice of Sgt. Johnson boomed over the line. "Gini? Hey, we were worried about you." He told her that Ruth Coe was trying to hire a killer and that they were afraid she was the target.

Her old fear of Ruth Coe jumped into her throat. She slid a hand over her Adam's apple and asked, "What—what can I do?" Johnson told her to be watchful, to try to stay at home and to report anything suspicious.

Gini and her brother Tom and sister-in-law Cary piled cinderblocks against the inside of the back door and furniture against the front. Cary made plans to fly her newborn son Paul back to her parents in the East till the scare was over. Gini brooded about the problems she was bringing into the lives of innocent people. The nightmare would never end. She began to get angry. She thought, Who the hell is Ruth Coe to treat me like some kind of trash? My family goes farther back in Spokane than hers. She remembered her return home from Denver a few weeks ago. The need to get a good job and pay her bills had forced her back, not any romantic notions about home. But as she'd driven into town late at night, crossed the Spokane River and noticed how the graceful old place seemed to float on its own pink light, she'd realized that her roots went deeper than she'd imagined, despite the bad memories. Spokane *was* home to her, and she didn't intend to leave.

By the time Gary Johnson called back to say that her house was being placed under surveillance, along with the homes of Donald Brockett, Sheriff Erickson, Judge Shields and Deputy Prosecutor Pat Thompson, Gini was angry. "Listen, Gary," she said, "you can tell Ruth Coe that if Spokane belongs to anybody it belongs to me, not her. *They're not gonna run me out of my own town!*" That evening when she left the house on an errand, she found that an old habit had returned. She couldn't take her eyes off the rear-view mirror.

115

Lt. Lynn Howerton looked and acted like a typical old-fashioned harness bull even though he was in charge of ADVIN, the Spokane PD's spook unit. His heavy face, strong nose and bristly gray mustache were as identifying as a shield with a number. Gruff of voice, deliberate in his movements, he was built like an aging discus thrower, strong and densely bodied. His temporary partner, plainclothesman Richard Jennings, looked like anything but a cop. He wore a thick black beard, the better to be an undercover man behind. Wiry, loose-jointed, given to boots and T-shirts and jeans, he was as comfortable with banter as the lieutenant was taciturn. In a game of stud poker, Jennings would be the favorite. Howerton would be the beefy guy in shirt-sleeves serving the beer.

This unlikely pair took on the job of finding out if Ruth Coe was serious about hiring a hit man and, if so, whom she wanted hit. First they drove thirty miles north of Spokane to a small home on Eloika Lake and called on Violet Cooper, a petite forty-six-year-old woman with brownish-red hair, high cheekbones, sloped dark eyes and a voice of a thousand sorrows. At first, the woman was understandably defensive. Back when she'd run the Touch of Finland massage parlor and the Executive Sweet Sauna, cops meant trouble. Once they'd booked her into jail on a sodomy charge, later dismissed. But this time she'd promised to cooperate in the interests of saving a life, and she kept her promise faithfully, repeating her entire story.

A few hours after briefing the men from ADVIN, Vi Cooper stepped up to a public phone at their request and called Ruth Coe at home. Howerton and Jennings waited alongside. When a female voice answered, Cooper asked, "Are you still in the market for doing harm to someone?"

"Yes, yes!" Mrs. Coe answered breathlessly. "Definitely, definitely!"

Cooper recited a tale to the effect that she'd been busy making inquiries in the underworld and expected some action any day now. "Who do you want hit?" she asked nonchalantly.

The woman mentioned Donald Brockett and Richard Olberding, then worked herself into a rage about the railroading of her son. Howerton and Jennings summed up the outburst in a report:

She said that her son's trial was a very political thing, because of OLBERDING & BROCKETT; went on talking about the OL-BERDING statement of "lay back and enjoy it," as how to prevent rapes. [She said] This caused OLBERDING to have problems. BROCKETT was also tied up in this some way, which caused BROCKETT problems and, in order to get the news media off their backs and to start to look a little better, they turned her son's trial into a political thing. Never before had BROCKETT allowed cameras in the courtroom and he had them in her son's trial. He has not allowed them since. . . .

She also mentioned that Judge Shields was just trying to get a Supreme Court judge job. COOPER asked her, "Your attorney—did he do a good job for you?" COE told her that she had wanted to have MR. DICK CEASE [chief public defender] represent her son, but that the attorney they got was the No. 2 man and did as good as he could.

She has had conversations with a private attorney, CARL MAXEY, and he told her that he should have been in on it from the first, because of the political climate created and some of the mistakes made, such as hypnotizing of the victims and their descriptions vary-ing from the description of her son; that he thought defending the boy would be "a piece of cake." COOPER asked Mrs. COE how she could be gotten in contact with in the future, by anyone who might get hold of her and COE replied, "At home," although she was gone a good deal.

Also told COOPER to only have someone contact *her*; and re-emphasized that only SHE should be contacted. COOPER terminated the conversation at 5:01 p.m.

It took three days of conferences among detectives, their superiors and the prosecutor's office to settle on a course of action and win the necessary court approval. At 10:48 on the morning of Thursday, November 19, Richard Jennings dialed the Coe home and asked for Mrs. Coe. A male voice explained that she was asleep.

Jennings left the name "Terry" and said he would call back. He tried twice later and got no answer. At 2:48 p.m. a team of detectives who had been watching the Coe house radioed that the couple had just returned home in a silver-gray Citation. Jennings phoned again, and a breathless voice answered his fourth call of the day with a musical "Hel-*lo*-oo."

"Mrs. Coe?" Jennings said.

"Yes." She sang the word in two clear notes, a high followed by a low: "*Yeh*-ess."

Jennings responded in kind, asking, "How are *you* today?"

"I'm fine, thank you," she responded cheerfully. "I'm sorry I—oh, let me catch my breath! I was outside and ran in the door." Her words trailed off in a peal of giggles.

"I see, I see," said the undercover cop as Lieutenant Howerton and Ser-geant Tom Morris recorded the conversation.

"Take me a minute," the woman said. "Go ahead and talk and let me catch my breath." She giggled again.

"Okay," Jennings said. "My name's Terry."

"*Yes*, Terry."

"And... and you've never talked to me before."

"No, and you *did* call this morning."

"Yes, I did."

"Ahhh, great!"

"... I understand from a friend of mine that, uh, you have a job that you need to be performed very discreetly."

"Yes. *Extremely* discreetly."

"Very well."

"Uh, yeah, of course I'm concerned with expense. I don't have an awful lot of money, but...." Her voice dropped to a lower register and turned almost grim. "The job I would like done would help humanity, too—"

"Um hmm."

"—Very much. Uh, uh, how could we talk about this, Terry, or find out the cost, and how it could be done and everything? Or can we do that right now on the phone?" She sighed heavily.

Jennings switched to his "hit man" voice. "I'm not gonna talk about things like this on the phone."

"No, I agree with you," she said quickly. "I don't think so either." She sounded deferential. She asked where he would like to meet and suggested, "I do think it should be away from my home, too, don't you?"

"Yes... someplace reasonably public."

They agreed to a rendezvous at 4:30 p.m. in a shopping center near her home. She said she would be driving a silver Citation and he said he would be in a silver Mustang with Illinois plates. "Great," she said, pronouncing it *"greet"* in her over-enunciated style. "I'll look forward to seeing you."

"I'm looking forward to seeing *you*," the policeman said. "I hope we can work something out."

"I do, too, Terry," she said, and added fervently, "Very much." She signed off with a friendly, "Bye-bye now!"

Watched by another pair of detectives, Ruth Coe left home at 4:16 and pulled into the Old National Bank parking lot five minutes early for her appointment. She stepped over to Jennings' car and said, "Terry?"

"Yes, it is," he said. "How are you?"

She said she was very fine. "But Terry, how do I know you're who you are and not police?"

"Pardon?" The conversation was being taped by Howerton in a nearby police van, and Jennings wanted to give the woman plenty of time to get into his car so her voice would be picked up by his body-pack mike.

"How do I know you're who you are and not police?" she repeated.

He switched to his street-tough voice. "Well, I guess you're just gonna have to take my word for it." He paused to let that sink in, then said, "But, um, from the information that I've got... you want a job done?"

"Um-hmm."

He said he couldn't see any problem. "That's great," she said.

"Uh, I can use the money."

"How much? That's the thing. See, I don't have a lot of money, but I mortgaged my soul for this one because, uh, it's very important." She was speaking slowly now, seriously, most of her theatrical accent gone.

"Well, let's talk about it for a while first."

"Okay. And you want to know...their background and everything. Uh, actually, two I'd like out—and they're both pretty big men, in fact, but they should be taken out. Uh—one is a judge. He is a very vicious, cold man—a vicious, *vicious* man.... He has visions of the Supreme Court.... And the other one I'd like out is the prosecuting attorney. And—"

Jennings said, "I take it you were very directly involved with it?"

"Yes. My son, my son. Uh, my son was used as a scapegoat. He was picked up, uh, as the South Hill rapist. I'm sure you're probably not from Spokane, you don't realize that there was a series of about three years where there were, oh, I don't know how many different rapes, uh, committed on primarily the South Hill.... Now it had gone along and they hadn't had much success, and, uh, the captain of the rape division, Capt. Olberding, said to, uh, one of the women broadcasters one day when she said, 'Captain, have you any advice for the ladies'—victims—and he said, 'Yes. Tell them to lay back and enjoy it.' And, of course, coming from him, it just infuriated the town. This town was inflamed and I blame them not—on a remark like that. They were inflamed, and his job was at stake, and he wanted somebody and he wanted somebody *fast*. And...the bar association wanted him *out*."

The explanation went on and on. The longer she spoke, the less stylized her accent became. Pedestrians strolled past as she said, "My son is innocent; there's absolutely no doubt about it. And he's taken on sick." In an annoyed voice she enumerated the lengthy prison sentences he would have to serve.

"Sounds like a heavy," Jennings said offhandedly.

"My son was *innocent*," she repeated, "and we tried to carry his innocence, but the public defender was honestly not the top man, unfortunately. That second fellow I really don't think cared because, uh, in the, uh, courtroom he tried to get me not to say *nothin'*. The judge and the prosecutor just, you know—just lined up. But, at any rate, uh, this filthy judge—what a difference, twenty, twenty-five, thirty and life. And he was doing it just to make a big man of himself."

She began to sound as though she were having difficulty putting words together. "Now, then he also said—listen to this—he said in his speech— whatever it's called—that, uh, if my son would plead guilty to even one, they said, um, would suggest sexual psychopathy for him. Now a very dear black attorney here in Spokane, whom we've known and dearly love, saw my husband and me, said he wanted...to be on this for the sentencing part because the judge had said that he will go for sexual psychopathy, and he offered this for one dollar. And we shook hands, and he came in right at sentencing...."

After a while the woman returned to the point of the meeting. "I want the prosecutor and I want the judge out...."

Jennings said they would have to agree on a few things. "Like I said, I'm leaving town," he said.

"Greet! Should be."

"Um, we'll set down some rules. You'll get your results."

"If I could do it myself, I would. But I can't, you see, because they know who I am. I could—if I could do it myself; that's how deeply I feel—I would."

Jennings said he needed front money. "How much?" she asked. "This is the hard thing for me."

He said it would depend on the people he would have to kill, "how much background I'm gonna have to do; am I gonna know who they are, where they work?"

"I have their addresses, even their home addresses, that I brought with me. The judge, of course, is not in the phone book, but I have looked in the city directory." She handed over a slip of paper from a spiral notebook. "The prosecuting attorney is the first one and he is in the phone book. I have his name, address, and his phone number there."

Jennings studied the neat handwriting and said, "Donald C."—

"—Brockett."

"Brockett?"

"Um-hmm. He's a little man. He's probably five-eight or nine, and he goes along with that description—very cocky, Napoleonic, kinda boyish face."

He asked if she had a photograph and she said, "I sure can get you one, 'cause his picture's there in the paper constantly." She added that the judge's picture had also appeared. "Our trial being everything on camera, my *God*, he was just, uh, like some young *ham*, posing for pictures constantly. So I can... get you pictures very easily."

Jennings asked, "This man is a judge?"

"Yeah. He's a judge in superior court and he has his eyes on the supreme court."

The conversation drifted back to the subject of a down payment. "How much cash are we talking about?" she asked.

"Probably four or five hundred dollars. Will that be a problem?"

"No—well—yes, but I can do it. I can do it." She hesitated as though thinking, and repeated, "I can do it."

The "hit man" explained that the eventual total payment would have to be at least $4,000. "I need some bucks."

Mrs. Coe said, "I can get four. It won't be easy but I can get it." She agreed with "Terry" that it sounded like a lot of money. "But I'm gonna *get* it because it's *worth* it.... We're not money people, but I'll get it."

"I'll guarantee you results."

"That's what I want."

"Because, like I say, I have no qualms about it. I'd rather kill a man than I would a deer."

"I'm *with* you," the woman said. "An animal, a deer, a dog, a cat—or mice." She muttered, "*People*."

They agreed on a 2 p.m. meeting the next day. Before she could leave the undercover cop asked, "Um, we *are* talking about the same thing? You want these people...."

"Gone!..."

"Dead?"

"Dead. Right.... If I had my *druthers*... I'd have that prosecutor just made

a complete vegetable so that he could never ever be anything but a vegetable"—
her voice sped up—"so that they had to care for him forever and he lived on
and on that way. And the judge—"

Jennings broke in, "Just tell me what you want."

"Well, uh, that judge, I'd like him gone, dead, and I'd like both of 'em
dead, really, except that with Brockett, I felt that—he's a man about forty-six
or -seven, and he has been so filthy, and my feeling for him is that I would
love to see him just an addle-pated vegetable that had to be cared for—that
his family had to take care of the rest of his life—that there was nothing—I
mean diapers and all the rest of it. . . ."

Her voice had turned casual; she could have been reading a grocery list.
"He wanted forty-two of my son's life gone. I'd like to see him sit forty-two
years in—uh, as a baby, but, uh—to have him gone would be great, too. I
mean, you can never be sure, I suppose, how you clobber them, that that
could be the way it would come out. So dead is great. But I do think he should
suffer."

Jennings asked, "Would you like to be there?"

There was a long hesitation. "Would that be dangerous for either of us?"
she asked.

"Neither one is gonna be a piece of cake."

She paused again. "I *would* like to be there. I don't want it to be . . . hard
on either you or me or the—"

"It's not gonna be hard on me," Jennings assured her. "It makes no
difference to me."

She said, "And I don't want it to . . . lead back to me. However, I feel this
way—I want this so badly that even if I *paid* for it in any way—you know, if
they caught me in any way, I would, uh, know it was worth it."

Jennings said he would guarantee the hits within a week of receiving
$500 front money. "Marvelous!" Mrs. Coe said. "*Marvelous!*" She said that she
felt fortunate to meet him. As she climbed out of his Mustang she told him
how much she admired the interior. It was 4:36 in the afternoon.

116

At lunchtime the next day, Friday, November 20, Richard Jennings called the Coe house again. When a familiar voice answered, he said, "Hi! I just wanted to call to confirm our two-o'clock appointment."

"You betcha!" Ruth Coe said. "I'm looking forward to it... very, very much. Terry, I wanted to ask you one thing that kind of bothered me that you said over the phone yesterday." He noticed that her speech was rapid and a little slurred. "Uh, I thought about it and I hate to ask you, and it's not really important, but if you cashed a check at that bank that we were next to and I was wondering if you were from out of town, how you could do that?"

"It was a traveler's check," Jennings said quickly.

"O-kay. That answers it."

"A traveler's check. No personal check. I don't have a personal checking account."

"Okay... that's what I was kinda wondering. I said, 'My goodness, he's not from here. How'd he do that?'" She said she would see him at two.

Everything was in readiness an hour early at the shopping-center parking lot. Jennings was on station in his Mustang, his bug checked out by test transmissions to a blue and white police van parked nearby. Inside, Lt. Howerton, Sgt. Tom Morris and Det. Don Johnson manned a tape machine and a video recorder behind one-way glass. Two policewomen waited in an undercover car.

At 1:30 p.m. a surveillance team advised that the subject had just left her house. She was five minutes early the day before, twelve minutes early today. She pulled in so close to the Mustang that the cars almost touched. Dressed in navy-blue slacks, a cream-colored V-neck sweater and gold lamé sandals, she arrived with a worry on her mind. "These two men are so closely associated with our case," she told Jennings, and "if both go out at a close time—I mean, can't it look like it's a heart attack?"

Jennings laughed and said, "No, it's not gonna look like a heart attack. No!"

"Uh, well, I really... the finger will be... go right to us...." She outlined a possible alibi. On Sunday, two days hence, she and Gordon would be visiting Fred in prison and having dinner with their daughter Kathleen in a Seattle suburb.

Jennings said, "That's fine. I felt that Sunday would be a good day for the judge, and Monday morning would be a good day for the prosecutor. Then I'm gone."

She whispered "Great!" and added fervently, "You're good, you're good!" She gave him her daughter's phone number in case he had to reach her, then produced a packet of pictures of the intended victims. "See," she said, "in one of these the headline was 'Star is Born'... because of all the television he had in the courtroom." She apologized for the quality of the pictures and added her own description of Brockett: "He's a little man. Well, I am five-six and a half, and with a heel, uh, what, I'm probably five-ten and I'm taller than he is.... He's got a kind of boyish face. This is kind of a stub nose." Then she turned over $500, explaining that she would raise the rest from "a piece of jewelry that was my mother's that I dearly loved and had all my life since she's gone—and that will bring the rest."

Jennings suggested that she pay the balance by check. She asked, "Do you think our names should be connected in any way—ever? I'd rather do it *cash*...." She added, "I mean, I'm not afraid of a check at all. We can have it postdated—"

"The only thing was, I was gonna say... let's see, today's the twentieth, Friday?"

"It's Friday."

"...You could write a check for the twenty-sixth and if the job wasn't done, which it will be—you just guaranteed his death—if the job wasn't done, you could stop payment on the check."

"Yes," she said in a dreamy voice, then explained that she didn't write checks.

Jennings asked, "Does your husband know about this?"

She took a deep breath. "Yes." She added, "In a way. He... *yes*."

The plainclothesman said, "He *does*?"

"Uh, yes. Not—fully. He does, yes. I'm gonna say it that way, because I got my... the five hundred from him. He, uh, we're very close. You don't have to worry about that."

"Okay."

"We have been married thirty-five and a half years." She laughed, and Jennings joined in. "Is that awful or good?" she asked, still amused at herself.

"Well...."

"See, and this is his son, as it's my son, and we... I, I don't think he thinks that I'm smart this way, and he is worried that the two going at the same time would point right to us, but, uh—how are they ever going to prove it?"

"That's right."

"How are they ever gonna *prove* it? And as far as I am concerned, those were the two who *ruined* our family. We have lived here all our lives.... I've just been a mother and a wife.... We've lived just a normal life and they crucified us. *Crucified us!* And they have really crucified my husband...and he's a *marvelous* man. It should never ever have happened to him. And my son isn't guilty. This I want to get across to you, too. My son is no rapist. He's a very attractive man, as you are. He has to run the other way"—she giggled—"to keep from being raped himself, as I know you probably do."

"I've never had that trouble," Jennings said blandly.

"Well, he really hasn't either. But he's attractive to women. I mean, he had no problem with dates, or anything like this. It was a scapegoat."

After she had said more about Brockett and the "ugly judge" and hypnosis and psychiatry and several other subjects, Jennings broke in, "I don't want to string this out. You're gonna be on the coast for an alibi?"

"Right."

"The reason I asked about your husband is because I want to know how many people know about this."

"*You. He. I.* And that's the end of it."

"Okay."

"He does know...we are close. We're very very close. He doesn't approve, but—he has never, uh, he knows how hurt, uh, we've both been very very hurt. And I'm still hurt....Now I'm getting mad." Her angry words were strangely unaccented; content and style didn't seem to match. "I think it's good when you get mad, 'cause you get a little bit of the hurt done. The hurt is awful to live with. But, uh, when you get mad and get in there and fight, and that's where I am, and—yes, he does know...."

Jennings told her to put the balance of the payoff in an envelope and tape it under the ledge of the phone booth. "Is that agreeable?"

"Perfect."

"Okay."

"Which booth?"

"Just the one on the right there is fine."

"One on the right. Okay."

"But, like I say, I'll talk to you prior to that, so—"

She started to ask a question. "Does that mean, uh, let's see...." Jennings spotted Lt. Howerton and the policewomen approaching the car. Mrs. Coe was mumbling, "Now, yes, tomorrow, uh—"

The car door opened. Howerton said, "Mrs. Coe?"

As he leaned in she said disgustedly, "I thought so. I thought so. That's right, I *really* did think so." It was as though she were more worried about being thought stupid than about being caught. "Well—"

Jennings said, "I'm sorry it had to be this way."

"I'm not," she said. "Because I told you that, uh—"

"That's enough," Jennings said. She hadn't yet been read her "CRs"—constitutional rights. The policewomen led her toward their car.

Two plainclothesmen sped to the Coe house on Dyer Rd. and read Gordon Coe his CRs. He waived his rights and asked the men in. "Your wife has just been arrested," one of the officers said.

He seemed genuinely surprised. "What for?"

"Solicitation to commit first-degree murder."

The officers took note of suitcases in a room and hallway. The questioning was short. Coe denied knowledge of his wife's offense but admitted that she'd mentioned killing Brockett and Shields in occasional fits of anger. He said he'd always counseled her to forget such ideas. As the men left the house he said, "First you fabricated a case against my son and now you're fabricating a case against my wife."

In the police car en route to jail Ruth Coe refused to answer questions but seemed eager to prove that she wasn't surprised by what had happened. She said she thought she'd seen "Terry" around the Public Safety Building when she'd gone there to visit "Son." She noted that Terry had told her the government had trained him to kill and that he must have been in Vietnam. "His eyes didn't look that cruel," she mused.

At headquarters a policewoman sat with her while Howerton conferred with superiors. Detective Denise Coker went down the hall to get her a cup of coffee. Then she was escorted to the jail on the second floor. At the booking area a clerk asked in a friendly voice, "Why, Mrs. Coe, what are *you* here for?"

She turned to Coker and asked if she should answer. "It's up to you," the detective told her.

Mrs. Coe said, "For trying to kill the judge and prosecutor."

Bail was set at $500,000 on two counts of criminal solicitation to commit first-degree murder, each punishable by imprisonment up to life. Gordon Coe immediately retained Carl Maxey, who rushed a psychologist to the jail. After a brief interview therapist Richard L. Dennie told the press that it was his opinion that Mrs. Coe was a sick woman, but not suicidal at the moment. "I think that she's doing pretty well under the circumstances," said Dr. Dennie, a favorite expert witness for Maxey. "When you think what these people have gone through in the last eight months, it's pretty hard to take. I think it's especially hard for a mother." His client, he said, had been driven by grief.

Reporters who watched as the jailed woman spoke to her husband in the visiting room noticed no overt signs of grief or regret. "Mrs. Coe appeared calm," one wrote, "maintaining the same self-assured, flamboyant manner that marked her behavior during her son's trial." Another witness said that she seemed to perceive herself as the celebrity heroine of a real-life production. She smiled and blew kisses as she chatted with her husband on the hand-set telephones. When she was led away to the jail commissary to buy a pack of cigarettes, she chatted gaily with a guard, as though they were old friends.

Gordon Coe brushed aside reporters' requests for comment. "Public knowledge is important," said the recently retired editor, "but what happens in the end is more important."

In his own isolation Fred Coe seemed to take the news hard, and his fellow inmates did their best to compound his aggravation. A reporter who went to Shelton to interview him heard "Your mother's coming in on the next chain!" "Hey, Fred Coe, you fucking rapo!" "They should burn him." "Hey, two-timer!... Tree climber!... *Rapo!*..."

A guard said that Coe had appeared upset when he heard the news about his mother on another prisoner's radio. "He said he couldn't believe something like that would happen. He said it was a frame job." He was placed on a routine suicide watch and his cell checked three or four times an hour. A prison official explained, "A person can only take so much harassment before it starts to get to him."

A few days after his wife's arrest Gordon Coe made himself available to reporters at Carl Maxey's suggestion. Of the latest arrest he said, "It seemed to me to be a clear case of entrapment because I had a severely disturbed and distraught wife, and they could have just informed me that she had gotten this idea and we could have seen that she got help. It's like handing a loaded gun to someone who said they were going to commit suicide."

Later he added, "She and I are the only ones who know the Fred Coe case from end to end, and we are the only ones who know Fred Coe thoroughly. Her opinion and my opinion as to the fact he's innocent can't be scoffed at because only we of all the people really know the case." He said that his wife had made occasional threats about Brockett and Shields, "but she always got over it and regained her perception, and she would have got over it again had they not set up this phoney baloney scheme.... They just happened to catch her at a point where she was emotionally over the brink and took advantage of her."

In an affidavit for the court he explained that he and his wife were in financial straits and had been preparing to move west to Tacoma when her arrest intervened. She hadn't been happy about leaving the house "which Ruth loved so much. We could no longer make our mortgage payments, so we were arranging to give up our equity and abandon the home by turning it over to the lending agency. Giving up this house that Ruth had worked so hard to decorate and landscape to her tastes was just one more crushing blow, which piled on top of so many others had driven her to the breaking point." Unmentioned were the facts that Mrs. Coe had soured on the house a year before and that their equity was minimal.

Three days after the arrest, the jailed woman appeared in court for a formal reading of the charges. She seemed disoriented as a matron led her into the courtroom wearing the clothes she'd been arrested in. She gripped a tissue and stumbled slightly as she was led to a seat next to Maxey. Her hand trembled as she smoothed her jet-black wig. A judge read the charges, informing her of her right to remain silent and to have a jury trial. Asked if she had any questions, she produced a meek, "No."

Two days later bond was reduced to $30,000. Gordon Coe scraped together another 10 percent bondsman's fee and bailed his wife out. She seemed to have regained her spirits, telling reporters, "I will be cooking the happiest turkey I have in a long time—which isn't even bought yet." Just after dark she was sneaked out a side door to avoid photographers and driven home by her husband behind a sheriff's escort.

Not long afterward the proprietor of the Backroom Boutique, a secondhand store on Spokane's near west side, decorated a little driftwood tree with a new offering of costume jewelry and baubles marked "Coe." Some of the jewels looked almost real, but most looked as though they had tumbled out of a supermarket slot machine. The Ruth Coe collection sold fast. A "poison ring," with a hinged cap and a depression large enough to hold a capsule, went for $3, a wedding band for $5.26, a pair of jade earrings for $8.45. Ropes of imitation pearls in aquamarine and coral were offered at $3.25 each. The centerpiece of the offering, a glittering rhinestone necklace, was snatched up for $36.75. The store manager explained that the goods were sold on consignment. The Coes would realize 50 percent.

117

Now that Ruth Coe had displaced her son at center stage, newsmen faced the task of digging up her background. They soon found that she'd had little impact on her native city. Like her husband, she apparently had shied away from close friendships, and the few who knew her story had been convinced to remain silent. Public records proved skimpy. A yellowing certificate registered the Spokane birth of "Mamie Ruth Enfield" on June 30, 1920, to Fred L. Enfield, thirty-four, a dry-goods merchant born in Iowa, and his wife Edna Turnley Enfield, thirty-two, a housewife born in "Arkansaw," both now deceased. Another document showed a marriage to Clyde D. Brown, a salesman, at the age of twenty-one. On the license, Mamie Ruth had listed herself as divorced. Her occupations were variously listed as salesgirl and assistant credit manager.

A *Chronicle* staffer did some research and memo'd, "Her dad ran a small drygoods shop on First near Jefferson and her uncle had a butcher shop on W. Garland on the north side of town." The family business, started in 1898, had been dissolved in 1938, the year she graduated from Lewis and Clark, and her father had gone to work as a salesman. Her late brother Edmon had been an executive with Penney's.

A few childhood friends checked in with information, but only after receiving promises of anonymity. Said one, "Mamie Ruth was raised by nice people in a big house on Sixth Avenue. The neighborhood was typical South Hill. In her childhood there were still a lot of substantial houses, a few mansions, places with upper balcony walks, big fences, porticoes, pillars. Everyplace she looked she would have seen affluence. But it didn't extend to her folks—they might have had a little money once, but by the thirties the chains were putting family drygoods stores out of business. Her father's store had been founded by Ruth's maternal grandfather, a great politician, a great talker. Mrs. Enfield, Mamie Ruth's mother, was a lovely woman, tall and stately, a beautiful and sweet person. She had one strict rule: her kids had to be in early. Mamie Ruth used to rush home for supper and bedtime."

Another early acquaintance recalled, "Ruth was a beautiful child and she got prettier with time. She had charm and personality—knew it, too. She was one of those women who form up pretty early. By the eighth grade she was attracting the pre-pubescent boys. I guess the words that described her best were 'luscious' and 'sensuous.' But she was never promiscuous, never cheap."

A female classmate chimed in, "Mamie Ruth Enfield was interested in boys, you bet! She liked their attention, but she was never in the top level of popularity in our class. She was flamboyant, given to overstatement and inappropriate response. If you ran into her downtown she would act excited at seeing you: effusive, I would call it. I remember what she wrote in my Nineteen Thirty-eight annual: 'Here's wishing the best to a perfect girl!' Well, I wasn't a perfect girl, but that was just the way Ruth put things."

Other information turned up, not all of it verifiable. Just before meeting Gordon in late 1945, Ruth had planned to leave Spokane for California; she'd never spoken highly of her native city and had felt rejected by its high society. Early in 1946 she'd married reporter Gordon Coe, just home from the war.

The neighborhood atop the South Hill where the couple raised their children was highly social, but word was that the Coes received few invitations. Mrs. Coe had quickly established a reputation for being different. "All the years that I knew her," said a childhood friend of daughter Kathleen, "Ruth remained consistently eccentric. You'd see her driving down the street in the family car and if Fred wasn't sitting next to her a big collie was. When I was in high school, I walked into a big department store and I saw this collie coming down the row, scented and coiffed, a bow around its neck. The sight stopped traffic. I started to ask myself, Who the hell would—'Oh,' I said, 'hello, Mrs. Coe!'"

A neighbor recalled, "When we kids were around twelve or thirteen, she taught us how to play bridge. She used positive reinforcement—overpraising us when we did good. You can't make a kid mad by praising him, so we had a hell of a time."

A woman whose child attended elementary school with Fred Coe remembered that the boy's mother would arrive for functions with every thread in place, her face carefully made up and her hair groomed. "You would *never* see Ruth Coe in her grubbies," the woman recalled. "She'd wear heels and stockings to a potato race. I always found her hard to talk to unless you mentioned her kids. Then she'd go on for hours."

A newspaper wife remembered, "She would show up at company parties, but she was always aloof. Maybe she knew that the other wives made fun of her speech. So *affected*. I felt sorry for her and tried to draw her out. Children and animals—those seemed to be her main interests."

A seamstress recalled the Ruth Coe of the mid-1970s. "She spent a fortune on clothes and drycleaning. She used to wear things a few times and then put them up for re-sale—on consignment. Did the same with jewelry. She would swish in and out of the shop in the wrong clothes—too loud, too young for her. Her hair was dyed and overdone. She would buy a dress and have me alter it. When she came in to pick it up, she would say, 'I love it, I love it!' She'd get so excited! She had fuzzy speech and a thick tongue, but I never smelled liquor on her."

That was the file on Mamie Ruth Coe. The most conspicuous fact about the accused woman was that not a soul outside her family claimed to know her well.

1982

118

Almost from the day Ruth Coe was charged with two counts of solicitation of murder, a blizzard of paper poured from the one-story brick Maxey Building a block west of the Spokane County Courthouse. Her three-man defense staff filed motions to throw the case out on the grounds that widespread publicity had made a fair trial impossible (denied), to bring in an outside judge and prosecutor (granted), to forbid the use of a Seattle prosecutor (denied), to bar all persons involved from talking to the press (granted), and to go straight to the state court of appeals on the issue of entrapment (twice denied).

The trial date was postponed and postponed again while the stories of Ruth Coe and "Son" were updated and re-hashed in such publications as the New York *Times, Newsweek, People, True Detective*. The London *Mirror* headlined, "Sex Shame of Town's Top Family—Rapist Given Life Plus 74 Years." As far away as Singapore and Hong Kong, the Coes were front-page news. Kevin never stopped working diligently on his image. He was interviewed by Paul Henderson, Pulitzer Prize–winning reporter of the Seattle *Times*, whose articles had resulted in the freeing of an innocent man convicted of rape. Henderson came away unconvinced of Coe's innocence. Coe advised friends to watch for his story on various network TV programs, but none appeared.

At their home in the Spokane Valley, Gordon and Ruth Coe stayed quiet. They retained their listed phone number but seldom answered calls. When they were seen in public, it was usually on a trip to a nearby supermarket or an occasional downtown store. There were reports that Mrs. Coe still seethed about her son's case and particularly about the way Jay Williams and Paula Whitmore had dropped out as character witnesses. It was said that in moments of anger she blamed the two of them for her son's conviction. A few conversations were held at police headquarters about providing protection, but the idea was discarded as impractical. Manpower was as short as ever.

In March, 1982, four months after the payoff to the hit man, Paula Whitmore was walking out of a downtown store when she passed a familiar figure. "At first I hardly recognized Mrs. Coe because her hair was so short," the realtor told a friend. "I kind of nodded but she didn't speak. I turned and realized she was following me. I got into my car and she got into a silver-gray Citation. That's when I knew for sure who she was. She followed me for three miles. I thought she might have a gun, so I made a couple of quick turns and ditched her. It bothered me for a long time."

119

Another Coe, another trial.

Just before Judge Robert C. Bibb entered the stuffy Spokane courtroom, one of defense chief Carl Maxey's associates dropped a white carnation on the table. "It symbolizes our feelings about our client," said Gordon Bovey, a thickset man with glasses and wavy gray-black hair and the friendly manner of a Rotarian toastmaster. He was one of three Maxey lawyers and several clerks and secretaries who made up the Ruth Coe defense team.

As Bovey was explaining his gesture, a secretary from the Maxey law firm pushed a portable file case into position just inside the bar, lending an impression of solidity and depth to the defense. Another Maxey functionary placed a four-foot-high "Trauma Chart" against the empty jury box, where it would be conspicuous till the end of the trial. In large letters it read:

MAR 10	FRED COE ARRESTED—IN JAIL 25 DAYS.
APR 4	MR. AND MRS. COE SOLD FAMILY CAR—TO PAY FRED'S BOND (1979 YELLOW CADILLAC).
APR 5	MRS. COE SUFFERED A SEVERELY BROKEN WRIST.
APR 20	DEATH OF MRS. COE'S DEAR FRIEND.
JULY 15	MR. COE'S LEAVE OF ABSENCE— FROM HIS POSITION AS CHRONICLE M.E.
JULY 15-31	FRED COE'S TRIAL. Incessant publicity—lost friendships—social ostracism—lost family home
AUG. 17	FRED COE'S SENTENCING—ON THAT EVENING THE COES BEGAN RECEIVING A SERIES OF GRUESOME ANONYMOUS PHONE

CALLS, RESULTING IN THEIR
HAVING A 'PHONE TRAP'
INSTALLED WITH AID OF POLICE
AND PHONE CO.

AUG. 28   MR. COE—KNEE SURGERY.
OCT. 1   MR. COE'S FORMAL RETIREMENT.
OCT. 31   FRED COE MOVED FROM SPOKANE
            COUNTY JAIL TO SHELTON—MR.
            AND MRS. COE DECIDE TO MOVE
            FROM SPOKANE, LIFELONG HOME,
            TO THE COAST.
App. NOV. 14   COES LEARN FRED TO GO TO
            WALLA WALLA.
NOV. 16   VI COOPER CALLED MRS. COE—AT
            POLICE INSTRUCTION.
NOV. 19   UNDERCOVER POLICEMAN
            CALLED MRS. COE.
NOV. 20   MRS. COE ARRESTED.

The "trauma chart," like the portable file cabinet, appeared to come under the heading of theater—props brought in to create or heighten an impression. As Carl Maxey confided to a reporter, "This trial is our chance to educate the judge."

Opening day was windy and unspringlike even though it was mid-May and blooming flowers fringed the courthouse. The modernized courtroom with its four big wafers of overhead light was only three quarters full; Ruth Coe's ordeal wasn't the hot ticket that her son's had been—at least not yet. Husband and wife looked exhausted as they entered the courtroom, Ruth leaning heavily on Gordon's arm. The former managing editor, dressed in a double-breasted navy blazer and a blue and gold rep tie, stared for several seconds at the press. In less than a year he had turned from proud journalist to angry mediaphobe. For a time, he'd spoken highly of the Seattle *Times*, but that relationship seemed on the wane. The *Times* wasn't even staffing the trial.

Mrs. Coe smiled and showed a shy interest in her surroundings. She glanced at the four prints depicting the seasons on the oak-paneled wall, the ficus and the Norfolk pine over by the two windows, the French shutters so like the ones she had installed during the Gallicizing of the old family house. The aging process that she and her son dreaded had loosened the skin of her chin and neck, and her torso had thickened in the fourteen months since her son's arrest. But in her sixty-second year of life she still turned men's heads as she stood waiting for the judge. Her dark-blue eyes were carefully made up beneath plucked black eyebrows that arched upward in flattened inverted V's. Her teased hair was ultra-black except for a whitish blaze in front. Her leg muscles were smoothly defined, her ankles slender, her bust modestly understated. She wore a light tan suit, backless four-inch heels, and heavy gold earrings. She looked like a stylishly conservative socialite.

Judge Bibb, a balding man with a faintly cherubic look, opened proceedings by asking over the soft hiss of the air-conditioner, "Counsel, are you ready?" At Maxey's request the visiting judge was hearing the case without a jury. The defense would be entrapment and diminished mental capacity, and the experienced Maxey trusted the jurist from coastal Everett to have a better understanding of such complex legal concepts than a panel of laymen. Diminished capacity, the argument that the defendant had been unable to form "specific intent" to harm anyone, was a defense usually reserved for drunks, although it had been used by Sirhan Sirhan. Its virtue was that the defendant went free if acquitted. Acquittal on an insanity plea might result in an enforced stay in a mental hospital, a contingency that Maxey's client had rejected.

The special prosecutor, Mary Kay Barbieri of Seattle, outlined the state's case in an opening statement as basic as an ax. She was a small brown-haired woman, a former English teacher with a reputation for doing her homework. When she pointed out that Mrs. Coe had wanted a fellow human made into a "vegetable," a young court clerk stopped scribbling and slowly raised her head to stare at the defendant from beneath dark brown bangs. The courtroom remained silent as the stocky Barbieri rearranged her oversize glasses and lobbed her next grenade: "She compared how many years his family would have to change his diapers to the amount of time her son would have to spend in prison." She went on to tell the judge that Ruth Coe was no pathetic psychological wreck, as the defense intended to argue; she was motivated solely by "hatred and revenge" and had known exactly what she was doing.

Not true, Carl Maxey replied. He painted a sympathetic picture of a woman "tormented by thoughts of self-destruction, at the peak of her anxiety"—a pill-popper of long standing and a manic-depressive, "like Napoleon." The defendant had had absolutely no defenses, he said, when the police stepped in to take advantage of her. "Law enforcement," he said, "exceeded its bounds and manufactured a crime." When he resumed his seat next to the defendant, she gave him a smile and a squeeze.

There were frost warnings overnight. Leaves turned brittle and pedestrians in summer clothes shivered as they hurried toward the warmth of the courthouse. Carl Maxey, wearing a colorful outfit highlighted by a silver-gray suede jacket and tasseled black alligator shoes, spoke briefly to reporters before the second day's session and gave the impression that his client had become little more than a rag doll, painted and propped up and led into court. "A couple days ago she fainted in my office," he said. "It was a hell of a job getting her ready for trial." Asked what he had told her about courtroom demeanor, he said, "I told her to sit down and be quiet."

She did, while plainclothesman Rich Jennings testified that during the hit-man conversations she had been "calm, very businesslike, very professional. She was eager, energetic, extremely serious. She was very, very bitter, very revengeful." When the time came for the first public playing of the undercover tapes, Maxey prevailed on the judge to let his client wait in a back room. In her lavender dress and tall ankle-strap heels, Ruth Coe walked unsteadily toward the rear door of the courtroom and disappeared.

Her husband remained in the front row. On the first day of the trial he had worn black and gray, but today he seemed caught up in the sartorial mood of the defense team and wore a plum outfit—unusually sporty for him. He was the only person in the courtroom who seemed to find the taped conversations boring. Spectators sat forward to catch every nuance of the crackling sounds. The judge's pink face looked as alert as a gerbil's. A hollow thumping sound on the tape came across like a heartbeat, adding a touch of Edgar Allan Poe. At the point where Ruth Coe began talking to the "hit man" about an alibi, Gordon Coe turned heavy-lidded. His eyes remained closed through the conversation about whether he knew of her assassination plans, snapped open when Ruth said, "They really crucified my husband," then closed again while she emphasized, "Yes, he *does* know."

Mrs. Coe returned from the lunch break looking drawn. Her facial muscles were slack and her walk unsteady as Maxey and her husband guided her to the defense table. Gordon Coe took the witness stand and fought as hard to save his wife as he had to save his son. He leaned into the microphone as Fred had done and sometimes his voice came out strained and thin. His wife, he testified, had always been "a sympathetic and kind person... a very kindly cheerful person... a kindly and thoughtful person of others and of animals, everything. Just sort of a kindhearted person." But her personality began to change after thyroid operations in 1953 and 1961, menopause in the 1960s, and "a vast quantity of uppers and downers and everything in between—an absolutely appalling jumble of chemicals."

Coe testified that in the fall of 1971 the woman who had always described herself as a "go person" went into a severe depression, sitting in the kitchen all day staring at TV—"doing nothing till I came home." The next year he took her to New York City, and the person who usually rushed off to fashion centers and boutiques sat listlessly in the hotel. In 1973 she went from depressed to excited, and Coe took her to a psychiatrist who prescribed pills. By the summer she was so high that she went out and bought an unneeded Chrysler Imperial. "I tried to prevent it, but there was no stopping her short of tying her up or something," Coe testified. He described a runaway trip to Las Vegas, where she spent $6,500 in a week and managed to lose the family Samoyed in a motel en route. "I mean it's totally unlike her," Coe testified as he dabbed at his eyes, "a person who was a tremendous animal lover and so kind to dogs and cats and every stray that came along."

The manic state, he said, returned the following summer. "She borrowed a thousand dollars from a loan company and didn't tell me. She bought many things. She traded our spinet piano in on an organ.... My daughter protested because she played the piano and so Ruth bought *another* piano." Medications like lithium helped, and by the late 1970s she seemed to be under control. Then came the arrest and trial of Fred Coe—"an uninhibited circus, extremely difficult for us."

Coe testified that his wife took the blame for losing the case and suffered terribly when outsiders claimed that she'd lied for her son. She felt "that she had not been a good witness, had not been an effective witness." A deep depression followed, or as Coe put it, "You didn't know from one minute to the next whether she was going to finally take the suicide step that had been looming over her horizon." He told of harassing calls to the Coe residence from a man who would shout, "Fred Coe has taken my fall and I'm *freeeeeee!*" Police found out who the man was, Coe testified, but he disappeared. "So we'll never know whether he was a rapist or a nut." He told of his son's transfer from jail to prison. "On the day he was shipped, just as an added bit of horror, they awoke him at four-thirty in the morning. He was still half asleep. They were taking him down the steel stairs and he fell and contacted his head, had a rather severe concussion. They went ahead and shipped him seven and a half hours all chained up." The effect on Mrs. Coe was traumatic. "It awakened her to the horrors of the penal system, and the things that can happen and the fact that there's very little attention paid to the inmates."

After that, Coe testified, his wife felt as though "the whole world was coming down on us and people who had been friendly had gone back on us. She had a feeling that she was hearing from her daughter and/or from God, and she could hear, I mean—two sides of her brain were competing for attention or telling her what to do." The crowning blow came on November 14, just five days before the undercover policeman's call. The Coes found out that their son was being shipped from Shelton to Walla Walla without benefit of the in-prison psychiatric treatment that Judge Shields had recommended. "Everything got worse," Gordon Coe testified. ". . . She frequently couldn't understand why God had done this to us."

The couple had made a mutual decision to get her away from Spokane. "It was perfectly obvious that she couldn't make it here with her nose being rubbed in this thing every day." At first they decided she would go to Hawaii, where she could "get a job and just maintain herself there for as long as it was necessary." But after she overslept her flight, she changed her mind about going. "If she had gone to Hawaii," the witness said in tones of deep regret, "none of this would ever have happened." Her subsequent conversations with the undercover cop were "a fantasy, a part of a hallucination."

Asked what condition his wife was in now, Coe said, "The shock of the arrest and imprisonment in the county-city jail for five days found her clear out of her hallucinations and paranoia and she came out of the jail back to the old Ruth for all intents and purposes." After intensive psychological therapy she'd improved even more, and now "she's made a rather exceptional recovery, but it's a long road back."

Carl Maxey asked, "Did you give your wife any of the money for the hit man?"

"I gave all of it to her," Coe testified. "We have been following a plan since March of 1981 . . . that the smart thing to do was to let Ruth handle all the finances. And we had found that when she handled the money she was very careful of it and rarely got into any kind of a manic problem where she would buy something she didn't need."

Under cross-examination Coe testified that he went to the bank on the morning of November 20, the day of the arrest, and drew $600 for his wife. The bulk of the money was for moving expenses on the trip to Tacoma. Mary Kay Barbieri asked, "Did you ever consider whether your wife should be committed to the psychiatric unit of a hospital?"

"She had a most terrible fear of something like that," Coe responded. "Too much discussion of that could push her over the brink to suicide. That was asking for it."

The prosecutor asked, "After your son's trial, did you hear your wife make threats of harm to people that had been involved in the trial?"

"Well, I originally kind of thought of them as threats. I think once she said, 'I'd like to go down and burn that courthouse down'... and she would say things like, 'I wish these people would be struck by lightning or the plague or something'.... She had a feeling that there had been great harm done to us and wrongs done to us."

Most courtroom observers reacted to the testimony with cynicism. Ruth Coe was widely perceived as an archvillainess who had committed perjury long before committing more serious crimes. Cynical comments about her and her husband could be heard at every recess. Said a veteran courthouse reporter, "Gordon didn't say anything about his wife that doesn't apply to half the wives in the country. She sits around the house, takes too many pills, spends too much money and has her ups and downs."

Some felt that the Coes had long since forfeited their credibility, especially after word came up from Walla Walla that Fred was taking credit for designing his mother's defense. When Ruth kissed Gordon after his testimony and her high-heeled foot kicked backward like an ingenue's in an old movie, observers wondered if they were looking at devotion or theater. They also wondered about Ruth's trembling hands. She had seemed so self-possessed at the other trial. Everyone agreed: It would take convincing psychiatric testimony and a strong performance on the witness stand to save her.

120

*The trial has made the whole Coe family look like a bunch of jerks—
all kooks. The truth is, I have no mental illness. I'm not crazy.*—Fred
Coe, May 26, 1982

For three consecutive days the courtroom rang with what the defense
characterized as legitimate medical testimony and the prosecution as "psy-
chobabble." Two types of expert witnesses appeared: those who had treated
Ruth Coe before her arrest and those who had been summoned by Maxey to
treat her afterward. The testimony of the first group seemed clear and com-
pelling, but the later observers only seemed to confuse. The problem, as the
prosecutors kept insinuating in cross-examination, was that there was no way
of telling whether the wily Ruth Coe had faked a whole new set of symptoms
to provide herself with an alibi.

Dr. Fred Viren, a Spokane internist, testified that he'd spotted manic-
depressive symptoms in the patient as far back as the early 1970s. He spoke
of her "flamboyance, her eccentricity, her bizarreness." But her mental problem wasn't obvious to all, he testified. "She kept a very strong mask on her
face. She presented herself very well to the public." Viren told the court that
his patient had contemplated a divorce in 1973 and had suffered "disordered
sexual functions" over the years. He told of her unnatural excitement about
going into franchising; he said he had warned her that this was "crazy behavior,
crazy talk." Asked if the real Ruth Coe would have ordered a pair of assassi-
nations, the Spokane physician said, "I don't understand what the real Ruth
Coe is at many different times because she is many different people."

The next witness was a psychologist, Dr. Richard L. Dennie, an ultra-
serious expert witness of the sort who repeatedly answer "That is correct"
instead of "Yes." He told the court that he'd been called to the jail at Maxey's
request and had seen Mrs. Coe several times since. He found her to be in a
"major depression with psychotic features" but with no signs of "manic behavior per se." At the time of her meetings with the undercover policeman,
she'd been too mentally ill to think rationally, he said, and hadn't been able
to form a "specific criminal intent" to cause their deaths. He listed some of

her symptoms: She had gained ten pounds in the last year; she sometimes screamed to relieve depression; she felt worthless, helpless and guilty for involving her son in the search for the South Hill rapist; she had the delusion that the judge and prosecutor were in collusion in persecuting her son, and she suffered from "hallucinations and distortions of perceptions."

She also heard voices, the therapist testified—her son saying over and over, "Do something, do something!" After she hired the hit man, "She heard a voice on the left side of her brain saying, 'It's a trap, it's the police!'" She felt "there was a ninety-five percent chance the hit man was an undercover policeman. She also said she believed it was probable there would be no bloodletting, but the judge and prosecutor would be shown up for what they really were. If the truth came out about what they did to her and her son, she believed everyone else could see what they really were."

"To me," the psychologist added, "that's an illusion." Mrs. Coe also suffered from a martyr complex, he went on, and was "willing to sacrifice herself in a recklessness brought on by her psychosis."

Several times Judge Bibb interrupted the direct examination. "Let's take another run at this," he said after suggesting to Dennie that his testimony was lacking in legal relevance. "We're not talking about psychotic delusion. We're talking about specific intent." He explained, "In the situation described to you on the tapes, this lady intended to pay a hit man five hundred dollars. She was able to get the five hundred dollars from her husband and take it with her to the meeting and intended to pay. Now what's the difference between that intent and her ability to form an intent to do something like go to the bathroom or drive down the street?"

The therapist answered that someone in Mrs. Coe's condition could form the intent to go to the bathroom or drive down the street, but in the area of her psychosis "her mind would be debased by her psychosis...deformed by her cognitive limitations on account of her mental illness." The judge blinked. When co-counsel Gordon Bovey stood up to resume the questioning, Carl Maxey slid him a one-word note: "QUIT!"

Deputy prosecutor Rebecca Roe, a slender marathoner very much at home in courtroom jungle warfare, asked Dennie if it weren't true that everything he knew about Mrs. Coe had come from her own lips. Said the psychologist, "When you interview with patients, you can have a feel for whether a person is trying to con you or not. Her statements were so earnest and she repeated them so many times. I can distinguish between people who are psychotic and people who are not."

An earnest young psychiatrist, Dr. Leonard Wildeman, took up where Dennie left off. He too had been called in to treat Mrs. Coe after her jailing. The patient, he said, suffered from manic-depressive illness, depressed phase. She was convinced that the devil was out to destroy the Coes and believed that she had seen horns on Judge Shields. "She felt there was a God-devil struggle going on," the doctor testified. "She was on God's side. She was willing to sacrifice her life."

Wildeman told of his first interview with Mrs. Coe. "She was obsessed with thinking about her son, obsessed with his innocence. She feels that the Coes are all gonna be killed. She was paranoid, agitated. She sat at the edge of her chair for the whole two hours. If I made any movement she would jump up wildly excited. She hit herself in the face a couple of times."

According to Wildeman, some of his patient's delusions dated as far back as her mother's death in 1956. "Mrs. Coe had been very ill that year," he explained, "and her mother was at her bedside, kneeling down. She heard her mother pray to God, plead that Ruth be spared, save Ruth and take her instead. Her mother died shortly afterward." Mrs. Coe, the psychiatrist testified, was left with the delusion that her mother had died in her place. "Ruth feels now that if she died she might save her son and punish herself for her guilt... and it might save the world from evil."

He insisted that Mrs. Coe couldn't kill—"she has a history of being kind to people and especially kind to animals." He said she was under the delusion that she was trying to save human life, and that she hadn't wanted blood to be shed; she'd simply wanted to get caught. Under cross-examination the young psychiatrist was asked why his patient had spent so much time discussing alibis if she wanted to get caught. He said he hadn't known about the alibis. Rebecca Roe asked if he believed that Gordon Coe was suffering from the same "psychotic delusion" as his wife. Dr. Wildeman said the two cases were different, since Mr. Coe wasn't mentally ill. Said Roe, "Jim Zorn, the Seattle Seahawks' quarterback, is quoted as saying, 'God made me play well.' Is that a hallucination?"

The psychiatrist said it wasn't, because Zorn was "expressing a statement of belief and not of delusion."

Roe managed to suggest by her questions that most of the expert witnesses were engaged in circular reasoning: Ruth Coe heard voices because she was psychotic and was psychotic because she heard voices. The judge's expression suggested that he didn't disagree.

121

After a tearful Kathleen Coe testified that her mother had raved that Judge Shields was the devil, the first psychiatrist who had ever treated Ruth Coe arrived from his home in Hawaii to take the stand. Dr. Delano Collins had started treating the defendant in 1973 and continued off and on for six years. The bespectacled psychiatrist testified that she had been referred to him for "low spirits, great fatigue, lack of endurance, hair loss, anorexia, inability to make everyday decisions, etc." He said his original diagnosis had been depression with neurasthenic and phobic features. Later the patient had gone into manic-depressive illness—"she felt very liberated and had plans to purchase an old house to convert it into a boutique. I felt professionally that it was preposterous. . . . During one interview she thought she would go to Spain, have a party, and divorce her husband practically all in the same breath. She regarded her husband as a bore and a stick in the mud and indicated, 'I must be free!' I remember her complaining at that time that her husband attended WSU football Cougar games in the rain, bad weather etc., and that she had been doing that for years and was tired of that pedestrian way of life."

He recalled an impulsive trip by his patient: "She returned with a number of schemes, including contemplating buying a store in Las Vegas, which was the only place that she could live because it was close to the sun. I might add 'sun' in two senses: sun and Son." The testimony was one of the few acknowledgments by defense witnesses that the problems of mother and son might be linked. Dr. Collins said that when Mrs. Coe's buying sprees began to get out of control, "I was on the phone with her husband several times. 'What can we do to stop this?' She did not recognize that this could end in divorce. In fact, she *welcomed* the possibility of divorce action."

He recalled that "external adornment" was very important to Mrs. Coe in the manic phase. She was also concerned about the appearance of others, including her daughter Kathleen, who she felt was eating too much and becoming "obese." He said his last visit with the patient was in April of 1979. "She was in a state of partial remission from her manic-depressive disease but with a residual hypo-manic tendency. That is, still some leftover expansiveness

and grandiosity with mild excitement punctuated by being at times very quer-
ulous and argumentative, highly irritated if she were thwarted by any re-
straining influences, particularly from her husband. She was also very angry
at her son, who had not lived up to her expectations, and had claimed she
was going to disown him."

In the short cross-examination Rebecca Roe asked, "You said she characterized herself as a 'go' person?"

"Yes, ma'am," the army psychiatrist answered.

"Would it be fair to characterize her as a 'go' person who was also reasonably flamboyant?"

"Yes, ma'am. I'm sure most of you in the room saw *Auntie Mame*....Auntie
Mame in the movie was a classical manic. Mrs. Coe even had some of the
physical characteristics: the words she used and a little bit of the huskiness
of the voice and what one ordinarily might say is flamboyant and showy." Eyes
turned toward Ruth Coe. Everyone could see that the woman who'd been
known as "Mame" and "Mamie" in grammar school bore a marked resemblance
to Rosalind Russell, the Auntie Mame of the movie. Dr. Collins summed up,
"To me it was all evidence of disease."

After more brief testimony court was recessed for lunch. At 12:01 p.m.,
the Spokane CBS-radio outlet, KHQ, began playing an excerpt from the hit
man tape in violation of an order by Judge Bibb. At a hearing a few days earlier
psychologist Anna Kuhl, another of the therapists hired by Maxey, had warned
the judge that any broadcast of the tapes would "facilitate a full-blown psychotic breakdown" and "literally destroy Mrs. Coe."

Kuhl, a cheerfully supportive woman with close-cropped light hair, had
just sat down to lunch at Milford's, a seafood restaurant three blocks from the
Maxey building, when she learned about the broadcast. She dropped her fork
and ordered a passing driver to rush her to Carl Maxey's office, where the
Coes lunched daily with their legal staff. Timothy Egan, covering the trial for
the Seattle *Post-Intelligencer*, also rushed from the restaurant. When he reached
Maxey's reception room, everything was quiet. Gordon Coe and his daughter
Kathleen sat in a side office listening to the last few minutes of the KHQ
broadcast.

Maxey emerged from the back and explained that he and the Coes had
been walking across the street when they'd heard a passerby shout that the
tapes were on the air. He told Egan, "I have a sick woman on my hands and
she's back there collapsing and refusing to go on with the trial." The Seattle
reporter wondered why he hadn't heard any commotion. He guessed he must
have arrived a few minutes too late.

Just before court reconvened, a KHQ newsman approached the lumbering
Maxey, a former intercollegiate boxing champion, and was told, "Go in the
back room and take a look at my client. You guys don't give a shit about
humanity!" Maxey informed the judge, "My client refuses to allow me to
present any evidence on her behalf....Everyone who has attended the trial
knows of my client's long-term mental illness, which the testimony indicates
she was beginning to recover from." He demanded a mistrial.

Anna Kuhl testified that a continuance was desperately needed—"so I
don't have a suicide on my hands. I just spent the last hour with her and she
is suicidal." When Ruth Coe learned that the tapes were being aired, Kuhl

said, "she went over the edge into the pit and doesn't feel she can come out again. I don't know if I can strongly enough relate to you the seriousness of her problem. The potential for Mrs. Coe to commit suicide upon hearing the tapes is extremely high." Kuhl said that her client needed at least forty-eight hours of intensive therapy before a decision could be made about continuing the trial. "The last defense Mrs. Coe has as a survival technique is not hearing these tapes played across the airwaves. For her that is the final straw." Psychologist Richard Dennie agreed.

Judge Bibb announced that he considered KHQ, owned by the well-known Cowles family, in contempt of court. He granted a weekend recess and cracked that if a news director had violated one of his orders back home, he'd have dispatched him to the "Snohomish County Hotel"—the jail. Later Bibb admitted that he was skeptical of defense claims about the defendant's suicidal condition, but "I decided I would be rather cavalier disregarding the sworn statements of the two psychologists. I didn't want her blood on my hands."

Members of the defense team rushed the stricken defendant to "8 North," the psychiatric center at Sacred Heart Hospital, where she remained incommunicado. Maxey told a reporter, "She's resting comfortably. Her doctors are with her. That's about all I can say." KHQ turned its tapes over to the three networks and airings were scheduled nationally. News of this was withheld from the patient.

After a weekend of rest Mrs. Coe returned to the courtroom on the arm of the supportive Kuhl, who had changed into a black smock and white collar that gave her a slight resemblance to a Sister of Mercy. To reporters Mrs. Coe seemed more at ease than at any time since the trial had begun seven days earlier. She wore a sleeveless white dress that looked a little small. As always she waited for the judge to enter before sitting down. Her daughter Kathleen sat just behind her in the front row and cast a few cold glances at the press. Gordon Coe sat alongside his daughter and appeared to be studying the walls.

The defense recalled psychologist Kuhl, who testified that the tapes of the meeting with the undercover policeman were proof that Ruth Coe's delusions had "completely consumed her." Kuhl cited the way the woman had raced from topic to topic in a "flight of ideas," and offered the professional opinion that Mrs. Coe could have been manic and depressive at the same time.

During an intermission a defense lawyer confided to reporters that Ruth Coe would not testify in her own behalf. He said, "All I can tell you is that it's always the client's decision, not the lawyer's. It might be she felt she wasn't in any condition to testify." He hinted that her decision had originated during the Friday blow-up and was therefore the fault of the media.

The state's major rebuttal witness proved to be an Oklahoma-born psychiatrist with a shock of gray-white hair. Dr. Isaac Jesse Lawless, another of Ruth Coe's many therapists, had been interviewed by both sides before the trial, and he testified haltingly and reluctantly under subpoena. The defendant, he said, was not a psychotic but "a neurotic with a character disorder."

He said he had entered the case after Dr. Delano Collins had moved from Spokane. Between May 18, 1979, and January 18, 1980, Lawless saw the patient ten times; "then she quit coming," he said. Consulting notes, he explained that Mrs. Coe had had two serious conflicts: "She was not accepting the fact that she was getting older" and she had "a very heavy relationship with her son.... They were two people closely glued together emotionally and there's an abnormal or atypical thriving off one another beyond what's normal or healthy or optimal."

The patient's bizarre behavior, Lawless told the court, stemmed from "anxiety caused by not acknowledging her two conflicts" rather than from manic-depressive illness. He said he'd listened to the undercover tapes and heard nothing suggesting psychosis, just a woman "clearly preoccupied with her task." He discounted testimony about delusions and hallucinations and testified that Mrs. Coe's anger toward Shields and Brockett related to a "very straightforward, real event in her life. They were harming her son, at least putting him in jail"—nothing psychotic or manic-depressive about that, the psychiatrist concluded in his slight Sooner drawl.

Mary Kay Barbieri's closing statement was as terse as the state's case. "What we have seen," she told Judge Bibb, "is a very frightening combination: Ruth Coe's burning belief in her son's innocence, a slow and consuming anger, and a wish for revenge." Testimony about the woman's psychological vulnerability was beside the point, the prosecutor argued. "She is no more vulnerable than thousands of others who experience crushing poverty and other difficulties that lead to crime." Barbieri told the judge, "Anger, revenge, determination is what you hear on those tapes. Her intention is stated over and over again. She intended that they be killed." And it was a mere accident that they hadn't been, the former English teacher went on. "It is a stark reality in this society that murder for hire happens."

Carl Maxey provided a fiery, oratorical finish. Striding up and down and waving his long arms, the white-maned lawyer quoted Carl Sandburg ("There were children in the ships, there were children in the town. War is for everyone. War is for children, too"), William Shakespeare ("He jests at scars who never felt a wound"), U. S. District Judge William B. Bryant ("Law enforcement exceeds its bounds when it manufactures crimes"), and others. He bore down on the entrapment issue; "the police done it for her and to her," he claimed. Mrs. Coe, he continued, hadn't advanced the death plot "except to respond to the urgings of the police in her childlike mental and emotional condition." He observed that he had two sons himself. "I'd go to the mat for 'em. But *I'm* not a manic depressive." He closed with a reference to Martin Luther King. "Think of a good man who the night before he was shot said, 'Don't mention that I have won the Nobel Peace prize or many others. Just say that I wanted to be able to have them say on that fateful day they bury me—that I tried to feed the hungry. I want you to be able to say that I tried to clothe the naked, that I tried in all my life to visit those who were in prison. I tried to love and serve humanity. Yes, sir, if you want to say it, say I was a drum major, a drum major for justice!' *That's what Ruth Coe was all her life until she became mortally wounded with a disease that prevented her from being able to form a specific intent.*"

In surrebuttal the wispy Rebecca Roe suggested that the judge scrutinize Gordon Coe's words carefully. "We have testimony that essentially doesn't make sense." She asked the judge whether Coe's claim that he was willing to hand his wife $500 for moving expenses squared with his earlier remarks about her spending sprees and her grave mental illness—"at the very farthest point away from reality." She chided some of the expert witnesses for coming to court without notes and for "incredible impreciseness." She called Dr. Lawless's rebuttal testimony "refreshing common-sense analysis" after some of the other experts' "psychobabble and mystical terms." She disputed Anna Kuhl's remark that the tapes showed Mrs. Coe skipping from subject to subject in a "flight of ideas." Said Roe, "The only topic on those tapes is *why* she wants these people dead and *how* she wants these people dead."

The young assistant prosecutor argued that motivation based on emotion rather than greed is no sign of insanity. "She hires a hit man because she's angry and disappointed over what happened to her son," Roe told the judge. "I hire a hit man to kill my husband because I want to inherit his money. Our motives may be different—but both of us intend murder."

Judge Bibb announced that he would announce his verdict in two days in his home courtroom three hundred miles away in Everett. Chatting in chambers, he gazed out the window at the warm spring sun and said he would be mowing his lawn while he considered the issues. Said Carl Maxey, "Judge, I hope you got a big lawn."

122

In the old mill city of Everett, where Boeing assembled 747s in cavernous sheds, the biggest media crowd in the history of the Snohomish County Courthouse assembled on the breezy afternoon of Friday, May 28, for Ruth Coe's judgment day. Most of the assembled journalists had driven over the mountains from Spokane to the Spanish-style courthouse with its terra cotta roof and rhododendron gardens in red and pink. Another contingent had driven up from Seattle, thirty miles south by freeway. And a few network news teams had flown in from San Francisco and Los Angeles.

Mrs. Coe looked exhausted but serene, resigned to her fate. Wearing a turquoise nylon blouse, cream ultrasuede suit and open-backed toeless "slides," she seemed to sag into her seat, as though the force of gravity were stronger here in coastal Everett than back home. She was closely flanked by members of her defense team. Now and then the bearlike Carl Maxey reached over and squeezed her hand.

Judge Bibb entered the courtroom twenty minutes late and read his findings to a standing-room audience. His glasses slid halfway down his nose as he reviewed the case and said that under normal circumstances the facts alone would have been enough to prove Mrs. Coe's guilt, but two defense arguments had to be dealt with: entrapment and diminished mental capacity. He made short work of the entrapment issue, noting that the defendant had grabbed at the hit man's offer "like a hungry trout snapping at a fly." He said it was true that the undercover officer had initiated the contact with Mrs. Coe—"but under the statute that does not constitute entrapment." Nor had plainclothesman Richard Jennings lured her into committing a crime she would not have otherwise committed. Said the judge, "The tapes speak for themselves."

He turned to the question of whether Mrs. Coe had been so addled that she'd been unable to form a specific intent to have someone murdered. As the judge began to explain his reasoning, Gordon Coe flexed his cheek muscles and shook his head from side to side as though already in disagreement. Seated next to him in the front row, Kathleen Coe displayed the same reaction. Both father and daughter seemed to be fighting tears.

The judge quickly confirmed what many had guessed: that he'd been unimpressed by most of the defense's expert witnesses. Drs. Dennie, Wildeman and Kuhl were "relatively new to their present professions," he noted. "Their testimony, in my view, lacked internal consistency and they appeared to be less than totally objective. This is no reflection on their competence as therapists." He said he found the testimony of Doctors Viren, Collins and Lawless "much more persuasive." They had convinced him that there was "no question that defendant has suffered a partially disabling serious mental illness since 1971." Superimposed on that mental illness, the judge went on, was the "severe stress caused by a series of highly emotional traumatic events." But neither problem had destroyed her ability to form a specific intent. Nor, he ruled, had she been delusional.

"This case reads a bit like a Greek tragedy by Euripides or Sophocles," the judge said, peering over the tops of his glasses at the packed courtroom. "A symbiotic family relationship, catastrophe caused by man or the gods, avengement, and the judging of the avenger again by the gods or fate or by a man or men, and the human emotions described by the ancient Greek playwrights of anger, hate, the desire for revenge—human emotions that exist today—I must find to be the precipitating cause of defendant's conduct, not a diminished mental capacity, whether with or without inducement from the police." Kathleen Coe shook her head again, in unison with her father's.

The judge cleared his throat and continued, "This is certainly not to say that defendant's mental condition and the tragedies that have befallen her should not or will not be considered by the court. There has to be a place for mercy in any civilized system of justice, and in my view the facts of this case will justify a substantial degree of mercy being shown the defendant, absent any showing that she presently presents a danger to others." He paused again. Ruth Coe stared up at him, unblinking. Gordon Coe brushed a finger across his forehead, and Kathleen Coe's eyes welled with tears. "I conclude," the judge intoned, "that defendant was guilty as charged."

In her sentencing recommendations Mary Kay Barbieri asked for a minimum of five and a maximum of twenty years' imprisonment—short of the possible life sentences that some had expected her to demand. "Any person who solicits the hired killing of another human being," she told the judge, "must be sent to prison. Our society must make a strong statement about that kind of behavior."

Carl Maxey said that when he'd first met his client, he found her "beset with the mental and emotional problem that rendered her hardly able to take care of herself, let alone the responsibilities of this trial." He spoke of her anguish and pain and accused the prosecution of seeking retribution. "We ask the court for the opportunity for a visitation of as much sympathy, not in the sense of ignoring the standards required for society in general—society in general isn't on trial," Maxey went on. "It's one little sixty-one-year-old lady who is a manic-depressive—who didn't meet, according to Your Honor's observations, the legal requirements but has nevertheless, by everybody's definition of pain and suffering, suffered immensely." He concluded by quoting Abraham Lincoln: "This too shall pass." As he said the words Ruth Coe spun around in her chair and smiled consolingly at her daughter. Kathleen smiled back through tears.

The judge asked if Mrs. Coe had anything to say. She stood up, cleared her throat and spoke in a tremulous voice: "First I would like to thank you, Your Honor, for having heard this case yourself." She paused, clenching and unclenching a lacy white handkerchief. "I appreciate it, and I can't let this case end without making a public apology to both George Shields—Judge Shields—and his family, and to Donald Brockett and his family, for the anguish and the harm that, in my illness, I brought their way. Thank you."

Bibb ordered a short *pro forma* recess to consider the final statements. When court was reconvened Maxey pulled his chair close to his client's and put his arm across her shoulders. The judge said, "Mrs. Coe, the crime which you committed demands a prison sentence in every case almost without exception." Then he began reciting a catalog of mitigating circumstances: "your emotional vulnerability...genuine mental illness of longstanding duration...sixty-one years of non-criminal non-violent conduct...the almost incredible series of misfortunes that you encountered...."

The sentence was in three parts: twenty years in prison, suspended; ten years on parole, and one year to be served in the county jail of her choice. It was close to the lightest sentence possible.

When the hearing was recessed at 3:11 p.m., Kathleen Coe hurried to her mother's side. Photographers and TV cameramen swirled around the convicted woman, and mother and daughter hugged and managed smiles. Ruth Coe's head was high and she appeared calm. Assistant defense counsel Gordon Bovey dropped a red carnation on the defense table and repeated what he'd said about a similar gesture on the day the trial opened: "It symbolizes our feelings about our client." The white carnation, he explained, had been for purity; this one was for sacrifice.

While Mrs. Coe was being fingerprinted in the jury room, newsmen stepped up front for a final word with the lawyers. Assistant prosecutor Rebecca Roe seemed disappointed. Of Maxey's final plea for mercy she said, "You just don't take a class-A felony and say she's a pathetic sixty-one-year-old lady and forget it. As long as she continues to be obsessed with her son's innocence, she continues to represent a danger to the community."

The frown that had covered Carl Maxey's face during most of the trial was now replaced by a warm smile. He told a friend, "I'd be crazy to appeal this one, wouldn't I?" A reporter asked if it was true that Fred Coe had helped prepare his mother's defense, as claimed in a prison interview. "Like the shark helps the swimmer," cracked Maxey as he walked away.

Donald C. Brockett, the prosecuting attorney who would have spent the rest of his life in diapers if Ruth Coe had had her "druthers," broke his public silence about the Coes to discuss the sentence with John Webster of the Spokane *Chronicle*. He admitted that the judicial system had worked to an extent, but only after far too much wasted time, game-playing and manipulation. "Deciding whether somebody is guilty or innocent ought to be simpler than it is," he went on. "Historically, it may be interesting to look back on this stage in criminal justice because it seems to me that almost anything, regardless of how ridiculous it might appear to be, is presented on behalf of defendants to show that what they really did appears to be different than what it really is."

Brockett harked back to the bail reduction that had enabled Ruth Coe to walk the streets for six months before her trial. "I thought it was rather unique that you can attempt to hire someone to kill the principal role players in the criminal justice system and yet not be considered a danger to the community.... Who's this system for? I think it was designed for the victims, not the defendants. Justice needs to be more swift and certain." The light sentence, the prosecutor insisted, was another proof that judges had too much discretion. He pointed out that under new guidelines being worked out by a committee of which he was a member, Mrs. Coe would have had to serve a minimum of five years. "Judge Bibb said justice needs to be tempered with mercy. As a person who's in the system who now can sympathize much more with victims, I think it might be well for judges to remember that mercy has to be tempered with justice.... The purpose of sentencing is to adequately punish the individual involved and to sufficiently deter others. I don't see how this sentence could possibly deter anybody."

At Judge Bibb's instruction, Ruth Coe remained free on her original thirty-thousand-dollar bond while she made plans to appeal. Carl Maxey informed his client that if she chose to appeal she would have to find another lawyer.

The Coes shopped around for the least oppressive jail. A half hour after midnight on Thursday, July 1, Ruth surrendered to the sheriff of Pend Oreille County, fifty miles north of Spokane in Washington's quiet north woods. There she was the sole occupant of the women's section with its six bunks, table, toilet, and shower, and access to a library and commissary. Each day she was allowed to use the jail's exercise yard and make two phone calls. Personal visits were permitted twice a week. Since the rural jail stocked no overalls for women, she was permitted to wear her own clothes. "Whether she's right or wrong," the sheriff said, "I don't want to degrade her."

The prisoner had hardly eaten her first jailhouse TV dinner before another controversy erupted. County officials insisted that someone had to pay for her board. After running up an unpaid bill of three hundred and twenty-five dollars, Mrs. Coe was quietly returned to Spokane county-city jail. A mystery woman described by receptionist Priscilla Achenbach as "beautiful and tear-stained" appeared in Carl Maxey's office with three one-hundred-dollar bills, a twenty and a five, and said the cash was for the unpaid bill in Pend Oreille County. Maxey told reporters that the stranger didn't know Mrs. Coe but felt "that whether or not Ruth did wrong, she deserved to be treated as a human being."

Gordon Coe commented that it was nice to have someone "show such good feeling toward us." His wife seemed to make a quick adjustment to the jail routine. Within a few months Judge Bibb granted her request to attend daytime classes in interior design and spend nights at a work-release center. Each afternoon she lunched with her husband, and occasionally she was seen downtown. With four months of her sentence remaining, the judge allowed her to move to Seattle with her husband and serve out her time on another work-release program. Officials described her as "a model prisoner."

The same words were used at Walla Walla to describe her son. F. H. Coe, #279538, remained in protective custody because of the general prison antipathy toward "rapos." In a letter to a friend he said, "I look better and feel better than ever. I work out constantly. They have a tremendous gym down here—brand new—with $2 million worth of Nautilus and Universal equipment. I'm finally getting to do what I've never had the time for! Three days a week I'm in the gym—running, shooting baskets, working on the Universal. I'm probably in the best shape I've been in since age 17, when I quit organized sports. My stomach is hard as a rock—diamond-sculpted.... In many ways prison is a trip. It ain't no biggie."

He said he was receiving heavy mail. "It's almost entirely favorable," he reported proudly, "and it's overwhelmingly from females." He claimed that he'd received a letter from a "beauty queen runner-up—a blond, very attractive young lady in the Washington, D.C. area.... She was very adamantly pro-claiming her belief in my innocence."

It wasn't long before reporters began receiving letters from other inmates echoing Coe's claims of frame-up and fix. The point of almost every note was that convicts enjoyed a special expertise on the subject of of guilt and inno-cence; they had made their own impartial study of their fellow prisoner and found him innocent. "Coe," a tiermate wrote, "ain't no rapo!"

Timothy Egan of the Seattle *Post-Intelligencer* found the convicted South Hill rapist friendly and optimistic in a prison interview. "He gave me a big handshake," Egan told a friend later. "It was like meeting a guy from the chamber of commerce. His hair was almost to his shoulders, his shirt open showing his chest. His eyes caught the faded blue of his shirt and the insti-tutional blue of the walls and a patch of sky-blue that showed through a window. He had an armload of notes. Before the interview started, I took the guard captain aside and said, 'How's he doing? What kind of things should I ask him?' He looked as though I had a hell of a nerve. I said, 'I mean off the record, between you and me.' The captain said, 'I'm not telling you *anything* about Kevin.' I expected Coe to sit next to me, but instead he walked around the desk and took the captain's chair. All through our interview he rocked back and forth like a executive."

Coe told Egan how shocked he was that his mother had been convicted in the Spokane "soap opera." He called the case "blatant entrapment" and wondered aloud why he hadn't been summoned to testify: "I would have been an excellent witness for her." He wrapped his hands tightly together and said, "Our cases are like this—inseparable."

His mother would have been pleased. She had always insisted, "He was *my* baby. He was *my* boy." He still was.

EPILOGUE

He may not stay long. Psychopaths know how to beat this game and are not about to be indefinitely trapped here [in prison]. They return home, and somebody, whoever they fall in with, will start to pay for the outlaw's damaged childhood.—Alan Harrington, *Psychopaths*

Decades will pass before the memory of the South Hill rape case slips from the minds of the good people of Spokane. The Lilac City took the national publicity as hard as it had taken the wave of rapes. "Slide on over, Peyton Place," wrote columnist Chris Peck in the *Spokesman-Review* shortly before accepting promotion to managing editor. "Your steamy reputation as America's mythical township of murder, rape and back-alley intrigue has been supplanted—by real events in Spokane."

Said John Lemon, retired assistant managing editor of the *Chronicle*, "Spokane was already in trouble from growing too fast, and suddenly we began to look like a sinkhole. It wasn't fair, but that's the way a lot of people felt."

A minister's wife named Darla Correll was equally upset. "Things are getting worse and worse in this city," she commented. "It's just what the Lord said would happen in the final days."

Many found the subject too painful to discuss. One wrote the *Chronicle*, "How long, O Lord, how long are you going to badger, club and harass us with that Coe family story.... Your obsession with this disgusting story has made Spokane a national butt of lewd jokes and snide publicity.... Drop it! Give us a rest! We are sick of that name and anything about them!"

Many would never forget.

Lois Higgins, her five-year-old daughter Becky and her new husband Bill packed up and moved to another state after the Ruth Coe trial. "I'm a lot better now," she said in her tidy new home. I was always a clean person, but ever since that night I've had to take a bath twice a day. I wake up feeling like I've got dirt caked on my body. I still see his face and have nightmares. Sometimes I get the feeling I'm completely worthless. He destroyed my peace of mind, my sex life, my self-confidence, self-esteem, pride, my trust in my fellow humans, my sleep. In many ways I'm getting better—thanks to Bill and all that therapy. For a long time I couldn't let him touch my shoulders and my upper arms, but it doesn't bother me anymore. I trust Bill, and I never thought I'd trust another man. Once in a while I regress for a few minutes, and he'll always leave the bedroom and go into the living room and wait. When it passes I call out, 'I'm fine. Will you hold me now?' It doesn't happen very often. We have another daughter now—Mary Ann. She weighed five pounds thirteen ounces, just like Becky. I weigh one-fifteen myself. Ten more pounds and I'll be back to what I weighed before the rape. It's taken four years."

Shelly Monahan, promoted to TV weatherwoman, also considered herself healed, but long after her rape she still carried tear gas on her keychain and insisted on a personal escort to the parking lot at night. Arriving at her little South Hill house with its quiet decor of plants and cats, she always ran from her car to the front door. "Night smells different from day to me," she explained. "Night smells like rape. For a long time I relived the whole thing. I would wake up yelling: 'No, no, no! Don't let him do it!' Then I'd cry for hours. But now I dream that I get away from him and I run along Fifty-seventh to a house, knock on a door stark naked—and they help me. The nice part is I don't get beat up."

The former parlor girl who called herself "Misty" recovered from her descent into drugs and began a more plebeian life with her husband Bob. It was a few years before she stopped condemning herself. "People might think that since I worked in a massage parlor I deserved it," she said. "I wasn't a low-life. There are some ladies who come off as low-life no matter what their profession, but I never asked for trouble and I conducted myself as a lady. And I didn't deserve what I got."

After her second rape by the same man, Lynn Barkley withdrew from society for a while. "I even cut off my best friends and my family, so I'd have time to think. I lived alone, and I turned in on myself. I never went out at night—I was too afraid. Little by little I changed my mellow feelings about him, especially after seeing him up on the witness stand lying to the hilt. I used to think he just needed someone to give him a good talking to. That was naïve. He needs a lot more than that, and he's where he belongs. I'll never know why I kissed him—some things in life are really hard to understand. Maybe I was glad to be alive. I've gained some perspective on what he did, some objectivity. My opinion of men—it's gone way down. It's hard for me to trust them now."

Marie Oldham suffered from agonies of self-doubt for six months after her rape. "That's part of the problem," she explained later. "Subconsciously, rape victims try to take the blame themselves. I kept asking myself, How should I have acted? One night my husband said, 'You know, honey, you're not the only one that's been victimized by this. I should have been there to protect you. I feel guilty, too.'

"He looked so sad. I said, 'Babe, it wasn't your fault. There's nothing you could have done.' I cried and cried.

"He said, 'Marie, this is the first emotion you've shown since it happened.'

"I said, *'Well, right now I just hate that man so much!'*" Her self-doubts began to dissipate that night.

Margot Terry openly discussed her rape and wrote about it in a national magazine, but no catharsis could take away the memory of that hour on the rocky slope below High Drive. "I have to live with it forever," she explained. "Uncertainties, dreads, nervousness. There's a big empty black fear in the back of my mind. Walking a dark street now, or getting off a bus, my heart beats fast. And I'm a person who's navigated Istanbul by myself, gotten off planes alone in international airports—a free spirit, someone who's always trusted people, someone who's never been fearful. It's so unfair. I can't believe there are women who don't report rapes, who don't do everything in their power to bring rapists to justice. For a while my husband seemed embarrassed by what happened, but he got over that. He found that our friends were proud of the way I spoke up and tried to help the police. *'Styrka'* has been a big help—'strength.' And I repeat my affirmations every day. 'I like myself unconditionally!' 'I am Margot Terry and I am *proud* of my identity and uniqueness.' Here's one I keep on the front of my refrigerator. 'Success means getting up one more time than you fall down.'"

Jay Williams still felt a sense of betrayal about his oldest friend but also relief that the hurt hadn't cut deeper. "But somehow it still weighs on me. I think about Fred and miss the things we didn't get to do together as adults. Throwing a football around, things like that. We were always too busy trying to make money. I used to think, When we're both fifty and wealthy we'll have a little time to enjoy ourselves. Now we won't. Somehow it's an attrition on me. I still feel upset that he did what he did—and then left. I guess we're not friends anymore. He's written a few letters, but none lately. I value the friendship we had. He's a unique human being, fascinating. He was eccentric but never boring. We could be friends again if he would only admit his guilt. But that's something Fred could never do. He denies himself the defense of mental disturbance. He'd rather be a convict for life than admit he has the slightest problem. A friendship becomes pretty hollow when lies like that stand between you.

"His sense of humor seems to have changed in prison. When he tries to be funny in his letters, it just sounds silly. His humor used to be very advanced—very sophisticated and subtle. He wrote some dirty stuff to me from prison, and he *never* did that in the old days. He's always shopping around for new personalities—I can remember three or four. It was part of his problem. Not long ago I saw him on TV and I was struck—he had a brand new way of talking, not effeminate but bordering on it. He kept showing his bottom teeth, stretching his mouth to pronounce his words. And he didn't carry himself the way he used to. Several of my friends noticed the same thing. He seems to be living a Walter Mitty existence in Walla Walla—bombastic statements, public fights with lawyers, demands for disbarment. That's not the Coe I remember. He used to talk about learning to be more assertive. I've seen him jacked around by mechanics and waiters, but he would *never* raise his voice. Now he's telling everybody off.

"A few months after Mrs. Coe was convicted I ran into Kathy Coe in a restaurant. She'd come over from Seattle to help her father move. At first she looked so enraged I thought she was gonna tear me apart—you know, the vein throbbing in the neck, eyes blazing, head trembling? But I've always liked her, and I tried to show it. We talked about inane things for a while, and then I said, 'Well, Kathy, I imagine you and your family could possibly misunderstand the things I did and *didn't* do in Fred's case. But has it ever crossed your mind at all—I'm not trying to antagonize you, please believe me—that your brother could be guilty?'

"She thought for a while and said, 'Well, I've considered the possibility, but the evidence is totally overwhelming that he isn't. If you only knew a *fraction* of what we know.'

"I said, 'Well, I'll have to admit I think he's guilty.' I wanted her to understand my position, so I brought up an analogy. I said, 'Do you believe Richard Speck was guilty of murdering all those nurses in Chicago?'

"She hesitated. 'I imagine he did,' she said.

"'Well, what would you think of his friends if they thought he was guilty and lied for him under oath?'

"'Oh, Jay, my family *never* expected that of you!'

"'Fred did. Your mother did.'

"Kathy said, 'When my mother criticized you over the phone she wasn't in her right mind. She had thyroid problems, hormonal problems. She was going through hell on earth. That wasn't my mother you were talking to, Jay. I hope you recognize that.'

"I said, 'I don't recognize it. Frankly, Kathy, your mother scares me to death.'

"At the end she said, 'Don't hold your breath thinking Fred will stay in prison. This was the greatest travesty of justice in history. My brother's getting out.'"

Williams paused in his reminiscences. "Funny thing," he said. "When Fred lived in California he used to tell people he was from Spokane, and nobody knew where Spokane was. So he started saying he was from Seattle and that didn't work much better. But he found that everyone seemed familiar with Walla Walla, maybe from all the old jokes. So he started telling people he was from there. Now he is."

On the Pacific side of the Cascades, Fred Coe's other high school pal remained unnerved about the case long after Ruth Coe went off to jail. Said John Nyberg, who was usually more interested in exchanging jokes, "I worry about retribution for talking about them. That's the way people get a bullet in the brainpan. Fred won't be in jail forever and neither will his mother."

When Nyberg and Williams talked on the phone, they agreed they were both lucky. As Nyberg put it, "I've been a lot of places, I've done things I'd rather not think about, I had to try it all, feel everything in life, but thank God I was able to pull back in the end and not wind up like Fred." He said he would never forget Coe's reaction "when I went to the wife-and-kids scene. It was like he was surprised by my priorities. Watching the way he lived his life was like watching a bad side of myself. I saw in Fred the uglinesses in myself that I was fighting constantly to defeat but he seemed unable or unwilling to. In school I knew that the way we acted toward women was a stage of life, but he seemed to think it was life itself. Ten years later he was still talking the same way, still doing the same things. He tried to model himself on the Frank Sinatras, the Dean Martins, the Howard Hugheses, people with power and money who were able to stay immature and egotistical and sexually oriented all their lives. But they'd paid their dues and he hadn't. Fred wanted everything right now. He couldn't wait."

The booking agent lifted his feet to a desk covered with account books and audition cassettes and said, "I think maybe he started raping when he saw how unreal his life was, how superficial and phony. Everything about him had been based on gaining control over others. Apparently his deepest childhood fears could only be controlled by total dominance. But he never even learned to control himself."

As Gini Perham sat in the front seat of a friend's car parked in front of the Manito Highlander laundromat, she kept glancing around. "It's a reflex," she explained. "Everywhere I go I scan the parking lot for a gray Citation or a yellow Cadillac. It's like the way chow dogs circle around to kill snakes on the rug." She brushed a curl of her hair from her blue-green eyes. "Whenever I walk into a public place, I look for Fred and Ruth. I keep thinking they're gonna get out of jail and head straight for me. It's nerve-wracking to live in such fear, but it's my life sentence."

For two years after Fred Coe's conviction, Gini kept moving from address to address and job to job. Real estate was closed to her now—a remote, glamorous part of her past when she had driven to work in her new blue Monte Carlo and worn the chic dresses and suits of a businesswoman. The only jobs available to her paid little more than the minimum wage. She worked as a telephone solicitor, a housecleaner, a veterinarian's assistant, a commission salesperson. Fear kept her moving. Once she thought she'd found the perfect hideout: a small apartment on the north side. No one but her closest friends and relatives knew the address and phone number. Within a few weeks she received two plain white typewriter-addressed envelopes, each containing a $20 bill. "It's Kevin," she told a friend nervously. "I *know* it's him. He owed me money. Don't ask me why he's paying it back like this. Or maybe it's Ruth, trying to make some kind of point about twenty pieces of silver. I don't know why, but it's *them*." She moved in with a girlfriend and left no forwarding address.

It wasn't only the Coes who made her apprehensive. "I was afraid of running into women Kevin had abused, and I was embarrassed about meeting people who'd heard my testimony. All that bedroom stuff. My friends—thank God for my friends!—they say it'll all be forgotten. When?"

A part of her insisted on believing that Kevin had loved her as she'd loved him, but another part had doubts. "I think he saw in me a person he could manipulate, a person he could use to gain certain ends. I helped give him a respectable front. He used my money. He used my reputation to help him establish credit and credibility. He used me to pacify his mother, to relieve her anxieties about his taking up with 'white trash' again. Of course she used that expression to describe me later on, and she's *always* used it about Jenifer. I guess it's because we both rode buses. I still think about Kevin, but I don't sit around and moon. All I feel is hurt and pain. I think of all those women trying to scream with his glove down their throats, swallowing blood. This is the first time I've gone near this laundromat. I'll drive a mile out of my way to avoid Twenty-ninth and Rebecca.

"I spent two years trying to figure him out and I'm as confused as ever. I kept reading all his quotes and press releases about how Don Brockett and twenty-seven other people conspired to railroad him to prison and how everybody else is a liar—only Kevin Coe is telling the truth. He knows he did the shoplift, the rapes, the other sex crimes, everything, but in his sick mind he doesn't think he's guilty, because he's not subject to the same laws as the rest of us. In his mind the Coes can do things that others can't—because they're the Coes. That's why he sounds so sincere—he really feels that he *is* a breed apart and he doesn't belong in jail. As he and Ruth both kept saying, those rapes were 'no big deal.' I still cry when I think about the women he hurt, the lives he changed and disrupted. God knows he changed mine. My ambition is still the same—to marry and settle down—but I'm thirty now and he's made me scared to meet anyone. I haven't the least desire to be intimate with a man. Once in a while a tiny feeling will crop up, but that's just loneliness. For a long time after he was arrested, I didn't date. I wasn't going to be victimized again. I didn't hate men—you can't hate a whole sex—but I was just careful.

"Before this happened I had a sense of humor—I used to be a practical joker, make people laugh, try to make 'em see there's hope for tomorrow. I lost that. Thank God it's coming back. I'm beginning to be open with people again, more trusting. For a long time my energy was gone. I felt tired, sapped. It was all too damned much. I guess I have a few things to feel good about. The relationship with Kevin taught me about myself, my limits. I learned how tough I can be, how resilient. After I found out what he'd been doing, I still loved him, but I didn't let my heart overpower my head. I did what I had to do—I testified, and I survived. I'm proud that I didn't let the Coes run me out of my home town."

She talked about seeing Kevin on the same KREM-TV interview that had made Jay Williams wonder if his old friend was changing in prison. "He seemed to be enjoying himself," Gini recalled, "but I think it was just another act. His long hair hadn't been washed in a day or two, and he hadn't shaved. He looked puffy, as though he'd been overeating. *That* old cycle. He spoke in his radio voice and some of the remarks he made would have been funny if they hadn't been tragic. At one point he said something like, 'Fame's a funny thing,' as though he'd finally made it to the top. He didn't seem to recognize the difference between fame and notoriety. At the end of the interview he did a little dance step going out of the room. It reminded me of the twirls his mother used to do. He held his arms out and posed as though to say, 'Get your last shot; we're striking the set.' I guess he thought he was Clark Gable in 'It Happened One Night,' Robert Redford as Gatsby, Warren Beatty—all the men he admired but never understood. One thing gave me heart. He said he would never come back to Spokane. Oh, God, I hope it's true."

"I still have deep feelings for him," Jeni Coe said haltingly. "I worry that I caused all this to happen. If I hadn't refused him, if I'd only stayed with him. I sit and think—why did I treat him like that? I should have helped him. He wrote a letter to my parents from prison, back when he was trying to convince us not to talk about him, and he told them they would always be part of his family and he loved me, he would *always* love me. He—"

She had to stop talking. Tears slid down her pale, chiseled face. She was forty-two and still looked like a model, but there was a lassitude about her. She'd returned to Spokane a few months after Fred's arrest and lived a fugitive's existence in her parents' house. Day after day she sat at home with her elderly parents, reading, playing solitaire, taking naps, watching TV, doing housework. Her social life consisted of long walks and twice-weekly visits to her sister Sonia. Her parents drove her to and from the rest home.

She was unable to think about Ruth Coe without rancor. "I read all that stuff about her in the paper. They said her mental illness went way back. I know better. It started the day Fred said he was gonna marry me—the day she thought she lost him. All her mental problems came from not being able to let go of her son. It shouldn't take a psychiatrist to see that. Sometimes people say Ruth and I were two of a kind—we both were involved with modeling, we both were pretty, we both were divorcees. But that's where the resemblance ends. I've done some crazy things, but I've never purposely tried to hurt somebody. I've never manipulated people; more often I was manipulated myself. When I married Fred, I didn't know I was getting his mother too.

"People ask if I miss men. Well, I can't go out, because I keep wondering who'll be the next madman I run into. My trust is about an inch high. And anyway, what do I have to offer? I'm washed out now, an old woman. All of a sudden the world seems too big. Fred took away my identity, and I still don't have it back. I used to think of suicide. Then everybody could say, 'Forget about Jeni. She was never here.' I thought of becoming a nun. God must have put me on earth for some reason."

Sonia was a comfort. One night Jeni told her, "I don't know how God can forgive me for some of the things I've done."

Sonia said, "That's what God is for."

Jeni thought about her sister's remark for a long time. Then she joined a Christian fellowship and began to meet a few people. In the summer of 1983, after the public defender's office had helped to get all charges against her dropped, she steeled herself and took a step she'd once thought impossible. After twenty-eight months of self-imposed house arrest, she rode the bus downtown to look for work. She said she felt like Columbus sailing toward the edge of the earth.

Jack Olsen is the author of twenty-two books, published in eleven countries and nine languages, including such noted works of nonfiction as SILENCE ON MONTE SOLE, NIGHT OF THE GRIZZLIES, THE BRIDGE AT CHAPPAQUIDDICK, THE GIRLS IN THE OFFICE, *and* THE MAN WITH THE CANDY, *and the novels* ALPHABET JACKSON, MASSY'S GAME, THE SECRET OF FIRE FIVE, NIGHT WATCH, *and* MISSING PERSONS. *His shorter works appear in many anthologies. An award-winning journalist in Washington, New Orleans, and Chicago, he was a chief correspondent for* TIME *magazine and senior editor of* SPORTS ILLUSTRATED. *He makes his home on an island in Puget Sound, Washington.*